Preserving Dance Across Time and Space

Dance is, arguably, the art least susceptible to preservation since its embodied, kinaesthetic nature has proven difficult to capture in notation and even in still or moving images. However, established frameworks and guidance are available for keeping dances, performances, and choreographers' legacies alive so that the dancers of today and tomorrow can experience and learn from the dances and dancers of the past.

In this volume, a range of voices address the issue of dance preservation through memory, artistic choice, interpretation, imagery and notation, as well as looking at relevant archives, legal structures, documentation and artifacts. The intertwining of dance preservation and creativity is a core theme discussed throughout this text, pointing to the essential continuity of dance history and dance innovation. The demands of preservation stretch across time, geographies, institutions and interpersonal connections, and this book focuses on the fascinating web that supports the fragile yet urgent effort to sustain our dancing heritage.

The articles in this book were originally published in the journal *Dance Chronicle: Studies in Dance and the Related Arts*.

Lynn Matluck Brooks is the Arthur and Katherine Shadek Humanities Professor of Dance at Franklin & Marshall College, USA. She holds a doctorate from Temple University and is a Certified Movement Analyst and dance historian. She has written for *Dance Magazine*, edited *Dance Research Journal* and *Dance Chronicle*, and authored several books including *John Durang: Man of the American Stage* (2011).

Joellen A. Meglin is Associate Professor of Dance at Temple University, USA. Her articles have appeared frequently in journals such as *Dance Research* (UK), *Dance Research Journal* and *Dance Chronicle*, and two essays have been published in Studies in Dance History monographs. She has served as coeditor of *Dance Chronicle* since 2008.

Preserving Dance Across Time and Space

Edited by
**Lynn Matluck Brooks and
Joellen A. Meglin**

Routledge
Taylor & Francis Group

LONDON AND NEW YORK

First published 2013
by Routledge
2 Park Square, Milton Park, Abingdon, Oxon, OX14 4RN

Simultaneously published in the USA and Canada
by Routledge
711 Third Avenue, New York, NY 10017

Routledge is an imprint of the Taylor & Francis Group, an informa business

British Library Cataloguing in Publication Data
A catalogue record for this book is available from the British Library

ISBN13: 978-0-415-63490-8

Typeset in Baskerville
by Taylor & Francis Books

Publisher's Note
The publisher would like to make readers aware that the chapters in this book may be referred to as articles as they are identical to the articles published in the special issue. The publisher accepts responsibility for any inconsistencies that may have arisen in the course of preparing this volume for print.

Dedicated to the memory of
Lesley-Anne Sayers, 1958-2010

Contents

Citation Information   ix

Notes on Contributors   xi

1. Introduction
   Lynn Matluck Brooks and Joellen A. Meglin   1

Part I: Choreography, the Archives, and Sustaining a Legacy

2. Choreographers' Archives: Three Case Studies in Legacy Preservation
   Cheryl LaFrance   6

3. The Choreographer's Trust: Negotiating Authority in Peggy Baker's
   Archival Project
   Allana C. Lindgren and Amy Bowring   35

4. A Bold Step Forward: Genevieve Oswald and the Dance Collection of
   the New York Public Library
   Lynn Matluck Brooks   64

5. The Choreographic Trust: Preserving Dance Legacies
   Francis Yeoh   104

Part II: Preservation and Creation

6. Gained in Translation: Recreation as Creative Practice
   Valerie Preston-Dunlop and Lesley-Anne Sayers   130

7. The Dancing Gaze Across Cultures: Kazuo Ohno's *Admiring La Argentina*
   Mark Franko   171

CONTENTS

Part III: Preservation in Diaspora

8. Celebrations During a Traditional Wedding on the Island of Rhodes
Patricia Riak   197

9. A Creative Process in Ethiopian-Israeli Dance: Eskesta Dance Theater
and Beta Dance Troupe
Ruth Eshel   231

10. Dance and Difference: Toward an Individualization of the Pontian Self
Magda Zografou and Stavroula Pipyrou   267

Index   292

Citation Information

The following chapters were originally published in the journal *Dance Chronicle: Studies in Dance and the Related Arts*. When citing this material, please use the original issue information and page numbering for each article, as follows:

Chapter 2
Choreographers' Archives: Three Case Studies in Legacy Preservation
Cheryl LaFrance
Dance Chronicle: Studies in Dance and the Related Arts, volume 34, issue 1 (2011)
pp.48-76

Chapter 3
The Choreographer's Trust: Negotiating Authority in Peggy Baker's Archival Project
Allana C. Lindgren and Amy Bowring
Dance Chronicle: Studies in Dance and the Related Arts, volume 34, issue 1 (2011)
pp.77-105

Chapter 4
A Bold Step Forward: Genevieve Oswald and the Dance Collection of the New York Public Library
Lynn Matluck Brooks
Dance Chronicle: Studies in Dance and the Related Arts, volume 34, issue 3 (2011)
pp.447-486

Chapter 5
The Choreographic Trust: Preserving Dance Legacies
Francis Yeoh
Dance Chronicle: Studies in Dance and the Related Arts, volume 35, issue 2 (2012)
pp.224-249

Chapter 6
Gained in Translation: Recreation as Creative Practice
Valerie Preston-Dunlop and Lesley-Anne Sayers

Dance Chronicle: Studies in Dance and the Related Arts, volume 34, issue 1 (2011) pp.5-45
Copyright © 2011 Crown copyright

Chapter 7

The Dancing Gaze Across Cultures: Kazuo Ohno's Admiring La Argentina
Mark Franko

Dance Chronicle: Studies in Dance and the Related Arts, volume 34, issue 1 (2011) pp.106-131
Copyright © 2011 Mark Franko

Chapter 8

Celebrations During a Traditional Wedding on the Island of Rhodes
Patricia Riak

Dance Chronicle: Studies in Dance and the Related Arts, volume 34, issue 3 (2011) pp.388-421

Chapter 9

A Creative Process in Ethiopian-Israeli Dance: Eskesta Dance Theater and Beta Dance Troupe
Ruth Eshel

Dance Chronicle: Studies in Dance and the Related Arts, volume 34, issue 3 (2011) pp.352-387

Chapter 10

Dance and Difference: Toward an Individualization of the Pontian Self
Magda Zografou and Stavroula Pipyrou

Dance Chronicle: Studies in Dance and the Related Arts, volume 34, issue 3 (2011) pp.422-446

Notes on Contributors

Amy Bowring holds a B.A. in fine arts studies from York University, Canada, and an M.A. in journalism from the University of Western Ontario. She is the director of research at the archives/publisher Dance Collection Danse, the founder/director of the Society for Canadian Dance Studies, and the copy editor for *The Dance Current*. She is a frequent contributor to *Dance Collection, Danse Magazine* and *The Dance Current* and has also published articles and papers in books, encyclopedias, and conference proceedings. Bowring teaches Canadian dance history at Ryerson University. She is currently writing a book on the Canadian Ballet Festivals (1948–1954), and is curating an exhibition on Toronto's twentieth-century dance history. She has curated virtual exhibitions on Nancy Lima Dent and Alison Sutcliffe for www.dcd.ca. She is an outspoken advocate for dance preservation in Canada and was the literary manager for Peggy Baker's The Choreographer's Trust.

Ruth Eshel is a scholar, choreographer, dance critic, editor, and author. She was awarded a Ph.D. from Tel Aviv University, Israel, for her thesis, "Theater Movement in Israel, 1976–1991." From 1977 to 1986, she choreographed and danced in recitals in Israel and abroad performing her own works. She is author of *Dancing with the Dream: The Development of Artistic Dance in Israel, 1920–1964*, dance critic for the daily newspaper *Haaretz*, and founder-editor of the dance journal *Dance Today* [*Mahol Akshav*]. Between 1991 and 2005, she taught dance history and movement composition at the University of Haifa. From 1991 to 1993, she conducted research on the dance of the Ethiopian-Israelis for the Dance Library of Israel. In 1995, Eshel founded Eskesta Dance Theater at the University of Haifa and later Beta Dance Troupe in the Neve Yosef community center in Haifa.

Mark Franko, professor of dance and performance studies and director of the Center for Visual and Performance Studies at the University of California, Santa Cruz, USA, is editor of *Dance Research Journal* and the Oxford Studies in Dance Theory book series. His books have been translated into French, Italian, and Slovenian; they include *Dance as Text: Ideologies of the Baroque Body*, *Dancing Modernism/Performing Politics*, and *The Work of Dance: Labor, Movement, and*

Identity in the 1930s. He edited *Ritual and Event: Interdisciplinary Perspectives* and co-edited *Acting on the Past: Historical Performance Across the Disciplines.* His choreography has been produced at the Lincoln Center Out-of-Doors Festival, the Berlin Werkstatt Festival, the Getty Center, the Montpellier Opera, the Toulon Art Museum, the Haggerty Art Museum in Milwaukee, the Akademie der Künste in Berlin, the Mozarteum in Salzburg, and at many New York and San Francisco dance venues. He is currently finishing a book on Martha Graham, antifascism, and mythology in the 1940s.

Cheryl LaFrance is a Ph.D. student in dance studies at York University in Toronto, Canada, with a research focus on Canadian women choreographers. Her fascination with choreographers' archival practices began with video recording of reconstructions and rehearsals of dances by choreographers David Earle and Santee Smith in 2008. She also has an interest in dance dramaturgy and practice-based research, which evolved from her 2009 M.A. project analyzing her own creative process in the course of developing choreography that reflected her experiences with Skinner Releasing Technique and her connection to Tchaikovsky's Sixth Symphony. She retired from a secondary-school teaching career in 2005, but continues to work as a consultant and mentor in teaching development with a focus on curriculum, backwards design, assessment, and evaluation.

Allana C. Lindgren is Assistant Professor in the Department of Theatre at the University of Victoria in Victoria, British Columbia, Canada. She was on the board of the Society of Dance History Scholars from 2007 to 2010. Her research, which addresses twentieth-century dance history in Canada and the United States, has been awarded grants from the Social Sciences and Humanities Research Council of Canada and the Canada Council for the Arts. Her articles have been published in the *American Journal of Dance Therapy, Canadian Dance: Visions and Stories, Canadian Theatre Review, The Journal of Educational Thought, The Encyclopedia of Theatre Dance in Canada, The Journal of Arts Management, Law and Society,* and *Theatre Research in Canada,* as well as on the website *The Worlds of Herman Voaden.* She is also the author of the monograph *From Automatism to Modern Dance: Françoise Sullivan with Franziska Boas in New York* (2003).

Lynn Matluck Brooks is Arthur and Katherine Shadek Humanities Professor of Dance at Franklin & Marshall College, USA, where she founded the Dance Program in 1984. She holds degrees from the University of Wisconsin and Temple University. A Certified Movement Analyst and practicing dance historian, she has held grants from the Fulbright/Hayes Commission, the Pennsylvania Council on the Arts, and the National Endowment for the Humanities. Brooks has been a performance reviewer for *Dance Magazine,* editor of *Dance Research Journal,* and co-editor of *Dance Chronicle: Studies in Dance and the Related Arts,* and is author of four books and many articles. Brooks remains active as a choreographer, researcher, and teacher while continuing to administer the F&M Dance Program.

Joellen A. Meglin is Associate Professor of Dance at Temple University, USA. Her articles have appeared frequently in journals such as *Dance Research* (UK), *Dance Research Journal* and *Dance Chronicle*, and two essays have been published in Studies in Dance History monographs. She has served as coeditor of *Dance Chronicle* since 2008.

Stavroula Pipyrou holds a Ph.D. in anthropology from Durham University, UK, where she is currently a teaching fellow. She has conducted extensive fieldwork among the Greek linguistic minority in Reggio Calabria, south Italy, focusing on civil society, politics and governance, kinship, and dance. Since 2004 she has been engaged in ongoing research in northern Greece examining the political aspects of Pontic dance. She is also a member of the dance research team for the project Aspects of Refugee Identity in Halkidiki.

Valerie Preston-Dunlop, author and practical scholar, studied with Rudolf Laban, performed with British Dance Theatre, and was a founding member of both The International Council of Kinetography Laban and the Society for Dance Research. Interested in reexamining Laban's praxis and concepts, she published translated texts from the Weimar Republic journal *Schrifttanz* (1990) and wrote the award-winning biography *Rudolf Laban: An Extraordinary Life* (1998). Dr. Preston-Dunlop is well known for her recreations of Laban's *Kammertanz* works of the 1920s, the latest being *Nacht 1927 to Night 2010* with Alison Curtis-Jones and dancers from Trinity Laban in London. Her books *Looking at Dances: A Choreological Perspective* (1998) and *Dance and the Performative: Laban and Beyond* (2002) are widely read. Of her DVDs, *An American Invasion 1962–72* (2005) documents the arrival of American modern dance in the United Kingdom, and *Living Architecture* (2008) presents Laban's interest in sacred geometry and the body. She is a consultant and an honorary research fellow at Trinity Laban, and her recent research on William Forsythe's dance-theater piece *The Loss of Small Detail* has been published as an interactive web file.

Patricia Riak received her Ph.D. in social anthropology, with a focus on the anthropology of performance, from La Trobe University in Australia. Researching traditional folk dance practices on the island of Rhodes in the Dodecanese, she won the Greek-Australian Award from the National Languages and Literacy Institute of Australia for her doctoral research. She has worked in the French Studies Department at the University of Melbourne and the Greek-Australian Archive and Learning Centre at RMIT (Royal Melbourne Institute of Technology) University, where she researched Greek-Australian students' maintenance of the Greek language and their aspirations in education. She has written articles on a range of topics including Greek dance, the traditional Greek island wedding, Greek Orthodox saint worship, first-generation Australian-born Greek identity, and the Greek community in Australia. Dr. Riak was recently appointed adjunct assistant professor of socio-cultural anthropology in the Department of Anthropology at Temple University, where she teaches a course on anthropology and art.

Lesley-Anne Sayers (1958-2010), in her short but packed career, was an associate lecturer on modern art at the Open University at Bristol and a visiting lecturer at Gloucester University, UK. She wrote essays for the books *Fifty Contemporary Choreographers* (1996), *Dance in the City* (1997) and *Soviet Society and Music Under Lenin and Stalin* (2004), and reviewed books for *Dance Now*, *Gender & History*, and *Dance Theatre Journal*. Immediately prior to her death in 2010, she had co-developed a new master's module for Trinity Laban and undertaken a project with the composer Michael Berkeley and the choreographer Melanie Clarke to rework the lost Massine/Nabokov/Tchelitchew ballet *Ode* (1928).

Francis Yeoh has completed his doctoral thesis, "Copyright Law Does Not Adequately Accommodate the Artform of Dance," at Birkbeck Law School, University of London, UK. He trained in law and graduated from the University of Singapore. In dance, he trained at the Royal Ballet School and then studied notation at the Benesh Institute of Choreology (1965 67) on a British Council grant. He founded and directed the Singapore National Dance and Theatre Company (1970–78). He has presented conference papers at meetings of the European Association of Dance Historians, the Society for Dance Research, and the project *Music and Dance: Beyond Copyright Text* (supported by UK Arts and Humanities Council).

Magda Zografou is professor of Greek traditional dance ethnochoreology in the Department of Physical Education and Sports Science at the University of Athens, Greece. She is also coordinator and tutor of Greek culture for the program in Greek music and dance at the Open University, Greece. Since the mid-1980s she has been engaged in fieldwork within Pontian communities in northern Greece, focusing on the politics of dance. She is director of dance research on the project Aspects of Refugee Identity in Halkidiki. She has published in Greek and English on Greek traditional dance with focuses on Pontic and Cretan dance as well as on the role of dance in Greek education. Zografou is the author of *Dance in the Greek Tradition* (2001). She translated and edited the Greek edition of Anya Peterson Royce's *The Anthropology of Dance* (2005) and edited the Greek edition of Richard Schechner's *The Theory of Performance* (forthcoming).

INTRODUCTION

LYNN MATLUCK BROOKS and JOELLEN A. MEGLIN

Dance flickers "at the vanishing point": the movement is performed and viewed, but cannot be fixed in time or memory. Rather, "a moment later, who could be sure" what it was—*that* it was?[1] Dancers know this, many finding ephemerality part of the thrill of the art, and writers—like Marcia Siegel, quoted above—faced with an assignment to discuss a dance work they have just seen immediately feel this truth. You cannot hold on to dance. Or can you? What constitutes the stuff of dance history? Can we legitimately talk about dance existing in time? Dance's relationship to place is also fragile. What William Hardy McNeil has described as "the indefinitely expansible basis for social cohesion among any and every group that keeps together in time"—this "muscular bonding"[2]—is connected inextricably to the ground and community from which this dancing sprang. What happens when a community migrates from that ground?

These questions shape the essays in this volume, resulting from a call for papers by the editors of *Dance Chronicle: Studies in Dance and the Related Arts* on the theme "Preserving Dance as a Living Legacy." In formulating this call we asked, Can we hold on to our dancing past? What value might dance have in spite of, or even because of, this very fragility? How are preservation and recreation to be achieved? Dancer and critic Fernau Hall noted the "poverty" of access to ballet's traditions when compared with the antiquity of available precedents in the fields of painting, literature, and music.[3] Commenting on the irretrievable loss of so many ballets old and—in his time—new, Hall bemoaned "losses caused by imperfect transmission (or complete failure of transmission)." These losses so impede the forward momentum of the art that, periodically, it must "be re-created almost from scratch."[4] Ballet, of course, is not the only dance art so troubled, according to a recent publication of the Dance Heritage Coalition (DHC): "From toe to toe, from hand to hand, from eye to eye, dance, more than any other of the performing arts, has been transmitted through time by human chains of dancers, choreographers, and others involved in its creation and performance." However, the fragility of that chain makes it imperative that we, according to DHC, "take advantage of new awareness, new technology, and new resources to lessen our dependence on the human chain of memory."[5]

It became evident that the questions and topics articulated in this *Dance Chronicle* call for papers were concerns shared by many in the dance world. So rich were the responses to this theme that we published two issues on the subject: volume 34, number 1, was titled, like the call for papers, "Preserving Dance as a Living Legacy," while volume 34, number 3, focused on "Preserving Dance in Diaspora." In these issues, we presented a range of voices discussing concerns that cross time and geographies. Preservation, as discussed in these articles, involves memory as well as artistic choice, interpretation, cultural continuity and flexibility, and the realities of dealing with institutions, individuals, communities, documentation, and artifacts. It is a challenging endeavor—rich with possibilities for generating new knowledge and even new art from the perspectives of both embodied memory and intellectual history.

In 2006, for example, Canadian dancers participated in an important gathering, "Endangered Dance: A National Dance Heritage Forum," held in Toronto, Canada, and spurred by the Danny Grossman Dance Company as it faced the retirement of its artistic director. This forum articulated goals for protecting, preserving, and sustaining Canadian dance and dance history. In "Choreographers' Archives: Three Case Studies in Legacy Preservation," Cheryl LaFrance explores how the objectives emerging from that forum have shaped the work of choreographers Karen Kaeja, Allen Kaeja, Rachel Browne, and Stephanie Ballard. Moving from the dancers' views to a different perspective, LaFrance also explores ways that Canadian archives, such as Dance Collection Danse, have responded to the needs of dance preservation and she offers views from archivists on strategies for artistic documentation and legacy maintenance.

Another Canadian artist, Peggy Baker, established a highly personal plan for preserving her dance legacy. In "The Choreographer's Trust: Negotiating Authority in Peggy Baker's Archival Project," Allana C. Lindgren and Amy Bowring investigate the give and take that Baker embedded in her preservation plan, which allows for artistic interpretation of her documented works and yet retains control of what is preserved and how it is presented to the public. Baker resists authoritative readings of her works, seeing the dances as opportunities for interpretive choice as artists of different backgrounds perform them. Yet the materials of the six selected dances—the steps, patterns, and musical choices—remain Baker's, supported by considerable textual documentation for each work selected for preservation. This plan results in "a paradox … as the traditionally privileged position ascribed to choreographers in relation to their work is both restricted and reinforced by Baker's efforts to archive her solos," these six being the only works she chose for her preservation project. Baker, like the artists discussed in LaFrance's article, was caught between the ongoing artistic urge for creating anew and the desire to preserve works already presented and she, along with her Canadian dance colleagues, faced the limitations of time and funding that forced choices about which works would be documented and the format for that preservation.

The trust has been a legacy-preserving choice for other artists as well. In fact, Francis Yeoh advocates the choreographic trust as the ideal legal construct for safeguarding, sustaining, and controlling a choreographer's work beyond his or her lifetime. In "The Choreographic Trust: Preserving Dance Legacies," Yeoh takes a close look at successes and failures in preservation of the *oeuvres* of George Balanchine, Frederick Ashton, Jerome Robbins, Merce Cunningham, and Martha Graham. Citing legal precedents and rulings as well as concerns and practical outcomes of these artists' plans (or lack thereof) regarding their own legacies, Yeoh makes a persuasive argument for the value of the trust, in its varied manifestations, as an instrument for artistic preservation. The responsibilities, rights, and privileges of the artist and legatees receive careful attention in Yeoh's concerns for appropriately constructed and sustainable trusts.

An institution that has played a central role in the preservation of dance of all types—theatrical, social, folk, and more—by means of the written word, material traces, oral histories, and film recording is discussed in "A Bold Step Forward: Genevieve Oswald and the Dance Collection of The New York Public Library" by Lynn Matluck Brooks. More precisely, the experiences and memories of that collection's primary founder and long-time sustaining curator, Genevieve Oswald, form the backbone of this article—part history, part memoire. How this collection has interfaced with and influenced dance trends, research technologies, choreographers and performers, and dance preservation is revealed in Oswald's wide-ranging comments on her work and on the field it helped to nurture.

Dance in academe, which depends on institutions like the New York Public Library's Dance Collection, plays an important role in preservation of the art's history. Trinity Laban is one such academic center that values not only new dance, but dances of history. In "Gained in Translation: Recreation as Creative Practice," Valerie Preston-Dunlop and Lesley-Anne Sayers consider *recreation*—with the emphasis on creative process—to fill the lacunae in information when no detailed transcriptions of movement or camera-recorded moving images of the original work exist. But their argument has implications even for reconstruction as traditionally understood, as they explore what lies beneath the "surface forms" of a work—what processes and intents created it and what meanings it has accrued within larger political, economic, sociocultural, and intellectual contexts, not to mention the specific circumstances of its production. Preston-Dunlop's recreation of Rudolf Laban's *Die Grünen Clowns* (Green Clowns, 1928) and Sayers's recreation of Georgi Yakoulov's Constructivist set design for Sergei Prokofiev's *Le Pas d'Acier* (1927) present new knowledge that could only be revealed through embodiment: the psychic-physical-spiritual connections made when a dancer inhabits a complete world, rich with visual-aural-kinetic intersections and replete with historical meanings. Notable about Preston-Dunlop and Sayers' approach is its focus on the learning community involved in the project, comprised of students and faculty-artists, arts and humanities scholars, and the general public; digital access compounds the interdisciplinary, interactive knowledge that can be generated by such projects.

Mark Franko's "The Dancing Gaze across Cultures: Kazuo Ohno's *Admiring La Argentina*" plumbs some of the paradox between the two components of the title of the initial call for papers: "preserving dance" and "dance as a living legacy." Is there something in the very concept of preservation that suggests freezing of a dance creation as it existed at a particular point in time? When a work "lives" (is recreated) or a choreographic artist is revisited, is it not always through the eyes and embodiment of the new artist(s), hence summoning memory and phenomenological experience, both individual and cultural? Franko's study of Kazuo Ohno's famous evocation of La Argentina (Antonio Mercé) explores the meanings that proliferate, recursively, iteratively, when one artist "admires" the work of another. In considering an extreme case—one artist remembering another across time warps, gender gaps, generational differences, geographic divides, and even cultures—Franko's philosophical–psychoanalytic perspective reminds us that the "gaze" is integral to the process. There must be *somebody* who "remembers." In alighting on *excorporation*—empathetic transcendence of self—as the psychoanalytic process underlying Ohno's tribute or memorial, the author's argument resonates with others in this anthology that investigate meaning in works of memory.

It is not only the individual artist who springs across divides in time and space, with the fluid medium of dance serving as their bridge; global migration or diaspora has also shaped dance practice and preservation. As populations move from their homelands to different cultural settings, they must find new understandings as well as methods of preservation and reconstruction for their traditional dances. As a Greek-Australian (now living in the United States), Patricia Riak has pursued "nostalgic ethnography" to uncover family heritage in the island of Rhodes, where her grandfather was a prize-winning *sousta* dancer. Because her focus is on the period between the two world wars, she interviews Greek citizens from her grandfather's generation, constructing her text from their memories, which results in a rich and warmly human description of the wedding ritual in which the *sousta* was embedded. She uncovers the dance's integral part in courtship and marriage, expressing central cultural values of honor and grace, legitimizing gender relations, and revitalizing a Greek village community.

Another inter-war migration affecting Greek populations was forced on the Pontians, who came to Greece from Anatolia, Turkey, as part of a massive population exchange mandated by the Treaty of Lausanne in 1923. Focusing on the celebrations of Panayía Soumelá, a summer feast honoring the Madonna, Magda Zografou and Stavroula Pipyrou explore the preservation not only of movement but also of cultural identity in this community's maintenance of the dance traditions connected with this holiday. These traditions mark the community of Pontians as distinct and individuated from surrounding Greek populations, even as they borrow from, allude to, and integrate with contemporary Greek society. Key to this investigation are the concepts of "major" and "minor" differences—the theoretical framework for this research—which facilitate or hinder a population's distinctness as well as tolerance of difference.

Some artists are concerned with sustaining the nature of a community's expression in movement, what Ruth Eshel calls the "DNA" of a people's dance language. In her article, "A Creative Process in Ethiopian-Israeli Dance: Eskesta Dance Theater and Beta Dance Troupe," Eshel explains the particular circumstances leading to the immigration of a large population of Ethiopian Jews to Israel, the challenges faced by this group to both sustain its traditions and to integrate into contemporary Western society, and her own role in nurturing a choreographic version of this delicate balancing act. What kinds of works can best represent these dancers, the roles they play in the creative process, and Eshel's drive as both an artist and a teacher to explore and sustain essential elements of this community's movement language? Investigating these questions yields insights relevant to other immigrant populations struggling with their own cultural sustainability. The relationship of "folk" to "theater" dance and the unique history of dance in Israel are factors in the development, presentation, and reception of this work.

Today's artists are aware of dance's slipperiness: "Everything that we do as dancers, as choreographers, is created and destroyed in the same moment," according to Crystal Pite, a Canadian choreographer who worked closely with William Forsythe at Ballett Frankfurt. As she watched older colleagues and teachers retire from the stage, she discovered, "I had nothing to hang onto, other than memories."[6] This led Pite to ask, in her work *Lost Action*, some of the very questions that have shaped this anthology: "What happens to a dance when it's over? Does it vanish, never to exist again? What if, like a painting, a dance could live on forever?" She concludes, "Dance is really a present-moment experience. It is always disappearing unless you are doing it. I think this could be what gives it its power, but it's also quite tragic."[7]

With the attention to preserving and recreating dance across time and space articulated by the artists and authors included in this volume, we grapple with this very loss—its implications and even its potential for dance's renewal.

Notes

1 Marcia Siegel, *At the Vanishing Point: A Dance Critic Looks at Dance* (New York: Saturday Review Press, 1972), 1.
2 William Hardy McNeil, *Keeping Together in Time: Dance and Drill in Human History* (Cambridge, Mass.: Harvard University Press, 1995), 2.
3 Fernau Hall, "Dance Notation and Choreology," in *What Is Dance?*, ed. Roger Copeland and Marshall Cohen (Oxford: Oxford University Press, 1983), 390.
4 Ibid., 392.
5 Dance Heritage Coalition, "Beyond Memory: Preserving the Documents of our Dance Heritage" (http://www.danceheritage.org/preservation/beyond.html#intro, accessed December 17, 2010).
6 Crystal Pite, quoted by Robert Johnson in " 'Dark Matters' Review: A Look at the Ephemeral Nature of Dance," *Star-Ledger*, Oct. 15, 2010 (http://www.nj.com/entertainment/arts/index.ssf/2010/10/dark_matters_review_a_look_at.html, accessed July 24, 2012).
7 Pite, quoted by Sara Bauknecht in "Kidd Pivot Explores Ephemeral Nature of Dance in 'Action,'" *Pittsburgh Post-Gazette*, March 16, 2012 (http://www.post-gazette.com/stories/ae/theater-dance/kidd-pivot-explores-ephemeral-nature-of-dance-in-action-360014/, accessed July 24, 2012).

CHOREOGRAPHERS' ARCHIVES: THREE CASE STUDIES IN LEGACY PRESERVATION

CHERYL LaFRANCE

Case studies of current practice in dance archives, preservation, and legacy-building among established Canadian choreographers are instructive for the field. The personalities, circumstances, and creative drive of each of these choreographers influence choices in maintenance of records for their own legacies. Viewpoints from archivists and the head of a national dance collection further illuminate this investigation.

What choices and concerns do established contemporary-dance choreographers face as they attempt to maintain a legacy of their historic records and past dance creations while they are still actively creating and presenting new choreography? Three case studies of choreographers who are wrestling with the everyday realities of simultaneously preserving the past, creating in the present, and planning for the future reveal some opportunities and limitations that other choreographers may wish to consider. Circumstances and preferences of the choreographers affect their choices of what to keep, where to deposit it, and how to ensure that it is passed on for use in the future. Each case demonstrates that a choreographer's legacy is both a historical record that resides in archived form and a cultural memory or experience that the choreographer envisions leaving behind for future audiences, educators, and scholars.

The terms *archive, preservation,* and *legacy* are used casually and sometimes interchangeably in the dance community, while to professional archivists they have strictly defined meanings. Many choreographers consider their archive to be all the "stuff" they have amassed over the years that is significant to their artistic life; their collections incorporate both primary and secondary source material in two- and three-dimensional formats. From a professional archivist's point of view, not all of this material may qualify for acquisition by a traditional archive. In addition, the creative process of choreographers is a challenge to document because it takes place in unrecorded or undocumented ways: in the choreographers' and dancers' bodies, and in ongoing dialogue between choreographers and dancers. To the dance community, the term *preservation* usually connotes having the material and personnel that allow for a dance's reconstruction. However, to archivists the terms *preservation* and *conservation* have specific implications about methods of maintaining records in an archive. *Legacy* can also be problematic because to some archivists, as well as to the choreographers interviewed in this research, the term seems to have subjective connotations and a broad range of meanings. The term *living legacy* is also often used in the dance community to describe the various ways dance artists and scholars employ documentation such as video recordings of performances, reconstruction projects, interviews, and oral histories to preserve a record of a dance, sometimes long after its original creation.

In Canada, as in the United States and other nations, there is a growing sense of urgency at both the national and grassroots levels about preserving dance heritage. The urgency in Canada was precipitated at the beginning of the new millennium by the realization that the current "senior" generation of choreographers, whose initial dances and companies exploded onto stages across the country in the 1960s and 1970s, were reaching retirement. These transitions could mean the potential loss of these artists' work and even of their documentation, as had happened with many of the preceding generations of choreographers. To date, the larger companies still operating either have continued to keep their own collections of material generated by their administrative and creative departments in the form of an in-house archive or have donated all or part of their historical records to collecting institutions. Primary among such institutions is Dance Collection Danse (DCD) in Toronto, the only national collection in Canada specifically for theatrical dance. It was founded in 1986 by the late Lawrence Adams and Miriam Adams, both of whom were dancers and choreographers. According to the DCD's website,

> programming combines ongoing activities in collections, preservation, research, publishing and education.... Through DCD's magazine, books and virtual exhibitions, DCD provides a context for the past and a foundation for the future of dance [in Canada]... the

archival holdings represent the work of dance artists, companies and events related to theatrical dance dating back to the nineteenth century. These include choreographic notes, moving images, oral histories, sets, props, personal correspondence, house programs and other artifacts.[1]

The collection is approaching 550 archival "portfolios."

Some companies and artists have donated their collections to other heritage repositories in their own provinces. The Archives of Manitoba holds records of the early years of Winnipeg's Contemporary Dancers. The Bibliothèque et Archives nationales du Québec (BAnQ) recently acquired the *fonds* of the late Jean-Pierre Perreault.[2] Canada's national repository, Library and Archives Canada, holds very few dance-related records. Instead, the expectation is that dance companies and artists will work with their regional institutions, universities, and municipal libraries to arrange acquisition of their records.[3] Generally, most institutions take a passive stance to this type of acquisition and respond to incoming inquiries only.

Historically, public archives in Canada functioned largely to collect the organizational records of their sponsoring body (for example, provincial government records were collected by the relevant provincial archival institution), along with complementary acquisitions of historical material from their jurisdictions. In practice, this has resulted in a very limited focus on local performing arts. Most federal and provincial museum and art gallery collections do not focus on collecting Canadian theater-dance artifacts. Nevertheless, owing to the keen interest of an individual librarian, such as occurred at the Toronto Reference Library, some municipal libraries developed theater or performing arts collections that included dance. There is no national initiative comparable to that of the Dance Heritage Coalition in the United States. Thus, the initiative for collecting dance archives in Canada has sprung primarily from dance communities themselves in the major cities nationwide. Aside from DCD and the in-house archives of the major companies, significant collections are held by various dance organizations. Many Quebec dance resources are in La Bibliothèque de la danse de Vincent Warren (formerly La Bibliothèque de l'École supérieure de danse du Québec) and the Tangente Centre de documentation in Montreal. Other Canadian resource collections are listed on the Society for Canadian Dance Studies website.[4]

Concern about the state of dance resources and collections in Canada prompted several federally commissioned studies that offer insights into archivists' and librarians' work with choreographers and their collections. In 1982 the then National Library of Canada (now Library and Archives Canada) published the study *Dance Resources in Canadian Libraries*, which serves as a baseline for the history of dance collections in Canada.[5] In 2000 the Dance Section of the Canada Council for the Arts, in conjunction with the Department of Canadian Heritage (Arts and Heritage Sector), commissioned the *Study of Dance Collections in Canada* by Theresa Rowat, now archivist at McGill University.[6] Rowat found that the dance community in Canada was generally not systematic in recordkeeping and record management. Another of Rowat's observations was that the types of material prevalent in dance collections posed some problems for archival repositories because they did not fit easily into traditional collecting practices. Three-dimensional objects such as costumes and artifacts are problematic as "records" for an archive. Additionally, because video recordings and audiotapes become obsolete and deteriorate they likely require extensive conservation and preservation measures.

Following Rowat's study, the Canada Council for the Arts and concerned members of the dance community took several initiatives between 2000 and 2006 to launch a conversation among all the parties interested in dance heritage—creators, educators, scholars, historians, administrators, and collecting institutions—in order to advance dance heritage collection and preservation. The LOGIN:DANC/SE symposium, supported by the Canada Council and facilitated by Rowat for these stakeholders in 2000, was the incentive for developing the document, "A Dance Heritage Strategy for Canada—2002."[7] Movement toward implementing the many strategies suggested has progressed slowly. The issues are complex since they involve both arts and heritage funding.

A third major report for the Canada Council for the Arts, in 2005, *Legacy, Transition and Succession: Supporting the Past and Future of Canada's Arts Organizations*, set a national context for further discussion of issues related to arts heritage, funding, and policy recommendations across and within seven arts disciplines, including dance. The report's basic definition of legacy across the arts is informative:

> The legacy of an arts organization represents the accumulated artistic capital, derived from its artistic mission, vision and mandate. Artistic capital is realized over time through the whole of the organization's creation, production and/or dissemination activities. Legacy also embraces relationships built with the organization's various communities; its intellectual property; archives documenting its creative work; and facilities or equipment essential to fulfilling its mandate.[8]

The definition of legacy emphasizes a broad picture of "accumulated artistic [and organizational] capital," archival records being only one of several components. A key recommendation in the report was that organizations applying for operating support grants be asked to "articulate their artistic and organizational legacy, along with plans to preserve that legacy."[9]

As part of this growing national focus on the importance of preserving dance legacy, Danny Grossman's Dance Company in Toronto had a particular sense of urgency in 2005 as its choreographer faced imminent retirement and the dissolution of the company after almost thirty years. It was thus appropriate that Grossman's company take the initiative in January 2006 to convene a grassroots dance community conference, "Endangered Dance: A National Dance Heritage Forum," in Toronto. Dance artists, choreographers, arts administrators, scholars, teachers, and archivists shared concerns and ideas and a website was created to summarize the presentations and recommendations: "Designed with three goals in mind, Endangered Dance drew attention to the critical need to protect our Canadian Dance Heritage, gain a better picture of the scope of preservation activities currently underway, including where collections are currently being held, and to collectively define goals that would lead us to the development of a dance heritage strategy."[10] Speakers and panels worked to clarify the role of dance documentation and preservation as more than just a concern for historical records. Documenting choreography was identified as integral to dance teaching, performances, and scholarship.

The seven themed sessions at the Endangered Dance forum addressed the fundamental aspects of fostering dance legacy through advocacy, artifacts, education, policy, technology, performances, and community. Each of the seven discussion groups identified short-term, mid-term, and long-term goals with time frames of approximately one, three, and five years. The goals generated by these panels, posted on the conference website, offer insights from across the spectrum of stakeholders in dance heritage and highlight the legacy concerns of practicing choreographers. It is notable, however, that this initiative came from the dance community rather than from collecting institutions, a fact reflected in the themes and goals. The conference illustrated that the dance community's focus on how and what to archive, preserve, and conserve is different from that of a collecting institution in that dancers are concerned predominantly with methods of fostering a legacy of living dances. The conference website can, perhaps, give archivists insights into choreographers' thinking about dance legacy priorities.

The three case studies of choreographers presented here shed some light on the reality of achieving the one-, three-, and five-year goals set out at the Endangered Dance forum. As Rowat wrote in her summary document distributed before the conference, there is a continuing competition for each choreographer's energy between "the immediacy of creation and performance" and the need for "documentation and the archival record."[11] She also observed:

> The interest in dance documentation and heritage preservation is growing as dance records are sought for the revival and reconstruction of works, for development and teaching methods that draw on studying past works, as well as for dance scholarship, literacy and promotion. Although the immediacy of creation and performance predominates, there is increasing historical awareness and recognition of the value of documentation and the archival record.

In order to compare the approaches of the three choreographers studied here, I use the framework of the Endangered Dance forum's discussion themes: advocacy, artifacts, education, policy, technology, performances, and community.[12]

The Choreographers' Perspectives

Interviews with choreographers Karen Kaeja and Allen Kaeja of Kaeja d'Dance in Toronto, Ontario, as well as with Rachel Browne and Stephanie Ballard, independent choreographers associated with Winnipeg's Contemporary Dancers and the School of Contemporary Dancers in Winnipeg, Manitoba, revealed that each artist's legacy and archiving goals are as distinctive as their dances. While it is almost unnatural for them to think "backward" about their records and how to bequeath their earlier dances when they are constantly thinking "forward" about creating new works, the choice of whether to collect records of their performances or to create legacy tools for remounting works has become a conscious choice, depending on each choreographer's circumstances and objectives. And, in each case, the goals set out at the Endangered Dance forum for sustaining a national dance legacy came up against the limited funding available for dedicated personnel and technical support needed to maintain an archive and for documenting the creative process.

Allen and Karen Kaeja of Kaeja d'Dance

Kaeja d'Dance, founded by co–artistic directors and choreographers Karen Kaeja and Allen Kaeja in 1991, is approaching its twentieth anniversary. The company has presented more than one hundred original works employing dynamically complex contact improvisation and their Kaeja partnering technique on the concert stage, in city parks, and in other community venues. Commissions for choreography come not only from other Canadian dancers, but also from troupes in England, Mexico, India, Sweden, the United States, and elsewhere.[13]

The Kaejas have been systematic about maintaining their archival records from the beginning of their dancing lives and during an interview and tour of their home office they explained their system of collecting records.[14] Allen said that his father's experience of losing everything as a Holocaust survivor influenced him from an early age to start collecting news clippings of his achievements, using scrapbooks as his archive. Karen is the unofficial Kaeja d'Dance company archivist who throws playbills, publicity postcards, and newspaper clippings in a large box that gets sorted out every summer into three piles: one for filing in the plastic sleeves of their own year-by-year archival binders, one for a box that goes to their file at DCD, and a third pile for the Performing Arts Centre's printed ephemera collection at the Toronto

Reference Library. The basement office in their home has book-cases full of their archival binders, some predating the found-ing of the company when they were students at the University of Waterloo (Ontario), York University, and Ryerson University (Toronto). The bookcases also house videotapes and DVDs of per-formances and the dance films they have created. Master copies of these tapes, films, and DVDs are stored at Creative Post, Inc., a Toronto film production facility. Office records are backed up every Friday on external hard drives brought in by the Kaejas' company manager. Posters are stored in portfolios of the size typ-ically used by art students or mounted on the basement office walls. Framed citations and awards are also hung on the office walls with photocopies placed in the annual binders. Wall space in the hallway outside the office is full of posters and photographs as well, and a bookcase holds binders of original publicity pho-tographs, negatives, and reprints from predigital days. Another basement room provides storage for a rack of recent costumes and even boxes of their children's archives. The garage holds boxes of extra publicity postcards, old paper office records, and more costumes.

The Kaejas admit to sharing a love for organizing their mate-rial, which makes the task easier. They use their archival binders and store of extra postcards to prepare material for press kits. But they find that keeping up is daunting. In the summer of 2009, for the first time that she remembers, Karen never did get around to sorting out the annual collection of "stuff" in the box. The bookcases are quickly filling up and they are outgrowing their home storage space. When queried about how they use their video recordings, they said that they do record rehearsals and use those videos in the creative process. They also record every stage per-formance with a single camera and Karen reviews these video-tapes afterward, marking on the case which version is the "best." Thus, their collection of video recordings is "huge" according to Allen.[15] For example, the piece *Resistance* toured off and on for five years after two years of development and rehearsal, and all of the creative process, rehearsals, and performances were video-taped. Their extensive video collection provides a "clear record" of each choreography so that they can recall the work when presenters or other companies ask to remount their works or when the Kaejas create dance films based on their choreography.

Figure 1. Karen Kaeja and Teena Walker in Allen Kaeja's dance film *Asylum of Spoons* (2005). Photograph by Albert Camicioli. Courtesy of Kaeja d' Dance.

Allen used performance footage from the cross-Canada tour of *Old Country* in 1995 to prepare dancers in 2003 for recreating the piece in a dance film. Similarly, stage performance videos were useful when the dance *Asylum of Spoons* was transformed into a major dance film in 2005. (See Figure 1.) Yet, despite all the video recordkeeping, Allen said the focus is always their future works. They are always looking ahead to the next major project.

In examining this archival activity in light of the short- and mid-term goals of the Endangered Dance forum themes of artifacts, technology, and performances, it is clear that the Kaejas are effective grassroots archivists. Their systematic approach to collecting all manner of records and artifacts generated in their creative and administrative practices predates by more than fifteen years the 2007 and 2008 workshops held by DCD to assist

Figure 2. Allen Kaeja. Photograph by Shira Leuchter. Courtesy of Shira Leuchter.

choreographers and dance companies in implementing "Grass-roots Archiving: A National Preservation Strategy for Dance" introduced at the forum.[16] In terms of technology they are experts with using video and film; based on his many years of making dance films, Allen(Figure 2) teaches a dance-film course at Ryerson University. Storing his master tapes and films in an off-site professional facility shows his awareness of "established archival standards," identified as a technology goal by the Endangered Dance forum.

However, with respect to the performance goals identified at the forum, Kaeja d'Dance took a different perspective. The forum set a short-term goal of remounting works at the annual Canada Dance Festival in Ottawa, Ontario, as a way of preserving "masterworks" with long-term goals of remounting works on student and emerging dance groups. The Kaejas did not keep a video record of their works for the express use of other dancers remounting their "masterworks" in the future. Allen felt that the Kaeja partnering technique is unique to the process and skills that he and Karen have developed and until recently he believed that the complex elevations in the partnering should not be attempted by those who had not trained with them. Thus, remounting their works in the distant future would have been problematic if their video-tapes were the only resource. However, he now feels that today's young dancers are training differently and have more access to instruction in complex partnering so that future remounting of their dances, based only on their archive of videos and without input from Allen and Karen, might be possible.[17]

While they are meticulous recordkeepers, creation and continued investigation propel the Kaejas forward. In her online commentary, "Making Dance," Karen articulates their mandate:

> With a personal vision at the forefront, we continue to trust our first impulse as well as that of our dancers. Our movement invention is a distinct blend of inspiration between the dancers and the choreographer. Whether we are creating or performing for stage or camera, investigation deepens each day. With the desire to open our eyes just that little bit wider, while we are in the studio and when we are teaching, we strive to reach a visceral core of impact within ourselves, our audiences, and our students.[18]

This philosophy embraces dance as a process experienced in the present moment. Furthermore, Karen adds, "as artists, Allen and I live in a beautiful place of open investigation. We are teachers and students, choreographers and performers, all in one breath. The intimacy we have with our own process is shared by our dancers who work with us." The emphasis is "open investigation," which they do through both the intimacy of the film camera and the immediacy of their live performances. It appears, then, that their main focus in meticulously maintaining their collection of records is to leave a complete historical record that will provide material for scholarly research about their work and lives. The archive of performance videos may prove helpful for future reconstructions by other dance artists, but this is not their primary purpose. The intensity of their choreographic vision and their dancing will remain alive in their dance films.

Rachel Browne of Winnipeg's Contemporary Dancers and the School of Contemporary Dancers

In contrast to the Kaejas, Rachel Browne's archival practice has been one of catch-up. Browne founded Winnipeg's Contemporary Dancers (WCD) in 1964 and began a tradition, which still continues, of presenting a contemporary dance repertory created by many Canadian and United States choreographers. As artistic

Figure 3. Rachel Browne performing in Stephanie Ballard's *homeagain* (2010). Photograph by Vince Pahkala. Courtesy of Vince Pahkala.

director of WCD for more than twenty years, Browne had little time for creating dances, but by the mid-1980s she became an independent choreographer with commissions not only from WCD, but also for other Canadian dancers. She continues to create new works, to remount earlier ones, and to perform on occasion. (See Figure 3.)

When Browne founded WCD more than forty-five years ago, she was responsible not only for the day-to-day survival of the company, but also for the establishment of the School of Contemporary Dancers (SCD).[19] Choreographing a piece or two each year and raising a family, she had no time for archiving WCD's history beyond videotaping performances and tossing a few mimeographed programs, hand-drawn posters, and newspaper clippings into a closet at home. She said that she "inadvertently saved" these items because she was a "pack-rat," not because of their importance.[20] Browne's story illustrates many of the concerns identified at the 2006 Endangered Dance forum regarding the themes of technology and performance: she has faced difficulties with updating old video formats to maintain her archive of performance videos and she has little existing documentation

of her creative process or remounted works for guiding future remounting of her dances.

In late 1982 Browne was fired by a hostile WCD Board but she
diplomatically managed to continue her connection with both the
company and school. A revered figure, she is widely acknowledged
for her longtime contribution to Canadian dance. With this major
shift in the company's artistic direction the WCD's records-to-date
were acquired by the Archives of Manitoba in the mid-1980s and
a student was hired to label newspaper articles and programs with
the year and location and mount the items in scrapbooks. Browne
assisted the student in this first attempt at organizing a company
archive. By 1987 she started presenting work as an independent
choreographer, but she also wanted to create a record of her past
choreography, created for WCD. She received funding from the
Canada Council for the Arts to make videotaped copies of her
earlier work. On attempting to review the videotapes from WCD
programs she was disappointed to discover that many had turned
to dust after twenty years. She had to track down equipment to
play those that were still viable and she found a sympathetic tech-
nician at a Winnipeg video shop, Fotovideo, who helped her transfer the WCD repertory as well as her own dances to Hi-eight cassette tapes and thence to VHS format. Three copies of each of
these videotapes were made—one for Browne, one for the Canada
Council, and one to be held at the Archives of Manitoba. In the
1990s the Canada Council returned their videotapes (1964–1992)
to Browne and she subsequently sent them to DCD's collection.
Their holdings of her videos now goes up to 1996. Throughout
this process, however, Browne admits that of "paramount importance was the new piece I was working on."[21]

Over a decade later Browne entered a third phase of archival
work with her video project for *Edgelit,* a piece she had developed between 1996 and 2000. She decided to document the
performance in 2000 with funding from the Margaret Laurence
Trust. She hired a professional videographer to film a performance of *Edgelit* and an editor from Midcan Productions in Winnipeg to create a high-quality VHS tape. Copies were sent to
universities and libraries across Canada. This venture—a shift in
her focus toward developing a lasting record of works she valued choreographically—continues to influence her vision of her
legacy projects. From 2002 to 2004 Browne developed another

piece, *Sunstorm,* set to Chopin's 24 Preludes. *Sunstorm* was also professionally filmed and edited, recorded in VHS and DVD formats. However, copies were sent only to producers who might want to present the work, not to educational institutions.

This third phase really began in earnest, however, around 2003, when Browne moved out of a house she had lived in for twenty-five years to a small apartment. She had to decide where to send the artifacts, video- and audiotapes, choreographic notes, and other papers accumulated in her closets and basement. The only items she decided to keep with her were videotape recordings of her dances. She entrusted the other material to Stephanie Ballard, longtime colleague and friend as well as official archivist for SCD and legacy adviser for WCD. Browne kept one copy of every dance she had made for WCD as well as those made for the school, boxed up the rest, and sent them to be stored in the school's new facilities. Another grant from the Canada Council for the Arts in 2006 allowed her to employ Kristin Haight, a WCD company member, to organize the boxes of videotapes that she had moved to her new residence and to create a coded inventory binder. The dance titles are listed alphabetically in the binder and Haight created codes to indicate the several tapes on which various performances of that dance are recorded.[22] Browne feels that this system, rather than a strictly chronological ordering, makes it easier for her, and for potential researchers, to find the dances. Finally, the videotapes were sent out for professional transfer to DVD format. Copies of each DVD are stored at Browne's apartment and at WCD. Browne has applied for continued funding to finish this phase of documenting her legacy. She has chosen eight to ten of her dances that she feels represent how she wants her craft to be remembered. Her goal is to have videotapes of these works edited professionally, as she did with *Edgelit,* so that she can also send these to libraries and other institutions for study by dance students and scholars.

In terms of a living performance legacy, several of Browne's works created since 1990 have been remounted by WCD. She is confident that these could be reconstructed by WCD without her presence because several dancers who recall these works are still in the company or located across Canada. Haight of WCD recently learned Browne's classic 1992 work *Mouvement* from videotapes and then through coaching by Alana

Figure 4. Kristin Haight in Rachel Browne's *Mouvement* (2009). Photograph by Rodney Braun. Courtesy of Rodney Braun.

Shewchuk, the original interpreter, who was no longer dancing with WCD but was available to consult. After refining the dance with Browne's assistance for the 2009 WCD tour On the Road, Haight began teaching the piece to another company member.[23] (See Figure 4.) Thus, even though videotapes were useful, the studio tradition of passing the choreography from dancer to dancer has continued. When interviewed, Browne said she had not thought about her dances "being spread further afield" for remounting. As part of educating preprofessional dancers at SCD she has created dances specifically for student performances. In these cases future students can rely on rehearsal and performance videos as tools for remounting works. Browne emphasizes that there are limitations at her age to the effort and energy she wants to put into preserving a legacy beyond her focus on sending a DVD collection of previously videotaped performances to interested institutions. She feels "impelled to make new dances" because that is what gives her the most satisfaction.

In February 2010 Browne came to York University to teach her dance *Ceremonies* (2007). She was invited by Mary Jane Warner, who had a grant from the Social Sciences and Humanities Research Council of Canada to document the work of four senior Canadian choreographers as they remounted dances of their choice with the York undergraduate B.F.A. students and several professional dancers. In addition, M.A. and Ph.D. students in the dance program participated in notating the dances, videotaping the reconstruction process (including commentary from each choreographer), and editing and transferring the video footage to DVDs. Finally, they compiled oral histories and interviews with the choreographers and some of the original dancers about the initial creative process and performance anecdotes. All this material was assembled into documentation packages for each choreographer and for supporting future reconstructions. The choreographers included in this research and remounting were Patricia Beatty and David Earle (two of the founders of Toronto Dance Theatre), Rachel Browne, and Danny Grossman.* This reconstruction process was intended to capture not only the movement phrases, but also the choreographer's intentions—information often unrecorded, hence lost, when passing on dances. The interviews also give a rich background about the inspiration and imagery significant to the choreographers, along with cultural connections to the era in which the

---

*Danny Grossman Dance Company also initiated a documentation project for teaching or licensing ten of his dances by means of written text, DVDs, notation, and computer animation. Co-artistic director Pamela Grundy presented a detailed overview of the documentation process, "Public Inheritance: A Framework for Remembering Dance," at York University on October 28, 2009. See also Rhonda Ryman's account, "Preservation of Danny Grossman's *Curious Schools of Theatrical Dancing, Part 1*," at http://www.endangereddance.com/pres_curious.html. Dances available for licensing are listed on the website http://www.dannygrossman.com/licensing.html.

works were created. In February 2010 Browne's *Ceremonies* was videotaped in the studio and in performance at York, with preliminary notation begun and editing started in the spring.

Browne's experiences show the difficulties of backtracking to establish an archive and to leave a record of one's dance legacy. Her situation, typical of so many dance artists, is precisely why the Endangered Dance forum was held. Her story also illustrates the need for funding from collecting institutions or public agencies to implement support for technical and archival assistance, particularly in the case of "catch-up" record collecting. Time, scattered records, and outdated technology endanger choreographers' legacies.

Stephanie Ballard: Independent Choreographer, Legacy Adviser, and Archivist

Ballard's career with WCD began in 1972 and has evolved from apprentice to company member, apprentice director, associate artistic director, independent choreographer, and legacy adviser. She has also had a long relationship with SCD, joining in 1997 as guest artist-in-residence and archivist.[24] (See Figure 5.) The responsibilities Ballard has taken on for various dance archives in Winnipeg over the last dozen years are extensive and ambitious. Her work reflects, yet predates, most of the goals set at the Endangered Dance forum.

Ballard's first Legacy Project began in 1997 with funding from the Canada Council for the Arts and Manitoba Arts Council as well as from private and corporate donations. The diverse initiatives she explored from 1997 to 1999 were related to her two major roles—as a dance educator at SCD creating a series of legacy courses and teaching workshops, and as an independent choreographer remounting, creating, and documenting her works. Ballard's *Final Report: Legacy Project, Phase One & Two, 1998*, prepared for the Canada Council for the Arts, details her undertakings for this project.[25] She choreographed seven new works (solos, duets, and group pieces) and mounted three reconstructions (*Prayer, Prairie Song*, and excerpts from *A Gathering*). (See Figure 6.) The reconstructions were videotaped along with interviews with the dancers about the working process and an edited final tape was produced. Finally, she began three archival projects: organizing

Figure 5. Stephanie Ballard. Photograph by Svjetlana Tepavcevic. Courtesy of Svjetlana Tepavcevic.

her personal archives; assisting with sorting WCD's thirty-six boxes of archival records and scrapbooks, and thirteen boxes of video-tapes (dating from 1964 to the mid-1980s) previously acquired by the Archives of Manitoba, plus organizing WCD documents and artifacts (from the mid-1980s to 1999) kept on-site in a vault; and organizing the SCD archives kept in the basement of the school's headquarters. Ballard recounted that after her initial sorting of WCD records at the Archives of Manitoba in 1999, the paper records remained uncatalogued until 2006, when volunteer Maureen Hamilton, in consultation with Ballard, sorted and recorded the WCD *fonds*.[26] The contents are now listed in a Finding Aid binder, but none of the Finding Aid information is accessible on-line to date.

Ballard's wide-ranging and creative approach to this early Legacy Project addresses many of the issues that came up almost ten years later at the Endangered Dance forum around the

Figure 6. Stephanie Ballard's *Prairie Song*, reconstructed (2003). Dancers: Kevin Coté, Emma Doran, Zachary Schnitzer, Alison Wersch, Brooke Noble. Courtesy of Stephanie Ballard.

themes of performances, technology, education, and artifacts. She treats the issue of legacy as both an archival endeavor and a reason for remounting her "masterworks" and documenting them on video. Nevertheless, she still feels strongly about the tradition of a choreographer "gifting" a dance to a dancer to carry forward into the future. So, while she acknowledges that videotaping a dance in a studio setting and capturing the choreographer's commentary may be a good idea for documenting her dance legacy, she hesitates to let go of the tradition of passing on a dance from one body to another. For her, the dances are living "beings." In the educational setting of SCD, Ballard continues to make dance legacy a part of the curriculum. In addition, when she creates her choreographies for the school, she videotapes rehearsals as a practical legacy for her use as a starting point for later restaging or for instructing new cast members.

Another part of Ballard's vision, which connects with the Endangered Dance forum's themes of performance, community, and artifacts, is her effort to establish what she calls a "living

archive." This has come about through her work on several anniversary celebrations for both SCD and WCD and her archivist
role with both organizations. For SCD's twenty-fifth anniversary in
1997 she created a calendar of photographs highlighting Rachel
Browne and alumni dancers in performance.[27] For SCD's thirty-
fifth anniversary in 2007 she created a comprehensive souvenir
booklet, A Living Legacy,[28] containing lists of all the graduating
class members, brief overviews of the apprentice and professional
programs, and many more photographs. There were also a poster
exhibition, screenings of archival film and video footage, and gala
performances featuring graduates returning from across Canada.
She has collected and mounted all the posters of SCD's major performance programs, currently displayed to celebrate public events
at the school.

The thirty-fifth anniversary of WCD in 1999 was celebrated in
two phases, both of which are examples of how Ballard combines
the themes of community, performance, and artifacts. There was
a festival of choreographies by Ballard, Browne, Ted Robinson,
and Tom Stroud, the latter three having served as artistic directors
of WCD. For this event, modeled after the Festivals of Canadian
Modern Dance held at WCD during the 1980s, guest artists were
invited to interpret the works, which were associated with WCD's
history. Also included was the premiere of The Garden, a new work
by then artistic director Tom Stroud. The second phase of this celebration comprised an exhibition of photographs, posters, and
company documents that Ballard had organized in her archival
work for her Legacy Project in the late 1990s. For the fortieth
anniversary of WCD in 2004 she had forty-three archival photographs of WCD dancers in performance framed and displayed.
About half of these are currently on permanent display in the
lobby of The Rachel Browne Theatre, now the home of WCD performances. These photographs, along with many others, were also
reproduced in the fortieth-anniversary souvenir booklet, a body of
work.[29]

Ballard's kaleidoscopic approach to legacy continues to reflect themes that emerged at the Endangered Dance forum since
she has taken on advocacy and community roles with her current
Winnipeg Dance Preservation Initiative (WDPI) project. Ballard's
inclusive community vision for dance in Winnipeg grew out of her
association with the late Margaret Piasecki, alumna of the Royal

Winnipeg Ballet (RWB), whom Ballard had met during the 1999 celebrations of the RWB's sixtieth anniversary. Drawn together by their shared affection for the late Arnold Spohr, former artistic director of RWB, and their love of promoting dance legacy, they began to share ideas for an archive of the "crown jewels" of Winnipeg dance—Browne and Spohr. In April 2009 Ballard's Mouvement/ Winnipeg Dance Projects presented SCD students in *Landscape Dances* at the provincial legislature buildings, followed by a photo opportunity to publicize International Dance Day. Included in the photograph, taken on the steps of the legislature building, were Manitoba minister of culture, heritage, tourism and sport, Eric Robinson, and Jennifer Howard, a member of the Legislative Assembly, along with RWB's executive director Jeff Herd and artistic director André Lewis, plus members of the Chai Folk ensemble and SCD dancers. Ballard saw this event as the first step toward creating large-scale participation for the April 2010 International Dance Day celebrations, which would include representatives from the schools of RWB and SCD, along with participants from Winnipeg's longstanding annual *Folklorama* ethnic dance celebrations.

Finally, Ballard continues to shoulder responsibility for the archive of her own thirty-seven years of material and for ongoing supervision of several other archives: the WCD company archives located on-site and at the Archives of Manitoba; some of Browne's artifacts stored at Ballard's apartment as well as at WCD and SCD; the SCD archives stored in three different on-site rooms; and Spohr's archives stored in his former office at RWB and in Ballard's apartment.

Some of her archival work involved retracing her steps because her 1999 inventory of the WCD archives had to be redone after the company moved to its new headquarters in 2002 and records became disorganized. Only in the summer of 2009 were the WCD archives permanently located in a secure vault room on-site. The task of continuing to sort through material from the past twenty to twenty-five years for both WCD and SCD, as well as setting up a system for handling current documents and artifacts, is overwhelming when Ballard is also working as a guest artist and teacher for SCD, attempting to carry on with the WDPI, and choreographing her own works. Ballard's creative energies embrace most of the broad themes identified at the Endangered

Dance forum by addressing issues related to advocacy, artifacts, education, performances, and community. However, she is stretched to her limit.

The Archivists' Perspectives

Not only do the choreographers have their own, individual perspective on what is important to keep and how they want their legacy passed on, but the archivists interviewed in this research do as well. Interviews for this research were conducted with Miriam Adams, co-founder and director of DCD, Theresa Rowat, currently archivist at McGill University Archives, and Michael Moir, archivist at York University. Supporting and educating choreographers about their records management and legacy is a pressing concern for each one.

Miriam Adams on the Role of Dance Collection Danse

Many dance artists and choreographers across Canada choose DCD as the final destination for their entire collection, especially since DCD is willing to consider accepting both archival records and artifacts, such as costumes, as long as DCD's space permits. All the choreographers studied in this research have had a long connection with DCD in Toronto, but they have used DCD's support for their legacy differently. The Kaejas make annual deposits to DCD of their company's published material such as programs, publicity postcards, copies of news articles, and reviews. Both Browne and Ballard have retained the bulk of their records in Winnipeg but Browne gave DCD copies of performance videotapes of her works up to 1996, along with lists of performance details. Ballard is an "honorary adviser" to DCD and her file there contains copies of the anniversary program booklets she has created for WCD and SCD as well as a copy of her Legacy Project report (1998). Ballard has been active in DCD's Grassroots Archiving workshops and in other meetings on national dance heritage strategies; thus her involvement with DCD is strongest within its education/outreach programs. These three different types of relationship with DCD illustrate the wide-ranging services it offers to the dance community.

As a national theatrical dance resource operating in Canada since 1986 with a focus on archives, publishing, research, and education, DCD grew out of the personal passions of the late Lawrence Adams and Miriam Adams. Both Lawrence and Miriam Adams had been dancers, choreographers, then videographers of dance, and they also became collectors of other dance artists' records and artifacts. Thus, as discussed earlier in this article, DCD evolved into a "hybrid" collection. In a recent interview, Miriam Adams indicated that part of their philosophy of making collected material "known" means that archival "portfolios," as they call them, are open to researchers even before cataloguing has been completed.[30] Other strategies for promoting dance history have focused on three pathways: books, a semiannual magazine, and web exhibitions. DCD has published thirty-eight titles to date about dance in Canada. Available on the DCD website is an archive of the semiannual magazine. DCD's online "Exhibitions" section is a "museum without walls," and the main focus of the 170,000 monthly visitors to the DCD website.[31] In future, however, DCD intends to publish only one title every other year and to shift toward creating more public exhibitions of items from the collection. Its goal is to raise funds to set up a comprehensive center for exhibitions, teaching, film screening, and remounting dances.

It is notable that DCD did not grow out of an existing heritage institution's initiative but rather out of the dance community itself. Many of DCD's projects developed in response to the dance community's requests. Before his death in 2003 Lawrence Adams had drafted *Building Your Legacy: An Archiving Handbook for Dance.*[32] He had also begun developing a manual and the prototype of a free software program, the *Canadian Integrated Dance Database* (CIDD) in response to dance artists' requests for tools to collect and manage all their material.[33] Both of these initiatives were completed by DCD's director of research, Amy Bowring, and are now used to assist far-flung Canadian dance communities. Bowring's advice is available for dance artists, choreographers, and companies who wish to create and maintain their own collections of records or databases. At DCD, volunteers and staff assist in cataloguing existing DCD holdings in its CIDD database. A list of DCD's archival portfolios is posted on the DCD website.

DCD also serves as an advocate for dance heritage support. After introducing the concept of "Grassroots Archiving" at the

Endangered Dance forum in 2006, DCD held follow-up work-shops in 2007 and 2008. DCD also sponsored a national "think tank" called "Movement for Canadian Dance Heritage" in November 2008 with the goal of developing a networking strategy. One outcome was that participant Colleen Quigley, dancer and archivist in St. John's, Newfoundland, organized a similar provincial think tank for Newfoundland's and Labrador's dance communities in 2009. Again, the participants and leadership for these heritage initiatives have come from the dance community itself.

DCD has been funded by municipal, provincial, and federal arts councils and by private donations, rather than by the Department of Canadian Heritage. Miriam Adams feels that the Canada Council for the Arts has been "very supportive" and sees "the value" of DCD's work, as evidenced recently by increased financial commitment to DCD. She also senses that proposals to the council for dance-related funding are increasingly shifting to include reconstruction and heritage projects, alongside funding for new works. The heritage initiatives of DCD's founders, staff, and board offer choreographers, dance artists, and their companies imaginative and simplified practical supports for meeting their archival, preservation, and legacy goals.

Theresa Rowat on Archival Issues for Choreographers

Theresa Rowat, McGill University archivist and author of the comprehensive *Study of Dance Collections in Canada* and other reports for the Canada Council for the Arts, emphasized that an archival *fonds* derived from systematic recordkeeping, through which records of historical value are retained, "reveals much about the workings of the organization or the creative process of the artist."[34] Thus, a "sustainable practice of recordkeeping underpins an archive." She feels that "creators need to see their records as corporate assets in the present while choreographing and operating a company" and as the source of their archival legacy in the future. She noted the need for choreographers to preserve master video recordings of the original performance experience. Rowat wondered why many dance artists have not stressed on-going documentation of their work as an integral part of the creative process and production. In her view, Warner's documentation project with Browne and other senior choreographers keeps dance works alive. She does, however, distinguish between the authenticity and evidential value inherent in the original records, and the documentation compiled in the course of re-mounting a dance. In Rowat's *Study of Dance Collections in Canada* she elaborated, "In strict archival terms, [oral history] must be understood as a record of memories and perceptions of historical experience, rather than historical fact. In dance, the absence of a recordkeeping culture in favor of oral tradition and teaching suggests that oral history approaches are particularly relevant to the dance legacy."[35] Her advice is that choreographers become aware of the importance of systematically maintaining original records that have "evidentiary" value from a historical perspective.

Michael Moir on Choreographers' Archives

Michael Moir, a historian and archivist at York University, explained his view of what makes a document a record for an archive. He believes that one of the key factors in this transition is "the decision by the individual who created it or received it to retain it for future activities."[36] Thus, he feels that if a choreographer retains a document in order to remount a dance, this choice invests the document with evidential value that must be respected by the archivist when deciding to acquire records for the archive. Examples of such documents would be the choreographer's notes or journals, correspondence discussing the reason for choices in choreography, casting, or production, photography or video taken during rehearsals, and any document explaining how the dance developed or evolved. He feels that oral histories are of use to historians who will look at the "quality of the evidence" in these recollections, bearing in mind that these reflections were made after the events occurred. Historians can add their "reservations," if appropriate, when they publish such recollections.

If the choreographer has been "selective in keeping documents," Moir finds that they have "assigned a value to the document." While he is aware of the Kaejas' methodical record-keeping from discussions with Allen, and prefers to receive material that is similarly organized by the donor, York's archive has also accepted boxes of randomly assorted papers. He notes that, in the process of sorting through these boxes, the archivist imposes a sense of order and perspective. Material organized by the original user "reflects the needs of the donor," as Theresa Rowat also pointed out, and thus gives insights to researchers. Moir commented that the Kaejas "recognize information as an asset, not an encumbrance" but that not everyone does, which will influence how they treat their records. In addition to paper records, videotapes, photographs, and hard drives of data, York's archive also accepts technical specifications, design drawings for costumes, and models for theatrical set designs. Descriptions of the holdings of York's Clara Thomas Archives are also sent to ARCHEION[37] (an electronic database of archival holdings in repositories throughout Ontario), which in turn submits the descriptions to the Canadian Archival Information Network.[38]

Conclusions

The personalities, circumstances, and visions of choreographers create distinct legacies with implications for stakeholders interested in their careers and their dances—the dance community, educators, scholars, and professional custodians of culture. The need to maintain a comprehensive record of choreographers' artistic and operational processes is often overshadowed by both their creative drive to look ahead to the next dance, rather than back to the last one, and the daily pressures of making a living, running a company, and teaching in the studio.

Allen and Karen Kaeja have the advantages of working as a team on their recordkeeping and employing a manager to help maintain the organization of their operational records. Rachel Browne, now in her seventies, concentrates on leaving a record of performance videos of her most significant works and continuing to create new work. Stephanie Ballard's dilemma is trying to find the support needed to manage the records of so many artists and organizations while in the midst of her own busy career.

To collect, archive, and make available a record of a personal dance history and legacy depends on the choreographer's readiness to think ahead and make preparations. It also depends on understanding the nature of comprehensive records management. Choreographers need to be methodical in the organization and maintenance of ongoing administrative office records, relevant correspondence, programs, playbills, photographs, biographies, critics' reviews, and other published material, all useful for creating press kits and grant proposals in the present, and for establishing the context of their work for future scholars and dancers. Effectively supporting a choreographer's legacy, so that audiences can continue to experience their art, requires documentation, which often occurs only in a reconstruction process. Archivists encourage choreographers to consider documenting their original creative processes in several formats.

What interferes with choreographers' abilities to meet these goals, according to Karen Kaeja, and evident in both Browne's and Ballard's dilemmas, is the lack of time and assistance in managing a growing body of records in the midst of an active artistic career. Without a structured approach to a national dance legacy strategy by collecting institutions or public agencies, our choreographers' archives will remain vulnerable to the vagaries of circumstance, leaving their dance legacies endangered.

Acknowledgments

I would like to thank Dr. Selma Odom, Professor Emerita, Department of Dance, York University, Toronto, Canada, for her guidance in my archival research and writing and for introducing me to Stephanie Ballard, Miriam Adams, Theresa Rowat, and Michael Moir. Thanks also to Dr. Mary Jane Warner, Chair, Department of Dance, York University, Toronto, Canada, for introducing me to Rachel Browne. I deeply appreciate the warm welcome, candor, and assistance of each of the choreographers I interviewed—Allen Kaeja, Karen Kaeja, Rachel Browne, and Stephanie Ballard. I am especially grateful to Ballard for giving me tours of the archival holdings at WCD, SCD, and the Archives of Manitoba, and replying to many e-mails. Kristen Haight of WCD was very helpful in explaining her organizational system for Browne's videotapes and DVDs. I am grateful also to Miriam Adams, Theresa Rowat, and Michael Moir for their interviews. Their input was invaluable in contextualizing this research.

Notes

1. Dance Collection Danse, http://www.dcd.ca/ (accessed July 22, 2010).
2. See "Welcome to the Fondation Jean Pierre-Perreault," at the website for Montreal's Fondation Jean-Pierre Perreault, http://www.fondation-jean-pierre-perreault.org/en/ (accessed June 27, 2010).
3. Theresa Rowat, McGill University archivist, telephone interview by the author, June 12, 2010.
4. Society for Canadian Dance Studies, http://people.uleth.ca/~scds.secd/Heritage/directorycoll.html (accessed June 28, 2010).
5. Clifford Collier and Pierre Guilmette, *Dance Resources in Canadian Libraries* (Ottawa: National Library of Canada, Collections Development Branch, 1982).
6. Theresa Rowat, *Study of Dance Collections in Canada*, unpublished report commissioned by the Dance Section of the Canada Council for the Arts, in conjunction with the Department of Canadian Heritage (Arts and Heritage Sector), for advance distribution to participants in LOGIN:DANC/SE 2000 (June 2000).
7. "A Dance Heritage Strategy for Canada—2002," prepared by the Committee for the Preservation of Canada's Dance Heritage: Lawrence Adams, Miriam Adams, Amy Bowring, Theresa Rowat, Philip Szporer, Vincent Warren, and Leland Windreich. Unpublished report supported by the Canada Council for the Arts (April 2002) and distributed during the 2002 Canada Dance Festival in Ottawa.
8. Roy MacSkimming with Francine D'Entremont, *Legacy, Transition, and Succession: Supporting the Past and Future of Canada's Arts Organizations*, report for the Canada Council for the Arts (March 2005), 8.
9. Ibid., 4.
10. Endangered Dance, www.endangereddance.com (accessed June 27, 2010).
11. "Review of Recent Approaches to Growing Dance Legacy: Summary prepared by Theresa Rowat for the Canada Council for the Arts" (October 2005), 2. Available at http://www.endangereddance.com/en_growinglegacy.html (accessed June 28, 2010).
12. See http://www.endangereddance.com/themes_en.html for details on the one-, three-, and five- year goals for each of the seven themes. See also "The Choreographer's Trust: Negotiating Authority in Peggy Baker's Archival Project," by Allana C. Lindgren and Amy Bowring, in this issue of *Dance Chronicle*, for another approach by a Canadian choreographer to documenting dance.
13. See the Kaeja d'Dance company website, http://www.kaeja.org/company.html, for more information. Allen Kaeja has also posted more than a dozen trailers and excerpts from his dance films on YouTube.
14. Allen Kaeja and Karen Kaeja, interview by the author, November 6, 2009.
15. Allen Kaeja, telephone interview by the author, September 15, 2010. Allen elaborated, with specific examples, on how extensively they video record their performances.

16. See http://www.endangereddance.com/grass_roots.html (accessed June 27, 2010).
17. Allen Kaeja, telephone interview, September 15, 2010.
18. Karen Kaeja, "Making Dance," http://www.kaeja.org/company/methodology.html (accessed November 26, 2009).
19. Rachel Browne's biography is available at http://www.thecanadian encyclopedia.com/index.cfm?PgNm=TCE&Params=A1ARTA0009033 (accessed June 27, 2010).
20. Rachel Browne, interview by the author, November 16, 2009.
21. Ibid.
22. Kristin Haight, interview by the author, November 14, 2009.
23. Ibid.
24. Ballard's website, http://mts.net/~sballard/, has information about her career beyond WCD and SCD.
25. Stephanie Ballard, *Final Report: Legacy Project, Phase One & Two, 1998,* unpublished report located in Ballard's file at DCD.
26. Stephanie Ballard, interviews by the author, November 16 and 17, 2009.
27. Stephanie Ballard, ed., *The Professional Program of Contemporary Dancers: Celebrating 25 Years of Dance* (Winnipeg: School of Contemporary Dancers, 1997).
28. Stephanie Ballard, ed., *A Living Legacy: The Professional Program of the School of Contemporary Dancers, Celebrating 35 Years of Dance* (Winnipeg: School of Contemporary Dancers, 2007).
29. Stephanie Ballard, ed., *a body of work: Winnipeg's Contemporary Dancers, 40th Anniversary, 1964–2004* (Winnipeg: Winnipeg's Contemporary Dancers, 2004).
30. Miriam Adams, interview by the author, June 2, 2010.
31. See more about DCD's "Exhibitions" at http://www.dcd.ca/exhibitions.html.
32. Lawrence Adams, *Building Your Legacy: An Archiving Handbook for Dance* (Toronto: Dance Collection Danse Press/e, 2004).
33. Lawrence Adams, Amy Bowring, and Clifford Collier, *Canadian Integrated Dance Database: Standards Manual and Collier Descriptor Thesaurus,* trans. Marie Claire Forté (Toronto: Dance Collection Danse Press/e, 2008).
34. Rowat, telephone interview.
35. Rowat, *Study of Dance Collections in Canada,* 8.
36. Michael Moir, interview by the author, June 23, 2010.
37. York University Libraries, Clara Thomas Archives and Special Collections, "The Benefits of a Donation to the Clara Thomas Archives," pamphlet (2007), 2.
38. The Canadian Archival Information Network is found at archivescanada.ca, a portal maintained by the Canadian Council of Archives. Michael Moir, e-mail, September 7, 2010.

THE CHOREOGRAPHER'S TRUST: NEGOTIATING AUTHORITY IN PEGGY BAKER'S ARCHIVAL PROJECT

ALLANA C. LINDGREN and AMY BOWRING

Peggy Baker's project, The Choreographer's Trust, raises questions about the creator's authority in the preservation process. Her dual goals—documenting her choreography while allowing for interpretive latitude—create an apparent contradiction in which the choreographer's traditionally privileged position is both restricted and reinforced. Baker's example provides an opportunity for reflection on such dance preservation issues as the significance of embedding uncertainty into the archiving process, choreography's resistance to authoritative readings, and the positioning of an artist in relation to his or her archival material.

The archive is first the law of what can be said.

—Michel Foucault

I realized that unless I passed my dances on, the hard-won lessons that were embedded in them risked being lost when I retired.

—Peggy Baker

What happens to a choreographer's works once he or she stops performing them? The Canadian dance artist Peggy Baker began to think about this question as her fiftieth birthday approached.[1] Her solution was to initiate a project in 2002 that she called The Choreographer's Trust. Supported by a multiyear grant from the Metcalf Foundation in Toronto, Baker selected six of her solo choreographic works to be staged and recorded. She then chose two dancers to learn each solo and, at the end of the rehearsal period for each piece, the dancers performed the works publicly.

In addition to teaching the choreography to a select group of dancers, Baker invited a choreologist, a dance writer, a visual artist, a DVD production team, and a website designer to work with her to produce multimedia records of the rehearsals and performances. The resulting documentation has been collected in

packages that include DVDs and booklets introducing The Choreographer's Trust and its participants. The booklets also contain
excerpts from the dance writer's journals and essays by Baker that
explain her theories about dance and performance. These packages are available for student dancers, dance artists, and choreographers to use for pedagogical purposes. Should a school or
artist wish to mount the works in a performance setting, a licensing agreement with Baker can be arranged. Baker has given each
of the dancers who participated in The Choreographer's Trust
permission to perform the solo she or he learned at fundraisers
and other similar events, although a licensing fee will be charged
if the dancer performs the work in a revenue-generating situation.
The original archival records are, at the time of writing, in the
process of being deposited with the archives and research center
Dance Collection Danse in Toronto and Baker intends to place a
duplicate set with the dance program at the University of Calgary.

Baker's archival project is part of a concerted effort, which
has been growing since the mid-1980s, to preserve Canada's dance
heritage. The Choreographer's Trust, however, is an unusual and
particularly interesting case study because Baker has repeatedly
conveyed a desire to frustrate any authoritative readings of her
work.[2] She attempted to thwart the possibility of archiving definitive interpretations of her solos through the manner in which her
work has been documented. While Baker has not identified her
archival process as poststructural, nevertheless the tenets of multiplicity, unstable meanings, and decentering of authority are apt
descriptors of the approach to preserving her work.

There is, however, some ambiguity between Baker's stated
rhetoric and her practice. Although The Choreographer's Trust
indicates that "passing on" her work ultimately means relinquish-
ing control over her work, the resulting archival documentation
also reveals that the choreographer is calibrating the interpretive latitude she would like her work to accommodate. As a result, a paradox emerges as the traditionally privileged position
ascribed to choreographers in relation to their work is both restricted and reinforced by Baker's efforts to archive her solos. In
the spirit of the poststructuralism that appears to define Baker's
project, we will leave the paradoxes unresolved rather than try
to impose a grand narrative of dance preservation. Indeed, far
from being problematic, the inconsistency of the limitation and

fortification of the choreographer's power in The Choreographer's Trust provides an opportunity to think about important questions related to dance preservation. First, what are the political implications of deliberately enfolding plurality and thus, uncertainty, into the archiving process? In answering this question, it becomes clear that more than steps are being archived. Values are implicitly conveyed. Second, although Baker has stated on more than one occasion that the performer's interpretation should not extend to changing the steps and movement sequences of her choreography, how does her *oeuvre* resist attempts to "set" or "preserve" it? That is, despite her claims, The Choreographer's Trust ultimately undermines the claim that choreography is ever truly "completed." Finally, what does The Choreographer's Trust—and, by extension, dance—contribute to discussions about how best to position an individual in relation to his or her archival material? In other words, what kind of power does a person maintain when acting as an archivist of her or his own work? Collecting and protecting historical records are not neutral activities; they inescapably involve making choices about what is valued enough to keep and what is dispensable—choices that, often unintentionally, disclose ideological priorities.[3] By retaining control over the central choices of what is preserved and how, and then by overseeing the packaging and distribution of her archival material, Baker demonstrates that the choreographer as archivist is what might be called a "double-creator"—a person who not only originates the material to be saved, but also crafts and directs the modes of communication of the saved documentation.

There are, of course, other choreographic trusts in existence, including the George Balanchine Trust, the Antony Tudor Ballet Trust, the Robbins Rights Trust, the Ashton Trust, and the Merce Cunningham Trust. Generally speaking, these trusts engage in preservation activities, licensing of performance rights, and maintenance of the artistic integrity and legacy of the respective deceased choreographer's creative work through remounting dances that are staged by approved repetiteurs.[*] Unlike these

---

[*]For further information on preservation activities in the broader Canadian context, see Cheryl LaFrance's article, "Choreographers' Archives: Three Case Studies in Legacy Preservation," in this issue.

better-known choreographers, Baker is representative of a generation of choreographers who have worked with less institutional support, but who are, nevertheless, undertaking the preservation of their own work. Moreover, what makes The Choreographer's Trust an especially intriguing example of dance preservation is that it facilitates a discussion about the creator's control—a discussion with implications for dance archiving beyond Baker's specific project. Many other dance preservation activities are concerned with protecting the choreographer's creative vision. Baker, conversely, uses archiving techniques not only to preserve the steps of her dances, but also to attempt to undermine her own supremacy as the choreographer. The result, as this article suggests, is a paradoxical negation and reassertion of the choreographer's authority.

Peggy Baker and The Choreographer's Trust

Born and raised in Edmonton, Alberta, in western Canada, Baker (see Figure 1) has received some of the highest civic honors in Canada and Ontario, where she now makes her home: the Order of Canada, the Order of Ontario, the inaugural Premier's Award from the province of Ontario, and the Governor General's Performing Arts Award, among others. Her long and productive career in dance began in 1971 when she moved to Toronto to begin her intensive studies as a student in modern dance at Toronto Dance Theatre. She soon joined the company and also was a founding member of Dancemakers in 1974, becoming the company's artistic director in 1979. Shortly after that date, Baker was invited by New York choreographer Lar Lubovitch to audition for him. Initially she turned down his proposal, but he persisted and from 1981 to 1988 she danced with his company. Upon leaving the Lubovitch company, Baker worked independently in New York. After a decade away, she returned to Canada in 1990 and began her solo career while also pursuing such projects as performing with Mikhail Baryshnikov and Mark Morris's White Oak Dance Project.

As a soloist, Baker's repertory consists of her own choreographic works as well as commissioned pieces by such artists as James Kudelka, Paul-André Fortier, Molissa Fenley, Tere O'Connor, and Doug Varone. Baker is also sought as a teacher

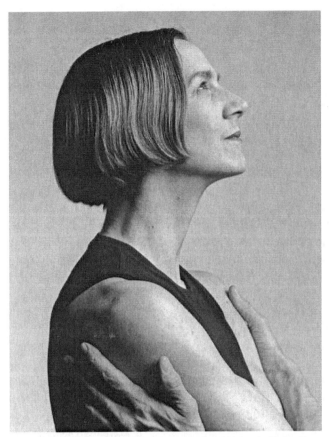

Figure 1. Peggy Baker. Photograph by Michael Slobodian. Courtesy of Michael Slobodian.

and rehearsal director (she is often brought to Juilliard to re-hearse pieces from the Lubovitch repertory). She was the first artist-in-residence at Canada's National Ballet School and contin-ues in that role. She also maintains strong ties with the school of Toronto Dance Theatre, where she often sets work on students.

Baker's experiences as a professional dancer learning and embodying choreography created for other dancers taught her the important lesson of finding ways to honor the choreography while personalizing her performance. This has intrigued her since 1981 when, as a dancer with Lubovitch, she was scheduled to learn his *North Star*, which had originally been set on company member Laura Gates.[4] Baker was surprised to discover that some of the basic steps had been augmented and enriched by Gates: "Some movements that seemed well defined for me when I watched Laura turned out to be more the by-products of intended gestures, movements that took place in the aftermath of prescribed choreography. It wasn't that Laura had changed the dance; it was simply that when she engaged in the choreography it produced other movements as well." Baker was encouraged to follow this interpretive approach by beginning with the "primary choreographic gesture" and then, as she recalls, to allow her engagement with the movement "to take an authentic pathway through my own body."[5]

Other experiments testing the elasticity of choreography followed. In 1983 Baker was learning the solo *Non Coupable*, which Québécois choreographer Paul-André Fortier had originally created for dancer Susan Macpherson.[6] Strategies that had allowed Macpherson to solve the technical challenges presented by *Non Coupable* were less successful for Baker. She realized that she had to find her own way to embody the steps. Another experience that contributed to her continuing consideration of the relationship between choreography and interpretation occurred in 1990 when she joined the White Oak Dance Project. She and Baryshnikov were both taught *Ten Suggestions*, a solo that Morris had originally choreographed for himself.[7] The differences in physicality between Morris ("a great big guy, soft and floppy," yet with an innate technical virtuosity), Baryshnikov ("like a greyhound, small and perfectly proportioned"), and Baker ("tallish, angular . . . androgynous") reinforced the idea for Baker that body types inescapably influence artistic interpretation: "I . . . got a better sense of the fact that sometimes it is simply the physique of a dancer that makes something work in a particular way. Mark's lush bulk was splendid for the Duncanesque dance with a ribbon. Misha was so low and compact for the somersault/crouch phrase that it read like the kind of optical illusion a clown uses to squash his height. And my extra long arms were perfect for the deco sequence with the hoop."[8] These experiences shaped Baker's thinking about how best to preserve her own work, turning her attention toward the choreography-interpretation issue, which had long interested her:

When I established The Choreographer's Trust in 2002, one of my major preoccupations was with disentangling the choreographic score of the dances I had created from my own dancing, with establishing what John Cage referred to as the identity of the composition. . . . I have emerged from that process with a very clear perspective on the issue of identity in relation to choreography. My philosophy is that the choreographic score is a construct that is distinct from its performance. I think of the choreographic score as less complex, nuanced, virtuosic, and subjective than any outstanding individual performance of it, but also as more open-ended, flexible, precise, and objective than all of the performances it will ever receive.[9]

To apply her theory, in the first year of The Choreographer's Trust, Baker chose to remount *Brahms Waltzes* (1992) and *In a Landscape* (1995), both of which are approximately ten minutes long. Both works were rehearsed during a five-day period and then performed for an audience on the last day. *Brahms Waltzes*, performed for The Choreographer's Trust by dancers Jessica Runge and Kate Holden, was inspired by the American dancer and choreographer Annabelle Gamson, with whom Baker first studied in the fall of 1988.[10] Gamson had been working with dancers Roxane D'Orléans Juste, Risa Steinberg, and Nina Watt when Baker joined the group. Gamson choreographed new works on the dancers and also taught them choreography by Isadora Duncan, Eleanor King, and Mary Wigman. The choreographies for *Brahms Waltzes*, including Brahms piano duets, opus 39, numbers 2, 3, 4, 5, 7, 8, and 15, were from the Duncan dances Gamson taught the group and Baker loved how it felt to move to this music. According to Baker, who views her own choreographic exploration of the music she had been introduced to by Gamson as little poems, "I made *Brahms Waltzes* in 1992 and it remains one of my favorite dances. I used the chorus/verse form that had struck such a chord with me, and pushed inside of the movement principles I had studied with Annabelle to see how they would resonate with my own spirit."[11] *In a Landscape*, the second solo to be archived, was dedicated to the movement researcher and pedagogue Irene Dowd and choreographed to John Cage's 1948 composition of the same name. Baker first encountered the music for *In a Landscape* when she received a compact disc of Cage's piano pieces as an opening night present from her long-term collaborator, pianist Andrew Burashko. Baker invited dancers Christopher Grider and Tanya Howard to perform this work, which the choreographer has described as "restrained and introspective."[12]

Among the people involved during the first year of The Choreographer's Trust was Peter Ottmann, a choreologist and ballet master from the National Ballet of Canada, who notated the works. Demands on his time at the ballet company were great following the project, so choreologist Natasha Frid completed the scores. Filmmaker Mark Adam videotaped the proceedings and dance writer–historian Amy Bowring, one of the authors of this article, recorded the process in journals. Lighting designer Marc Parent, a frequent collaborator of Baker's, created different lighting designs for each of the solos. Pianist Andrew Burashko performed the music for *Brahms Waltzes* and the John Cage score.

For year two, Baker reconstructed *Sanctum* (1991) and *Yang* (1998), which together totaled over twenty minutes of dancing. Again, the choreologist, dance writer, lighting designer, pianist, and filmmaker as well as a visual artist, Jerry Silverberg, attended the rehearsals. The work period was expanded to six days and again included a performance on the last day. Baker had choreographed *Sanctum* in the spring of 1991 and it became her homage to Martha Graham (who died on April 1, 1991) because its movement lexicon evoked corporeal memories for Baker of how Graham technique felt on her body.[13] In creating the work, she collaborated with the musician and composer Ahmed Hassan, whom she had married in December 1990. Together, the couple decided that Baker would restrict her movements to the same amount of space covered by the carpet Hassan used for his "stone age" instruments—"wood, clay, twine, pebbles, shells, seed pods." If Baker was limited to the area allotted to Hassan, he in turn extended his performance into the realm of the dancer by choreographing his hand movements into a silent and visually rhythmic gestural dance. Baker and Hassan always performed the piece on stage together, so in addition to inviting two dancers—Nova Bhattacharya, who is trained in bharata natyam, and Helen Jones, a dancer fluently conversant in Graham technique—to participate, Baker arranged to have two musicians interpret the music: Ed Hanley accompanied Bhattacharya and Debashis Sinha performed with Jones.

Baker had originally created *Yang*, the other solo preserved during the second year of The Choreographer's Trust, for dancer Sylvain Brochu in 1998. The title refers to the Taoist philosophy of yin-yang equilibrium. As she created the work, which is set to Thierry de Mey's *Frisking Prolationum for 11 Percussionists,* the theme of masculinity emerged and the characteristics traditionally associated with yang—"masculine, round, odd-numbered, and upward moving"—became the structural core of the piece.[14] For The Choreographer's Trust, Baker knew that she wanted to include Brochu in the process, but that she also wanted to teach the solo to a woman. As a result, the other dancer to learn *Yang* was Shannon Cooney, a dance artist who had previously performed with Dancemakers.

Year three presented a challenge. *Brute* (1994) and *Unfold* (2000), the works Baker chose to include during this last phase of The Choreographer's Trust, were each approximately thirty minutes in duration and could not be rehearsed and remounted in a week. Consequently, Baker opted to teach the dances as part of her normal rehearsal process in preparation for scheduled performances and the dancers learning the pieces would each have an opportunity to perform the work during one of Baker's productions in Toronto. As a result, dancers Andrea Nann and Kate Alton alternately performed *Unfold* during the May 2004 season in Toronto for Baker's company, Peggy Baker Dance Projects. Rex Harrington, a former principal dancer with the National Ballet of Canada, and Sasha Ivanochko, an independent dancer who had previously performed with the Toronto Dance Theatre, were cast in *Brute* (see figures 2 and 3). As in her solution for *Unfold,* Baker scheduled the performers on alternate evenings for the Peggy Baker Dance Projects February 2005 season in Toronto, which was called Music for Piano and Solo Dancer. Baker has stated that, for her, *Unfold* was an opportunity to consider "the art of listening with my body."[15] Moreover, for the 2000 premiere of the piece, she placed pianist Andrew Burashko and herself close to the audience, as she said she was interested in exploring how audiences might react to the artistic conversation that occurs between dancer and musician during a performance.[16] If *Unfold* provides an opportunity for the dancer to investigate how her body responds to music and invites the audience to think about the relationship between movement and music, the source for *Brute* is more visual and intertextual because it was inspired by Pablo Picasso's 1937 painting *Guernica.*

The longer rehearsal period for *Unfold* and *Brute* had implications for the other collaborators and thus for the preservation

Figure 2. Sasha Ivanochko rehearsing Peggy Baker's *Brute*, The Chore-ographer's Trust, 2005. Photograph by David Hou. Courtesy of David Hou.

process. It was not practical for filmmaker Mark Adam to be in-volved, since he was based in Montreal, so the rehearsals were not videotaped. Choreologist Peter Ottmann could not get away from his rehearsal schedule at the National Ballet. Amy Bowring attended as many rehearsals as possible while juggling other responsibilities. Jerry Silverberg, the visual artist Baker invited to attend rehearsals, was present more regularly. Marc Parent designed the lights, which remained the same no matter who was performing. Andrew Burashko performed Scriabin's Opus 11 preludes for *Unfold* and Prokofiev's Sonata No. 6 for *Brute*. The performances were recorded on video and Benesh notator Natasha Frid has been completing the notation scores for both pieces.

Decentering the Choreographer's Power

Baker makes a firm distinction between choreography and interpretation, and she advocates multiple readings of her work. When launching The Choreographer's Trust, she did not want her own interpretations of her solo work to become authoritative readings: "Mindful of the possibility of confusing choreography with interpretation, we need to be sure that we are working toward the reconstruction of a choreography, rather than the replication of a performance."[17] Similarly, in the booklet for *In a Landscape*, Baker outlined how her performance experiences have shown the interpretive latitude possible within the confines of the choreography.[18]

Baker's views on the relationship between interpretation and choreography evoke the debates that accompanied dance reconstruction during the 1980s and early 1990s, when concerns were raised about the extent to which interpretation should alter or dominate a choreographed work.[19] Roger Copeland, for example, brought to the discussion Nelson Goodman's concepts of "constitutive elements"—those aspects of a work of art that are crucial to its identity—and "contingent elements"—those that can be changed without fundamentally altering what is essential about the work.[20] Similarly, Jack Anderson has suggested that an "idealist" approach to reconstruction positions the essence of a work of art as its "concept" or "intention," whereas the "materialist" approach advocates the sacrosanct nature of the steps, all other elements being considered negotiable.[21] According to these categories, Baker is clearly oriented to the materialist's position since she appears to see production elements as contingent and choreographed steps as constitutive.

Beyond simply exemplifying existing dance typology, however, Baker's approach to dance preservation has more to offer. Others have noted that interpretation is an active agent that affects choreography in performance. According to Selma Jeanne Cohen, "Unlike a painting or a novel, a dance cannot be experienced directly as an intimate encounter between work and perceiver. When a work must be transmitted through an intermediary, through the person of a performer, then its material is constantly rethought, reshaped, reinterpreted."[22] Yet, as Helen Thomas has astutely noted, the main goal underpinning most of the dance preservation "industry" and attendant attempts to reconstruct, revive, recreate (and so on) lost or archived dance is "the search for a definitive, authentic version."[23] By positioning itself in opposition to this premise, which instigates many reconstruction projects, The Choreographer's Trust creatively challenges the assumption that authenticity is desirable or even possible by embedding plurality into the preservation process.

Throughout the rehearsal processes for the solos in The Choreographer's Trust there are numerous examples of Baker's resisting the impulse to make her interpretation of her work authoritative. Most notably, Baker did not use video to teach the work because she did not want the dancers' interpretations to be influenced by her own performance of it.[24] Similarly, the desire not to dictate interpretation caused Baker to refrain from depositing videotapes of herself performing the works with the audiovisual material that has been archived with The Choreographer's Trust.[25] This choice is designed to prevent privileging her own performance as an authorial reading. Even in the studio, Baker often sought to limit interpretive cues to the dancers. When she performs *Brahms Waltzes*, for example, Baker's face is very expressive, but during the rehearsals the dancers could not see her face because they were learning the dance behind her and the studio had no mirrors. When asked if she was going to demonstrate her facial expressions to Tanya Howard and Christopher Grider, Baker responded that she deliberately did not show them her face in order not to influence their interpretations.[26*]

---

*Interestingly, Baker does not consider facial expression—a kind of gesture—to be part of her set choreography, but other types of corporeal gestures, including those for the hands, legs, arms, and so on, are treated as set.

Figure 3. Sasha Ivanochko and Peggy Baker rehearsing Baker's *Brute*, The Choreographer's Trust, 2005. Photograph by David Hou. Courtesy of David Hou.

In addition to trying to excise the influence of her interpretation of her works included in The Choreographer's Trust, Baker deliberately added variation and choice to the production elements. For most of the pieces, for example, Baker put each of the dancers engaged with her pieces in different costumes and used different sets—if sets were used at all—with different lighting for some of the solos. For *Brahms Waltzes* Kate Holden wore black cropped pants with a black tank top.[*] The lighting for Holden's interpretation was a morphing series of "hues of blue, purple, orange, yellow, and pink."[27] As Bowring wrote in her journal, "Sometimes we see the cyc blush, at other times it looks like dusk." The accompanist and the piano remained on stage in the same place for both pieces, but for Jessica Runge's performance, a scrim was lowered in front of the pianist. In further contrast to Holden, Runge wore a long, sleeveless, empire-waist dress made of lush

---

[*]Holden was supposed to wear a black mock turtleneck top, but it was misplaced and a substitute—the black tank top—had to be located shortly before the public performance.

blue velvet material that was echoed in the bluish tint of the cyclorama. A diagonal rectangle of light that fell across the stage suggested illumination from an open door.

Perhaps the most obvious and arguably the most important way that The Choreographer's Trust subverted the desire for an authoritative reading of Baker's solos in order to offset the temptation to (con)fuse interpretation with choreography was the choreographer's decision to double-cast dancers and to invite dancers to participate in the project who represented a range of social demographics and dance experiences. As Sasha Ivanochko told one interviewer about her experience of learning *Brute* with Harrington, "We've both been in pieces that have been double- or triple-cast. You can't think about how you'll compare to someone else. That will drive you crazy."[28] Indeed, although the convention of multiple casting for performances is a standard practice in dance and a factor that many dancers ignore in preparing for their own performances, Baker's process conveys a theory of dance preservation in which the diversity of bodies able to access the same choreographic work is key. For example, she taught *In a Landscape* to dancers of different genders, body types, and movement qualities. National Ballet of Canada dancer Tanya Howard was described as "delicate, slender and long—lithe yet strong, poised, and balanced."[29] Conversely, Christopher Grider, the other dancer Baker invited to learn *In a Landscape*, has worked for a ballet company but more recently has pursued opportunities in contemporary dance; he was noticed for his "chiseled physique—he is solid and powerful, grounded."[30] As previously mentioned, in addition to casting both a man and a woman to learn *In a Landscape*, Baker had, in year two, cast Shannon Cooney in *Yang*, which she had originally created for Sylvain Brochu, the other dancer to perform the work as part of The Choreographer's Trust. The final piece "passed on" by Baker was set on another male-female couple, Rex Harrington and Sasha Ivanochko.

Although most of the dancers invited to participate in The Choreographer's Trust had training backgrounds similar to that of Baker (a variety of Western ballet and contemporary dance influences) and most, like Baker, have had careers as professional dancers in contemporary dance companies and/or as solo dance artists, there were some exceptions. Howard was not the only member of the National Ballet of Canada to participate.

Harrington was a former principal dancer with the National Ballet. Bhattacharya, one of the dancers Baker wanted to perform *Sanctum*, trained in bharata natyam and had a career performing for eleven years with Menaka Thakkar & Co., a bharata natyam-based company in Toronto.* More recently, Bhattacharya has performed as an independent dance artist who moves fluidly between contemporary Western and South Asian dance communities.[31]

The dancers were also representative of a broad spectrum of ages from the twenties to the fifties. Holden, Howard, and Grider were all in their twenties; Runge, Cooney, and Bhattacharya were in their thirties; Ivanochko, Alton, Harrington, and Nann all in their late thirties or early forties. Jones was two years older than Baker. Despite the range, none of the dancers expressed a fear that their ages were an impediment to learning the choreography. In an interview prior to the performance of *Brute*, Harrington voiced his concerns about the physically draining movement in the work: "It's a brute of a solo, like doing *The Four Seasons*, a full-evening ballet. It's a new vocabulary for me. And it's performed barefoot, so I'm working my feet open daily. In a way, I feel like I'm putting myself out to slaughter"[32] (see Figure 4). Yet, Harrington noted that Baker had been forty-two when she first performed the piece, the same age he was at the time—a fact he used to buttress his confidence.

Baker's casting choices have implications beyond celebrating the interpretive possibilities in the choreographer's work. As Nicholas Mirzoeff and other scholars have argued, "Western visual culture has evolved several icons to represent the perfect body" and in so doing has normalized some bodies and ostracized others.[33] By multiplying the types of bodies appropriate for her work as a means to prevent a singular and authoritative interpretation of the solos, Baker also challenges the history of aesthetic reduction through idealization. Granted, despite Baker's desire to demonstrate that her choreography is accessible to a wide range of body types and movement training, the choreography is not open to all dancers. The level of kinetic expertise

---

*Menaka Thakkar & Co. has collaborated numerous times with artists schooled in other dance techniques, so working with non-bharata natyam colleagues was not new for Bhattacharya.

Figure 4. Peggy Baker and Rex Harrington rehearsing Baker's *Brute*, The Choreographer's Trust, 2005. Photograph by David Hou. Courtesy of David Hou.

demanded by her dances requires a dancer with training that has emphasized core strength, technical skill, and sensitivity in musical phrasing. Nevertheless, the traditional categories of exclusion in dance (race, gender, age, etc.) have been made less rigid.

Diversity of Archival Sources

In addition to encouraging a plurality of readings of her solos by casting more than one dancer to learn each piece and by choosing dancers from diverse demographics and movement backgrounds, Baker also used several archival methods to record and disseminate information about her choreography. This observation, however, is not intended to ignore that the traditional "performative manner" of passing a dance from dancer to dancer was central to Baker's process.[34] Conventionally, dance preservation occurs in a studio. A choreographer or dancer teaches a role to another dancer. Memory is embodied and that body ensures a living legacy for the choreographic work.[*] Certainly, Baker's process in The Choreographer's Trust accesses and perpetuates this traditional type of preservation. This established process of dance preservation, in which one dancer teaches another dancer through movement, demonstrates how corporeality can function as cultural memory.[35] Paul Connerton has suggested that "in habitual memory the past is, as it were, sedimented in the body."[36] While Connerton is referring to acquired skills like swimming, his comments also apply to the traditional method of passing on dance as practiced by artists like Baker.

Yet her approach to dance preservation also invites observers to think about the role of bodies in the archival process because, through her inclusion of multiple sources of preservation, the hegemony of the dancer's body as a dance archive is displaced in The Choreographer's Trust. The dancer's body is one source of memory among others that Baker used to record and comment on her work, a situation found in other preservation examples as well. Moreover, in moderating the authority of bodies in the transaction of dance knowledge, the project provides an opportunity to consider that more than just dance steps and the performance event comprise a choreographic work. Contexts are constitutive, too. Aligned with the philosophy that the layering and diversity of documentation is key to dance preservation—a belief shared and put into practice by other organizations, including the Dance Notation Bureau and the American Dance Legacy Institute—an important noncorporeal archival source included in The Choreographer's Trust is the series of essays by Baker in the booklets that accompany the DVDs. (Each choreographic work will be framed by an essay, although because the DVDs and the text of the booklets for *Unfold* and *Brute* are currently still in production, there is as yet no commentary for these works.) Based on the texts available, it is clear that Baker has the ability to transpose her experience as a dancer and choreographer to the page with the same eloquence that defines her choreographic works and stage performances. Indeed, the essays make clear that, for artists like Baker, dance is a cerebral as well as corporeal endeavor.

---

[*]Similarly, Diana Taylor has asserted that performance is a form of accruing and conveying embodied knowledge. See Diana Taylor, *The Archive and the Repertoire* (Durham, NC: Duke University Press, 2003).

Most of the essays in The Choreographer's Trust booklets do not directly refer to the dances with which they are paired, but instead provide philosophical contexts for the works as Baker expounds on her views about different aspects of dance. The two companion essays for *Brahms Waltzes* are examples. The first, "Video vs. Imagination: Leaving the Archival Tape Behind," reiterates Baker's belief that choreography exists "like a score or script, as a construct that is distinct from its performance."[37] In the second essay, "Individuality in the Dancer: Working with What is Unique," she discusses the equilibrium that the dancer needs "to master the specific and challenging demands within the choreography, while navigating the elements that require a personal response to complete them."[38] For the second year, Baker wrote "Listening to the Worlds Inside and Out" for the *Yang* booklet, in which she argues that the skill of listening is paramount for the performer: "[M]odes of listening, to the world outside of us, and to the inner world of our own bodies, are crucial to the refinement of our expressive capabilities."[39] Thus, by moving beyond the simple transmission of steps to include contextual information in her archival process, Baker challenges the reader, viewer, and dancer to embrace dance as a way of analyzing ideas and not just as a visceral art.

Another part of the archival process that involved constructing and commenting on movement was Baker's decision to invite Bowring to act as the literary manager for the project and to attend rehearsals in order to keep a journal of the process. Free to roam around the rehearsals as long as she did not disrupt the work in progress, Bowring was privileged in the sense that she, unlike most audience members, had access to the "reverse" side of performance. Her presence was defined by her engaged invisibility. Extended excerpts from Bowring's journal are included in the DVD booklets and describe the atmosphere of the rehearsals for the different choreographic solos. For example, she began her journal for the first rehearsal for *In a Landscape*, which was also the very first rehearsal for The Choreographer's Trust, by conveying the sense of expectation: "There is a certain electricity in the air. The moment of the first rehearsal has arrived and everyone prepares to fulfill an individual role. I don't know how the others feel but I have been anticipating this moment for months."[40] At other times in the process, she offers her creative responses. Reacting to a moment during the rehearsals for *Sanctum* (see figure 5), Bowring expresses movement shapes and dynamics in poetic language:

> Words and images come to mind as I watch: a woman confined, sticks representing barriers, a series of sculptures pulsing with the low breathy echoes of the didgeridoo, faster gestures, sobbing, pulsing, prayer, gestures repeat, palms unfolding to reach the earth, plant a seed in silence, bean pods shake as skirt flies, lilting, curving, embracing, an arm curves over around and side, barrier removed, sticks whip, lies prostrate, fast hands, arching, curving, sticks thrown, skirt, fire, black.[41]

In the excerpts from her journal, Bowring becomes a surrogate for the audience—observing, thinking, kinetically constructing meaning as she writes in her notebook. Bowring's writing suggests that Baker's rehearsal process was analogous to an open, or what Barthes termed a "scriptable," text, which positions and encourages the reader to be an active agent in the production of meaning.[42] In producing journal entries that are then included as documentary evidence, Bowring's participation in The Choreographer's Trust serves as a reminder that in dance, and in the arts more generally, meaning is contingent on audiences as much as

Figure 5. Helen Jones in Peggy Baker's *Sanctum*, The Choreographer's Trust, 2003. Photograph by Ian McMaster. Courtesy of Ian McMaster.

artists—that audiences have an important role to play in the construction and maintenance of artistic memories. Similarly, during the talk-backs with the audience after the first performance, Baker was reluctant to answer a question about her motivation or inspiration for a particular section of *In a Landscape* because she did not want to influence viewers' interpretations of the work.[43]

The Unfinished Choreography

The ability to rethink the original costumes, sets, and lighting is something Baker wants to encourage. In the letter of agreement between Baker and the dancers invited to participate in The Choreographer's Trust, she explicitly grants permission for the dancers to commission new designs.[44] What Baker was—and is—adamant about is that the steps of her choreography not be altered. To this end, the letter clearly states that "[t]he Artist will respect the original creation and will not make changes to the choreography without the permission of Peggy Baker." Similarly, Baker has implicitly conveyed an essentialist view of choreography in her essays: "The beautiful and unsettling irony of the stable choreographic structure producing shifting associations and variations in meaning for everyone who engages with it is one of the greatest glories, deepest mysteries, and truest hallmarks of dance."[45] In another section of this essay, she elaborated further, discussing the process by which she feels that choreography is set and meaning emerges:

> Knowing when a dance is finished could be based on anything from the choreographer's hunch to having run out of time to work. Once the choreography is complete, it is considered to be an established structure, and from that point on great efforts are made to maintain its integrity through the physical and mental precision of the dancers. For its rendering, the finished choreography is completely dependent upon the performers' embodiment of the movement vocabulary, and their navigation of space and time, all within a prescribed aesthetic. . . . Speaking directly about meaning, and grooming one's performance to communicate a particular and specific meaning, generally does not support the choreographic structure in contemporary dance, because while a dance is stable and definite, the possibilities for meanings it might convey are as numerous as all of the people who will ever see it or be involved in staging and performing it.[46]

Her forceful advocacy of avoiding set meaning and embracing multiplicity of interpretations, while at the same time insisting that choreography can be "complete," "finished," "stable," and "definite," is echoed repeatedly in her essays accompanying The Choreographer's Trust DVDs:

> Movement vocabulary, compositional structure and style emerge, are developed, and become established as rehearsals progress. The steps, spacing, and timing provide a stable structure that we identify as the dance. An audience watches the dance, and each individual in that audience perceives it differently, notices different elements, makes their own associations, attaches their own meaning. A second viewing might shift the reading of the dance subtly, or a change of cast alter the reading dramatically, for that same audience member. . . . [M]eaning can also emerge and impress itself upon choreographers in unexpected ways. In spite of their original intentions they may discover associations in their work that they did not in any way expect.[47]

However, upon closer examination, the steps for the solos included in Baker's archival project are never entirely fixed, despite Baker's attempts to "preserve" them. At a few different moments throughout The Choreographer's Trust, there were instances when Baker could no longer do a movement—the mind remembered but the body could not oblige. In discussion with the audience in between dances during the dress rehearsal for *In a Landscape*, Baker noted that aspects of the choreography had been changed to accommodate the different body types of the dancers.[48] For *Yang*, Baker told Cooney that she was not wedded to the number of rolls performed during one section of the work, but that she was more interested in ensuring that the phrasing was correct.[49] Moreover, sometimes the multiple readings were unintentional. During one rehearsal, for example, Baker forgot the counts for a phrase of *In a Landscape*.[50] At another rehearsal, she needed a moment to try to remember a section in *Brahms Waltzes*.[51] *Brute* includes sections that are structured improvisations; the dancers have the rhythm of the music to guide them and they know where they need to finish, but the shapes of the movement during these specific phrases are to be improvised by the performer.[52]

Creatively compensating for physical limitations or the fallibility of memory are routine occurrences when transferring a dance from one person to another. Even the choice to incorporate structured improvisations into choreographic works is not particularly unusual. In and of themselves, these examples are unremarkable, but in the context of The Choreographer's Trust, they gain importance because they signal the indeterminacy of choreography that emerges despite the choreographer's claims to the contrary. Granted, the integrity of the whole remains, but finality is unachievable when dealing with living, breathing bodies. Instead, choreography always modulates slightly as it passes from one dancer to the next.

The Choreographer's Trust also demonstrates that many artists—even those engaged in preserving their work—often cannot resist the creative impulse to rework ideas. For *Yang*, Baker reconfigured the solo into a duet. *Yang* is the work Baker originally choreographed on Sylvain Brochu. Because this was not a work that she had created for herself or performed, she felt it had to be structurally altered during its transmission to another dancer. She decided to present *Yang* first as two solos and then to show the audience a version where both Brochu and Cooney danced on stage together. Baker also wanted to make sure that the two versions worked well together on stage because she did not want to see the same phrases performed simultaneously. Baker kept the integrity of the phrases intact but altered the order in which they were performed and changed some of the pathways in space. In the duet, Brochu performed the work as it had originally been choreographed and Cooney learned the variation of *Yang* in which the original movement phrases were all included, but reordered (see figure 6). While not the same kind of indeterminacy as that practiced by Cunningham and Cage, since the new order was fixed in the studio, the exercise underscored the malleability of the choreography and the multiple readings possible even for the creator.[53]

Reasserting the Authority of the Creator

The Choreographer's Trust demonstrates the benefits of working with dancers who represent a range of body types and dance training, the richness of interpretation that is made possible by introducing a plurality of archival sources, and the impossibility of truly finalizing embodied choreography. Baker's method also simultaneously reasserts the authority of the creator. Indeed,

Figure 6. Shannon Cooney in Peggy Baker's *Yang*, The Choreographer's Trust, 2003. Photograph by Ian McMaster. Courtesy of Ian McMaster.

any time choreographers are directly involved in preserving their own work, their authority will be reinforced, as historian and archival educator Tom Nesmith has written in relation to archiving: "[A]ny work of archives-making *is* a type of authoring or creating of the archival records" because archivists "co-create and shape the knowledge in records, and thus help to form society's memory" (emphasis in the original).[54] Nesmith's words bring to mind those of Jacques Derrida in his seminal text, *Archive Fever*, where he states that "archivization produces as much as it records the event."[55] Thus, some of the choices that Baker made throughout The Choreographer's Trust project emphasized that she never fully relinquished control of how her work might be interpreted.

In this light, Baker is still clearly working out where interpretation fits on the continuum between her and other dancers who might perform her work. As she taught the choreography for The Choreographer's Trust, she often gave corrections to the dancers, praising them when they had done a movement "correctly" or got the quality of phrasing "right." In these works, movement qualities were seen as integral to the steps, not part of the performer's interpretive range. While rehearsing *Sanctum*, for example, Bhattacharya had trouble curving her spine in a Grahamesque contraction.[56] Baker and choreologist Peter Ottmann spent considerable time working with Bhattacharya to help her achieve this type of movement and aesthetic. The result is a movement quality more aligned to the way Baker performed the work, but the process to achieve this result contradicts Baker's philosophy of letting the dancers interpret the movement.[57] (See figure 7.) As a result, Baker's rehearsals can be seen as a process of establishing what Connerton has called the "proprieties of the body," meaning that there is a correct or acceptable way for the body to act that is learned through practice and correction.[58] These observations are not intended as a criticism of Baker's rehearsal process, but rather they are intended to illustrate the difficulty of truly divesting the choreographer of authority over his or her dances in a traditional rehearsal setting.

Baker also retains control over the preservation process by archiving only a small number of her choreographic works. The decision to focus on archiving a few dances was dictated in part by financial exigencies. Baker originally received a strategic initiative grant from the Metcalf Foundation consisting of $20,000 per year for three years. After the initial grant ended, she received another $20,000 per year in a three-year grant that allowed her to complete the DVDs. The costs involved, from hiring dancers to the production of the DVDs, booklets, and website design, necessitated that Baker choose between in-depth archiving strategies and simply recording as many choreographic works as possible. Clearly, Baker felt that the former choice was right. The practical limitations

Figure 7. Nova Bhattacharya in Peggy Baker's *Sanctum*, The Choreographer's Trust, 2003. Photograph by Ian McMaster. Courtesy of Ian McMaster.

imposed by limited funds, however, have significant implications for Baker's legacy as they inadvertently reinforce her authorial control through restricting the availability and access to her entire body of work. Placing any of the pieces included in The Choreographer's Trust in the larger context of Baker's choreographic *oeuvre*, for example, will be challenging for future scholars and dance artists.

Similarly, Baker's interest as a choreographer has been to explore the possibility of solo works primarily for herself. She has acknowledged that the "stripped down" and "distilled" nature of solo choreography was advantageous while she and her archival collaborators were still discovering how best to coordinate and maximize the effectiveness of their preservation methods.[59] Nevertheless, Baker has created a few duets and group pieces. The omission of a representative sample of her work intended for more than one dancer is another way that choices made for practical reasons function to underscore the interpretive control of the choreographer, at least when attempting to position individual works within that choreographer's entire career.

Beyond the work in the studio and the choices about what to preserve, Baker's participation in the packaging of the archival material also shows that she maintains a significant level of authority over her work. The creation of the booklets, the companion DVDs, and the inclusion of information about The Choreographer's Trust on Baker's webpage are all examples of this. Although other people contributed most of the text for the booklets, edited the DVDs, and designed and programmed the website, Baker nevertheless wrote essays included in the booklets and oversaw all aspects of the production process. Writing, compiling, editing, and programming all involve choices, and choices reflect opinions about what to include, what to exclude, and how to present, disseminate, and physically preserve the archival material and the attendant contextual information. All archival material, including that preserved in The Choreographer's Trust, is the product of selection and organization and, therefore, of editorializing. To a certain extent, then, choice remains within the choreographer's purview, revealing what is important to Baker about her work and how she would like others to engage with her archival documents. For example, the DVDs for each dance mostly recorded Baker teaching the dancers the choreography in rehearsal as well as the resulting performances. There are sections in which Baker discusses her work, but these moments are quite limited in comparison to the recorded interaction between Baker and the dancers. It appears that the dance community (as opposed to other types of communities—scholarly, general public, etc.) is her intended audience.

Conclusion

The word "trust" has a range of meanings for Baker: it refers both to "the notion of a body of work as wealth that may be endowed" and to the resulting organization—The Choreographer's Trust—she created to oversee the preservation of her choreography.[60] Equally important is the "faith placed in the dancers to keep the works alive and well" and, one might argue, her trust in the durability of her work to sustain the multiple readings that her archiving methodology encourages. Although the extent of

Baker's trust might appear mitigated by the ways in which she retained control over her choreography during the preservation process, the word "trust" also invites observers to have confidence that the contradictions embedded in The Choreographer's Trust are integral to the preservation process.

Notes

1. Peggy Baker, "The Choreographer's Trust," *Peggy Baker Dance Projects, The Choreographer's Trust, Year One—In a Landscape* (Toronto: Peggy Baker Dance Projects, 2002), 4. This essay is also included at the beginning of all of the DVD booklets developed for the trust. See also, http://www.peggybakerdance.com/trust/trust.html (accessed March 31, 2010).

2. Ibid., 4.

3. For examinations of the politics of archival practices, see H. Bradley, "The Seductions of the Archive: Voices Lost and Found," *History of the Human Sciences*, vol. 12, no. 2 (1999): 107–22; Richard Harvey Brown and Beth Davis-Brown, "The Making of Memory: The Politics of Archives, Libraries and Museums in the Construction of National Consciousness," *History of the Human Sciences*, vol. 11, no. 4 (1998): 17–32; Louise Craven, ed., *What Are Archives? Cultural and Theoretical Perspectives: A Reader* (Aldershot, U.K.: Ashgate, 2008); Jacques Derrida, *Archive Fever: A Freudian Impression*, trans. Eric Prenowitz (1995; Chicago: The University of Chicago Press, 1996); Helen Freshwater, "The Allure of the Archive," *Poetics Today*, vol. 24, no. 4 (December 2003): 729–75; and Reuben Ware, Marion Beyea, and Cheryl Avery, *The Power and Passion of Archives* (Ottawa: Association of Canadian Archivists, 2005). For a discussion about the distinctions between intentional and unintentional evidence, see Marc Bloch, *The Historian's Craft*, trans. Peter Putnam (New York: Vintage Books, 1953), 60–61.

4. Peggy Baker, "Interpretation and Identity: A Preoccupation I Share with John Cage," *Peggy Baker Dance Projects, The Choreographer's Trust, Year One—In a Landscape*, 9.

5. Ibid.

6. Ibid., 10.

7. Ibid.; see also Carol Anderson, *Unfold: A Portrait of Peggy Baker* (Toronto: Dance Collection Danse Press/es, 2008), 136.

8. Baker, "Interpretation and Identity," 10–11.

9. Ibid., 11.

10. Peggy Baker, "Brahms Waltzes," *Peggy Baker Dance Projects, The Choreographer's Trust, Year One—Brahms Waltzes*, 5.

11. Ibid., 5.

12. Peggy Baker, "In a Landscape," *Peggy Baker Dance Projects, The Choreographer's Trust, Year One—In a Landscape*, 5.

13. Peggy Baker, "*Sanctum* Introduction," typescript, *Peggy Baker Dance Projects, The Choreographer's Trust, Year Two—Sanctum*, n.p.

14. Peggy Baker, "*Yang* Introduction," typescript, *Peggy Baker Dance Projects, The Choreographer's Trust, Year Two—Yang*, n.p.

15. Peggy Baker, quoted in Anderson, *Unfold*, 87.

16. Anderson, *Unfold*, 88.

17. Baker, "Interpretation and Identity," 11.

18. Ibid., 9–11.

19. For a detailed chronicle of this debate, see Helen Thomas, *The Body, Dance and Cultural Theory* (Basingstoke, UK: Palgrave Macmillan, 2003); and Helen Thomas, "Reconstruction and Dance as Embodied Textual Practice," *Rethinking Dance History: A Reader*, ed. Alexandra Carter (London: Routledge, 2004), 32–45.

20. Nelson Goodman as discussed in Roger Copeland, "Perspectives in Reconstruction: Keynote Panel," *Dance ReConstructed: Modern Dance Art, Past, Present, Future, Conference Proceedings* (1992; New Brunswick, NJ: Rutgers University, 1993), 12.

21. Jack Anderson, "Idealists, Materialists, and the Thirty-Two Fouettés," *Ballet Review*, vol. 5, no. 1 (1975–1976), 12–21. Anderson's concepts are also discussed in Copeland, "Perspectives in Reconstruction," 13.

22. Selma Jeanne Cohen, *Next Week, Swan Lake: Reflections on Dance and Dances* (Middletown, CT: Wesleyan University Press, 1982), 7.

23. Thomas, "Reconstruction and Dance," 42.

24. Amy Bowring, "Amy's Journal," *Peggy Baker Dance Projects—In a Landscape* (Toronto: Peggy Baker Dance Projects), 19.

25. Peggy Baker, "Video vs. Imagination," *Peggy Baker Dance Projects—Brahms Waltzes*, 9.

26. Bowring, "Amy's Journal," 11.

27. Ibid., 17.

28. Sasha Ivanochko, quoted in Glen Sumi, "Moving the Work Around," *NOW*, vol. 24, no. 23 (February 3–10, 2005), http://www.nowtoronto.com/stage/story.cfm?content=145686&archive=24,23,2005 (accessed March 20, 2010).

29. Bowring, "Amy's Journal," 12.

30. Ibid.

31. "Four at the Winch, 2007: Choreographers and Costume Designers," http://www.tdt.org/4AW/choreo_costume_nbhattacharya.html (accessed March 20, 2010).

32. Rex Harrington, quoted in Sumi, "Moving the Work Around."

33. Nicholas Mirzoeff, *Bodyscape: Art, Modernity and the Ideal Figure* (London: Routledge, 1995), 3.

34. This description of the way that choreography is often handed down from one dance generation to the next is borrowed from Thomas, "Reconstruction and Dance," 33.

35. See Thomas J. Csordas, ed., *Embodiment and Experience: The Existential Ground of Culture and Self* (Cambridge: Cambridge University Press, 1994).

36. Paul Connerton, *How Societies Remember* (Cambridge: Cambridge University Press, 1989), 72.

37. Baker, "Video vs. Imagination," 9.

38. Peggy Baker, "Individuality in the Dancer: Working with What is Unique," *Peggy Baker Dance Projects—Brahms Waltzes*, 10.
39. Peggy Baker, "Listening to the Worlds Inside and Out," typescript, *Peggy Baker Dance Projects—Brahms Waltzes*, n.p.
40. Bowring, "Amy's Journal," 12.
41. Amy Bowring, "The Choreographer's Trust Year Two: Literary Manager's Journal," typescript, *Peggy Baker Dance Projects—Sanctum*, n.p.
42. Roland Barthes, *S/Z*, trans. Richard Miller (New York: Hill and Wang, 1974), 4.
43. Bowring, "Amy's Journal," 19.
44. For example, see Peggy Baker to Chris Grider, "Letter of Agreement," Peggy Baker Dance Projects, June 29, 2002.
45. Peggy Baker, "Emergent Meaning: Stable Structures/Shifting Associations," typescript, *Peggy Baker Dance Projects—Sanctum*, n.p.
46. Ibid.
47. Baker, "Emergent Meaning: Stable Structures/Shifting Associations," n.p.
48. Bowring, "Amy's Journal," 18.
49. Bowring, "The Choreographer's Trust Year Two: Literary Manager's Journal," n.p.
50. Bowring, "Amy's Journal," 15.
51. Ibid., 14.
52. Sumi, "Moving the Work Around."
53. Baker, "*Yang* Introduction," n.p.
54. Tom Nesmith, "Postmodernism and the Changing Intellectual Place of Archives," *The American Archivist*, vol. 65, no. 1 (Spring–Summer 2002): 32, 27.
55. Derrida, *Archive Fever*, 17.
56. Bowring, "The Choreographer's Trust Year Two: Literary Manager's Journal," n.p.
57. Ibid.
58. Connerton, *How Societies Remember*, 82, 83.
59. Baker, quoted in "Peggy on The Choreographer's Trust," online DVD, http://www.peggybakerdance.com/trust/trust_features.html (accessed June 28, 2010).
60. Baker, "The Choreographer's Trust," 4.

A BOLD STEP FORWARD: GENEVIEVE OSWALD AND THE DANCE COLLECTION OF THE NEW YORK PUBLIC LIBRARY

LYNN MATLUCK BROOKS

One of the world's most renowned centers for dance research is the Dance Collection of The New York Public Library (NYPL), and at the center of that library's vision, founding, development, collections, prominence, and range has been Genevieve Oswald. Now called the Jerome Robbins Dance Division, it "is the largest and most comprehensive archive in the world devoted to the documentation of dance."[1] While many people have contributed guidance, expertise, and support to this institution, Oswald's persistence and dedication were primary in shaping its growth, evolution, and stature.* While this essay cannot cover every one of the wide-ranging stories and achievements recounted by Oswald, now retired with the title Curator Emerita of the Dance Collection, the highlights selected touch on the development of the Dance Collection, the process of acquiring the collections, significant figures who contributed to the institution, its major achievements, and Oswald's personal experiences in the course of her work.[2] The following general outline of Oswald's career serves as a chronological reference for the article's themes.

Oswald was hired at NYPL in 1947 by the curator of the Music Division, Carleton Sprague Smith. All research libraries were

---

*Oswald called the creation of archives of cultural records "a bold step forward— ... a gesture which expresses how deeply communities care about their traditions, giving them an historical dimension as they preserve them in a meaningful way as an enrichment for future generations." See Genevieve Oswald, "One Approach to the Development of a Dance Archive," in *Libraries, History, Diplomacy, and the Performing Arts: Essays in Honor of Carleton Sprague Smith* (Stuyvesant, N.Y.: Pendragon Press, 1991), 79. Interviews for this research were conducted by Lynn Brooks and Ishani Aggarwal on May 16, 29, and 30, 2007 at Oswald's home in Ardsley, New York, with follow-up conversations over the course of the next several years. Unless otherwise credited, all quotes are from transcriptions of these initial interviews and are cited in the text as parenthetical numbers corresponding to the page in the transcript from which the quote, sometimes slightly revised, is taken.

then located at the main branch, 42nd Street and Fifth Avenue. Oswald was hired as a musicologist, having recently graduated from the University of North Carolina at Greensboro with a B.S. in music; at the time of her hiring, she was in the midst of graduate studies at the Juilliard School. Smith initially offered Oswald a few hours a day for work on the nascent dance archive, the rest of her time being devoted to the Music Division. After 1950, her time was devoted entirely to dance, except for her service at the Music Division reference desk and its rare-books section. By 1956, Oswald's progress, at the Music Division, in establishing a dance archive and developing awareness of dance as a research field earned her the Capezio Award, one of many honors she has received.[3] With the opening of Lincoln Center in 1965, the performing arts research libraries moved to what was then called the Library-Museum of the Performing Arts. In the year prior to that move, the Dance Collection had become an independent division of NYPL, at the same level as the Music Division, with its own location in the Lincoln Center library complex. Oswald retired from NYPL in 1987.

Background

Oswald's background, while primarily in musicology and composition, prepared her for a career devoted to supporting dance. In college, Oswald wrote reviews of visiting dance companies, composed music for local theater-dance productions, organized a festival of new art that featured José Limón as well as William Schuman, participated in a theater club and in music events, and took dance classes (pp. 39, 74–77). In fact, she recalled the "wonderful dance program" at the University of North Carolina (p. 76), where modern dance teacher Jean Brownley inspired students by not only teaching technique in her classes but also keeping students up to date on the New York dance scene, reading them reports from *The New York Times* on the latest modern dance events (pp. 74–75). In New York, while working on music and dance materials at the Music Division of NYPL, Oswald continued her education in dance by attending performances, meeting important figures in the dance world, and hearing lectures by scholars interested in dance, including musicologists Gustave Reese and, particularly,

Curt Sachs (pp. 62, 75). Smith had helped to bring these European musicologists to the United States in 1938, saving them from the Nazi threat. Sachs, as resident musicologist at the Music Division, had a desk near Oswald's and became her mentor.* Oswald's collecting and cataloging of the Dance Collection was itself a deep and broad education in dance, preparing her to teach dance history at New York University (1970–94), write and edit dance essays, organize dance exhibitions, and speak authoritatively on dance as well as library matters.

But, when Oswald arrived at the Music Division, the Dance Collection was barely visible. Smith told her, "We'd like to do a little something with dance. You can only do it a couple of hours a day." The suggestion inspired Oswald with a "wonderful sense of elation, because I loved the dance" (p. 62). Smith recognized that the dance material in the Music Division should be treated as a collection of its own, and he foresaw the need to create a separate division devoted entirely to dance material and research. At this critical juncture, Oswald was guided by a prescient and mentoring director.

A start had been made prior to Oswald's arrival: in 1933, dance-related books at the library began to be identified and placed in the Music Division. Two important dance collections were donated in the late 1930s: the Roger Pryor Dodge photographs of Vaslav Nijinsky and the Walter B. Graham collection of dance books.[4] As additional dance books, clippings, and visual material were added, more hours were needed for the collection's maintenance. Alan Schulman, who had devoted some time to this work in the Music Division before Oswald's hiring, created a short catalog of dance titles. While she was aware that there were some rare and ancient dance books in the library's Lenox and Astor Collection, Oswald initially thought that "all the great historical collections were in Europe"—and therefore unattainable. So she decided to turn to American modern dance as her first foray into collecting and thus initiated a formative influence on the Dance Collection.

---

*Sachs wrote a seminal, if now controversial, dance history and ethnography text, *World History of the Dance* (New York: Norton & Co., 1937).

Collecting

American Modern Dance

To begin this project, Oswald turned to Walter Terry, dance critic for the *New York Herald Tribune*. He introduced her to Ted Shawn (see Figure 1), who proved an enduring friend to the Dance Collection, donating his own material to the nascent organization and becoming a trendsetter for other modern dancers. For example, Ruth St. Denis's life and career were represented in the collection by a donation in 1951 of archival material.[5] Oswald recalls, "We seemed to get one collection after another during the next four years. It was very exciting to me because I had studied modern dance … and I was deeply impressed to meet these people" (p. 62).

Oswald actively pursued Isadora Duncan's legacy: "I … tried to find out what she was doing in every month of her life, where she was, and with whom. And then I wrote down everybody's name that I found and went to various sources including the

Figure 1. Genevieve Oswald and Ted Shawn at the New York Public Library Dance Collection at Fifth Avenue and 42nd Street, with a poster for the exhibition *Ted Shawn: American Dancer* in 1950. Courtesy of Genevieve Oswald.

telephone books of different cities and wrote to everybody whose name I found. Eventually, we received the Irma Duncan Collection [1957] .... It was really magnificent" (p. 33). In late 1956, Oswald, her husband and young son, along with dance critic Doris Hering, went to Irma Duncan's lovely home near Albany, New York, and "had an Isadora Duncan afternoon." Oswald asked, "'Irma, could you *be* Isadora Duncan? ... Come into the room, waltz, move about, dance, be her.' And she did, and my son was thunderstruck" (p. 47). Irma Duncan became not only a donor and advisor, but "She would tell us who the 'true' Isadora Duncan dancers were, from her point of view" (p. 33). To further document Isadora's work, Irma Duncan and Oswald developed a plan for Irma "to rent a studio for six weeks, with a blue curtain, a piano, carpet, and everything. She wanted to ... recreate some of the dances of which she knew the choreography cold .... And then we were going to film them" (p. 33). The Ford Foundation agreed to fund the project, an offer to which Oswald had prepared a draft response. "And then [the Ford Foundation] made a grant to the New York City Ballet [NYCB], and [Irma] said, 'I wouldn't think of working with them, or taking their money if they would fund the New York City Ballet,' and she wrote them a letter telling them so" (pp. 33–34). Thus did early rivalries interfere with documentation and collection.

Oswald sought to interest an author and a publisher in bringing Duncan's letters out for the public. Through colleague David Erdman, editor of NYPL's *Bulletin*, Oswald met Doubleday editor Ann Freedgood. Oswald brought along copies of a few of the Duncan letters, which Freedgood found "wonderful" (p. 34; see also pp. 92–93). Freedgood in turn suggested to author Francis Steegmuller that he stop by the Dance Collection to look at the full set of letters, which he quietly did. Although primarily a Gustave Flaubert scholar, he found the Duncan letters so fascinating that he decided to write a book incorporating them: *Your Isadora: The Love Story of Isadora Duncan and Gordon Craig*, originally published in 1974 by NYPL. This was one of the earliest research-based books to bring Duncan's personal story to light.

Other first- and second-generation modern dancers gave their material to the Dance Collection, among them Doris Humphrey, Charles Weidman, and Hanya Holm (p. 27). Louis Horst, a strong supporter, donated his collection, including original scores he had written for Martha Graham, although Graham herself "was not a friend of the collection" (p. 51). Oswald spoke with Graham, but at the time Graham "did not want a record and she said so: 'I don't want people snickering'—these are her words—'snickering over me after I am dead . . . and don't try to do anything about it.' So, naturally, I said, 'We can't not do it, Martha'" (p. 51). Oswald found a way: "Quite a bit later, we became friendly with Leroy Leatherman, the Martha Graham Company administrator . . . . We did a couple of favors for the company. They needed something that we could get for them." Oswald asked Leatherman about Graham's press scrapbooks, which she recognized as an important historical record. He lent these to the Dance Collection for filming.

To supplement this kind of collecting, and in a broad sweep to cover other important modern dancers of Graham's generation, Oswald undertook an oral history project in 1967, initiated with a modest grant from the National Dance Guild. Oswald created what she called a "cluster system," for which she found support through a grant from the Andrew W. Mellon Foundation (pp. 31–32, 79):[6] with Graham, for example, Oswald interviewed her set designer, artist Isamu Noguchi, and composer Hunter Johnson, as well as the dancers in her works (p. 32). This cluster of interviews would "create this unit with [Graham] as the centerpiece." Oswald found, talking to Graham and other dance artists of her stature, that "they had given so many interviews that often they told you the same things, and what you got wasn't anything new. So the only way to find anything new about the way they worked, what their principles were, how they felt about things, was to go and talk to the people they worked with" (p. 32). The oral history movement was fairly new at this time, with Columbia University's Oral History Research Office, under Allan Nevins, serving as a center for developing this work. Oswald trained herself in this methodology, eventually using oral history procedures, with her staff, to gather interviews for the Dance Collection (pp. 18, 69).

Doris Humphrey was another important dancer of the period whom Oswald sought to document (p. 47). Because few women at that time in the dance world had children, Humphrey and Oswald found a common bond in discussing their families, which led to a closeness valuable for dance research as well: "I would go up and have her [Humphrey] identify photographs for me, because she was very kind and willing to do so. When we got the Denishawn collection, it seemed all mixed up. Ted Shawn had it brought down from the Museum of Modern Art [MoMA]" (p. 48), where in 1941 Lincoln Kirstein had spearheaded an attempt to create a repository and center for dance research.[7] In 1948, after this effort failed to achieve permanent archival status, most of the material was given to the Dance Collection. Walter Terry was influential in convincing Shawn to make a first transfer. For a year after Shawn's donation, Oswald sorted and cataloged the material, which proved so frustrating that she had to request that Shawn come to the library to help out. Their work together led to an enduring friendship (pp. 47–48). Oswald asked him about some photos she could not identify. "Every Sunday," Shawn recalled, "we didn't have anything to do, so we'd go down to the White Studio and we'd put [on] a headdress of this and the leggings of that and we would just dress up any old way." He also promoted the importance of the Dance Collection to other dancers.

Charles Weidman was another Denishawn descendant who contributed significantly to the Dance Collection. "I remember, the first time I went to see Charles Weidman in his apartment, he had this terrible noisy radio on a high level—concert music, which I love. But it was so loud that I had to shout to him, 'Charles!'" Weidman came right to the point: "If I give you the collection, who is going to answer the questions?" Oswald responded, "'We will.' We were already answering questions on his career." He gave his collection to NYPL and became a good friend (p. 48). Jack Cole, another Denishawn student and important innovator in jazz dance, donated to the Dance Collection his complete archive of books, memorabilia, and working material. Because of his study of world dance, particularly the dances of India, his collection was unusual in its range. Oswald went to Cole's home in California to pack and ship this precious material.[8]

The Dance Collection played an important role in supporting the Alvin Ailey company at a critical juncture. After early successes, the company ran out of money, a fact publicized in the *New York Times*, which reported that Ailey would be forced to disband his company. Oswald recollects, "I called his office and asked his secretary, 'Look, do you want us to film your repertoire?'" Ailey was eager to proceed, and the whole repertory was filmed. This convinced the company's board of the importance of sustaining the work and "eventually they raised the money to go on" (p. 30). When asked whether he would leave his material to the Dance Collection or to NYPL's Schomburg Center for Research in Black Culture, Ailey told Oswald, "Well, I am black, but you know I am a dancer first.' And so he said, 'I want you to have my stuff, I really do.'" However, "what we tried to do was to share it" between the Dance Collection and the Schomburg Center (p. 88), Oswald observed.

Before beginning her work in East St. Louis, Katherine Dunham, already a celebrated dancer, befriended Oswald at the Dance Collection (p. 47). Dunham material now held at NYPL includes photographs, programs, interviews, clippings, and books. Oswald met Merce Cunningham through one of the Dance Collection's graduate-student assistants, Bruce King, then studying at NYU and also a student and dancer with Cunningham. "Bruce said, 'You know, you ought to invite Cunningham out to supper. Just invite him.'" This was at a point in Cunningham's career when he was still making little money. He proved a friendly supporter, "interested in what we were doing with earlier modern dance figures" (p. 52). David Vaughan later became Cunningham's archivist, but the Dance Collection was able to buy some of Cunningham's material after Oswald's retirement. Working with Paul Taylor was a different story: "I went to visit him when he had a big studio, and he lived at one end of it" (p. 53). Oswald was particularly interested in documenting and saving the various versions of Taylor's major works that she had seen. She asked him, "Don't you want to have people look at the variant editions of this work?" He responded, "No Gegi, that's what I *don't* want to do." The Dance Notation Bureau (DNB) had also, at that time, been pressing Taylor to have his dances notated. Taylor eventually did permit the DNB to create scores for several of his works, and he also started filming his dances: "He understood, he knew that he had to save everything, all versions of a work. I was afraid that he was going to discard all the films except the one he preferred, destroying the earlier versions . . . . But as far as I know, he didn't do that."

Ballet's Records

The American and international ballet worlds were flourishing at the same time that modern dance was emerging and becoming well established. Oswald realized that the comprehensive nature of the Dance Collection should embrace all facets: concert dance in all its manifestations, classical forms from the world over, social and ritual dances, pedagogy, history, anthropology, and so on. Ballet, both that of the distant past and that unfolding as Oswald developed the collection, became an important subject of acquisition. A critical core of that collection was donated in 1955 by longtime Dance Collection friend Walter Toscanini, son of the renowned maestro Arturo Toscanini and husband of Italian ballerina Cia Fornaroli.[9] NYPL's online catalog summarizes this collection as "more than 3,300 rare books, and tens of thousands of libretti, scores, manuscripts, prints, photographs, clippings, and playbills."[10] An early and steady financial supporter of the collection, Toscanini invited Oswald and dance historian Lillian Moore to lunch, after the death of his wife, to tell them he intended to donate his remarkable collection of historical dance material to NYPL. Oswald recalled that, "barely breathing, I said to him, 'Why aren't you giving it to an Italian library?' And Lillian kicked me under the table! But I did want to know that and he did tell me" (p. 88). Toscanini was impressed by the systematic collecting and cataloging that Oswald had undertaken. Oswald was delighted. Toscanini's donation helped the Dance Collection to fulfill the future he envisioned, making possible the study, in an American library, of the great legacy of European ballet.

Toscanini's friendship proved utterly dependable. In 1960, collector George Chaffee, a New York dance teacher and brilliant collector of dance books, prints, and related material, was in serious need of funds. Oswald, with Toscanini's support, was able to help: "I knew that the collection was to go to Harvard—George said it was, which was fine. ... I never thought we'd get that collection, and I never really tried. But we were really friendly with Chaffee and they [Chaffee and partner Richard Doobs] were down to the Dance Collection and I was up at their place a lot." One memorable day,

I got a call from George Chaffee and he was weeping, and he said, "If I don't get ten thousand dollars before tomorrow morning to pay a year's rent, my collection is going to be taken by the sheriff and it's going to be sold unidentified in boxes at a sheriff's sale," and there would be no way that it would be distributed or sold as a dance collection, since people who go to the sheriff sales just buy things in bulk. This was incredible, this great collection of memorabilia, all of the prints—the American prints, ... a bust of [Anna] Pavlova, the whole business was going to be lost! He had tried Harvard Theatre Collection and others for funds. I said, "I'll see what I can do." I thought, the library doesn't have ten thousand dollars. But, I went to the administration and asked .... George had also told me that it was not enough for me to get the money but I had to go down and take a check to a certain city office. I thought, "This is crazy!" (pp. 83–84)

As Oswald had expected, the library did not have the cash at hand, so she turned to another possible resource: "I decided I would call Walter Toscanini," who had not only donated his magnificent collection, but also "was a great mentor" to Oswald. This was not an easy call to make, because competition between Toscanini and Chaffee as collectors had created mutual suspicions.

I said, "Seriously, I need ten thousand dollars," and he [Toscanini] started to laugh .... I said, "You probably want to know what it's for." He said, "No, if you call me and ask me for ten thousand dollars, I think it is dead serious, life and death." And I said "Yes." So he said, "Meet me at the RCA Victor [studios] ... in the parking lot." ... I met him there and he smiled and took out his checkbook and wrote a check for ten thousand dollars to the city office downtown. And then I told him it was for the Chaffee collection, and of course he was just jubilant. I went to George and I said, "We have ten thousand dollars," and we went downtown .... I said, "We do not want to infringe on what you promised to Harvard ... but Walter Toscanini has a right to come and look at this material," and he agreed. Toscanini got the most ravishing collection, ... all the American prints, the European prints, the libretti, the playbills, the unusual items like the wonderful statues of [Marie] Taglioni and [Fanny] Elssler, and the cigarillo cases and castanets. (pp. 83–84)

Toscanini purchased the collection and the following week had it delivered to the library. There is also a George Chaffee collection at the Harvard Theatre Collection.

The Diaghilev era also became the subject of collections donated to or acquired by the Dance Collection. The diaries of Vaslav Nijinsky were purchased (pp. 36, 60), while donations included the letters of Serge Diaghilev, the archive of documents held by Diaghilev's secretary, Gabriel Astruc, and material from choreographer Michel Fokine, whose son, Vitale, donated important press material, letters, and contracts, including Diaghilev's

communications with his company (p. 91).[11] The archive of ballerina Nathalie Branitzka was an early donation to the library, sup-
plying information about the off-stage life of Colonel de Basil's
Ballets Russes de Monte-Carlo through scrapbooks and informal
photographs, along with other records Branitzka provided. The
hours the dancer spent at the library reviewing the material with
Oswald gave the young librarian a rich education in this period
of ballet history.[12] The fine collection of Serge Denham—who
directed the last of the Diaghilev successor companies, the Ballet Russe de Monte-Carlo, for many years—came to the library
through donations by Denham's daughter, Irina Pabst, beginning
in 1974; Pabst also provided a grant for processing the material.

To supplement this growing collection on ballet history, Oswald sought microfilm copies of precious items held abroad, a
goal she had identified in her initial years at the Music Division. "I
wanted to get the one hundred and fifty great early works in the
dance repertoire completely documented, with music, stage sets,
designs, photographs or prints if they existed, with the libretti and
production notes" (p. 96). Oswald's objective was, "if you wanted
to look up *Swan Lake* or *Giselle,* you not only had references to all
the versions ... that we do, but you had the libretti, stage designs,
production notes, everything you could find in various European
collections." The project was realized in the 1980s. Personal assistance was essential in this process because ordering this kind of
material or microfilms was a long and uncertain process at NYPL:
"You ordered an item through the order department, and the order ... would go on a list, and all the other divisions of the library
had things on this list; you just moved up the list and you might
get your item in ten years or you might not" (p. 42). Thus, Oswald sought assistance from mathematician and Columbia University professor Hubert Goldschmidt, son of a member of the
Committee for the Dance Collection (discussed later). A dance
lover, Goldschmidt went to Paris regularly.* Oswald broached her
plan: he would look up and report back to her on the material
she sought from the various archives, and he would be free to investigate other items that came to his attention. Once Oswald had
Goldschmidt's list, she would investigate funding for whatever she

---

*Goldschmidt's involvement with the Dance Committee has continued. He was, at the time
of this writing, the committee's chairman.

wished to purchase; when that was secured, she would order the material directly, with the Acquisition Department's cooperation, and Goldschmidt would bring it back on his next trip to Europe. He first went to the Paris libraries, where he ordered copies "of every single score that was a choreography of a dance work, ballet, or social dance, and we got thousands of frames of this material on microfilm, which has largely been cataloged.... Then we started on the 150 ballets—to get the set designs, the music, and the stage directions" (p. 43). Oswald had, at her Ardsley apartment during our interviews, a copy of the major source she used for this project, a musicological and archival catalog of the great French archives compiled by Théodore de Lajarte,[13] which gave some idea of the riches that were microfilmed for the Dance Collection. Oswald explained that she would comb through this text, select the ballets, and investigate where the libretti and other information could be found, often in the music department of the Bibliothèque Nationale. This project was funded largely by the Andrew W. Mellon Foundation, a strong supporter of the Dance Collection.

Microfilms were also acquired of the outstanding P. J. S. Richardson Collection, a core of the Library and Archives of the Royal Academy of Dancing in London.[14] While Richardson never visited NYPL himself, he corresponded with Oswald and was eager to make material from his collection available there. Oswald also wished to support scholars beginning to work in the field of "early dance"—European Renaissance and baroque dance. Unfortunately, her attempt to bring these artists and scholars together to create a set of historical film documents that could be disseminated was unsuccessful because of their rivalries (p. 9).

The ballet riches held at the Dance Collection attracted the attention of visiting ballet companies and stars, and the library served as a meeting ground for artists from all over the world. For example, during the Royal Ballet's first American tour (1949), Oswald arranged a reception for the company at the Dance Collection. Artists from both sides of the ocean, who had been kept apart through World War II, heard speakers such as composer and conductor Constant Lambert and Ninette de Valois, founder of the Royal Ballet, which had opened in New York the previous evening. "[I]t was interesting to observe that red-haired Moira Shearer was very shy and deferential to Fonteyn because Shearer had already danced and had gotten tremendous praise, and Fonteyn was not to dance until the next night. But everybody was there—Nora Kaye—everybody. [The American dancers] had never met these British dancers and it was just wonderful to see them meet, introduce themselves, and begin talking and laughing together quickly" (p. 57). When designs for an exhibition of sets for *The Sleeping Beauty* and other works were delayed in customs the day before the show's opening, Oswald and other library officials went to the customs office to verify their use and arrange their release. Oswald had organized the show, "British Ballet," which she and her then-fiancé, Dean Johnson, hung. Oswald's efforts during this demanding period were rewarded: "Every year when she came back on tour, Ninette de Valois would visit us. She would come to the back workroom at Fifth Avenue and 42nd Street, sit down at the table, and say, 'What have you got for me today?' Perhaps I'd bring her Noverre's stuff ... or something of Diaghilev—letters, programs, pictures, a libretto—and she'd talk about when she'd been with the company" (p. 58).

Marie Rambert, another major figure in establishing ballet and nurturing emerging choreographers in England, also developed a warm working relationship with Oswald, who was seeking films of the work of new British choreographers, including Frederick Ashton. "I decided that I should go see Marie Rambert when I was in Europe again. Well, it was wonderful; I got to see her two years in succession and because I was married and had children, and she had the same, she walked me around and showed me all the places that had to do with her children and her marriage. It was one of the most cherished experiences of my life" (p. 59). Upon broaching her request for choreographers' films, Oswald was delighted by Rambert's "blithe" response: "Oh yes, why don't you go out to Ealing Studio, I'll call the company.... Tomorrow morning, I'll put you in a taxi." The Dance Collection received about thirty-five films as a result of this venture.

Another important European company, the Royal Danish Ballet, also had a warm connection with the Dance Collection. Oswald recalled that Erik Bruhn "was there frequently. He was a friend of Lillian Moore's, and he invited both of us up to see him perform at Jacob's Pillow ... and when we were down in the village of Lee, he came and had supper with us" (p. 59). Moore

Figure 2. Lillian Moore, dance historian; Niels Bjørn Larsen, ballet master and artistic director of the Royal Danish Ballet; and Genevieve Oswald, at the New York Public Library Dance Collection at Fifth Avenue and 42nd Street, ca. 1956. Courtesy of Genevieve Oswald.

generously donated years of research material, including interviews with Bruhn and memoirs of the Royal Danish Ballet, to the Dance Collection (see Figure 2). But Oswald recalled that her first encounter with the Danish dancers had been "bizarre.... I was sitting at my desk and I got a call from a former library employee on the staff of our press office, now at the American-Scandinavian Foundation, and she said, 'I have got a couple of Danish dancers here and they want to dance in the United States. Can you give me any idea of what I can do with them?'" Oswald agreed to contact Ted Shawn about presenting the pair at Jacob's Pillow. That year, 1955, Shawn offered to host the dancers in his own house and present them in performance. The next year, he invited the company. Through this kind of support for the field—"just doing whatever we were asked to do"—dance artists and donors "came to believe that we were all right, that they could give us their records, their archives, and not be afraid" (p. 59).

Contemporary ballet artists began contributing material to the Dance Collection. Ruth Page, a leader in the Chicago ballet community, donated a fine personal collection (p. 91). Much material related to the entire history of dance, and especially to the NYCB and the work of George Balanchine, came through Kirstein's generous support and donations. Rudolf Nureyev gave a large portion of his material as well as generous financial support. Oswald recalled that "when [Nureyev] was in London, after he did his film in Australia, *Don Quijote*, we were going to have one of our benefit evenings arranged by the Dance Committee [Committee for the Dance Collection] (see below) .... Nureyev was wonderful. He flew over to come to our evening as our guest, and because he was performing, he flew back the same night" (p. 50). Moore had amassed an extensive archive of dance prints, libretti, and particularly a remarkable collection of Elssler memorabilia. This material came to the Dance Collection after Moore's death in 1967.[15] Her research notes, files, catalogs, and books form an integral part of the Dance Collection today, as they served also in educating Oswald during Moore's almost daily visits to the library, where the two dance lovers became great friends.

Another memorable figure at the Dance Collection from the ballet world was Agnes de Mille, who, Oswald recalled, "became a very good friend, a really good friend. She understood exactly what we were doing. She was a born archivist." De Mille donated films of her works and other significant material (p. 54). Unfortunately, in the late 1970s the IRS found de Mille behind in her tax payments because of controversy over whether films were choreographic documents of value. A nasty court case ensued in which Oswald was asked to support de Mille, even to testify in court. "We worked hours developing arguments about the value of the films and what she had done for American dance" (p. 55). Oswald recalled the hostility of the IRS lawyers who came to the library to interview her about de Mille's case but refused to hear her references to dance as an art form.[16] The judge decided he would admit the choreographic documents as records of value but de Mille would have to agree never to use these again in staging her works. This decision devastated de Mille emotionally and financially. Oswald was shocked not only at the decision but also at "the glee of the IRS team, who danced and clapped each other on the back, a big win for them." De Mille stayed in close touch with Oswald and eventually donated manuscripts of her books, her correspondence, and other items.

Many other great ballet figures of the age made their way to the Dance Collection for their own research as choreographers or performers. A memorable example was a "little, slight woman in this nondescript print dress" (p. 48). She told Oswald that "'Mr. Tudor said for me to come in . . . . My name is Makarova and I am going to dance with the company.'" Choreographer Antony Tudor had instructed Natalia Makarova to look at filmed works of his in the Dance Collection. Oswald made sure the ballerina was set up with a full collection of Tudor's filmed work, which she carefully watched in its entirety. "She thanked us; she was always very familiar with us from then on. But, at that first visit, she didn't look anything like a ballet dancer." (p. 49) A few weeks later, "Tudor came and said, 'What have you done to me? . . . You showed Makarova those old Nora Kaye movies, and she's now got all these mannerisms that I can't stand.' I said, 'But you sent her in here to look at the films!'" Although momentarily angry, Tudor proved a "great friend" to the library, eventually willing a large part of his own material to the Dance Collection along with the income from performances of some of his ballets.

Balanchine, too, was often quietly present, reading scores at the Music Division, and he knew the library as a whole. Oswald particularly recollected a visit he made to the Dance Collection while it was at 42nd Street, during a period when Tudor was choreographing for NYCB (p. 49). Balanchine requested Italian scores, *ballabile* from nineteenth-century Italian opera scores. The request was a pleasure to the music-trained Oswald, who provided Balanchine with a library truck full of the scores. Unfortunately, Tudor failed to appear at that meeting, which was arranged so that the two choreographers could choose a score for Tudor to choreograph. "So Balanchine, a marvelous musician, read through all the scores on the carts. He thanked me, and about three weeks later, Mr. Tudor called and he needed the same scores. So, we took the room upstairs, which had a piano in it, and he brought in a pianist and had the scores played for him." Other ballet artists, including Jerome Robbins and Mikhail Baryshnikov, visited, appreciated, and supported the Dance Collection (p. 50).

World Dance

"When I first came to the Dance Collection," Oswald recalled, "I talked with Carleton Sprague Smith and told him that I was interested in all of dance, not just ballet, not just modern dance" (pp. 1–2). She collected material and created catalogs on popular, ritual, social, and therapeutic dance, and she was interested in global coverage. Among the greatest successes Oswald had in this breadth of coverage was the Asian Collection.[17] Oswald's interest in Asian dance was stimulated early in her career at NYPL by programs presented at the Museum of Natural History by Hazel Lockwood Mueller that included Asian dance (p. 1). Upon beginning her work on dance at the library, Oswald visited La Meri (Russell Meriwether Hughes), who "had a wonderful school of Asian dance at that time. It was in the old Isadora Duncan studio, which was the same studio that later would house the New York City Ballet when they first started" (p. 2). Oswald remembered La Meri as "a beautiful woman. She was a wonderful teacher; she had a tremendous core of young people, young Americans that were studying all forms of Asian dance—Indian dance, Indonesian dance." La Meri desired to pass on her love and knowledge of Asian dance to others since, in the late 1940s, Asian teachers were not able to travel to New York. Some years later, however, La Meri told Oswald that she was giving up her studio because Asian artists were, at last, able to come to the West and teach their own dances. Indeed, Oswald's work at the Dance Collection helped facilitate such visits.

In the mid-1970s, Porter McCray of the John D. Rockefeller III Fund invited Oswald to lunch, although the Dance Collection had never applied to the fund for support. In the middle of their elegant meal, McCray asked if she would like to create an Asian Dance Archive at NYPL. "I was stunned. I still can feel the thrill that I felt, the excitement. . . . We would be going back to some of the foundations of dance if we could do that." McCray offered her a grant to fund creation of such an archive, along with his full support and assistance. In response to her query about his motivation for this generous offer, he said, "I think the people at the Dance Collection are passionate about dance and I feel that if we can create an archive of documents and films here we will save them for the Asian countries themselves," since, Oswald commented, "they were engaged in other aspects of their development and much was being lost." Oswald learned that McCray "was considered a real prince among Asians, a man of phenomenal stature, a force for the arts in Asia. His contacts ranged from presidents to dancers and teachers. When he said that he was going to help me, he did" (p. 2)

The project required that Oswald take a six-week trip through Asia. Her husband and family encouraged her to go. To prepare, Oswald hired Elizabeth Miller (later McCue). Supported and informed by McCray's extensive Asian connections, Oswald and McCue wrote to dancers, companies, and dance authorities in every part of Asia, explaining their intentions and requesting interview appointments. After establishing a rigorous daily schedule, the time for the trip arrived. "It was New Year's Day and I went to the airport, to the French airlines gate, and literally there was nobody there. Later, there were two passengers in the plane. It was snowing.... As we took off, I saw the deep snow outside and I said, 'What am I doing here? Why am I going to Asia?'" (p. 4). The long journey's first leg took her to Paris where, in a bleak mood, "I decided ... I would go see when the first flight back to the United States left, and so I did." Returning to the airport the next morning to catch a plane home, she "decided just for fun that I would go and see where the airplane to Thailand was taking off much later.... The plane was sitting outside this big glass window. And it was gorgeous, a beautiful airplane. The wonderful tail was painted like a Garuda [mythical Hindu bird], a bird's tail." Still, she was determined to fly home. "As I was turning to go back to my gate for the New York plane, I met a friend of mine from NYU, where I was teaching dance history. We were amazed to find each other and she said, 'What are you doing here?' I said, 'Well, I am supposed to go to Asia but I have decided I am going back home to New York.' She said, 'You can't. I will not let you get on the plane.'"

With this friend's encouragement, Oswald boarded the plane to Thailand. "It was a Thai plane and everything was colorful silk, beautiful. This was the beginning of the New Year, when all the young Thai men were coming back from studying in Europe and they were such a handsome group." At the Oberoi Hotel in Bangkok, Oswald prepared to make her telephone calls, struggling with "an unfriendly telephone system. I had a great big, thick book listing appointments with everyone important to dance in every city, every country I was to visit. This was the start—several hundred people, at least, in six weeks. I *had* to meet them all. I had a translator. It ... was intimidating—the range of people and places was terrifying" (pp. 4–5). Oswald arrived amid political chaos: university students were demonstrating in the streets against food price hikes. Oswald feared that her first interview, with the Thai prime minister, would be cancelled, but she was escorted to the meeting in a private car, surrounded by soldiers. The prime minister "had been, in his youth, a dancer of the refined style and he was a great friend of Porter McCray.* He sat, oblivious to the chaos outside—it was unbelievable—for about an hour and talked to me about the refined dance, with a few members of his staff also sitting about us, and it was recorded on tape and film. Then he kindly asked what he could do" to help (p. 5). Owing to McCray's influence, Oswald also met with royalty, foundation heads, diplomats, and dance artists.

This generous reception was repeated in other nations she visited—Bali, Japan, India, Indonesia, and elsewhere. In Japan, an officer of NHK television network gave her what was to become a collection of seven hundred films (p. 6); in Jogjakarta, Java, she was treated to a performance by the prince's professional company and introduced to the school's teachers (p. 6). Funding through the Jerome Robbins Film Archive (see below) allowed support for filming classes of an elderly Balinese teacher whose legacy was thus preserved (p. 8). The dance films, donated by professionals in many countries, were shipped directly to the library as Oswald continued on her itinerary. She also collected manuscripts, visual material, articles, microfilms, audiotapes, and books in many languages (p. 10). In India, she visited Sangeet Natak Academy of Kerala, falling so ill during the journey that, she recalls, "I almost died on the way" (p. 7). Such famous artists as Birju Maharaj and Rukmini Devi met with and graciously assisted Oswald. The Spencer Collection at NYPL held important Asian dance manuscripts, which had resulted in a fine public exhibition, "Asian Dance Images from the Spencer Collection" in the summer of 1977. Oswald's travels deepened and widened existing holdings.

A goal of Oswald's trip and collecting had been to preserve Asian dance traditions that were disappearing because of modernization or political chaos. One such poignant case was that of the

*M. R. Kukrit Pramoj, thirteenth Prime Minister of Thailand (1975–1976), was of an aristocratic family. The British-educated Kukrit was a scholar of Thai culture, including dance, visual art, and literature, as well as an award-winning author and leading intellectual in Thailand. Judy Stowe, "Obituary: Kukrit Pramoj," *The Independent* (London), October 11, 1995.

Khmer dance. In 1971, "When the classical Khmer company came to Brooklyn, we filmed every one of their performances. And later on, after the revolution and the destruction in that country, we were able to give the dancers who were teaching classical Khmer dance these films and those we had collected in Asia so they could continue to teach. The first time we sent them films, they were in refugee camps; the second time, they were in California where they were successfully teaching. Having these films really meant everything to them" (p. 12).

Oswald also befriended Beate Gordon, programming director of New York's Asia Society, and the two women worked together to create a presence for Asian dance at both institutions (pp. 8–9). Under Oswald's leadership, the library organized a two-day meeting in 1976 at which American and Asian scholars from all over the world were invited to share work, information, and plans related to the building of the Asian Archive.[18] During that weekend, the Asian scholars attended a NYCB performance, and, as Oswald recalled, "They loved Balanchine" (p. 9). They were "almost mesmerized."[19]

Oswald hoped to repeat the success of the Asian Archive with other dance research areas. However, the Dance Collection had only limited success in covering dance in South America and Africa. Cultural attachés in those areas, perhaps distracted by political and economic turmoil in their nations, were less responsive to requests for help in finding dance professionals and acquiring information on their work. The Dance Collection did purchase whatever could be bought in books and films to cover these regions, however. It also developed a fairly representative archive on Native American dance (p. 17).

Yet if the success of Oswald's Asian odyssey was not fully repeated in some other areas, that collecting experience had positive results beyond the magnificent material in NYPL (pp. 11–14). Oswald was invited to sit on the board of the Institut für den Wissenschaftlichen Film in Göttingen, Germany, where she helped to raise awareness of dance and to bring Asian dance experts on board (p. 11). Musicologists and ethnologists took note of Oswald's expertise, inviting her to speak at gatherings. She served on a committee in Pune, India, for the Archive and Research Centre for Ethnomusicology of the American Institute of Indian Studies. In Doha, Qatar, she met with Arab leaders seeking to establish a cultural museum (p. 12). This was the era of Ayatollah Khomeini's ascension to power, a time particularly uncomfortable for an American woman to travel alone in such areas. Aside from Oswald, there was just one other woman in the group: "She was a beautiful Iraqi who lived in Paris. And there were about sixteen or seventeen sheiks, older but with some younger men in beautiful kaftans of the finest wool." During their three days of meetings, Oswald gave a presentation on archival development. Despite her anxieties about this "male-oriented world," she was kindly and well received.

The Chinese government also took note of Oswald's successes. Oswald undertook a trip in 1978 with Ross Parkes, of the Martha Graham Dance Company, who taught master classes and led lecture-demonstrations. (See Figures 3, 4, and 5.) During their two-week visit to Beijing and Shanghai, Oswald met with writers, scholars, editors, and dance leaders, visited places of interest to Chinese dance, and gave lectures on American modern dance. She remembers, "When I walked into my hotel, I realized with a jolt that I was staying in the hotel that Ruth St. Denis and Ted Shawn had stayed in when they went there many years before.

Figure 3. Welcome ceremony for Genevieve Oswald, at the dais seated third from left, and Ross Parkes, seated second from right, in China, 1978. Courtesy of Genevieve Oswald.

Figure 4. Genevieve Oswald, standing second from left, and Ross Parkes, seated right, at welcome ceremony in China, 1978. Courtesy of Genevieve Oswald.

That was very personal to me" (p. 13). The visit was a success: "Chinese officials had assembled about 450 young dancers and teachers of dance throughout the provinces to learn about American modern dance" through Oswald's lectures and Parkes's classes.

Figure 5. Genevieve Oswald, being greeted in China, 1978. Ross Parkes is behind and slightly to the left of Oswald. Courtesy of Genevieve Oswald.

The visit concluded with a performance by participants in Parkes's workshops.

Visual Documentation

Oswald made visual documentation of dance a primary concern; she sought to document "not only the history of the art, but also the choreography itself in tangible form," that is, "the actual steps and sequence of steps."[20] Owing to the ephemeral nature of dance, its lack of a historically continuous notation or recording, and the paucity of written records, Oswald viewed collecting in the broadest light, embracing libretti, posters, scores, books, manuscripts, scrapbooks, oral histories, notations, prints, films, photographs, clippings, designs, playbills, and even costume items. She sought to bring these records together in one location where the researcher could find the visual, aural, descriptive, and material information on any one dance or subject. Dance as a moving art is well represented in the Jerome Robbins Film Archive. Yet her early efforts to establish this portion of the Dance Collection met with opposition from two influential and often difficult individuals: Kirstein and—ironically, considering the collection's eventual name—Robbins.

Kirstein argued tradition as his objection to the film archive at the Dance Collection, which, by the early 1960s, had already filmed NYCB rehearsals: "He came in one day and said, 'I see you are going to go on with the film archive,' and I said, 'Yes, I am.' He said, 'This is crazy. Dancers don't want it.' He stood at my door and stormed for five minutes, giving a brilliantly reasoned exposition on the way dance had been, and should be, transmitted. But he was always angry in a fond way" (pp. 71–72). After a good lunch, he returned and said, "But I suppose you are going to do it anyway." Some years later, in Kirstein's catalog for *A Decade of Acquisitions*, an exhibition he was organizing for NYPL, he called the Jerome Robbins Film Archive "the most useful and profound testimony to dance ever planned and executed," a statement that Oswald found "amazing. ... He always came around. If you were right, he saw it and told you so."

Like Kirstein, Robbins was far from enthusiastic when Oswald approached him for support of the film archive project (p. 29). He planned to establish his own dance film library. Oswald found seed money to begin the film library's archive from the National Endowment for the Arts and the New York State Council on the Arts. A few years later, however, Robbins saw the advantage of working through an established organization and gave Oswald a grant. In 1964, he extended his support remarkably, donating a percentage of the proceeds from *Fiddler on the Roof* to maintain the film and video material, hire staff, purchase films and viewing equipment, document significant works, and develop guidelines to protect against copyright violation and plagiarism (p. 70). This gift allowed the collection to grow and be available for research use. Appropriately, the film library at the Dance Collection was named the Jerome Robbins Archive of the Recorded Moving Image,* but after his death, the entire Dance Collection was named for him—a move Oswald protests, although she reveres Robbins.†

Not only did the library purchase films of existing works, such as the many copies of Asian films that Oswald acquired in the course of her travels, but also the Dance Collection actively filmed teachers, dancers, and works to ensure that artistic and cultural legacies would not disappear.‡ In the case of American professional companies, such filming presented delicate problems, particularly for the musicians' union, which was wary that others might use their work for financial gain when the musicians were not paid royalties, a situation they had encountered before (p. 72). Oswald, a musician herself, worked sympathetically to meet the musicians' concerns. When filming the NYCB repertory, Oswald had support from company administrators, including Kirstein and Betty Cage. Other companies, such as the Joffrey Ballet, proved equally cooperative. For these archival records, dancers performed in rehearsal clothes and films were never

---

*Initially, Robbins donated some money to the fund in honor of his mother, Lena Robbins, but his major support came through the royalties from *Fiddler*. Florence Tarlow explains the connection with the Lena Robbins Foundation in "Miss Oswald of the Dance Collection," *Playbill*, New York City Ballet Program, January 15, 1967, 66–67.

†Oswald fought against naming the Dance Collection for any individual person because she felt such a move would cause any dancer who wanted to donate material to feel that it was someone else's collection (p. 29). The renaming occurred after Oswald's retirement.

‡Oswald estimated, in "One Approach to the Development of a Dance Archive" (p. 83), that the Dance Collection had produced about 770 films, covering wide-ranging themes.

released commercially, but they provide an outstanding performance record of American dance companies in their prime. Moving image material covers works from all dance genres—ritual, social, children's dance, and many other categories. It has been the most heavily used of all the Dance Collection holdings.

Preserving and Cataloging

Oswald's enormous circle of acquaintances in the dance world and beyond has included scholars of music, dance, and various world cultures. Dancers and choreographers, critics and administrators, teachers and students, funders and dance lovers, writers and editors—all were part of her network and contributed to shaping the Dance Collection. Perhaps the individual most frequently named in the course of our interviews—and already mentioned in this article—was Lincoln Kirstein, co-founder of the School of American Ballet and NYCB, a dance writer, administrator, and influential arts thinker. Although Oswald experienced his famously difficult personality,[21] she also came to appreciate deeply his shrewd intelligence and critical support: "If he thought you were doing a good job, he was on your side" (p. 26). While the dance archive that Kirstein had begun at the Museum of Modern Art had not flourished there, that effort eventually contributed important material to the NYPL Dance Collection. Perhaps Kirstein's disappointing experience at MoMA made him initially skeptical of Oswald's plans for the Dance Collection, but in due time he was so impressed with the library's success that, "sometimes for months at a time, he would come in every day just to see who was working, doing research in the reading room" (p. 57). He had been a leader in establishing dance as a field of scholarly endeavor with his book, *Dance, a Short History of Classic Theatrical Dancing*,[22] and his founding in 1942 of the periodical, *Dance Index*. As the Dance Collection acquired more rare and fragile items—books, prints, clippings, photographs, and so on—Oswald became concerned about preservation. It was Kirstein who gave the funding for a small conservation laboratory to address Oswald's concern (p. 37). He regularly donated stock from his family's company, Filene's Department Store, to the Dance Collection for the purpose of maintaining the laboratory, the first in the dance field and the first at NYPL.

Kirstein also proved a supporter in another major initiative: developing what Oswald refers to as the "Dance Book Catalog" or the "ABC" (Automated Book Catalog) but which is more formally titled *Dictionary Catalog of the Dance Collection*.[23] Although she cannot prove it, and he never admitted it, Oswald is certain that Kirstein spoke with officials at important foundations, among these the Ford Foundation's W. McNeil Lowry, to garner funding amounting to millions of dollars for work toward this landmark catalog. Ford Foundation support for the project began in 1965 and continued as the work proceeded for ten years leading to the catalog's publication. Funding for special Dance Collection catalogs had earlier been given by the Rockefeller Foundation.

Oswald considers the creation of the *Dictionary Catalog* to be one of her greatest contributions to the fields of dance and library science, since performing arts cataloging was in its infancy when she began work on the project. Because the Dance Collection was relatively small for an arts collection, the NYPL administration felt it was a good laboratory for experimenting with computer technology and with categories, headings, and procedures. Working in a virgin field—dance cataloging—with two computer assistants, Oswald dug into the work. She approached the Library of Congress for guidance, but found little interest there in her project.* Her plan necessitated creation of a broad set of subject headings for the multiplicity of dance and the subdivisions under which dance material could be properly arranged: "I decided that what I would have to do was look at every book ... in our collection, at the chapter and section headings and the index, where the load of information was found, and at the way that information was arranged and subdivided. After a while, I began to get a sense of it all, of the richness and variety of dance subjects" (pp. 19–20). To bring the dance headings into conformity with library practice, she explored other large subject headings, like furniture and visual art, to match formatting and categorization. "I spent six months on it. The library gave me a leave of absence to do these headings and I finally came up with 46,000 subject headings for

---

*NYPL uses its own classmarks and subject headings, distinct from the Library of Congress or Dewey Decimal systems. Since the Dance Collection is specialized, the precision of its subject listings is considerably greater than that afforded by systems created for general libraries.

dance that were indeed the framework or structure for our catalog."

Oswald's goal was to create an integrated catalog in which all
material, of whatever sort (text, image, music, film, etc.), would be
brought under each subject heading. She explained that "in the
Dance Collection, we used dance as a mosaic. ... We wanted to
have the pictures, the prints, reviews, the program, all the books
and oral tapes, and everything that is relative to that production,
or that person" (p. 89). Organizing and interconnecting all of this
material was a monumental task. Because of the wide range covered by the collection, Oswald had to distinguish different kinds
of dances from one another: "To show that they were a folk or
a social dance, I put in parentheses the word 'dance' after it.
That meant that the reference listed had information on a particular folk or social dance. For the title of a ballet or a modern
dance work, I put the name of the choreographer after the title
of the work. That allowed us to organize choreographic works by
choreographers under the title" (p. 20). All versions of Petipa's
Swan Lake fell under '*Swan Lake* (Petipa),' and were listed with
the work's films, books, music, reviews, photographs, and libretti.
Computer cataloging was in its early stages and Oswald investigated all options then in process, from a library in Boca Raton,
Florida, to IBM in New York. She developed a coding system to
identify elements in each type of reference in the Dance Collection. With funding first from Ford and later from the Rockefeller
Foundation, Oswald and a creative group of systems analysts and
project assistants (first, Barbara Palfy and, later, Dorothy Lour-
dou) completed the huge job, only to discover, in proofreading, a
small glitch: "Ruth St. Denis was left out [of the main catalog]; I
couldn't believe it. It was high tragedy; she would have loved it! A
prank on us, perhaps?" (p. 22).

Oswald's system for the *Dictionary Catalog* was groundbreaking: "If you have at hand twenty-five lithographs of Marie
Taglioni—if you put them under the name of the lithographer,
which you would, if you were in an art catalog—then every time
a reader wanted the Taglioni material, one would have to go
through twenty-five different portfolios to bring everything on
Taglioni to that reader" (p. 23). Instead, Oswald cataloged all such
prints under the dancer's name, "Taglioni." She spoke at meetings
of the Special Libraries Association to introduce the field to "the

special needs of dance .... I remember one cataloger who said, 'Gegi, you can't do this. This is against library science—treason!' But we had to." Oswald's innovation—thinking of the material from the standpoint of its subject matter—is a practice now standard in the library field.

The Dance Book Catalog was the first such publication in the United States converted into a computer database. It quickly entered the reference rooms of public and university libraries around the world, making the service reach of the Dance Collection as international as is the material it holds. When asked if other dance libraries have adopted the method developed by Oswald and her assistants, she replied, "Oh, yes. Not only that—this is the joyous thing—I learned one day that the director of the Library of Congress was sending a committee to look at our catalog.... The senior committee member came up to me and said that we had created a benchmark in the world of library science. We had successfully invaded the upper reaches of library science" (p. 23).

Exhibitions and the Committee for the Dance Collection

The Dance Collection itself was a pioneering effort; the *Dictionary Catalog* was a further landmark. Yet another of Oswald's major achievements was the series of exhibitions presented by the library drawing on material she had acquired for the Dance Collection. The list is extensive and the kinds of material covered, as well as the geographic and temporal range, breathtaking.[24] Oswald's work on the Asian collection resulted, in 1977, in an exhibition of rare and unusual manuscripts (p. 10), while the visit of the Royal Ballet (1949) was honored by an exhibition of British ballet design (p. 58). The opening of the exhibition *Stravinsky and the Dance* (1966) was graced by the presence of the composer and his wife (p. 35).

A strong advocate of dance notation and collector of notated dance scores, Oswald arranged exhibitions on Labanotation and other forms of dance writing (1952, 1960). The Diaghilev period was beautifully represented by a show featuring the collection of Boris Kochno, the impresario's secretary (p. 81). Some exhibitions were on themes from the distant past, such as *French Court and Opera Ballet* (1948) or *The Jewish Dancing Master* *and Theatrical Society* (1986), while others were current, including *The New York City Ballet* (1959) and *Avant-Garde Dance* (1968). Exhibitions focused on significant figures of modern dance, including Shawn (1950), Horst (1984), Graham (1984), and Mary Wigman (1986), and honored renowned ballet artists such as Elssler (1951), Pavlova (1956), Marius Petipa (1958), Galina Ulanova (1962), Salvatore Viganò (1984), and Balanchine (1985).*

Exhibitions not only showcased acquisitions, but also served as fundraisers, many sponsored by the Committee for the Dance Collection, which Oswald and others often referred to as the "Dance Committee."[25] The NYPL Research Libraries, as public-private institutions, were funded by foundations created by philanthropists John Jacob Astor, James Lenox, and Samuel J. Tilden at the turn of the twentieth century, and they are largely dependent on ongoing private donations and grants (pp. 26–27). Oswald proved an excellent fundraiser, winning grants from such private foundations as Ford, Gould, Mellon, Pew, and Rockefeller, and from public sources such as the National Endowment for the Arts and New York State Council on the Arts. Yet funding needs were a constant concern. While working under Smith, Oswald had told him of her shortage of staff to process the material the collection had received on modern dance. A man of impressive experience and acquaintance, Smith helped Oswald to cultivate the dance interests of individuals influential in cultural circles, leading to the founding in 1957 of the prestigious and unusual Committee for the Dance Collection. Smith started with two cultural leaders, Marjorie Graff and Elizabeth Houghton, whom he invited to lunch at the Harvard Club. These passionate lovers of dance "started this committee" (p. 95), and went on to organize fundraising events, contribute money, become informed about acquisitions, and work actively to procure important donations or purchases. In addition to Graff and Houghton, the Dance Committee came to include Anne Bass, Randall Bourscheidt, Kirstein, William S. Lieberman, McCray, Terry, Pabst, Shawn, Jean

---

*As part of its mission to bring dance and dance research out of the Dance Collection itself, NYPL published books or monographs in the 1960s and thereafter on dance themes ranging from Isadora Duncan to early American ballet; authors included Selma Jeanne Cohen, Irma Duncan, Marian Eames, Lillian Moore, and Christena Schlundt (Treem, "Descriptive Study," 76–77).

Sulzberger, Toscanini, Helen Wright, and other well-placed individuals, eventually numbering in the range of ten to twenty members at a time.

The Dance Committee helped to organize benefits, public events (such as film showings or conversations with noted dance artists), exhibitions, and receptions, which publicized the collection and also secured money for such important acquisitions as the Nijinsky diaries (p. 36) and some of the Duncan collection (p. 93). Oswald called the Dance Committee members "true dance lovers. They went to the performances. They were on committees of other cultural organizations, they were very serious. They loved knowing what we were doing because they could actually visit the archive, see the conservator at work or the film being cataloged, right away" (pp. 35–36). Oswald kept members well informed of the results of their efforts, and respected their passion for dance. This kind of support was another pioneering effort of the Dance Collection; not long after establishment of the Committee for the Dance Collection, a broader, more affordable category, Friends of the Dance Collection, was created for those who wished to offer support on a smaller scale. Over time, following the Dance Committee's model, NYPL established a Friends of the Library category for other collections (p. 38).

The Dance Committee proved crucial in the early 1970s, when the entire NYPL system experienced a financial crisis so severe that the research libraries, including the Dance Collection, nearly closed their doors.[26] The Dance Committee rallied to organize a Gala Dance Benefit in January 1972 that brought together a wide range of artists: "This was the first time that New York City Ballet, the American Ballet Theatre, Fonteyn—all these dancers—had ever danced on the same stage [together]. Merce Cunningham came and danced; Erick Hawkins came and danced. It was amazing, all of them on the same program, and it was due to their wanting the Dance Collection to survive" (p. 94). Others, including critic Walter Terry and Broadway choreographer Donald Saddler, also supported the event. As Oswald remarked, "It's hard to believe. For example, Gelsey Kirkland, just beginning her career, opened the program with a pas de deux and when she came on stage, her leg trembled; it was the first time she had had that kind of exposure. And the committee found a man who was a corporate executive stationed in Atlanta, where Fonteyn was

touring. The committee got him to fly her up for that performance." Fonteyn stated that she came to support the collection
she had first seen in 1949 at the Royal Ballet's reception there.

Teacher and Mentor

During this productive if sometimes difficult period, Oswald also
taught dance history at New York University's graduate program
in dance education, an experience she found enormously stimu-
lating.[27] Who could better bring the materials of dance history to
students than the curator of one of the world's greatest dance collections? Similarly, Oswald was ideally suited to fill another role
from 1977 to 1987—associate editor of NYPL's research quarterly,
Research in the Humanities, which she regards as "one of the biggest
honors" of her career (p. 92). As if her plate were not sufficiently
full, she wrote regularly throughout her NYPL career for newspa-
pers, magazines, and scholarly journals.

Oswald also mentored many aspiring dance scholars from
her desk at the Dance Collection, where she kept abreast of the
graduate theses, choreographic projects, and scholarly books underway as artists, students, and researchers worked with library
material (p. 80). Lillian Moore, a pioneer in the field of dance history research, has been mentioned several times in this essay; she
"was there every day"* (p. 58) and Oswald became deeply interested in her research. For example, when Moore was investigating
the "Duport mystery," she and Oswald often went together to the
Woolworth's across the street from the main library at 42nd Street:
"We went over there every day and we had tea and a piece of
cake and spent what must have been a hundred hours discussing
Louis Duport, trying to figure out where he was in every period
of his life, if he had gone back to Europe, whether there were two
dancers of the same name," and other questions (p. 78). Moore's

---

*NYPL's online finding aid has a snapshot biography of Lillian Moore (1911–67), a pro-
fessional dancer who, upon retirement from the stage, became a major dance researcher.
Among her many publications are *Artists of the Dance* (1938); "Ballet," in the Encyclopaedia
Britannica; *Bournonville and Ballet Technique* with Erik Bruhn (1961); *Bournonville's London
Spring* (1965); *The Duport Mystery* (Dance Perspectives, no. 1, 1960); and *Images of the Dance:
Historical Treasures of the Dance Collection, 1581–1861* (1965). See http://www.nypl.org/ead/
742 (accessed June 10, 2011).

enormous treasure of research notes and findings are now available at the Dance Collection. Another renowned dance historian, Ivor Guest, was a frequent visitor in his early trips to New York (p. 58), mining the Dance Collection (and other archives) to gather information for his books on the Romantic ballet in England and France.* Another important figure in this period when dance history research was still nascent—Marian Hannah Winter†—was often at the Dance Collection and occasionally, during her research travels, scouted material that Oswald might wish to acquire (pp. 58, 78). Marian Eames worked closely with Kirstein in editing *Dance Index*, an important journal of dance history and analysis, and, with Oswald, on exhibitions and collections at NYPL. Oswald also recalled "a scholar in Georgia named Gladys Lasky‡ who did good work and now is completely forgotten" (p. 58). This was a period when there was just a handful of dance scholars. When they could afford to do research in Europe, they would copy out by hand reams of information, which they shared with one another. They formed a close-knit, if sometimes argumentative, community. In the 1970s, a NYPL survey yielded the information that "98 percent of the books published in dance had the Dance Collection as a primary source" (p. 49)—an impressive record.

Oswald warmly acknowledges the support she received from staff, dancers, and the community at large in the work of building the Dance Collection: "This collection was not built by me. It was built by the field. And I was here. As a vigorous force, but more a guiding force."[28] That guidance shaped the material collected, its cataloging and public access, and the work of scholars

---

*Guest's extensive list of publications on ballet history include *The Ballet of the Second Empire* (1953), *Fanny Cerrito: The Life of a Romantic Ballerina* (1956), *The Dancer's Heritage: A Short History of Ballet* (1960), *The Romantic Ballet in Paris* (1966), *Fanny Elssler* (1970), *The Divine Virginia: A Biography of Virginia Zucchi* (1977), *Jules Perrot, Master of the Romantic Ballet* (1984), *The Ballet of the Enlightenment* (1996), and *Ballet under Napoleon* (2002).

†Marian Hannah Winter published *Le Théâtre du Merveilleux* (1962), *The Pre-Romantic Ballet* (1975), and articles on ballerina Augusta Maywood, Juba and American minstrelsy, and other themes in early American dancing and mime.

‡According to Harvard's Houghton Library, Lasky came to the United States from London in 1954, after extensive ballet training throughout Europe. She taught in Macon, Georgia, and founded the Macon Ballet Guild. She was elected a member of the Royal Academy of Ballet and served on the Georgia Arts Commission," http://oasis.lib.harvard.edu/oasis/deliver/~hou01572 (accessed December 22, 2010). Several of Lasky's articles were published in *Ballet Today* and *The Dancing Times* (London).

in the field. At the same time, as Oswald hired specialists and assistants, she mentored and trained many in the library field who went on to make important contributions. Anne Wilson Wangh, founder of the Dance Library of Israel, was among those whose objectives Oswald supported[29] (pp. 19, 80–81). Others who worked with Oswald before moving to various library positions include Ruth Carr, who became Chief of the United States History, Local History and Genealogy Division at NYPL, and Nancy Shawcross, who became Curator of Manuscripts at the University of Pennsylvania's Rare Book and Manuscript Library. Following the example of the Dance Collection, dozens of other libraries began to collect and organize dance material, each enormously indebted to Oswald's pioneering work.

While acknowledging that the "basic function" of any archive is to provide a convenient repository for "retrieving sought-for material," Oswald has also written that "archives of records, including verbal and iconographic material, cannot help but extend the range and depth of contemporary understanding and practice."[30] The Dance Collection has had a profound impact on the worlds of dance, dance research, and cultural awareness through collecting, cataloging, and curating; publicizing, fundraising, and directing—skills and achievements that Oswald brought forward in the course of her career. Yet, when asked about factors or challenges that shaped or altered her vision for the Dance Collection over time, she commented, "It's funny that you say 'vision' and 'challenges.' I came to work every day, and there was so much to do and I knew what I wanted to do. The ideas were just 'there' and that was the vision. . . . I knew we had to collect original designs as well as photographs, make oral tape interviews and films. I knew we had to do these various kinds of things" (pp. 78–79). Oswald saw herself as a practical doer, rather than as a visionary: "we knew what we had to do, and we just threw ourselves into it. And if there was anything that was [the cause of] our success it's the fact that I always put a great deal of effort into figuring out what was really needed, what value it had, and when I understood the material or the problem in a fundamental way, I talked to people. We never went to anyone for money or to any foundation, unless we had thoroughly thought through what we were asking for." This practicality and planning underlay the shaping of this remarkable dance collection.

After Retirement

Oswald was able to relinquish, with grace, the leadership of the phenomenal collection she had built and guided. Although she was asked to chair the committee to choose her successor, she refused and instead "suggested a committee to be created from the dance world." Once Madeleine Nichols was in place as curator, in 1988, Oswald "didn't go back for a year because I wanted Madeleine to just do it all. I knew she could" (p. 44). Clearly, Oswald's presence at the library, even after retirement, would be a powerful force for a new chief to face, so she wisely gave plenty of elbow room to her successor. Yet it was not only for Nichols's sake that Oswald kept her distance: "I remember the first time I went back, I had a real physical response, I had heart palpitations—to walk into that room again was quite moving to me . . . . I think I needed to stay away. I wanted to, because everybody told me that the Dance Collection was my life and I found that it wasn't; I had a wonderful family and I knew that. I needed to stay away" (p. 100). She remained available for phone calls or consultations initiated by library staff or by the Dance Committee, since her depth of knowledge of the collection was unmatched, but she relinquished any sense of control. Over time, changes were made, such as creating a combined reading room for the three performing arts research collections: "It was difficult to go back when the changes were made that are there now, because I had fought strenuously in the early plans for the building in 1964 against having common reading rooms" (p. 101). Oswald had wished to retain "the individual nature of the collections," despite early pressures toward "a more generalized approach." She feared the possibility of losing the expertise of specialized dance librarians handling Dance Collection material. In the recent reorganization such dance specialists are still available, fortunately, since each collection has its own information desk and staff.

After her retirement, devoting time to her family was a priority, but Oswald did not leave the dance world bereft of her knowledge and energy. She became deeply involved in another wide-ranging venture to support dance: the World Dance Alliance (WDA). Oswald involved the network of dance leaders she had developed, in her decades of Dance Collection work, to help create an umbrella organization that would bring together dancers from every field, nation, and interest group to share information, concerns, experience, and contacts. She worked closely with Carl Wolz,* to form this new service organization, the seed for which was germinated at a joint conference of the American Dance Guild and the Congress on Research in Dance at the University of Hawaii in 1978.[31] The vision was, again, global and all-embracing, from theater dance to folk forms, from ballroom to books. "I've always felt that there was a need for a dance organization that would bring together the different groups, the different kinds of dance. It upset me that dance people in the erudite performing areas of dance really didn't appreciate the Dance Masters of America and the work they do, the conference that they have had every year for dance teachers. ... I was concerned that there was no interchange between the various groups" (p. 101).

From 1989 to 1994, Oswald served as coordinator and first president of the WDA Americas Center. In June of 1993 the first General Assembly of American nations met at the Walter Reade Theater at Lincoln Center, with attendees from the United Nations along with 150 dance representatives including teachers, scholars, administrators, dancers of all kinds, and government officials from thirteen nations in South and Central America and the Caribbean, fifteen states in the United States, and four Canadian provinces.[32] Oswald recalled the "fantastic success" of the gathering (p. 102), which took three years to plan. The WDA's goal was to become a member organization of UNESCO, a nongovernmental organization. The Americas Center continues its worldwide dance outreach and gatherings and participates in WDA Global Assemblies as well.[33]

Oswald has continued to serve the dance field in the 1990s and 2000s, sitting on the editorial boards of the Göttingen Encyclopaedia Cinematographica and *Dance Chronicle: Studies in Dance and the Related Arts,* and on boards for several dance and library associations. After retirement from the Dance Collection, she remained active at conferences, presenting papers and moderating

---

*Carl Wolz, a Juilliard-trained dancer, founded the Dance Department at the University of Hawaii, was dean of the Hong Kong Academy of Performing Arts, and taught at Japan's Women's College of Physical Education and at Washington University in St. Louis. He led the World Dance Alliance Asia-Pacific Center for several years. See http://www.wda-ap. org/wda-ap/wda/Carl%20Wolz.htm (accessed December 21, 2010).

panels for such organizations as the International Theatre Institute (Essen, 1988), International Festival of Dance Academies (Hong Kong, 1989 and 1990), Society of Dance History Scholars (1991, 1992, 1994), Fundação Calouste Gulbenkian (Lisbon, 1992), and others. Throughout her career, and continuing into her retirement, Oswald's lively range of interests, depth of knowledge, network of acquaintances, and engaging personality have made her a sought-after and esteemed participant at gatherings large and small, informal and official.

From the vantage point of a long, productive retirement, Oswald looks back on her life's work with both satisfaction and concern. The Dance Collection is a rich and renowned resource used by dancers and scholars from the world over, acknowledged as "the most impressive of all"[34] dance research facilities anywhere. Shortly after her retirement, Oswald commented that the creation and proliferation of archives like the Dance Collection would allow us to "begin to ask the great questions: How does dance fit into society, and where does society fit into dance?"[35] To help dancers and researchers to both ask and answer such questions, she had undertaken decades of a "vast program of collection" in order "to pierce the myth of illiteracy that has surrounded dance and provide a continuing history for this elusive art."[36] Where do we stand now in meeting this goal?

While the Dance Collection has been much used by dancers, choreographers, and researchers, Oswald commented, "One of the great disappointments to me is that we struggled so hard to have in-depth research materials like the kind that could be found in great European libraries, but I don't know whether they are being used as they might be" (p. 45), since dance history books are not being widely published. Oswald cites several glaring lacunae: "there is no biography of the great Taglioni.... There is no history of the Taglioni family, which is a spectacular story. We have a tremendous archive in microfilm of Gasparo Angiolini, a celebrated choreographer who was the Balanchine of his day, all of his works.... And nobody seems to want to do it."

Because the dance research field was nascent when Oswald began her work, she directly nurtured and encouraged dance scholars. "We always talked about wanting to have a great historical library, but now we are not using it as much as we might" (p. 45). A few themes—gender-related analyses, Balanchine—seem to have attracted publication interest, but many important figures, periods, and issues in dance history have been little studied. While recognizing that the dance field "refreshes, renews, and strengthens itself" (p. 95), Oswald is dismayed that historical material—books, prints, letters, clippings, programs, and so on—are much less used than films, which constitute 80 percent of requests submitted at the Dance Collection. Oswald reflects that, early in her career, Bournonville was little known to the dance world, but owing to the work of several fine dance scholars, "Bournonville has risen out of the ashes and ... we now know all about him" (p. 96). Other figures, also important and influential, "are just waiting" to be brought to light as he was. An encouraging development in the dance research world is the small but vibrant movement in early dance reconstruction, since many dancers who do this work are also deeply knowledgeable about the dances' contexts. Yet few are also widely published scholars.

Oswald wondered if the publishing houses are partly responsible for this discouraging picture: "One of the most revealing statistics I learned some years ago was that there are more books published in one week on film [than] there are on dance in a whole year" (p. 45). Is there too little of any worth proposed to the publishers? Does a book subject have to be current, trendy, or popular to be published? Are people unwilling to spend years in research with little hope of achieving publication? Another issue she identified "is that many people don't have languages needed for much historical research; that's a great problem" (p. 97).

On a bright note, Oswald is pleased with the greater seriousness given to documentation of their work by contemporary dancers and companies. "I think it's so much better than when we started" (p. 99). Similarly, other libraries—whether devoted exclusively to dance or incorporating dance into broader collections—are now able, largely owing to the groundbreaking work of Oswald at the library, to collect and catalog material that documents dance, often with a focus on dance types, choreographers, companies, or productions particular to the location of the library.

From documenting today's cutting-edge dance troupes to restoring the reputations of history's dancing masters, and from the most classical choreography to purely recreational dance forms, the Dance Collection reflects the depth and range of

Oswald's inquiring mind and intrepid collecting. Oswald's vigor, curiosity, drive, and intelligence helped to shape this outstanding collection of dance research material. A remarkable legacy by a remarkable woman!

*   *   *

I offer my deepest gratitude to Genevieve Oswald for her generosity in these interviews and in reading versions of the essay, to which she offered comments and corrections. Many thanks also to Barbara Palfy for important information and editing.

Notes

1. New York Public Library for the Performing Arts, Jerome Robbins Dance Division, http://www.nypl.org/locations/lpa/jerome-robbins-dance-division (accessed June 10, 2011).
2. Several sources provide overviews of the Dance Collection: Francis L. Mc-Carthy, "A Study of the Founding and Operation of the Research Library of the Dance, Located at the Museum and Library of the Performing Arts at Lincoln Center, New York City," presentation for the master's degree in library science at Villanova University, spring 1978; H.W. Pierce, "History of The New York Public Library Dance Collection, 1944–1974," paper prepared for a course, Research in Dance, at New York University, August 6, 1974; Frances R. Treem, "Descriptive Study of the Dance Collection of the Research Library of the Performing Arts of the Library & Museum of the Performing Arts at Lincoln Center," master's thesis, Graduate Library School of Long Island University, Brookville, N.Y., 1968; and Sam P. Williams, *Guide to the Research Collections of The New York Public Library* (Chicago: American Library Association, 1975). Genevieve Oswald has written extensively about the Dance Collection; see, for example, her essay, "One Approach to the Development of a Dance Archive: The Dance Collection in the Library and Museum of the Performing Arts (The New York Public Library at Lincoln Center)," in *Libraries, History, Diplomacy, and the Performing Arts: Essays in Honor of Carleton Sprague Smith* (Stuyvesant, N. Y.: Pendragon Press, 1991), 77–84.
3. See "Capezio Dance Award Recipients," http://www.capeziodance.com/foundation/dance_award/recipients.php (accessed December 20, 2010). A list of Oswald's honors and recognitions, in "Genevieve Oswald: Biography (Selected)," an undated document given to the author by Oswald, includes, among others: the American Dance Guild Award (1970), the William G. Anderson Award of AAHPERD/National Dance Association (1987), the Distinguished Achievement Award of the Congress on Research in Dance (1997), an Honorary Fellowship in the Society of Dance History Scholars (1998), and the World Dance Alliance Genevieve Oswald Award, named for and awarded to Oswald in 2003.
4. Williams, *Guide*, 150–51.

5. Treem, "Descriptive Study," 4, 20; Williams, *Guide*, 151.

6. See also Oswald, "Recent Developments in the Dance Collection, The New York Public Library," *Research in Dance*, Proceedings of the First Conference on Research in Dance, Riverdale, N.Y., 1967, 19–23.

7. Martin Duberman, *The Worlds of Lincoln Kirstein* (New York: Alfred A. Knopf, 2007), 370, 427; and Treem, "Descriptive Study," 2–3.

8. Oswald, note to author, Dec. 22, 2008.

9. Patrizia Veroli, "Walter Toscanini, Bibliophile and Collector, and the Cia Fornaroli Collection of The New York Public Library," *Dance Chronicle*, vol. 28, no. 3 (September 2005): 323–62.

10. See NYPL Digital Gallery Collection Guides, http://digitalgallery.nypl.org/nypldigital/explore/?col_id=522 (accessed June 10, 2011).

11. See also Treem, "Descriptive Study," 19–20 and Williams, *Guide*,156. Oswald, note to author, December 22, 2008, information on Vitale Fokine donation.

12. Oswald, note to author, Dec. 22, 2008, information on Brantizka.

13. Théodore Lajarte, *Bibliothèque musicale du Théatre de l'opéra: catalogue historique, chronologique, anecdotique / publié sous les auspices du Ministère de l'instruction publique et des beaux-arts et rédigé par Théodore de Lajarte ... avec portraits gravés à l'eau-forte par Le Rat* (Paris: Librairie des Bibliophiles, 1876).

14. Clement Crisp, "Archives of the Dance: The Library and Archives of the Royal Academy of Dancing," *Dance Research: The Journal of the Society for Dance Research*, vol. 9, no. 1 (Spring, 1991): 58–60.

15. NYPL, Finding Aid for Lillian Moore Dance Research Finding Aid, http://www.nypl.org/ead/742 (accessed June 10, 2011).

16. Oswald, note to author, December 22, 2008.

17. Oswald, "The Development of an Asian Archive in the Dance Collection of the Performing Arts Research Center, New York Public Library, Lincoln Center," *Dance Research Journal*, vol. 9, no. 2 (Spring/Summer 1977): 33–35.

18. Oswald, "Development of an Asian Archive," 33.

19. Oswald, note to author, December 22, 2008.

20. Oswald, "One Approach," 80. In this essay, Oswald estimated that 97 per cent of the Dance Collection's holdings are nonprint materials.

21. See Duberman, *The Worlds of Lincoln Kirstein*, for ample evidence of this point.

22. Lincoln Kirstein, *Dance, a Short History of Classic Theatrical Dancing* (New York: G. P. Putnam's Sons 1935).

23. *Dictionary Catalog of the Dance Collection: A List of Authors, Titles, and Subjects of Multi-Media Materials in the Dance Collection of the Performing Arts Research Center of The New York Public Library* (New York: New York Public Library, Astor, Lenox and Tilden Foundations, distributed by G.K. Hall, Boston, 1974). On Ford and Rockefeller Foundation funding, see Treem, "Descriptive Study," 5, 32, 34; Williams, *Guide*, 151.

24. Some information on exhibitions is from "Genevieve Oswald: Biography (Selected)."

25. Treem, "Descriptive Study," 82–84.

26. Pierce, "History," 7–10.

27. See Genevieve Oswald, "Some Random Observations on the Teaching of American Dance History," *CORD News*, vol. 2, no. 2 (December 1970): 17–21.

28. Quoted in "Her Legacy Speaks Volumes," by Jennifer Dunning, *New York Times*, September 8, 1987, C 15.

29. See http://www.dancelibrary.org.il/ (accessed December 21, 2010) and Talia Perelshtein, "The Dance Library of Israel: Thirty-Five Years Serving the Field," *Dance Chronicle*, vol. 33, no. 3 (2010): 442–52. On other dance collections and libraries, see Genevieve Oswald, "A Chest of Dance Treasures in American Libraries," *Dance Chronicle*, vol. 18, no. 2 (1995): 239–47.

30. Oswald, "One Approach to the Development of a Dance Archive," 79.

31. Oswald, conversation with the author, December 14, 2009. On WDA history, see http://www.wda-ap.org/wda-ap/wda/aboutWDA.htm (accessed December 22, 2010).

32. "Genevieve Oswald: Biography (Selected)." See also Muriel Topaz, "First General Assembly of the Americas Center of the World Dance Alliance," *Dance Research Journal*, vol. 25, no. 2 (Fall 1993): 62–63.

33. For the Americas Center, see http://www.wda-americas.net/; for the Asia-Pacific Center, see http://www.wda-ap.org/wda-ap/wda-ap.htm; and for Europe, see http://www.wda-europe.net/engchisiamo (all sites accessed December 21, 2010).

34. Sandra Hammond, *Ballet Basics*, 5th ed. (New York: McGraw-Hill, 2004), 137.

35. Oswald, "One Approach," 84.

36. "Library Gets Grant for Dance Division," *New York Times*, March 7, 1956, 12.

The Choreographic Trust:
Preserving Dance Legacies

FRANCIS YEOH

This article assesses the growing use of choreographic trusts to secure proper management of a choreographer's dance legacy, focusing on the legal status of those of George Balanchine, Frederick Ashton, Jerome Robbins, and Merce Cunningham, with consideration also given to Martha Graham's will. Such trusts are ideally suited to controlling the licensing and restaging of dance works and to sustaining long-term preservation programs. The nature of trusts and issues relevant to dance copyright and preservation are reviewed.

Choreographers must secure records of their choreographies not only for the preservation of their works, but also for propagating their dance legacies While some in the dance community express a reluctance, for a range of reasons, to preserve works, others have taken steps to do so. Some choreographers have expressed doubts that their works will survive in acceptable form for any period of time after their demise. George Balanchine stated his belief that, without his personal supervision, his works would eventually lose integrity and identity: "I don't want my ballets preserved as museum pieces for people to go and laugh at what used to be. *Absolutely not*. I'm staging ballet for today's bodies. Ballet is NOW."[1] Frederick Ashton likewise voiced doubt about his dance legacy. In 1999 David Vaughan wrote that Ashton believed his "works would be considered passé and would fall into neglect."[2] Vaughan suggested that "this was typically self-deprecating, yet it proved to be not too far from the truth, and shockingly soon. There was a sense that those who took over the direction of the Royal Ballet did indeed find his work silly and irrelevant. Whether or not this was actually the case, the number of his ballets in the company's repertory certainly declined." This phenomenon may be attributed to the pressure of maintaining a "balanced" repertory of

---

* See *Preserving Dance as a Living Legacy*, a special issue of *Dance Chronicle*, vol. 34 no. 1, in which this subject is discussed from a range of perspectives.

old and new works by the Royal Ballet and the Birmingham Royal Ballet, but the loss of so many Ashton works is disheartening and, perhaps, irrevocable.

The proposition I offer is that the task of preserving the legacy of Ashton and other choreographers should be centrally managed by a choreographic trust that devotes itself exclusively to this function. It is crucial, therefore, that choreographers choose appropriate types of choreographic trusts to manage their legacies, either in the form of comprehensive organizations or in tandem with a complementary entity, as is the case with the Jerome Robbins Foundation and the Robbins Rights Trust, which together ensure the comprehensive realization of the choreographer's intentions. Balanchine and Ashton, on the other hand, gave custody of their dances to those who worked closely with them because they believed that these people would be best equipped to safeguard the works. This left their dance works in danger of being restaged and preserved without benefit of centralized control and management. This was the principal concern behind formation of the George Balanchine Foundation and the George Balanchine Trust.[*]

The value of documentation is recognized in the many projects that champion preservation of the dance heritage.[3] Yet, owing to financial and time constraints, many choreographers are unable to sustain such a program. When undertaken, documentation often includes notation,[†] video or film recording, and collection of other material traces of the work (notes, scores, drawings, photographs, costumes) to assist stagers in establishing the identity and integrity of the works. The Cunningham Living Legacy Plan has adopted an innovative approach to preservation through the use of digital "dance

---

[*]   In this regard, the relationship between the George Balanchine Trust and the George Balanchine Foundation in the management of Balanchine's legacy is symbiotic: "The George Balanchine Trust is the entity responsible for licensing the ballets of George Balanchine. The Trust protects the copyrights of George Balanchine, including all media rights and live performance rights worldwide." On the other hand, "The mission of The George Balanchine Foundation is to utilize the Balanchine legacy to advance the development of dance and its allied arts worldwide. The goal is pursued through a broad range of activities and programs, including concentrated research, ballet reconstructions, publications, lectures and videos, and other innovative projects." See http://balanchine.com/content/site/show/faq// (accessed March 9, 2010).

[†]   Lynne Weber, executive director of New York's Dance Notation Bureau (DNB), noted that the DNB finalized and signed contracts for forty performances of notated dances in February 2010 alone (interview by the author, February 16, 2010). The DNB library houses 776 scores of dance works by 251 choreographers, including forty-four Balanchine works. See Mei-Chen Lu, "The Dance Notation Bureau," *Dance Chronicle*, vol. 32, no. 2 (2009): 291–301. Works by some choreographers in Europe and Australia are preserved through employment of in-house Benesh notators by a number of companies. The works of Balanchine, Robbins, and Cunningham that enter these companies' repertories are consequently notated. See T. Inman, *Benesh Movement Notation Score Catalogue* (London: Benesh Institute, Royal Academy of Dance, 1998).

capsules," which "assemble in uniform and stable digital form the array ⟨ creative elements that comprise each choreographic work, enabling works ⟨ be studied in perpetuity with knowledge of how they originally came to life.

Ray Cook points to a common situation faced by reconstructors, speci ically with reference to a retrospective in the late 1980s of Jerome Robbins works on Broadway. Robbins spent "several millions to bring dancers fro around America to help him remember the choreography from some of h past successes on Broadway."[5] Regarding this project, Maya Dalinsky write "Near the end of his career, Robbins staged an extravaganza of his be Broadway work in an effort to preserve the original staging and choreo raphy. His ballets were already well documented with video and notes, y even he could not remember all the details of the original productions. Had he earlier employed notation, film, and other documentation method to record his musical theater works, the staging process would have bee shorter and less costly. Lynne Weber noted that Ann Hutchinson Guest Labanotation score of "The Charleston Ballet" from *Billion Dollar Baby* cor tributed to the reconstruction process.[7]

Maintenance of Balanchine's ballets raises similar concerns. In 198 Marcia B. Siegel noted threats to the integrity of that repertory: "The safe of the ballet repertory is always in doubt. Ballet changes all the time, a ste here, a notch of tempo there, a smoothed-out accent, a shade of emphasi These never get noticed in the day-to-day performance of repertory, but they're not corrected, they accumulate until the work is transformed. Ball needs constant shoring up. It needs the prod of personal imperative, th systematic scrutiny of an eye that knows what to look for and sees wha wants changing."[8] The recourse is for custodians of a choreographer's danc legacy to ensure that every possible aid to the staging process be secure not only for licensing purposes but also for posterity. As Barbara Horgar Balanchine's longtime assistant, noted, "Balanchine will live as does Mozar the art is so strong.... Through a combination of notation, video and hanc to-hand, mind-to-mind and body-to-body teaching, the ballets will survive." The recording of "living memories" of Balanchine works by the Balanchin Foundation, under the direction of Nancy Reynolds, ensures preservation ⟨ these precious resources.[10]

When permission is given by trustees for documentation, the centralize management of dance legacies facilitates appropriately drafted licenses tha contain stipulations to secure the interests of the choreographer. The futur use of such documentation must be clearly defined in the contract alon with the ownership of the recordings. If the recording is to be commerciall available, contracts are more complex. Derivative works arising from th original dance work can generate further income for the trust; therefore such uses must be centrally controlled. Expertise in both legal and artisti matters must be assembled to support the custodians of a choreographer dance legacy. The trust is a means of securing such expertise and control.

TRUSTS

The trust, a form of English property law, "is based on a separation between ownership in law and ownership in equity."[11] The rationale advanced for the employment of appropriate trust organizations for management of the choreographer's dance legacy is that trustees possess the legal powers needed to fulfill the choreographer's plans efficiently. Another vital feature of the role of trustees is that they have a fiduciary obligation to the beneficiaries: each trustee must "act for the benefit of the beneficiaries rather than him or herself."[12] Similarly, trustees of private and public charitable organizations must ensure that the assets and funds of the trust are separate from their own. Trustees possess legal authority to carry out functions that may be beyond the means of an individual beneficiary. Recognition of this value is evident in actions taken by some choreographers or by the executors of their estates, although the intended outcomes of the chosen trust plans may not always be completely fulfilled.

Trusts created by a written document during the choreographer's lifetime (*inter vivos*) are often referred to as a "living trust," as in the case of the Merce Cunningham Trust, created in 2000. On the other hand, the intention to establish a trust can be stated in the choreographer's will; this is a "testamentary trust," as in the case of the Robbins Rights Trust. Trusts can also be created by a court order and by an oral declaration in which the donor hands over tangible property to another with verbal instructions to hold it in trust for designated beneficiaries—not an ideal method, since the beneficiaries will have no written proof of the declaration of trust.[13]

Robbins and Cunningham set useful patterns for others to emulate. Robbins chose to vest the rights to his works in the Robbins Rights Trust to enable trustees to secure the proper administration of his legacies. He made arrangements that, on the fulfillment of these duties, the rights transfer to the Robbins Foundation,[14] a private foundation under section 509(a) of the Internal Revenue Code, which is exempt from federal income tax under section 501(c)(3). As Christopher Pennington, executive director of the Robbins Rights Trust, noted, "A private foundation is different from an operating foundation in that a private foundation does not solicit or raise funds from the public as an operating foundation may."[15] The Robbins Rights Trust, as a noncharitable private trust, does not enjoy tax exemptions or raise funds for its projects.[*]

---

[*] Ellen Sorrin, director of the Balanchine Foundation, confirmed that the foundation is also exempt from federal tax under Section 501(c)(3) (e-mail to the author, January 24, 2011). Because of its charitable status, the foundation fundraises for its preservation projects. Christopher Pennington wrote that support for the Balanchine Foundation has also been given by the Jerome Robbins Foundation (e-mail to the author, January 26, 2011).

The Cunningham Living Legacy Plan provided for a two-year tour by th. Merce Cunningham Dance Company. Then, as Daniel J. Wakin has state "the Cunningham Trust will take control of Mr. Cunningham's dances fo licensing purposes; the dancers will each receive a year's salary as severanc and extra money to help find new careers" and "staff members and th musicians who play for his performances will also receive payments."[16] Othe choreographers were less well prepared with regard to their legacies: "Lest Horton and Erick Hawkins died without leaving wills. José Limón had on but didn't mention his works, which were divided among his heirs and sol back to the José Limón Dance Foundation. Alvin Ailey left his dances t his mother and the rights to his name to his step-brother. The Ailey boar eventually bought back those rights."[17] The custodians of the Ailey and Limó estates had to take the necessary steps to secure centralized management c each artist's dance legacies.

Private Trusts

The private trust serves the interests of an individual, a group, or a clas of persons, while a charitable trust is for the benefit of the public.[18] a trust is required to distribute its income to designated beneficiaries, may be constituted as a private noncharitable trust and will not qualif for tax exemptions. On the other hand, charitable trusts may apply for ta exemptions and other benefits. The Robbins Rights Trust is a "simple trust, which in U.S. tax law means that "it pays all of its income to its beneficiarie annually."[19] A "complex trust," on the other hand, need not pay out all of i annual income to beneficiaries and may also make charitable contribution of its own.[20] The Balanchine Trust was formed as a "for profit" entity.*

In those cases where the choreographer limits the bequest to the life c the beneficiaries, the private trust will exist until the last of the beneficiarie dies. However, there are cases where provisions are made to enable inhe itance of rights by the original beneficiary's heirs.† Nevertheless, the terr of copyright of the works lasts for only seventy years, which will limit th duration of such trusts. After that time period, the works are in the public dc main and no longer enjoy copyright protection.‡ On the other hand, a publi trust, such as the Balanchine Foundation and the Robbins Foundation, ca

---

* Sorrin stated that the Balanchine Trust "receives income from the licensing of his balle and other business, and that income goes to the heirs or in Tanny's [Tanaquil Le Clercq] case the income beneficiaries designated by her" (e-mail to the author, January 24, 2011).
† Pennington confirmed that two of Robbins's beneficiaries may pass on their equitabl rights to their heirs (interview by the author, February 18, 2010).
‡ Copyright is enjoyed for a term of seventy years from the end of the year of th choreographer's death (U.K.: The Duration of Copyright and the Rights in Performance Regulations, Statutory Instrument 1995, no. 3297; U.S.: Sonny Bono Copyright Extension Ac 112, Stat. 2827 [1998]).

exist in perpetuity because its objects are much wider in scope. The legal instrument creating the choreographic trust will determine the organization's duties and status. The Robbins Foundation was established in 1958 "to support dance, theatre and their associative arts," while the Robbins Rights Trust was established in 1999 "to license and protect the artistic works of Jerome Robbins."[21]

Robbins created his trust with powers to administer the licensing and restaging of his works and to distribute the profits to designated beneficiaries. Because control of the licensing of the choreographer's works is a complex process, the trustees require the support of a team of legal and artistic experts. Control of dissemination of the choreographer's repertory is exercised through appropriate license agreements that ensure that performances of the works are properly staged to retain their integrity. The stipulated supervisory powers include casting rights and rehearsal schedules. An advisory committee assists with identifying competent stagers.

Charitable Trusts

Charitable trusts such as those adopted for management of the legacies of Balanchine, Robbins, and Cunningham are organizations with charitable ends as their main object. Owing to their status and the public benefit they serve, these trusts enjoy such privileges as tax exemption. Charitable trusts "provide benefits for the public; any private benefit must be incidental to the public benefit. . . . Charities do not exist to make profits for participators or to provide income for specified private individuals; any surplus which is made must be applied for the public charitable purposes."[22] Unlike the noncharitable trust, it can exist in perpetuity because of its public service functions. Because the preservation of the choreographer's dance legacy must be a sustained and long-term program, it requires the services of a charitable organization. The charitable trust can attract sponsorship from other charities, individuals, or corporations for its projects. Thus, its objectives must be stated with certainty. Yet uncertainty may result when "the purposes are not prescribed with sufficient precision or conceptual clarity. Alternatively, the means by which the trustee is to achieve or to attain the specified purpose may be ill-defined or unacceptably broad. In addition, the classes of beneficiaries, or those people intended to benefit, must be sufficiently certain."[23] A trust may be voidable if its objects are deemed administratively unworkable.

The public benefit is found in the objects as stated in the legal instrument that creates the foundation. The Balanchine Foundation's stated mission, an example of clarity, is to "utilize the Balanchine legacy to advance the development of dance and its allied arts in the United States and throughout the world on behalf of the dance community at large. This goal is pursued through a broad range of activities and programs, including concentrated

research, ballet reconstructions, publications, lectures and videos, and oth
innovative projects."[24]

While Martha Graham's work was supported by a nonprofit corpora
organization, the Martha Graham Center of Contemporary Dance, her situa
tion was different from those just discussed and will be explored separatel

SECURING COPYRIGHT STATUS AND RIGHTS OF OWNERSHIP

The Graham case increased the dance community's awareness of the nee
to understand the intricacies of copyright and contract law.[25] Among othe
matters, the case dealt with questions about the copyright and ownership c
Graham's dance works. The decisions of the court clarified some legal issue
surrounding the question of dance copyright. This seminal case highligh
the need for considerable sophistication in making plans for the managemer
of choreographers' works* and serves to warn choreographers that qualifyin
for copyright status is crucial to management of a dance legacy.

Under copyright protection, choreographers enjoy rights that give ther
powers to prevent reproduction (copying), performance, recording (film
video, notation, and so on) and its distribution, and adaptation of the work
without prior agreement on terms and conditions for use of their work.
Choreographers, their executors, and trustees must attend to the statutor
prerequisites for copyright protection, a vital requirement of which is fixa
tion or documentation of the dance work.† The Graham case revealed tha

---

* The only two cases on copyright of dance works since the U.S. Copyright Act of 197
are the Graham case and Horgan v. MacMillan Inc., 789 F/2d 157 (2d Cir. 1986). In th
latter case, Barbara Horgan, as executrix of Balanchine's will, applied for an injunction t
stop MacMillan Publishers' *The Nutcracker: A Story and a Ballet*, authored by Ellen Switze
The book contained sixty photographs of the ballet, taken by Steven Caras and Costa
and interviews with ten New York City Ballet dancers. The case was settled out of cour
but the court findings on many dance-related issues have provided useful guidelines to th
dance community. See also Julie Van Camp, "Copyright of Choreographic Works," *1994–9
Entertainment, Publishing and the Arts Handbook*, ed. Stephen F. Breimer, Robert Thorne
and John David Viera (New York: Clark, Boardman, Callaghan, 1994), 59–92; also availabl
at http://www.csulb.edu/~jvancamp/copyrigh.html (accessed February 13, 2011).
† Works must be fixed "in writing or otherwise" (U.K. Act 1988, s.3.2) or, put somewha
differently, "fixed in any tangible medium of expression, now known or later developec
from which they can be perceived, reproduced, or otherwise communicated, either directl
or with the aid of a machine or device" (U.S. Act 1976, 17 U.S.C. 102 a). The U.S. Copyrigh
Office Circular No. 51(b) states, "The particular movements and physical actions of which th
dance consists must be fixed in some sort of legible written form, such as detailed verbal de
scriptions, dance notation, pictorial or graphic diagrams, or a combination of these . . . . Eve
a textual description of a dance would not seem to constitute a . . . work of choreograph
if the description is so general and lacking in detail that the dance could not be performe
therefrom" (cited in Bengt Häger, *The Dancer's World: Problems of Today and Tomorrou
Report on the First International Choreographers' Conference, New York (1978), organize
by the International Dance Council and UNESCO, 96–97.

some of her works did not gain copyright status because they were not documented. In 1978 Barbara Kibbe, executive director of California's Bay Area Lawyers for the Arts, stated, "To enable a creator to reap the benefits bestowed by the copyright laws, his or her dance must exist in a tangible form which is accurate enough to permit the reproduction of the dance without depending on the memory of the choreographer or troupe."[26]

Tangible evidence of dance works can be made available through film, video, and computer technology. These recordings are generating readily accessible, speedier, and perhaps, in comparison with notation, cheaper methods of recording dance that satisfy the statutory fixation requirement. Yet Francis Sparshott contends that such methods are not totally able to establish the identity of a dance work because, he believes, a recording "does not distinguish between choreographer's intention and dancer's execution, or between correct and incorrect practice."[27] He argued that "a notational record gives information but does not show what the dance is like." Arguably, any record is better than none, since each trace of a dance work will provide assistance to the stager of that work.* Custodians of a choreographer's dance legacy must, therefore, ensure that a comprehensive documentation program is put in place.

The work must also be deemed "original." This concept is fundamental to the doctrine of copyright law but the case University of London Press Ltd. v. University Tutorial Press Ltd. (1916), addressing literary works, held that "the standard of originality required is a *low one*."[28] Judge J. Peterson stated that "the word 'original' does not in this connection mean that the work must be the expression of original or inventive thought. Copyright Acts are not concerned with the originality of ideas, but with the expression of thought.... [T]he Act does not require that the expression be in an original or novel form, but that the work must not be copied from another work—that it should originate from the author."[29] In dance terms, this means that commonplace steps and combinations may not be considered original, just as the letters of the alphabet and common verbal phrases cannot enjoy copyright. However, a choreographer's use of these to express ideas in his or her own style would be deemed original. The test would be whether the choreography is "copied" from others.† In its revision of the copyright law,

---

* Lewis Flacks, Special Legal Assistant to the Register of Copyrights, United States Copyright Office, Washington, D.C., states, "Even a dance rehearsal record should satisfy the fixation requirement of the statute, at least insofar as the work exists at the time of that record.... I recently examined a Xerox copy of 'Graduation Ball' [a work by David Lichine], which is in a small, student examination note-book with elegantly crafted stick figures with the commentary and description of the activity in French. That was an adequate deposit copy for the registration of copyright in the work" (cited in Häger, *The Dancer's World*, 34).

† Anthea Kraut raised the fact that Hanya Holm, choreographer of *Kiss Me, Kate* (1948), registered with the Copyright Office in Washington, D.C., in March 1952 a microfilmed copy

the U.S. Congress received a submission that choreographic works shoul
fail to be original if the movements are "so simple or so stereotyped as
have no substantial element of creative authorship."[30] Furthermore, "idea
procedures, natural processes, systems, concepts, laws of nature, principle
information and utilitarian works (such as recipes or instructions) are a
generally outside the scope of legal protection."[31] Other factors relevant t
a dance's originality are "the choreographer's treatment of rhythm, spac
and movement in the work. As long as the dance bears the choreogra
pher's individual stamp, it is irrelevant that his dance uses well-known c
often-used steps."[32] The choreographer or custodians of the choreographer
dance legacy must consider such factors when they determine whether work
qualify for copyright protection.

Another vital matter that confronts the choreographer is determinin
the ownership of a work that is commissioned by an employer, be tha
a dance company, Hollywood producer, private sponsor, or in the cas
of Graham, the Graham Center, a nonprofit corporation. The Graham cas
centered on the intricacies of the "work for hire" doctrine.* The complica
tions that can arise from the relationship between the creative artist an
the nonprofit organization were well illustrated in this case.[33] Judge Miriar
Cedarbaum concluded that the Graham Center has exclusive rights to use c
the "Martha Graham" trademark and name for all purposes. In her length
decision, Cedarbaum confirmed that Graham had assigned the ownershi
of not only her pre-1956 works to the Graham Center but also that it own
those works created thereafter by Graham as an employee of the Cente
that she had formed.[34] The initial furor surrounding the Graham case be
came a rallying point for choreographers to rethink their contract template
"Shortly after the Second Circuit's ruling, Dance NYC, a professional danc
organization, posted boilerplate contracts on its website for choreographer
and artistic directors."[35] Francis Mason pointed out that the responsibility t
secure rights to their works rests with the choreographers: "This lawsuit i
a reminder to the dance community that choreographers who wish to ow
their own dances can copyright them or make arrangements to do so witl

---

of the notated score by Ann Hutchinson Guest. Because Holm had inserted an Amer
ican "specialty" act, Kraut contends, "Holm's legally sanctioned status as sole choreog
rapher of *Kiss Me, Kate* masked the labor of additional dancers as well." See "Race-in
Choreographic Copyright" in *Worlding Dance*, ed. Susan Leigh Foster (New York: Palgrav
Macmillan, 2009), 90. Holm ought not to have legally claimed copyright of the interpolate
dance unless she provided evidence that it is her "original" work. In fact, the performers ma
claim copyright if the choreography is their original work. Kraut also observed that "[Free
Davis and [Eddie] Sledge's tap dancing was not included in the Labanotated score" (Ibid., 89

* "In the case of a work made for hire, the employer or other person for whom th
work was prepared is considered the author for purposes of this title, and, unless the partie
have expressly agreed otherwise in a written instrument signed by them, owns all the righ
comprised in the copyright" (17 U.S.C. §§ 101 and 201 [b]).

their organization or with the organization that commissions dance by them. Martha Graham chose not to do so."[36]

Nancy S. Kim posited that the problems with the court's decision "result, not from its application of the work for hire doctrine, but from the statute itself."[37] She suggested that the doctrine "undermines the intent of the parties in 'creative genius' situations"[38] because the court failed to recognize the intent of the parties: the nonprofit company is unlike a for-profit company in that it has no wish to own the dance works but, rather, its prime purpose is to support choreographers' creative work. The court's decision could be seen as "a dangerous precedent for excluding the Center's non-profit status from the work for hire analysis. Consequently, this may chill the creations of artists who depend on non-profits created exclusively to support their art."[39] Therefore, a vital preliminary step in choreographers' planning for their dance legacy is satisfying the statutory prerequisites to establish copyright and ownership of their works.

AN OVERVIEW OF SEVERAL CHOREOGRAPHERS' PLANS

It is advisable that choreographers themselves establish the chosen infrastructure for maintaining their dance legacies, either directly, as in the case of Cunningham, or by means of their wills, as in the case of Robbins. Most choreographers are more concerned with maintaining the aesthetic standards of performances than with entrepreneurial exploitation of their works, an attitude that may be generated by the sociocultural and financial environments in which they work.

The difficult conditions experienced by Agnes de Mille in 1956 illustrate the choreographer's plight: "A choreographer's life is slow in developing and more expensive than any other creative worker's. (Any composition involves studio space, music, and living bodies, generally paid by the hour.) Taxes annually take all but the smallest profit. Money from good years cannot be set aside for study periods or privately financed experimental projects; losses incurred in rehearsal one year may not be applied against gains in the next."[40] By and large, these conditions still pertain today. Perhaps as a consequence of this working environment, choreographers are understandably generous in allowing their works to be performed, as in the case of Balanchine.[41] Further, this attitude is reinforced by a culture of sharing, which explains why there is a paucity of dance litigation cases. As Eliot Feld has said, "It may be a lawyer problem, but in my life it has not become a problem.... I wish people were stealing my work left and right, and it became an enormous issue for me."[42]

Choreographers like Robbins, who cross into Broadway and Hollywood, typically gain a better appreciation of the need to secure copyright and appropriate management of their dance legacies. Confronted with the danger

of exploitation of their talents in these commercial industries, choreographe
are forced to become more astute in their professional dealings. With th
burgeoning dissemination of dance through film, video, and the Interne
choreographers and their trustees are becoming more conscious of contr
and management of their dance legacies, including protection of copyrigh

Works such as Balanchine's *Jewels* are regularly performed in majo
cities on different continents and recordings of performances of such worl
are disseminated in different media and on the Internet. Such great exposu
increases opportunities to infringe on the choreographer's copyright. There
fore, surveillance of the use of works requires sophistication. A recent furo
resulted from the prompt action taken by the Balanchine Trust to discontinu
unlawful postings on the YouTube Ketinoa channel of one of the choreog
rapher's dances, a testimony to the effective use of trustees' legal powe
to prevent unlawful treatment of works. The trust contacted YouTube t
prevent the posting of segments from *La Sonnambula* and *Night Shadow*
The posted segments were unlawfully obtained from an archival tape of a
American Ballet Theatre performance. Ellen Sorrin, director of the Balanchin
Trust, stated that it was not the Trust's intention to shut down the Ketino
site, but YouTube automatically closed it down after five transgressions.
This action prevented all access to the 1,300 postings, many of which wer
taken from recordings of performances by the Russian Kirov (Maryinsky
and Bolshoi ballet companies. Sorrin stated that the trust will not in futur
take such drastic action, but will instead warn the offending party directly i
order to give them the opportunity to withdraw the postings before furthe
action is taken. However, the recordings in question were intended sole
for archival and restaging purposes and should not, therefore, be expose
to public viewing. The action taken demonstrates the vigilance that can b
exercised by the custodians of the choreographer's dance legacy.

George Balanchine (1904–1983)

Rather than trusting his legacy to the New York City Ballet, Balanchin
bequeathed his dances to those with whom he had worked and whor
he could trust to act as custodians of his dances, including several of th
ballerina "muses" who had inspired his works. Balanchine's action may b
attributed to a desire that his legacy not be tied to the possibly uncertai
existence of a dance company, but it could also have been influenced b
concerns that company policies may not always favor the choreographe
in the choice of repertory. Of greater import, the ballet company woul
not be the appropriate organization to propagate his works more widely
Balanchine chose Horgan, his personal assistant from 1963 until his death
as executrix of his estate. Horgan has been described as "the definition c
institutional memory."[44] Although Balanchine made no arrangements for

trust organization, Horgan sought legal advice that led her to understand that "if we put our rights into a trust, we would be able to execute those rights and make decisions about who could dance the ballets."[45] A centralized organization could avoid a situation that Horgan feared: "Clearing the rights to just one ballet could involve six different heirs and with their deaths, future dealings could become even more complex."[46]

For most of the choreographer's works, Karin von Aroldingen and Horgan were named joint beneficiaries, often with Tanaquil Le Clercq, who was bequeathed the American performing rights to designated works for which media and foreign rights were given to Horgan and von Aroldingen. Sheryl Flatow provided these details:

> Balanchine left Le Clercq the American performing rights to more than eighty ballets—including *Apollo, La Valse, Swan Lake, Scotch Symphony, The Nutcracker, Square Dance, Agon, Jewels, Who Cares?, Symphony in Three Movements, Coppelia, Chaconne* and *Union Jack*—and divided the media and foreign rights of those ballets between Horgan and von Aroldingen. (Media rights include photographs and the written word, not just video).[47]

Balanchine left rights to one or more works to a number of individuals.* The Balanchine Trust was created in 1987 to consolidate "the domestic, foreign and media rights" to the choreographer's works and "offered membership to all the legatees of Balanchine's will to avoid the administrative chaos of licensing the complicated performing rights."[48] Initially, only Patricia McBride and Rosemary Dunleavy joined the trust, which was administered by Horgan. However, Sorrin, current director of the trust, confirmed that the organization now administers ninety percent of Balanchine bequests.[49] The interests of other beneficiaries, including the Le Clercq Trust (Le Clercq died on December 31, 2000) are now embraced by the Balanchine Trust, allowing further centralization of the licensing process. The trust continues Balanchine's generous provision for performance of his works. For example, the fee to California's Diablo Ballet for performance rights was kept at "rock bottom," according to Horgan, because "they are small and they don't have

---

* Balanchine devised full rights in specified ballets to the following individuals: Diana Adams (*A Midsummer Night's Dream*); Suzanne Farrell (*Meditation, Don Quixote,* and *Tzigane*); Patricia McBride (*Tarantella, Pavane,* and *Etude for Piano*); Kay Mazzo (*Duo Concertant*); Jerome Robbins (*Firebird* and *Pulcinella*); Mrs. André [Leda Anchutina] Eglevsky (*Sylvia Pas de Deux, Minkus Pas de Trois,* and *Glinka Pas de Trois*); Betty Cage (*Symphony in C*); and Rosemary Dunleavy (*Le Tombeau de Couperin*). Also, Lincoln Kirsten (*Concerto Borocco* and *Orpheus*), Edward Bigelow (*The Four Temperaments* and *Ivesiana*), and Merrill Ashley (*Ballo della Regina*) share their rights with von Aroldingen and Horgan (Ellen Sorrin, e-mail to the author, May 9, 2011).

any money . . . . So we try to help them. After all, you can't hang ballets c a wall. Ballets are meant to be performed."[50]

The Balanchine repertory continues to be disseminated widely. Horga stated that, while "at the time of his death more than sixty troupes throug out the world were performing his ballets, today more than one hundre companies perform at least one Balanchine work."[51] Sorrin reaffirmed th licenses are normally issued for a two-year period but they are extende to three when there is a gap in performances. However, for works suc as *Jewels* and *The Nutcracker*, where the initial outlay to stage the work large, performing rights may be extended to five years.[52] Sorrin noted th the Trust will cease functioning when the last of the legatees dies; at th time, the Balanchine Foundation will inherit all rights.[53]

The task of staging Balanchine works depends on those who have in timate knowledge of them, but this is not an everlasting resource. The tim will come when documentation such as videos (both commercially pro duced and those made as archival recordings) are the only widely availabl evidence of his works. In this light, it is worth considering the dangers c restaging works without notated scores. Hutchinson Guest writes, "The cus todians of the choreography, working from their own notes, admit—so w hear—there are passages they don't remember and have to make up, thu small changes are occurring . . . . But in time the drift inevitably sets in . . . What then? Will the label 'Choreography by Balanchine' still be accurate?"* Thus, preservation of all available traces of Balanchine's works is essenti while the dancers and others are still available for records to be made The Video Archives Project, directed by Reynolds, comprises the Archive of Lost Choreography and the Interpreters Archive. The Balanchine Founda tion makes available an electronic edition of *The Balanchine Catalogue* tha provides data about the works and it created *Dancing Balanchine/Watchin Balanchine*, a series of lectures featuring Merrill Ashley, that aims to pro vide guidance on the Balanchine style. It is intended that these records wi ameliorate the deterioration of the works.

Yet Hutchinson Guest questions the neglect of notated scores of Balar chine ballets: "Why are the many Labanotation scores not being used? The sit, gathering dust, while the guardian dancers continue to ignore them. Why Because of the prevalent theory that any performer who has danced in th piece is a better source . . . . The notator had the advantage of capturing vit details expressed by Balanchine, his concepts of the movements, his par ticular statements and explanations.† Surely this notator produced a scor

---

* Toward this end, the foundation has received support from the National Endowment fc the Arts, the New York City Department of Cultural Affairs, and Capezio/Ballet Makers Danc Foundation.

† Horgan stated that Balanchine had direct input into few notated scores and that th majority of Labanotation scores were assembled after his death (Sorrin, e-mail to the autho

worthy to preserve the Balanchine heritage?"[55] One limitation to the value of notated scores as a tool for establishing the identity of dance works is the small population of dancers who read notation. Scholarly research, recordings, and other tangible traces of the dance works that are more accessible will continue to be critical to the preservation programs conducted under the auspices of the Balanchine Foundation and the Balanchine Trust.

Jerome Robbins (1918–1998)

Robbins, whose meticulous attention to detail in conducting his affairs is legendary, designed his legacy plan with clarity and vision. According to Sorrin, a member of the advisory committee established by Robbins's will, and Pennington of the Robbins Rights Trust, the infrastructure that Robbins set up for management of his legacy benefited from Horgan's experience with Balanchine's will.[56] Yet Robbins had always sought appropriate legal advice for his undertakings and secured favorable terms, as revealed by Robbins's private documents, held at the Jerome Robbins Dance Division of the New York Public Library.* He asserted his status as a choreographer and director and demanded just recognition not only in monetary terms, but also in publicity credits and billings on posters and programs, insisting that the size of lettering and the placement of his name be appropriately prominent. Robbins's actions are particularly understandable because of the wider dissemination of his works, since he was actively engaged not only in ballet, but also in musicals. His works enjoyed successes on Broadway, were later adapted into film musicals, and continue to play all over the world, necessitating careful surveillance in protecting his legacy and avoiding copyright infringement. Robbins ensured the proper administration of his dance legacy by creating the Robbins Foundation and the Robbins Rights Trust. According to Amanda Vaill, one of Robbins's biographers:

> He left monetary bequests (some of them substantial) to forty-one different family members, ex-lovers, friends, godchildren, colleagues, and staff. Most important, he set up a trust to administer the copyrights to his ballets and other choreography, and he directed that the royalties from his ballets be paid to an inner circle of family and the close friends—many but not all lovers—who were his surrogate family. Finally, he left all his

---

January 28, 2011). Scores by notators who have worked closely with choreographers, such as Sandra Aberkalns (Labanotation) and Monica Parker (Benesh) for Paul Taylor and Kenneth MacMillan, respectively, contribute greatly to establishing the identity of the choreographers' works. For a fuller discussion of the subject, see Francis Yeoh, "The Value of Documenting Dance," *ballet-dance magazine*, June 2007, http://www.balletdance.com/200706/articles/Yeoh200706.html (accessed March 25, 2011).

* The author is grateful to have been granted access, in February 2010, by the Robbins Rights Trust to Robbins's private papers housed at the New York Public Library.

papers, plus a bequest that amounted to $5 million, to the New York Public Library, making him (said the library's president, Paul Le Clerc) the largest personal benefactor in the library's history.[57]

The designated objects of the Robbins Rights Trust include ensuring th licensing and integrity of Robbins's works are centrally controlled and di tributing income to his designated beneficiaries.

Since the embodied knowledge of the stagers who closely assisted th choreographer is critical, the original advisory committee included dance Victor Castelli, Jean-Pierre Frohlich, and Susan Hendl. Stagers do not gene ally use notated scores, although some may. The restaging program is su tained by the continued training of new stagers to take over when the old ones retire. Pennington commented on "capturing the mood" of Robbins works: stagers not only explain the movements but also the motivation fo the movements, in the manner that Robbins had employed when he himse meticulously taught his works.[58] Pennington underlined the trust's concer that Robbins's works not become "museum pieces" and noted that, after ex piration of a license period, the trust may extend a contract but it will sen the ballet master "to ensure the cast is appropriate" so that the works do no "degrade." Ballets are therefore recorded on video at rehearsals as well as a first performances to assist other stagers.[*] Recordings are also available fro the 1990s, when Robbins was alive, for many of his ballets. Pennington als noted the assembling of scores, notes, and other records for archival an teaching purposes so that ballet masters can have material "from here, the and everywhere including selections of 'versions'" of the same work.[59]

The opportunities for dance companies to continue performing Robbin works with integrity are testimony to the stagers' successes. On March 1 1999, barely eight months after Robbins died, the Paris Opéra Ballet pe formed a gala tribute to him; Robbins had contributed twelve ballets to th company's repertory.[60] Among the works performed at the gala were *In th Night, Other Dances*, and *The Concert*, mounted by Jean-Pierre Frohlich. I an article written in 2009, Alastair Macaulay recorded that the New Yor City Ballet spring season included "no fewer than 33 Robbins works, rang ing chronologically from 'Fancy Free' (1944) to 'Brandenburg' (1997)."[6] Macaulay noted as well the performances of Robbins works by companie "from Seattle to Sydney, from San Francisco to Paris." The measures take by the Robbins Rights Trust to secure preservation of the choreographer' legacy have made a valuable contribution to sustaining this portion of ou dance heritage.

---

[*]   Six of Robbins's works have been recorded in whole or part in Labanotation, according t Weber of the Dance Notation Bureau (interview by the author, February 16, 2010). Robbins' ballets in the Royal Ballet repertory are recorded in Benesh Notation, the usual compan practice.

Merce Cunningham (1919–2009)

Cunningham may have noted the legal battles ensnaring the Graham legacy but it is more likely that his legacy plan was influenced by the experience of his inheritance from John Cage, his collaborator and longtime partner. Laura Kuhn, appointed by Cunningham as trustee of the John Cage Trust, may have been instrumental in his planning process, as she had urged him to consider adopting the same path taken for Cage's legacy. Cunningham "made sure that his trust, which licenses his works, is not part of the non-profit entity that supports the activities of his company. Should the company fold, his work, thanks to the trust, will live on."[62] Upon Cunningham's death, his assistant, Robert Swinston, took over direction of the company, which "will perform only Mr. Cunningham's choreography, raising the issue of whether audiences and donors—and the dancers themselves—will support it without the lure of something new."[*]

The Cunningham Trust was formed in 2000 with Cunningham himself as sole trustee. Eventually he appointed other trustees: Kuhn, Allan Sperling (a lawyer and member of the Cunningham Dance Foundation), Swinston, and Patricia Lent (former dancer and director of licensing with the foundation).[63] The mission of the Cunningham Dance Foundation, formed before the Cunningham Trust, is "to support, sustain, and further the wide ranging creative activities of the Merce Cunningham Studio. This includes the Merce Cunningham Dance Company, the Cunningham Repertory Group, the Studio Performance Program for Young Artists, Educational Outreach, and the Merce Cunningham Archives."[64]

In 2005 board members asked Trevor Carlson, executive director of the Cunningham Company, to produce a "long-range plan." Carlson called the resulting Living Legacy Plan "comprehensive, multifaceted, and—like Merce himself—precedent setting. It offers a new model for dance companies and other artist-led organizations transitioning to a post-founder experience."[65] An eight-million-dollar campaign was launched by the foundation to provide financial support for the "ongoing production and performances" as well as preservation of the Cunningham dance legacy in the form of digital dance capsules. Yet Weber of the DNB expressed concern: "Digital capsules may not be the best method for preserving Cunningham's works, as computer programs are constantly upgraded and these records will require continued maintenance and its associated costs, as computer systems change."[66] The

---

[*]   This article was prepared prior to the conclusion of the Legacy Tour by the Merce Cunningham Dance Company (MCDC) in December, 2011, after which the company disbanded. According to the prepared plan, "Following the closure of the MCDC, the Cunningham Dance Foundation will also close in June 2012, and its assets will be transferred to the Merce Cunningham Trust, a separate nonprofit organization established by Cunningham in 2000 to hold the rights to his work and manage his artistic legacy in perpetuity." See http://www.merce.org/p/ (accessed May 12, 2012).

Legacy Plan provided for the Cunningham Dance Company to undertak
a two-year international tour, beginning in February 2010, to feature maj
works, including revivals, from the course of Cunningham's choreograph
career. The choreographer arranged that, after the final performances by h
company, the Cunningham Dance Foundation will no longer function an
its assets will vest in the Cunningham Trust, which will "hold and administ
all rights to his choreography."[67] The trust's mission is to "promote educatic
and artistic development in the field of modern dance through instructic
and performance of works choreographed by Cunningham, and by makir
his choreography available to dance companies."[68]

Arthur Lubow raised doubts about the feasibility of the Legacy Pla
asking, "can Cunningham's scheme really be carried out? Can the dancers an
the dances he choreographed be disentwined? Those whom Cunningha
has entrusted with his legacy are now groping to work out the Zen koa
he left behind."[69] While the maintenance of Cunningham's dance legac
will not be an easy task, the Cunningham Trust will ensure that, when h
works are revived in the future, stagers will have the benefit of the digit
capsules and other support services. It is too early to evaluate the impact c
the Legacy Plan but the trustees possess the necessary framework and th
means to fulfill Cunningham's intentions since the trust "will be financed b
Mr. Cunningham's Estate, which includes artworks by the artists he hired a
set designers early in their careers, among them Robert Rauschenberg an
Jasper Johns."[70]

Frederick Ashton (1904–1988)

Ashton's will bore many similarities to Balanchine's. Anthony Russell-Robert
Ashton's nephew, executor, and residual legatee, explained Ashton's sent
ments: "Fred often said to me that it would be really mean to give a ballet ju
for one lifetime; [the legatees] and their loved ones should have it outrigh
and make as much money as possible. Also, the friends he left ballets t
meant so much to him that he felt he couldn't just give them the works i
part. He did consider that and he was advised to take that course of actior
but he chose not to do so."[71] Russell-Roberts's comments elucidate Ashton'
decision to designate specific works such that his beneficiaries could enjo
rights to the income for life and bequeath the rights to their heirs:[72] Ma
got Fonteyn (*Ondine* and *Daphnis and Chloe*); Michael Somes (*Symphon*
Variations and *Cinderella*); Anthony Dowell (*The Dream* and *A Month in th*
Country); Alexander Grant (*La Fille Mal Gardée* and *Façade*); Brian Sha
(*Les Patineurs* and *Les Rendezvous*); and Anthony Dyson (*Monotones I an*
II and *Enigma Variations*).

The absence of centralized management of Ashton's dance legacy re
sulted in the ad hoc licensing of his works by individual beneficiaries

Russell-Roberts endeavored to set up a trust but his efforts were unsuccessful because he could not persuade two of the legatees to adopt his plans; Somes and Shaw rejected the proposal "on the basis that, as they knew the ballets better than anyone, a trust was unnecessary."[73] Yet this attitude was shortsighted: "Their view, of course, becomes less convincing as time moves on and those who originally danced Ashton ballets themselves die off. ... Russell-Roberts' hope is to establish at least a loose association to protect the work, although even that will need money, and where funds for this might come from is uncertain."[74]

The original beneficiaries were intimately associated with Ashton and his works. They may seek assistance from Royal Ballet colleagues to provide advice and support for restaging the works. Somes's designated works were inherited by his widow, Wendy Ellis, a former principal dancer of the Royal Ballet. Likewise, Derek Rencher is Brian Shaw's successor.[75] As longstanding members of the Royal Ballet, both Ellis and Rencher are conversant with their respective ballets but, when they are succeeded by their heirs, who may be laypersons, the situation will be less favorable. Lavinia Hookham, heir of her late father, Felix Fonteyn (Margot Fonteyn's brother), "has been admirably passive. She has neither proposed nor made any changes to the ballets; she delegates responsibility for their stagings to those deemed by the Royal Ballet to know best."[76] Nonetheless, the Royal Ballet's support cannot be presumed and may not always be available, particularly when its experts are required for its own productions.

Problems in the upkeep of Ashton's repertory may be attributed to the lack of control and safeguards in management of the choreographer's legacy. Dance writer Gerald Dowler has remarked, "Frankly, it is in a mess; there are eight legatees who control the entire Ashton inheritance but have no formal co-ordination of approach or indeed agreement about performance standards."[77] A step toward remedying this situation was taken when Dyson, one of Ashton's legatees, announced establishment of the Ashton Trust, to include as trustees Ellis, Rencher, Phoebe Fonteyn (wife of Felix Fonteyn), Dowell, Grant, and Russell-Roberts.[78] However, no further progress has been reported. Many of Ashton's works are notated in the Benesh system, the result of Ninette de Valois's decision to employ that notation to record works of the Royal Ballet repertory in the mid-1950s.[79] Her foresight has ensured that a major part of the British dance heritage is documented. Ashton's *La Valse* (1958) was his first work recorded in Benesh notation. Thereafter, his newly created works and those revived were also notated, but earlier works were not and will be irretrievable when those who danced them pass away.[80] "Imbalance" in the restaging of Ashton's work is "deeply ingrained now in the Ashton repertoire as seen at Covent Garden. In the actual dancing itself, one may often regret lost nuances and enlightening moments, but notation and video seems at least to ensure that most of the technical choreography is retained. It is in the interpretation of roles that there is constant pain

for anyone with a long memory. ... Ashton ballets that should, still, b
relevant and important can easily run downhill into oblivion if they are n
properly conserved."[81] Shortcomings of the restaging process will be furth
exacerbated when the performances are staged without the home team
experts. This fact highlights the urgent realities facing the Ashton lega
as the living traces of the choreographer's work diminish. Documentatic
must be organized while embodied knowledge is available. The trust,
this regard, must prioritize these projects and seek funding to train a po
of stagers who can then benefit from the sustained documentation of th
Ashton legacy.*

When special effort is given to the restaging process, as was the case f
the Ashton centennial celebrations, some success is evident from the review
Dowler observed that the Birmingham Royal Ballet "was simply stunning i
Enigma ... and these performances were in no way inferior to any th
have gone before."[82] The company also performed *Five Brahms Waltzes* an
The Two Pigeons, and Dowler went on to urge that the newly revived *Dan
Sonata* "must continue to be revived and not languish as much Ashton h
done in Birmingham; the company still have the style and the audience love
them in this repertoire."[83] Critic Daniel Jacobson noted that the centenni
celebrations generated "much needed" revivals of "long dormant and sem
forgotten works."[84] And, he observed, it was "not a moment too soon: thes
precious works were destined to fade from memory, and finally to be lo
entirely, without the needful resuscitation of dancers close enough to the
original presentations to assure their survival with any degree of fidelity
Jacobson suggested that the Royal Ballet "seemed all too ready to allo
Ashton's legacy to wither in benign neglect." A highlight of the festival wa
the revival of *Sylvia*, which Ashton originally created in 1952. An importa
factor in the success of the revivals was Christopher Newton's participatio
As one of the earliest dancers trained in the Benesh system, his notator's ey
for detail greatly aided the reconstructions.[†]

Revivals of Ashton works for special occasions have been welcomed b
these cannot replace the advantages of sustained care by a centralized organ
zation. The call for resuscitation of Ashton's ballets suggests that preservatio
of his legacy must not rely solely on the efforts of individual beneficiarie
or of the Royal Ballet and the Birmingham Royal Ballet companies. Th

---

* Note the contrast with Frederick Ashton's contemporary, Sir Kenneth MacMillan. Su
taining a pool of qualified stagers to ensure the integrity of the work is a concern of Lac
Deborah MacMillan, his wife, who plays a major role in the licensing of his ballets and th
training of stagers. Liz Cunliffe, director of the Benesh Institute, states, "The MacMillan canc
is nowadays staged by a team of notators, including Monica Parker, Julie Lincoln, and Ka
Burnett (also Yuri Uchiumi, Grant Coyle, Denis Bonner)." E-mail to the author, March 2
2010.

† This information was acquired during my employment as administrator and compar
secretary of the Benesh Institute between 1979 and 1987.

frameworks created by Robbins and Cunningham and the formation of the Balanchine Trust for the management of dance legacies might be instructive models for custodians of Ashton's ballets.

Martha Graham (1894–1991)

Graham's will created a unique set of problems. Although she left her entire estate to her longtime friend, Ronald Protas, Julie Van Camp has observed, "There is some indication that Graham wanted to change her will before her death."[85] Nancy S. Kim contended that "his [Protas's] inheritance raised the specter of undue influence as she made him the beneficiary of her will when she was elderly, isolated, and in poor health."[86] The legal battles over ownership of Graham's works illustrate the essential role of the choreographer in clarifying ownership of his or her works and ensuring the best legacy management.

There is evidence that the process of protecting the Graham legacy was not adequately sustained by a number of parties concerned. Van Camp noted, "From the record reported in the court proceedings, it appears that many board members of enormous good will and great interest in promoting and preserving the Graham legacy struggled with poor record-keeping, apparent attempts at deception by Protas, and shifting personnel who offered accounting and legal advice."[87] Van Camp also found that the Graham Center's board members lacked understanding of legal matters regarding ownership of Graham's works: "There is evidence that as late as 1999, the board still had not fully challenged Protas' claims, even entering into a new twenty-year contract, providing $100,000 in salary in exchange for the use of the works."

Protas, a photographer, became Graham's confidant in the 1960s when she was recovering from alcoholism. He became an employee of the Graham Center in 1972 and an associate artistic director in 1980. The legal battles between Protas and the Graham Center commenced in 2000; the board had asked Protas to resign as artistic director, but when the parties could not mutually agree on his replacement, Protas terminated the license agreement with the Graham Center, denying further access to the repertory.[88] The relationship between Graham and the center began in 1956 when she sold her school, originally founded in 1926, to the newly incorporated Martha Graham School of Contemporary Dance. She signed a ten-year part-time contract as program director with overall control of the educational program. At this time she was creating works that were funded by many charitable organizations. Graham's contract with the school was extended for another ten years and, more significantly, she was employed as artistic director by the Graham Center. Her duties specified that she was responsible for the maintenance of the repertory and for creation of new works. In 1976 this

arrangement was again extended and remained in place until her death
1991.

Evidence offered in court indicated that Graham was fully aware
the legal implications of the creation of the Graham Center.[89] Van Cam
suggested that "Tax consequences and the security of the regular salary
an employee might be valuable trade-offs to the artistic freedom to contr
one's work and possibly to benefit from future licensing of the rights
that work," but the complexity and multiplicity of issues involved in Gr
ham's situation, over a long span of years, became further complicated l
"poor record-keeping, and several major changes in copyright law durir
that time."[90] Judge Cedarbaum held that the center had exclusive rights
use of the "Martha Graham" trademark and name.* In her lengthy decisio
Judge Cedarbaum determined that works created by Graham before ar
since the incorporation of the nonprofit Graham Center were assigned
the center and that the works created after 1966 were works for hire.[91] Fe
legal systems worldwide share the work-for-hire doctrine. The relevant fa
tors considered by the court in determining this status for Graham's wor
were provision of studio facilities, dancers, pianists, sets, and costumes fr
rehearsals and performances, as well as payment of "a fixed salary" wit
"no separate compensation for the creation of dances."[92] Organizations rep
resenting choreographers reacted positively to the findings in this case. Fr
example, the Stage Directors and Choreographers Society (SDC) has playe
an active role in providing advice on contracts.[93]

Yet Kim found a disparity between the court's findings and the er
trenched views of members of the dance community and suggested a
amendment to the law to accommodate "the reasonable expectations r
the parties rather than the existence (or nonexistence) of an employmer
relationship."[94] The proposal to reverse the presumption in the employee
favor was considered by the court: "Whatever the intrinsic merit of such a
approach, we conclude that its adoption is a matter of legislative choice fr
Congress in the future, not statutory interpretation for a court at present."
Noting that the Graham Center was treated by the court in the same manne
as a profit organization, Anne Braveman suggested that "the court can vie
any composition created during this time as created outside of the perime
ters of the non-profit's purpose."[96] Thus, she argued, "The court's assumptio
that the employer-employee relationship is the same for both types of o
ganizations is misguided and the uniform application of the work for hir
doctrine does not best reflect each organization's goals."

---

* Some Graham works were in the public domain owing to noncompliance with the stat
tory prerequisites of U.S. copyright law. Van Camp provided a detailed account of the leg
shifts regarding registration of dance works and renewal of registration under the Copyrig
Act (1909) in "Martha Graham's Legal Legacy," 76. As a note of interest, registration is not
statutory requirement in the U.K.

The sole reliance on a nonprofit organization by choreographers, as in Graham's case, for the management of her dance legacy presents a number of problems. Primary is the conflict of interest confronting the Graham Center as it serves two connected but separate functions: the center's prime duty is to advance the interests of the dance company and school, an undertaking that will occupy the greater part of board members' attention, while the center's other duty—the launching of preservation programs—could well be marginalized, thus affecting dissemination of the choreographer's works to other users. This concern may have influenced Balanchine's choice not to bestow his works on the New York City Ballet. Fortunately, confirmation of the ownership of Graham works and the resultant centralization of its management under the umbrella of the Graham Center's infrastructure resulted in a revitalization of the repertory while the propagation of Graham's "living legacy" contributes greatly to the preservation process. The requisite control needed to ensure the integrity of the Graham repertory is now, arguably, in place. Writing about the Graham legacy in 2007, Macaulay stated that "controversy about whether the best works were being well enough performed was already lively in the 1970s. And all these arguments reached larger dimensions after her death. The Graham company today is still rebuilding itself from the civil wars and lawsuits through which it has passed in recent years."[97] The Graham case demonstrated dramatically the outcomes of a poorly organized legacy and serves as a warning to choreographers to exercise caution when making plans for the preservation of their work.

CONCLUSION

This assessment of the role of choreographic trusts in preserving dance legacies has revealed that the task is difficult, in large part because of the ephemeral nature of dance and the entrenched oral tradition adopted in the creation, restaging, and preservation of works. Dance legacy preservation requires the exercise of skill and expertise to sustain a comprehensive program that includes maintaining the integrity of the works in performance and providing support and documentation for stagers, now and in the future.

The infrastructure provided by choreographic trusts not only coordinates but also sustains the preservation of the dance legacy—a task that cannot be undertaken by individual beneficiaries. Siegel's warning, quoted earlier, about the slippage of style that results in loss of a work's identity, continues to be relevant. Current models of choreographic trusts provide guidelines for other choreographers to consider, both to ensure that their gifts to beneficiaries are properly managed and to secure the preservation and propagation of their works.

NOTES

1. Cited in Richard Buckle (in collaboration with John Taras), *George Balanchine: Ballet Mas* (London: Hamish Hamilton, 1988), 327. Emphases in the original.

2. David Vaughan, "Celebrating Ashton," *DanceView* (Spring 1999), http://www.danceview.or archives/ashton/vaughan1.htmo/ (accessed February 16, 2009).

3. See the articles in *Dance Chronicle*, vol. 34, no. 1, and Catherine J. Johnson and Alleg Fuller Snyder, *Securing Our Dance Heritage, Issues in the Documentation and Preservation of Dan* (Washington, D.C.: Council for Library and Information Resources, 1999); Allegra Fuller Snyder, *Dan Films: A Study of Choreo-Cinema* (Albany: State University of New York Press, 1973); Glenn Lone "Broadway Dancin'" (interview with Lee Theodore), *Performing Arts Journal*, vol. 4, nos. 1–2 (M 1979): 129–41; and Libby Smigel, *Documenting Dance: A Practical Guide* (Washington, D.C.: Dan Heritage Coalition, 2006), http://www.danceheritage.org/publications/DocumentingDance.pdf (access May 8, 2011).

4. "Dance Capsules," http://www.merce.org/p/ and http://www.merce.org/p/dance-capsules.pl (accessed February 19, 2011).

5. Ray Cook, "In Response: Janet Karin's 'Copyright Preservation or Embalmment?'" *Brolga*, no. (June 1998): 63.

6. Maya Dalinsky, "The Dance Master: The Legacy of Jerome Robbins," *Humanities*, vol. 25, n 5 (September/October 2004), http://www.neh.gov/news/humanities/2004–09/robbins.html/ (accesse March 8, 2010).

7. Lynne Weber, e-mail to the author, January 26, 2011.

8. Marcia B Siegel, *Mirrors and Scrims: The Life and Afterlife of Ballet* (Middletown, Conn.: We leyan University Press, 2010), 136–37.

9. Cited in R. M. Campbell, "Preserving Balanchine Is a Matter of Trust," *Seattle Post-Intelligence* February 2, 1991, Entertainment, C1.

10. Nancy Reynolds, interview by Alexandra Tomalonis, "The Balanchine Archive Project," *Bal Alert*, no. 1 (October 1997), http://www.balletalert.com/magazines/BAsampler?Reynolds.htm (accesse October 12, 2006).

11. George L. Gretton, "Trusts without Equity," *International and Comparative Law Quarterly*, vo 49, no. 3 (2000): 600.

12. Jonathan Hilliard, "The Flexibility of Fiduciary Doctrine in Trust Law: How Far Does it Stretc in Practice?," *Trust Law International*, vol. 23, no. 3 (2009): 119.

13. Gretton, "Trusts without Equity," 600.

14. Christopher Pennington, interview by the author, February 18, 2010.

15. Christopher Pennington, e-mail to the author, January 18, 2011.

16. Daniel J. Wakin, "Merce Cunningham Sets Plan for His Dance Legacy," *New York Time* June 9, 2009, http://www.nytimes.com/2009/06/10/arts/dance/10merc.html?ref=merce_cunningham/ (a cessed December 13, 2010).

17. Diane Solway, "When the Choreographer Is Out of the Picture," *New York Times*, January 2007, Arts and Leisure, 2.

18. Philip H. Pettit, *Equity and the Law of Trusts*, 11th ed. (Oxford: Oxford University, 2009), 66; Jea Warburton, "Charitable Trust—Unique?," *Conveyancer and Property Lawyer*, no. 20 (January–Februar 1999): 21.

19. Pennington, e-mail.

20. Ibid.

21. The Jerome Robbins Foundation and the Robbins Rights Trust, http://jeromerobbins.org/ (ac cessed March 11, 2010).

22. Warburton, "Charitable Trust—Unique?," 21. See also Michael Haley and Lara McMurtry, *Equi and Trusts* (London: Sweet & Maxwell, 2006), 159; Jill E. Martin, *Hanbury and Martin: Modern Equi* (London: Sweet & Maxwell, 2009), 392.

23. Haley and McMurtry, *Equity and Trusts*, 136.

24. See *The George Balanchine Trust*, http://www.balanchine.com/content/site/show/faq, http:/ www.balanchine.com/content/, and http://www.balanchine.org/ (accessed May 13, 2011).

25. The following documents pertain to the case Martha Graham School and Dance Foundatio Inc. v. Martha Graham Center of Contemporary Dance, Inc.: 153 F. Supp. 2d, 512 (S.D.N.Y. 2001); 224 F

Supp. 2d, 567 (S.D.N.Y. 2002); 380 F. 3d (2d Cir. 2004); 380 F. 3d (2da Cir. 2004), petition for cert. filed, 73 U.S.L.W. 3570 (U.S. Mar. 21, 2005) (No. 04–1277); U.S. Dist. LEXIS 12241, 8–24 (S.D.N.Y 2005); U.S. App. LEXIS 17455 (2D Cir. 2006).

26. Cited in Bengt Häger, *The Dancer's World: Problems of Today and Tomorrow*, Report on the First International Choreographers' Conference, New York (1978), organized by the International Dance Council and UNESCO, 29.

27. Francis Sparshott, *A Measured Pace: Toward a Philosophical Understanding of the Arts of Dance* (Toronto: University of Toronto Press, 1995), 422.

28. University of London Press Ltd. v. University Tutorial Press Ltd. (1916), 2, Ch 601. Italics added.

29. Cited in *Copinger and Skone James on Copyright*, ed. Kevin W. Garnett, Gillian Davies, Gwilym Harbottle, Walter Arthur Copinger, and E. P. Skone James, 15th ed. (London: Sweet and Maxwell, 2005), 40.

30. See Julie Van Camp, "Copyright of Choreographic Works," *1994–95 Entertainment, Publishing and the Arts Handbook*, ed. Stephen F. Breimer, Robert Thorne, and John David Viera (New York: Clark, Boardman, Callaghan, 1994), 59–92, 63; also available at http://www.csulb.edu/~jvancamp/copyrigh.html (accessed February 13, 2011).

31. David R. Koepsell, *The Ontology of Cyberspace: Philosophy, Law and the Future of Intellectual Property* (Chicago: Open Court Publishing Co., 2000), 16.

32. Barbara A. Singer, "In Search of Adequate Protection for Choreographic Works: Legislative and Judicial Alternatives vs. The Custom of the Community," *University of Miami Law Review*, vol. 38 (1994): 300–1.

33. See Julie Van Camp, "Martha Graham's Legal Legacy," *Dance Chronicle*, vol. 30, no. 1 (2007): 67–99.

34. Francis Mason, "The Legacy of Martha Graham," *Ballet Review*, vol. 30, no. 3 (Fall 2002): 33–72.

35. Anne W. Braveman, "Duet of Discord: Martha Graham and Her Non-Profit Battle Over Work for Hire," *Loyola of Los Angeles Entertainment Law Review*, vol. 25 (2005): 496.

36. Mason, "The Legacy of Martha Graham," 33.

37. Nancy S. Kim, "Martha Graham, Professor Miller, and the Work for Hire Doctrine: Undoing the Judicial Bind Created by the Legislature," *Journal of Intellectual Property Law*, vol. 13 (2006): 339.

38. Ibid., 340.

39. Braveman, "Duet of Discord: Martha Graham and Her Non-Profit Battle," 491.

40. Agnes de Mille, *And Promenade Home* (Boston: Little, Brown and Company, 1956), 257.

41. Ellen Sorrin, interview by the author, February 17, 2010.

42. Cited in Joseph Carman, "Who Owns a Dance? It Depends on the Maker," *New York Times*, December 23, 2003.

43. Sorrin, interview.

44. Ria Catton, "Balanchine's Right-Hand Woman: Barbara Horgan," *New York Sun*, July 7, 2004, 18.

45. Quoted in Sheryl Flatow, "The Balanchine Trust: Guardian of the Legacy," *Dance Magazine* (December 1990): 58–59.

46. Quoted in Jann Parry, "The Next Generation, an Exercise in Trust—The Americans Are More Legalistic in Protecting their Balletic Inheritance than the British," *The Observer*, December 2 1990, 61.

47. Flatow, "The Balanchine Trust: Guardian of the Legacy," 58.

48. Cheryl Swack, "The Balanchine Trust: Dancing Through the Steps of Two-Part Licensing," *Villanova Sports and Entertainment Law Journal*, vol. 6 (1999): 270, n. 19.

49. Sorrin, interview. See also *The George Balanchine Trust, Licensing the Ballets*, http://balanchine.com/content/site/show/licensing (accessed May 8, 2011).

50. Quoted in Rita Feliciano, "The Balanchine Trust at Ten: Building a Better Future for Companies Nationwide," *Dance Magazine* (June 1997): 154.

51. Quoted in Flatow, "The Balanchine Trust: Guardian of the Legacy," 60.

52. Sorrin, interview.

53. Sorrin, interview; Flatow, "The Balanchine Trust: Guardian of the Legacy," 59.

54. Ann Hutchinson Guest, "And the Choreography Is By . . . ," *Dance Now*, vol. 11, no. 4 (Winter 2002/03): 43.

55. Hutchinson Guest, "And the Choreography Is By . . . ," 45.

56. Sorrin, interview; Pennington, interview.

57. Amanda Vaill, *Somewhere: The Life of Jerome Robbins* (New York: Broadway Books, 2006), 524.

58. Christopher Pennington, e-mail to the author, March 7, 2011.

59. Pennington, interview.

60. Alan Riding, "In Paris, Paying Tribute to Jerome Robbins with Pomp and Humor," *New Yo Times*, March 12, 1999, Arts, 1.

61. Alastair Macaulay, "Robbins's Legacy of Anguish and Exuberance," *New York Times*, April 2009.

62. Solway, "When the Choreographer Is Out of the Picture," 3.

63. Arthur Lubow, "Can Modern Dance Be Preserved?" *New York Times*, November 8, 2009, 38.

64. See http://www.merce.org/foundation/index.php/ (accessed January 20, 2011).

65. "Merce Cunningham Announces Precedent-Setting Plan for Future of His Dance Company a His Work" and "Merce Cunningham Dance Company to Launch Final World Tour in February 201(both at www.merce.org/p/documents/CDFLegacyPressRelease.pdf (accessed February 28, 2011).

66. Lynne Weber, interview by the author, February 16, 2010.

67. "The Legacy Plan," http://www.merce.org/foundation/index.php/ (accessed January 20, 201

68. "Merce Cunningham Announces Precedent-Setting Plan."

69. Lubow, "Can Modern Dance Be Preserved?" 38.

70. Solway, "When the Choreographer Is Out of the Picture," 2.

71. Quoted in Gerald Dowler, "Fred Steps Out in New York," *The Dancing Times* (September 200-13. See also Kathrine Sorley Walker, "Ashton Now and Then," *DanceView* (1994) in the Ashton Archi series, 8, http://www.danceview.org/archives/ashton/walker1.html (accessed October 16, 2009).

72. Sorley Walker, "Ashton Now and Then."

73. Suzanne McCarthy, "Report of the Interview between Anthony Russell-Roberts, Administrati Director, and Phyllida Ritter at a Lunch and Listen Friends event, 23 May 2002, Royal Opera House, Lo don," *ballet magazine*, http://www.ballet.co.uk/magazines/yr_02/jul02/sm_ rb_russell_roberts.htm (a cessed October 16, 2009).

74. Ibid. The Frederick Ashton Foundation has been established since the preparation of this artic "Launch of the Frederick Ashton Foundation," press release, October 8, 2011, http://balletnews.co.uk/th royal-opera-house-the-frederick-ashton-foundation/ (accessed November 16, 2011).

75. Jane Simpson, cited in Brendan McCarthy, "Ashton Trust," *Ballettalk, Discussion Forum* (Septer ber 17, 2004), http://www.ballettalk.invisionzone.com/index.php?showtopic=17654/ (accessed Octob 16, 2009).

76. Alastair Macaulay, "The Uncertain Future Life of Ashton Ballets," *New York Times*, June 19, 200 5.

77. Gerald Dowler, "A Foot in Two Camps, Interview with Anthony Russell-Roberts, Administrati Director of the Royal Ballet and Frederick Ashton's Nephew," *The Dancing Times* (November 2004): 1

78. McCarthy, "Ashton Trust."

79. Rudolf Benesh and Joan Benesh, *Reading Dance: The Birth of Choreology* (London: Condc 1977), 6.

80. Amanda Eyles, "Artistic Testament," *Dance Gazette*, vol. 1 (2001): 19.

81. Sorley Walker, "Ashton Now and Then," 5, 7.

82. Dowler, "Fred Steps Out," 11.

83. Ibid.

84. Daniel Jacobson, "*Sylvia*: Can These Bones Live?," *Ballet Review*, vol. 33, no. 1 (Spring 2005 21.

85. Van Camp, "Martha Graham's Legal Legacy," 70.

86. Kim, "Martha Graham, Professor Miller, and the Work for Hire Doctrine," 339.

87. Van Camp, "Martha Graham's Legal Legacy," 81–82.

88. Martha Graham Sch. & Dance Found. Inc. v. Martha Graham Ctr. of Contemporary Dance, Inc 224 F. Supp.2d, 567 (S.D.N.Y. 2002).

89. Van Camp, "Martha Graham's Legal Legacy," 86.

90. Ibid., 71, 68.

91. Mason, "The Legacy of Martha Graham," 33.

92. On work for hire, see Louise Nemschoff, "Authorship and Employment: Life in the Entertainme Industry after CCNV v Reid," *Entertainment Law Review*, vol. 4, no. 3 (1993): 80. On the Graham decisio see Sharon Connelly, "Authorship, Ownership, and Control: Balancing the Economic and Artistic Issue Raised by the Martha Graham Copyright Case," *Fordham Intellectual Property, Media and Entertainme Law Journal*, vol. XV (2006): 849.

93. Society of Stage Directors and Choreographers, http://sdcweb.org/ (accessed January 10, 2011).

94. Kim, "Martha Graham, Professor Miller, and the Work for Hire Doctrine," 339.

95. Martha Graham School and Dance Foundation, Inc. v. Martha Graham Center of Contemporary Dance, Inc., 380 F. 3d (2d Cir. 2004), 640.

96. Braveman, "Duet of Discord: Martha Graham and Her Non-Profit Battle Over Work for Hire," 490.

97. Alastair Macaulay, "Portraits in Grief after Graham and Jungian Torment in Greek Legends," *New York Times*, September 13, 2007.

GAINED IN TRANSLATION:
RECREATION AS CREATIVE PRACTICE

VALERIE PRESTON-DUNLOP and LESLEY-ANNE SAYERS

Valerie Preston-Dunlop and Lesley-Anne Sayers, from Trinity Laban Conservatoire of Music and Dance in London, recently recreated very different dance works from the 1920s. In this article they discuss the value of recreation as creative practice and the discoveries they have made regarding "lost" works, for example, Rudolf Laban's Die Grünen Clowns *(Green Clowns) and* Nacht *(Night) and Sergei Prokofiev, Georgi Yakoulov, and Léonide Massine's collaboration for* Le Pas d'Acier *(The Steel Step). Considering the potential of educational centers specializing in recreation as research laboratories for the profession, they reflect upon, from two different perspectives, the need to document and disseminate knowledge about creative processes as opposed to simply recording performance.*

Valerie Preston-Dunlop on Recreating Rudolf Laban's Kammertanz Works of the 1920s

Archeochoreology

The word *archeochoreology* suggests what it means: archaeological methods used to "find" lost dances. With archaeology defined as "the technique of studying man's past using material remains as a primary source,"[1] this paper looks at what an archeochoreological approach might pose for recreating the works Rudolf Laban made with his Kammertanzbühne (Chamber Dance Group) in the 1920s for audiences of the twenty-first century. As Mike Pearson points out, in considering the discipline of drama:

> The term theatre archaeology is a paradox: the application of archaeological techniques to an ephemeral event. However while performance may leave limited material traces, it does generate narratives. . . . Archaeology is not just excavation (analysis). It must in some way synthesize (reconstruct, represent, simulate) the past.[2]

The task for me, as the archeochoreologist, was to discover from the resources what kind of reconstruction, representation, or simulation was appropriate for Laban's Kammertanz. Being a founding Fellow of the International Council of Kinetography Laban, I had listened to many discussions on the relationship of a notated score to the dance work it represented, and to the endeavors of reconstruction directors to overcome the gap that inevitably exists between marks on paper and flesh-and-blood movement. Muriel Topaz, a veteran reconstructor of American modern dance works from the score, took for granted that "the text" of Doris Humphrey's master work *Day on Earth* was "the movement itself," details of which would be available in the notation.[3] Kenneth Archer and Millicent Hodson, discussing authenticity, asked a question of their own reconstruction of Vaslav Nijinsky's *Le Sacre du Printemps*: "Is there sufficient evidence to ensure the reconstruction will be a reasonable facsimile of the original?"[4] In essays written for the volume *Preservation Politics*, edited by Stephanie Jordan, these scholars presume that the surface form—that is, what is visible by an outside eye, what is captured on a film or videotape of a performance, what is transcribed in a Laban or Benesh notation score—is the essential template for a facsimile, and that making a dance as near as possible the same again is the only dialogue with the past to have validity.

But is this approach the only valid one, or is it the case that for those particular dances, Nijinsky's *Sacre* and Humphrey's *Day on Earth*, surface form is paramount and must be regarded as "the work"? For some other works, particularly those that are "open" or include improvisation, would another kind of dialogue be appropriate?

In "Issues in revivals and re-creations: a choreological enquiry,"[5] I focused on the distinction between the kind of ballet that can be remounted as a facsimile, with the aid of a score directed by someone with corporeal knowledge of the work, and Laban's Kammertanz, which cannot. In this case the works in question were Frederick Ashton's *Symphonic Variations*, reconstructed and rehearsed by Judith Maelor Thomas, and Kurt Jooss's *The Green Table*, remounted by Anna Markard, both with the Birmingham Royal Ballet. Most ballet companies function with repertory that must be repeatable with different casts. My inquiry pointed to the very different kind of theatre and engagement with the spectator that Laban was seeking by working as a Kammertanzbühne in residence, performing weekly, to regular audiences with season tickets: "To put together such a varied programme on a regular basis was a task that needed new thinking. Sharing responsibility and co-authorship were Laban's solutions, so that the creativity and time required were not shouldered entirely by Laban."[6] Clearly the approaches of Topaz, Archer and Hodson, Thomas, and Markard, right for the artists they were dealing with, were inappropriate for my engagement with Laban's practice. But I had to discover that by painstakingly collecting data and researching practically in the studio.

Later in this paper, when discussing another way to document dances beside score writing and filming (or videotaping), I look at the allographic work of William Forsythe and the open-installation work of Sarah Rubidge, both of whom would find the notion of "facsimile" alien to their work, which celebrates otherness rather than sameness. It seems that Laban's Ausdruckstanz and the postmodern methods of these two twenty-first-century artists have much in common, sharing a relish for exploring process rather than making a fetish of the product.[*]

The Context for the Research on Laban's Theatre Work

As is well known, the Third Reich decimated European dance theatre, which had been vibrant in the 1920s and early 1930s. Norbert Servos writes in his book on Pina Bausch, "Our own Ausdruckstanz tradition with such names as Mary Wigman, Rudolf von Laban, Harald Kreutzberg and Gret Palucca, had all but died since World War II. Striving for an apolitical, supposedly timeless theatre, people avoided confrontation with the provocative ancestors."[7] Laban's theatre works had indeed all but died and could have remained lost and forgotten, were it not for the dance scene in London, which provoked another outcome. By the end of the 1970s American modern dance was in vogue in European dance centers and that included The Laban Centre in London,

---

[*]"Fetishizing" is Forsythe's term for venerating a premiere. See "The Loss of Small Detail Project," in *Mapping Creative Procedures in Multimedia Works Using Choreological Perspectives* (Cheltenham, Gloucestershire: IDM Ltd., 2008), Map 3.

at the time under the joint artistic leadership of Laban-trained Marion North and American Bonnie Bird. A profound shift was taking place within dance practice and dance education in the United Kingdom, as a result of a clash in the professional dance world between ballet—for years the dominant professional dance form—and the burgeoning Graham-oriented London Contemporary Dance Theatre. In dance education Laban's creative dance methods, firmly established since the early 1950s,[8] were under siege by the training and choreographic methods of Martha Graham, Doris Humphrey, Charles Weidman, and Merce Cunningham.[9] With dance history at college level in danger of being taught entirely as the history of ballet and American modern dance—with the European heritage all but ignored—I decided to apply for research support to find and recreate works of the Ausdruckstanz tradition, which I believed had something significant to offer. I was successful in gaining support, and so began a twenty-year adventure in archeochoreology.

Archeochoreology in Action

Locating and Studying Archival Materials

In the first half of the 1980s, as a German- and French-speaking research faculty member at The Laban Centre, I was commissioned to search for and collect archival evidence of Rudolf Laban's activity in Europe between 1910 and 1938, when he arrived in England, and to gain interviews wherever elderly dancers and associates from his Tanzbühne Laban, Kammertanzbühne Laban, and Berlin Choreographisches Institut could be found.[*] The interviews,[†] not all coherent, were with Fritz Klingenbeck in Vienna, Gertrud Snell in Hanover, Lola Rogge in Hamburg, Kurt and

---

[*]The print, film, and sound materials from this search are now archived as The Laban Collection housed at Trinity Laban.

[†]Fritz Klingenbeck was *Kammertanzer*, teacher, and notation assistant. Gertrud Snell was *Kammertanzerin* and notation and secretarial assistant to Laban. Lola Rogge was the lead dancer of the Hamburger Bewegungschöre. Kurt Peters was the curator and archivist of Ausdruckstanz documents. Gisela Peters is a dance educator trained by Lola Rogge. Ilse Loesch was *Kammertanzerin* and movement choir leader. Herta Feist was *Kammertanzerin* and director of the Laban Schule in Berlin. Aurel Milloss was a student at Laban's Choreographisches Institut in Berlin and latterly choreographer at the Rome Opera House.

Gisela Peters in Cologne, Ilse Loesch and Herta Feist in Berlin, and Aurel Milloss in Rome, along with longer interviews with Sylvia Bodmer, Albrecht Knust, and Kurt Jooss.* What I uncovered was evidence of Laban's artistic experimentation in dance-theatre making on a scale and breadth unimagined, and at that time undocumented and unresearched.† The evidence convinced me there was sufficient data to enable a beginning to be made in connecting archive with practice. I believed that bringing into focus this forgotten heritage could provide a tranche of cultural, aesthetic, and choreographic discourse valuable and challenging to scholars and practitioners.

The Kammertanzbühne Laban was a chamber dance ensemble in Hamburg that created and performed small-scale repertory in their resident space, under Laban's leadership along with the day-to-day direction of Dussia Bereska. Of Bereska he wrote, "Only this dancer was still with me from the dance-farm [Monte Veritá] days and completely involved with my work. The style of her movements was inspired, and her strong gift as an art-educator made her particularly suitable to help me with the tasks I had set myself."[10] The young music and drama student Kurt Jooss joined him, as did the World War I veteran and folk dancer Albrecht Knust, and Sylvia Bodmer, Herta Feist, and Gertrud Loeser, all to become key figures in Ausdruckstanz, together with able performers Jens Keith, Julian Algo, and Edgar Frank. Bodmer's interview[11] reveals that their way of working was an extension of the experiments in alternative art making at Monte Veritá in 1913 and 1914, where as director of arts Laban eschewed tradition, valued the movement (and sonic) voice of each individual, and encouraged improvisation freed from "steps" and from music.[12] The dynamic body in space was sufficient for him to explore a new form of the movement art for the twentieth century.‡

---

*Sylvia Bodmer, Albrecht Knust, and Kurt Jooss were all dancers in the Kammertanz and long-term professional associates of Laban.

†Evelyn Dörr had not completed her doctoral dissertation, "Rudolf von Laban: Leben und Werk des Kunstlers (1879–1936)," at Humboldt Universität, Berlin, until 1999. A copy is housed in Trinity Laban Library.

‡Käthe Wulff, Monte Veritá dancer and participant in the dada art events at the Cabaret Voltaire, Zurich, at ninety-four years of age gave me a movement class in her studio in Basel, Switzerland. She used her gong and tambour to accompany me as I followed her instructions for simple movement improvisation tasks.

The Sources on Laban and His Context

For *Die Grünen Clowns* it was necessary to place Laban in his immediate context in the Weimar Republic turmoil that postwar Germany was, with its financial and political crises, street violence, and growing racial unease. These conditions are by now common knowledge in principle.[13] More specifically, the daily turmoil in Hamburg, Laban's base from 1922 to 1926, is well documented in the *Hamburger Nachrichtung* and the Hamburg Communist Archive collection. Laban's response to the longer-term issues of the loss of traditional ways of life through industrialization and the loss of spiritual certainty through the demise of established religion is recorded in his autobiography. In the chapter on his time in the railway workshops as a cadet at the Wiener Neustadt Military Academy, he wrote:

> I saw with growing clarity how man will come under the domination of the machine. Wasn't the magic word "Soul"? But hadn't the soul already withered and died in our spurious culture, in the turmoil of the big city? Wasn't it irreparably and irrevocably lost? Wasn't it the task of the arts to reawaken it, to keep it alive? And didn't I belong much more to those whose task it was to arouse the soul through their dreams and prayers, than to those who increased the power of the machine by diligently tending its screws and chains?[14]

Meanwhile, the artistic climate surrounding Laban shifted from the Theosophy-oriented arts such as the sculptures of Herman Obrist* to the Secession in Vienna, particularly Oskar Kokoshka's theatre work and the city opera house productions. (Vienna was the city of Laban's teenage induction into the arts and society.) He embraced the subjective priorities of abstract expressionism, particularly those of Der Blaue Reiter, which included Wassily Kandinsky and Paul Klee in Munich (where Laban lived and worked as a graphic artist and Karnival pageant director from 1910 to 1914).[15] He participated in the community in Monte Veritá, with its members' experiments in free love, vegetarianism, creative arts of all sorts, and a life close to nature,† and from there, he moved to the anarchy and nihilism of Dada in

---

*Laban was a pupil of Obrist in Munich at the turn of the century.
†Laban led the school of the arts at Monte Veritá in the summer months.

Zurich.[*] Then the Neue Sachlichkeit (New Objectivity) in Germany emerged after the calamity of the hyperinflation of 1923 and Laban's *Tanzschrift*, presented to the assembled dance world at the Second Dancers' Congress in June 1928, was his contribution to notating and analyzing dance objectively.[16]

It was also crucial to place Laban alongside other movement modes of the time, by contrasting his corporeality with Oskar Schlemmer's abstraction of the body,[†] and his insistence on dance as art with Rudolf Steiner's *eurhythmy*, in which dance was a form of prayer, and with Émile-Jaques Dalcroze, for whom it was a means for musical education. It was important to differentiate his dance for amateur men and women as art from the Korperkultur groups—Hinrich Medau, Rudolf Bode, Bess Mensendieck, for example, who prioritized "hygienic movement" for health and beauty, primarily for women.[‡]

It was also essential to know what kind of choreographic works Laban had previously created and performed in order to discern what could be assumed to be within his palette in 1928. Had he kept his works, toured them, remounted them, or made them as one-offs? I needed to understand his attitudes to music, site and set, movement vocabulary, dancers, and costuming. His 1935 autobiography *Ein Leben für den Tanz*, translated as *A Life for Dance* by Lisa Ullmann in 1975, offers many pointers.

---

[*]Laban was a noted visitor to the Cabaret Voltaire in Zurich during the war years. See Hans Richter, *Dada Art and Anti Art* (London: Oxford University Press, 1965).

[†]*The Letters and Diaries of Oskar Schlemmer*, ed. Tut Schlemmer, trans. Krishna Winston (Evanston: Northwestern University Press, 1972). Schlemmer refers to the Laban community's work as "the body dance" (185).

[‡]See Mary Wigman's description of Laban's work in dance as art in *Die Fahne* (1921), quoted in Valerie Preston-Dunlop, *Rudolf Laban: An Extraordinary Life* (London: Dance Books, 1998), 67. Steiner, Dalcroze, and Laban addressed the question posed by Kandinsky in 1912: How can we embody the spiritual in art? Steiner commenced eurhythmy (*A Lecture on Eurhythmy*, published by the Anthroposophical Publishing Company in 1926), and Dalcroze produced *Orfeo* at Hellerau in June of 1912, which Laban attended. See "How to revive dancing 1912," in *Rhythm, Music and Education* (Woking: Dalcroze Society, 1921). Laban rejected their solutions and opened his own first school as *Der Freier Tanz* in 1913. Contrasting his dance with that of the body-culture groups, Laban wrote of the content of a movement choir for a large amateur group: "a dance-play telling of the strength of the common hope which lies in a common will to achieve something better. This is *Titan.*" Laban, *A Life in Dance*, 156. Hedwig Müller and Patricia Stöckemann discuss Korperkultur in *... jeder Mensch ist ein Tänzer: Ausdruckstanz in Deutschland zwischen 1900 und 1945* (Giessen: Anabas-Verlag, 1993).

Especially revealing were the chapters named after a particular choreography: *Nacht* (Night, 1927), *Der Schwingende Tempel* (The Swinging Cathedral, 1921), *Gaukelei* (Illusions, 1923), *Der Spielmann* (The Fiddler, 1916), *Titan* (The Titan 1927), *Alltag und Fest* (Everyday and Festival, 1929), in which he discusses the life experiences that were the impetus for each work.

The Body as Living Archive

As a teenage student at the Art of Movement Studio when it opened in Manchester soon after the end of World War II with Lisa Ullmann at the helm, Bodmer assisting, and Laban directing from the background,* I experienced the improvisatory method. Individual and group improvisation was balanced by daily classes in eukinetics (dynamic studies) and choreutics (space studies). Laban started all the dance work I ever experienced with him by focusing on the intention of each movement, whether narrative or purely kinetic. You worked toward the intention, giving rise to vividly dynamic movement (eukinetics), which Laban harnessed into spatial form within your kinesphere's crystal-like "scaffolding" (choreutics). It was a collaborative process dependent on the dancer having a thorough corporeal command of effort rhythms, inner attitude, and space harmony principles. When he felt you understood his method, he would leave you to it and say nothing except "You do it." I was therefore able to engage with the archival evidence with a muscle memory and perspective informed by four years of close practice with Laban.†

This mode of being was what I set out to revisit in ten days of Kammertanz workshops at The Laban Centre in 1987, a very different dance culture from that of either post–World War I Hamburg or post–World War II Manchester. Each day we started with a Labanesque warmup outside on the grounds of neighboring

---

*Being classified during the Second World War as an enemy alien, Laban was not permitted to engage in education, only agricultural and industrial work, so Ullmann had to be the face of his work.

†Laban himself did not teach. He appeared from time to time and engaged us with whatever research issue he was grappling with at the time from his work in drama, industry, psychotherapy, space harmony, effort notation, or dance history. Where he saw potential he gave you responsibilities as an apprentice: Geraldine Stephenson in performance, Warren Lamb in movement behavior, Hettie Loman in choreography, and myself in choreology.

Goldsmiths College, wearing as little clothing as was decent to feel the freedom of the grass under our feet, the sun and breeze on our skin, and the sky as our limit, just as the Kammertanz dancers had done in "a big meadow near the lake" at their summer residence at Gleschendorf in 1922.[17] For ten days we functioned as an Ausdruckstanz commune, sharing the responsibility of getting together a program of the kind indicated in the Kammertanz brochure of 1924. My aim was to recreate, at least in first-draft form, four solos, *Krystall* (The Crystal) and *Orchidée* (The Orchid) for women, *Marotte* (Obsessed*)* and *Möndane* (The Chic Thing*)* for men, *Marsch,* a quartet, and two group pieces, *Oben und Unten* (Above and Below) and *Die Grünen Clowns,* opening with a Dionysian group study, *Dithyrambus.* I added the male duos *Bizarrer* (Bizarre) and *Ekstatischer Zweimännertanz* (Ecstatic Male Duos) two years later.

Product or Process

There being no film of these pieces, except for a phrase of Bereska performing *Orchidée,* and no notation,[*] the exact surface form had vanished. The Kammertanz repertory was ostensibly lost. The recreation of the dances relied on connecting scattered evidence. Had Laban regarded his works as polished products, I would not have been able to retrieve them. But that was neither his method nor what he valued. *Die Grünen Clowns,* for example, was sometimes danced by seven people and at other times by thirteen, appearing as three, one, or six scenes.[18] The photographs show dancers masked in one production and unmasked in another, barefoot in one and shod in another (Figure 1). The Kammertänzer might repeat a dance but with a totally different costume and title,[19] and show it danced by a man and then by a woman. Spontaneity, the availability of dancers, and what opportunities to perform might arise in what kinds of spaces ruled the day in the time of turbulent uncertainty that characterized the Weimar Republic.

Dances are allographic by nature; even the most rigid choreography changes with each performance, each casting, and each

---

[*]These dances were created before the journal *Schrifttanz* published the first draft of Laban's notation system in 1928.

Figure 1. War memorial in *Die Grünen Clowns, 1928* to *Green Clowns, 2008*, performed by Trinity Laban dancers. Photograph copyright © Kyle Stevenson.

venue. A choreographer has to choose when to minimize change and when to embrace it. Laban did both, the latter in much of his choreographic work while at the same time introducing a notation system that enabled the ephemerality of dance performance to be captured. "Otherness" is an integral part of casting and Laban had a point of view on it. Artists and thinkers of the 1920s valued the individual against the onslaught of industrialization with its capacity to dehumanize. Individualität was a call from Friedrich Nietzsche at the turn of the century that still resonated.[20] Individual differences mattered; they were perceived as something in danger of being annihilated. Laban cherished the movement voice of each member of his Kammertanzbühne; that is, he valued their creativity, movement solutions, capacities, physiques, and creative input. The process of making dance with them was his interest, while the performance was a mere fleeting occasion. While a few of his works, such as *Gaukelei* and *Don Juan*, were toured, most addressed a particular specification (*Fausts Erlosung* with speech choir) or mode of theatre (*Nacht* as a "dynamic materialization") and thus were one-off performances.

I had more information about *Marotte* than the other solos. Aurel Milloss, a renowned Hungarian dance artist who ended his long career as choreographer at the Rome Opera, had seen Laban perform *Marotte* in Konstanz, Germany, in 1926, as I discovered when I visited Milloss. It had made a huge impression on the young man, who, although a ballet student, had enrolled in Laban's Berlin Choreographisches Institut as soon as it opened, *Marotte* was danced mostly on the spot and as a rondo, he recalled, demonstrating a churning motion with his right arm over his gut that formed the A motif of the solo. The solo had no music but vocal cries, laughter, and body sounds. Together, in Milloss's library, he and I put together a sketch of the motifs, including obsession with hand washing, with self-harm, fear of being watched, and the comfort of thumb-sucking and the fetal position. The main difficulty back in London was to cast a man with the will to enter into the recreation of this challenging role.

The 1920s reviews reveal that Laban was a consummate man of the theatre. He knew how to entertain and to shock; he used satire and pathos, and he created ornamental and grotesque images. As we worked I had to take into consideration the mode of theatre Laban visualized for each solo or group piece.[21] For example, *Marsch* should amuse, *Marotte* should horrify. *Ekstatischer* should mesmerize as two masked priestly figures enact their geometric ritual in transfixed bodily states of spiritual ecstasy with Egyptian, Russian Orthodox, and Dervish movement material.* *Die Grünen Clowns,* as a suite, should shift from one mode to another with each scene.

Some casts in our 1987 performances thought they were under-rehearsed but that was how Laban worked. He would thrust responsibility onto the dancers, who, acquiring group improvisation skills, could live vividly in the moment and create the work on stage.

From *Die Grünen Clowns*, 1928 to *Green Clowns*, 1987 and 2008

Die Grünen Clowns is a work that my colleagues and I have re-created several times, sometimes in complete form, sometimes condensed, always using the same method, always with a different outcome.† It was a suite, an ensemble piece, the dancers depersonalized in white masks and skullcaps, dressed in uniform green, shapeless overalls.[22] I managed to glean enough information to attempt to recreate four of the six sections. The crux of the first scene, "Maschine," was Laban's response to the newly introduced and dreaded conveyor belt, which forced workers to labour at a vicious pace (Figure 2). I did not know exactly how the conveyor belt had been embodied so I experimented until my collaborator Dorothy Madden‡ offered a solution: dancers on all fours in a follow-the-leader line, the cheek of one joined to the rump of the one in front as they lurched forward and backward. The discomfort was real. In the second motif the dancers, now on their feet, were engaged in manufacture on a conveyor belt. Here I did not know just what operation Laban had used, but I did know the

---

*As a student Laban embraced Rosicrucianism. Study of forms of spiritual enlightenment since antiquity is part of the secret Rosicrucian discipline. Christopher McIntosh, *The Rosicrucians* (Boston: Weiser Books, 1998). No doubt *Ekstatischer* was informed by these studies.

†In Rio de Janeiro at a Laban International Conference with conference members in 2002, in Osaka with students of Kinki University in 2001, and in Volgograd, Russia, with Transitions Dance Company in 1997.

‡Dr. Dorothy Madden, professor emerita of University of Maryland, whose early training was with Wigman dancers Mary Lou Lee and Pola Nirenska, in Washington, D.C.

Figure 2. "Machine" in *Die Grünen Clowns, 1928 to Green Clowns, 2008*, performed by Trinity Laban dancers. Photograph copyright © Kyle Stevenson.

workshops at Pilkington's Tile Factory where Laban took me as an apprentice to assist him in his work as an industrial adviser.[*] All day long women turned sand into tiles using power pressure machinery and a conveyor belt that took the tiles for firing. It was arduous and tiring, repeating endlessly a sequence of action lasting approximately eleven seconds. I knew it well for I had observed the operations and written their sequence in minutely detailed movement notation. For *Green Clowns* this phrase was ideal. We found the dynamic effort rhythm of scooping sand awkwardly into a mould, flattening it hurriedly with a flickering stick, reaching for a handle, pulling it forcefully down, stepping on a pedal for an upward thrust, and lifting the delicate "tile" to deposit it on the belt. We discovered the points of discomfort in wrist, shoulder,

---

[*]Laban approached the problem in direct contrast to the Frederick Taylor–inspired work study managers who, with stopwatch in hand, encouraged workers to speed up. Laban set out to humanize an inhumane work situation, applying his principles of movement harmony by inserting a relief gesture at all the stress points, thus lengthening the phrase slightly but decreasing the cumulative stress and enabling operators to keep working for longer hours. See the booklet by Laban and F. C. Lawrence, *Lilt in Labour*, in The Laban Collection.

neck, and knee; felt the stress of speed, of force, and control; and we exaggerated their awkwardness.

What was lost by using material from the Pilkington factory instead of a mass-production factory in Germany of the 1920s? What was retained? The discomfort and tenor of the scene was what mattered and needed to be retained in order for spectators to empathize with Laban's rage at the dehumanizing mechanization of work.[23] Through my first-hand knowledge of the intricacy of the eleven-second phrase the dancers could experience the impact of mechanization on their bodies in exquisitely uncomfortable moves that could be exaggerated to enable spectators to feel the discomfort and dehumanization. Laban's form of expressionism required that the dancers show what they were actually experiencing, rather than mime an imagined event. It was his way of critiquing the culture surrounding him.

The second section of *Die Grünen Clowns* is a fast, frantic, athletic battle scene, "Krieg" (War). You hear the dancers' gasps, their footfalls, panting breath, and cries as masked and barely seeing they grapple with one another, fall to the ground, leap, and lash out (Figure 3). It is based on a simple improvisational structure for

Figure 3. Rehearsal of "War" in *Die Grünen Clowns, 1928 to Green Clowns, 2008*, performed by Trinity Laban dancers. Photograph copyright © Peter Sayers.

pairs of dancers who advance, engage, and retreat repeatedly, in a crescendo of force and speed and volume, progressing from a single, mildly antagonistic gesture to virtuosic, manipulative phrases of up to five "impacts." With timing open to the group's sense of crescendo, with a cry, they stop climactically. The dancers are literally exhausted and the audience hears it and cannot fail to feel it. In the Kinki University recreation in Osaka this scene was performed by male physical education students—more than a hundred of them in a huge drill hall. The martial arts techniques they had learned in their training automatically flavored their material, just as the Trinity Laban students brought contact improvisation to theirs. The former soldiers from the First World War who were in the Kammertanz production would have brought their own embodied experiences. As a student who had danced in Laban's *Chaos, Fight and Liberation,* clearly a reiteration in part of "Krieg," I had brought our vigorous eukinetic vocabulary. Using these differences reflects an ethos of Individualität; they were to Laban's taste in that he valued what the individual brought.

"Krieg" ends with a procession of the dying people (Figure 3). There exist two photographs of the procession from which its organization can be gleaned. The sound is of sighing as the last breath of life leaves each body. The method of improvisation is the same as before: a structure is repeated over and over again, in this case, experiencing a catastrophic blow somewhere in the body—producing an impulsive gasp that dies away in weakness—counterpointed with moments of supporting each other's trauma. With that intent, the dancers' eukinetic skills create the expressive phrasing and choreutic skills mould the three-dimensional form.

In the following scene, "Romanz" (Romance), a young man and woman who have been fighting and dying encounter one another and dare to love (Figure 4). Their masks are removed to reveal them as individuals, while their fellow Clowns anonymously watch and comment. It is a Romeo and Juliet romance situation. The audience has to be brought in to their dangerous but compelling attraction, to wonder if the relationship will blossom or fail, to appreciate the dilemma of the commenting Clowns, who egg them on, disapprove, are shaken by what they see, or hope for a better future (with performers deciding for themselves what their response might be). My task was to help a young man and

Figure 4. "Romance" in *Die Grünen Clowns, 1928 to Green Clowns, 2008*, performed by Trinity Laban dancers. Photograph copyright © Peter Sayers.

woman of the swinging 1980s find the intention for this attraction in a war-driven culture where free love was shameful and hidden, contraception unknown, and racism rife. This was even more an issue when Alison Curtis-Jones recreated *Clowns* again in 2008. A tentative approach and shock at cross-cultural liaisons were less easy to engender. Perhaps it was the recent Bosnian conflict that offered the duo, the commenting Clowns, and the spectators a point of entry.

The duo was recreated with structures provided by relationship analysis in Laban's notation (aware of, approach, retreat, near to, touch, surround, share weight, lift), nothing more, nothing less, in an order that could embody the ebb and flow of first love. The pair had to find the intention for each change, and to find the dynamic that spoke of tentativeness or eagerness. Ausdruckstanz is not acting. It is created by feeling in every pore of your skin and every muscle of your being the dynamic tensions that arise from a response to the world, diffused throughout your body. In 2010 four duos were rehearsed, all different in surface form, all identical in process and content. They were each danced at different performances, the watching Clowns responding to the differences.

Did it matter that we did not know the exact order of the improvisation? Did we lose something by that? To my mind it was far more important for the dancers to discover how to create Ausdruckstanz that could draw the spectator into an expressionist duo. The exact surface form of the duo of 1928 paled in comparison, in my view. What came through was the scene as a whole, the young couple exposed by their lack of mask and the Greek choruslike Clowns framing them.

The fourth scene, *Klub der Sonderlinge* (The Club of the Eccentric People), is a fast-moving satire on human weakness. The Clowns enter unmasked with a phrase of non-sequitur moves: a goose step, noisy kissing, petulant finger wagging, teetering on tiptoe. As the scene evolves they are revealed in moments that should be private: they scratch, bite, poke, shake, lick each other; they spit, shout, and laugh; they follow pretentious leaders like thoughtless sheep and end haranguing the audience, advancing toward them in structured vocal mayhem. The tone is not amusing but gross, daring, infused with digging irony and provocative *rausch.**

What Was Lost and What Was Gained and By Whom?

For Laban's heritage we gained the beginning of a shift in attitude toward the man—a realization that he was a theatre artist, not only the creator of a notation and analysis system. My purpose in 1987 was to demonstrate to dancers and spectators that this man's forgotten work was worth refinding, both for educational

---

*The material for this scene was drawn from photographs and from Laban's seventieth birthday party, where he reenacted, informally, fragments of scenes from his comedies and revues with members of Theatre Workshop and students from the Art of Movement Studio. There is no adequate English equivalent to the German word *rausch*, popular among the German expressionists; the closest approximation is "provocative raucousness."

and cultural reasons. For the dancers it was an absorbing process. Here was a work that engaged them with human issues they found relevant. Here was a method that allowed them to discover how to speak with their whole being—mind, body, soul, and critical self—and how to dialogue with the past. In the dance culture in London of 1987, the vogue for American work was too strong for an impact of any significance to be made by these first-draft performances. My aim was to keep the research alive and pass it on, to keep Laban's image as a man of theatre in focus.

It was not until 2008 that an opportunity arose for a well-funded performance to be mounted as a part of the celebrations of Laban-based work worldwide fifty years after his death. On that occasion the concept that surface form was not the most significant issue of authenticity was brought to the fore through juxtaposing *Clowns* with a reconstruction of Yvonne Rainer's *Trio A* from, among other documentary materials, the Labanotation score, and a remounting of Graham's *Diversion of Angels* from film, score, and memory, all of which were undertaken in the same season. Each project was a matter of getting the balance right in the process/product continuum. Curtis-Jones's recreation of *Clowns* was received with acclaim. Such juxtaposition enabled the value of recreating the Laban work to be judged in terms of what it offered the institution named after him as well as spectators in 2008.

Trinity Laban as an institution had moved on since 1987, as had dancers and the public. European dance heritage was recognized once again through, among others, the Tanztheater of Pina Bausch and the radical dance theatre of William Forsythe in Frankfurt, both of whom ackowledged a debt to Laban: Bausch through her association with Kurt Jooss, Forsythe through his use of choreutics. Trinity Laban is now a world-class conservatory so the ratio of value given to performance over everything else is high. The dancers have a capacity for performing articulate movement and Curtis-Jones had to turn that into a capacity to create articulate movement from intent. Contemporary dance in London is a postmodern if not a post-postmodern art form where anything goes, so the public is ready for something new. Spectators and dancers are less used to the kind of expressivity that Laban's method offers but they received it with open arms.

147

Issues in Recreating Rudolf Laban's *Nacht*, 1927

For spring of 2010 Curtis-Jones and I prepared, and she put into action, a first draft of a suite from Laban's *Nacht*. Recreation of any sort begs the question: is the new production sufficiently imbued with the originator's style to warrant his or her name being attached to it? Will *Night, 2010* be a Rudolf Laban work or will it be an Alison Curtis-Jones work? We have examples from Matthew Bourne in *Swan Lake* and Mats Ek in *Giselle* of reworking a classic and developing an updated interpretation of it with the original choreographer's name replaced by their own. There have been productions of *Les Noces* using Stravinsky's score that have paid attention to the narrative in the music but have abandoned Bronislava Nijinska's original choreography. We also have Ann Hutchinson Guest's refinding of Nijinsky's *L'Après-midi d'un Faune* in which, for her, the visual image achieved was more significant than how Nijinsky did what he did. Where were my collaborator and I on this continuum in our recreation of *Nacht*? The grant I obtained was quite clearly to bring forward a work of Laban and the opportunity for production lay in the historical studies by the Trinity Laban students, so we set about it within those constraints and opportunities.

One important difference between the *Green Clowns* and *Nacht* recreations was that Curtis-Jones had not had first-hand experience of working with Laban. However, she had studied with me at master's level, had danced in performances of *Green Clowns*, and had recreated Laban's work for two seasons. Nevertheless, we had to ensure that this gap was addressed. While her credentials for undertaking a recreation were impressive, she was also a choreographer in her own right. Once the rehearsals started, I had to ensure that the emerging work did not tip over from Ausdruckstanz into Curtis-Jones's style of twenty-first-century postmodernism.

The resources we amassed included the chapter entitled "Night" in Laban's autobiography about the dark side of city life in Paris and Munich between 1899 and 1910: "The rottenness and decadence of our so highly praised culture stared me harshly in the face." Of the work *Nacht* he wrote, "The play opened with a crowd of mechanically grinning society men and women, followed by all I had felt when I first met life in the big city." He tells the reader that the piece is about greed and covetousness and the adoration of three idols: dollars, depravity, and deceit. The critics stated that there was no letup in the onslaught on the audience. The spectators of 1927 were shocked and they booed. Laban admits the work was an "absolute flop" because "they appeared to be touched in their secret craving."[24] Considering this performance history, why did I decide to propose it for recreation?* The theme of *Nacht* seemed near to the realities of our time. Deceit and "greed for dollars," as Laban expressed it—people making money out of others—seemed only too real in a time of bankers' bonuses, risk-heavy stockbroking, and innocent people losing their jobs. The drink-and-drugs culture that he witnessed and loathed in Paris, reiterated in the Berlin cabaret culture of the 1930s, was only too obvious in the habits of urban youth in city centers in 2010. *Nacht* was a work about people of all eras, as the 1927 program note stated. Laban saw the work as a critique of the ever-recurring bleak side of human nature.

The resources included headdress and facial makeup designs from the Tanzarchiv in Leipzig; detailed rehearsal notes from the original production written by Elinor Warsitz, the rehearsal director, housed in the National Resource Centre for Dance in Guildford; and a photograph, press reviews, and programs from The Laban Collection. Despite a search in the Berlin Akademie der

---

*I could have chosen plenty of other works, perhaps *Gaukelei* (1923) or *Ritterballett* (1927). For any recreation there has to be something in the work that is not so bound to its time that viewers can make theatrical sense out of its original context. How might a 2010 audience take to a ballet about knights and their ladies, ghosts and jousting, nuns and peasant girls, pageboys and maidens dancing together? The music for *Ritterballett* was an orchestral score of that name by Beethoven said to have been written after a visit to the knight's castle at Mergentheim. Laban made the original for an event in Bad Mergentheim, a spa town dominated by its castle, in which Laban rehearsed the work. The company repeated it on the same weekend that *Nacht* and *Titan* were performed. As Laban wrote, "In the *Ballet of the Knights* the past is caught, in *The Night* the present of our time and in *Titan* I saw the promise of the future" (Laban, *A Life for Dance*, 180). The performances of *Ritterballett* "aroused great delight" and appealed to the bourgeois members of the public and press in contrast to *Nacht*'s loud rejection. *Ritterballett* was a safe work with a remote theme requiring a live orchestra, and I saw no purpose in bringing it forward for today.

Gaukelei had already been rechoreographed twice, in 1930 by Kurt Jooss for the Essen Opera House with his own company and in 1935 by Aurel Milloss for the Dusseldorf Opera House ballet. As a critique of tyrannical and fickle leadership, its theme was particularly relevant for the political struggles of the 1930s in Germany. Laban clearly wanted his theatre work to arouse his audience, but in 2010 tyrannical leadership on the scale of *Gaukelei* was not a topic in the news. I could see no way to make *Gaukelei* speak as it had done, so it fell away as an option for recreation.

Künste, no trace was found of Rudolf Wagner Regeny's music for the piece.

The original production had been a full-evening work. We would have twenty-five minutes maximum. I took courage from one critic of the period who surmised that, were *Nacht* radically condensed, it would have a sharp statement to make. That sharp statement needed to be a clear contrast to the chic dances about depravity that had appeared in Paris. Parisian chic and Berlin crudity were distinct modes of theatre for distinct spectators. Serge Diaghilev's ballets were performed in prestigious venues for the smart set, while Laban's works were intended for everyman. I recalled the contrast between Oskar Schlemmer of the Bauhaus and the Ausdruckstanz community. The figures in Schlemmer's *Triadic Ballet* were "abstract figures, completely divested of corporeality"[25] while Laban's were social, gendered, and thoroughly corporeal. The Berlin cabaret culture with the grotesque dances of Valeska Gert or outrageous nudity and eroticism of Anita Berber were nearer Laban's comment in *Nacht*.

Study of these contrasts was part of the preparation for *Nacht*, made more pertinent because Lesley-Anne Sayers was studying the Ballets Russes 1928 production of *Ode* concurrently with our own research. We had to think of the audiences to which Laban's mode of theatricality was pitched if we were to find its worth as a statement with the capacity to disturb. Curtis-Jones had to find fresh movement material for the different scenes. Warsitz's rehearsal notes showed that clear groupings and floor patterns mattered, that precision mattered, and that individual treatment of the "steps" also played a part. Gestural material was included as were social dance steps and facial expression. Of the original thirteen scenes, only one was identified in Warsitz's notes. Moreover, there was scant indication of how the movements described fitted into the work as a whole, and no indication of intention or narrative or mode of theatrical treatment. While clearly useful to Warsitz the notes did not take our research very far.

We settled on attempting four scenes for the 2010 draft of *Nacht*. Laban's scenes had no names so we devised our own working titles. The first was "Smart Set," a scene critiquing "the absolute peak of useless pretence" of the chattering classes and their rivalry to be smarter and more noticeable than anyone else.[26] The second scene, "Stockbroker," took as its theme making money from others through gambling, by rival jobbers jostling in the stock exchange,[27] through competitive dice and cards, by touts' hand signals at the racecourse, through greed to grab what others have. The third scene was set in a sleazy "Tanzbar" with cabaret singer, where the undercover sexual freedom so subtly stated in Berlin cabaret songs[28] was the material.[29] The fourth scene was the reality of the monotony and dehumanization of work and worklessness, "Monotony" being the one scene named in Warsitz's notes.

We looked at the balance between the semiotic content that the themes would offer and the method of transforming them into expressionist phenomena. Theatre in essence entails finding the proportion of sign to phenomenon (the so-called "binocular vision") of theatre as articulated by Bert States.[30] How open and accessible would the signs of "depravity, deceit and greed for dollars" be? Did Laban want to make the work an obvious depiction for the spectators to take in, or did he want them to bring their own imagination and knowledge to their engagement with the performance, in other words, to make their own transaction with it?[*] It was the latter approach that Curtis-Jones would seek to put in place by transforming the sign-rich movement sources into eukinetic and choreutic phenomena, as we believed Laban had done in his 1927 production. How Curtis-Jones achieved this is her part of the dialogue and remains to be written. Our collaborative preproduction research was devised to give her practice a solid starting point.

Documenting Process or Product and the Digital Age

Concerned with the ever-present problem of how to document, in the same medium, the concepts, the studio work, and the

---

[*]We had to decide whether the signs in *Nacht* would be "in the trace," that is, embedded in the media of the work and accessible to attentive spectators, or *poietic*, that is, known to be there by the makers and performers, but partially hidden from the average spectator although accessible through knowledge of the culture surrounding the performance, or *esthesic*, that is, not there at all in the work's fabric but imagined to be there by the spectators. Jean-Jacques Nattiez, *Music and Discourse: Toward a Semiology of Music*, trans. Carolyn Abbate (Princeton, NJ: Princeton University Press, 1990); Preston-Dunlop and Sanchez-Colberg, *Dance and the Performative*, 268.

performance that make up a dance work, I set out in 2007 to research how digital means might offer a solution. Supported by the Arts and Humanities Research Council[31] my task was to look at the challenges of documenting creative processes. William Forsythe's multimedia work *The Loss of Small Detail* was the exemplar since Trinity Laban had been given the archives on *Loss* by the Forsythe Foundation. That offered a unique opportunity (1) to record how this iconic choreographer worked and (2) to develop a documenting method useful to the profession as a whole.

This is not the place to present the interactive digital maps of Forsythe's work that were the result[32] but rather to point to significant issues that arose from it. The first concerns the method. With Plymouth University's Institute of Digital Art and Technology unit we decided on a mapping process on screen, using readily available software, to be illustrated by visual, moving, and sound image clips. Creating twenty-nine maps on screen, I addressed Forsythe's way of working with his company, the concepts he focused on, and the transformative modalities he used to make the solos, duos, and quintets with his dancers. Further maps addressed the spoken texts and their transformation and performance, Thom Willems's role as composer of a sonic environment, the concepts and references that fed Willems's curiosity, Forsythe's experiments in lighting, his ideas on the film and scenographic elements, and what he expected from his spectators. Visual and sound clips and scans of original drawings were selected from the archival holdings and placed within the maps to connect concept with practice. The whole package was transferred digitally into an interactive web file. The reader could choose any map from the index, and navigate through to pop up film fragments of rehearsals or texts or film loops or discussions about lighting, and so on. The *Loss* maps have a clear use for anyone curious to know how this astonishing work was made and for dance professionals considering how to document their own creative processes.

The research revealed a pertinent aspect of recreation, for Forsythe is a recreator of his own work. The original *Loss* was produced in 1987, version two in early 1991, and version three in late 1991. When I saw it in 2005, it had a new version of its opener, "Second Detail." Looking at the film clips of the versions, a casual observer would say they are not the same work but Forsythe views them all as *Loss.*[*] Why? *Loss,* like *Green Clowns,* is a process work. Its authenticity lies in a repeated coherence of source and procedure. The sources remain the same for each version; the concept of loss through translating and retranslating one thing into another is the prime concept,[33] embodied in the strands of multimedia theatre: film, snow falling, text, dancing. Further sources are Forsythe's use of images and words from marked books, the five characters and what they say, and the choreographer's drawings for *Loss,* a selection of which appear translated into set and props in each version. The authenticity of the dancing lies in Forsythe's original movement combinations that never appear in their raw state, but are nevertheless there, modified by the dancers as solos and doubly modified as duos and quintets. Forsythe is demonstrating that there is "a loss of small detail" in recreation while simultaneously celebrating the result.

Another practical scholar is Sarah Rubidge. Her research on the open work interrogates existing philosophical theories of identity. She argues that

> radically "open" works have no "original" author-determined performance or instantiation against which all other performances can be compared. . . . The very point of such an open work is that each performance is merely one performance amongst many variant performances generated from the same set of instructions.[34]

Rubidge's interactive installations, Forsythe's multimedia work *Loss,* and Laban's expressionism all share the attribute that their authenticity lies in their processes rather than their products. Through their methods they demonstrate that the works are not in "oblivion" at all but are alive and well.

As to the mapping process itself, it is seen as a breakthrough in the problem of integrating concept with practice in a user-friendly way for a digitally dependent culture.[35] This kind of detailed mapping for and by the practitioner may be complemented by a documentary directed by an outside eye and that

---

[*] In *Expedition Ballet,* Eva Elizabeth Fischer's documentary on Forsythe for Süddeutscher Rundfunk in 1987, Forsythe states his view that "the premiere is not the end of the process but the beginning."

is where Lesley-Anne Sayers and I began to discuss our different experiences of recreation and its documentation strategies or
processes—mine from the artists' perspectives, hers from the outside eye of the dance and visual arts historian.

Lesley Anne-Sayers on the Recreation and Documentation of Ballets from the 1920s

I have several interests in recreation from studying its applications
in historical research to exploring how we might creatively inter-
act with our dance legacy and how we can document and make
transparent its processes and dialogues for a wider audience. In
recent years I have participated in recreation in two ways: the
staging of "lost" works and the documentation of the recreative
process. In 2005 I acted as artistic coordinator of the Princeton
University staging of *Le Pas d'Acier*, a ballet whose original collaborators were Sergei Prokofiev, Léonide Massine, and Georgi
Yakoulov, performed by the Ballets Russes in 1927. This work involved a substantial amount of reconstruction but also offered
new choreography by Millicent Hodson; its status in relation to
preserving, rediscovering, or simply interacting with our dance
legacy was fascinating and ambiguous. I received an Arts and Humanities Research Council grant to document the recreation of
the work in the form of a DVD documentary.[36]

Since then I have made a second documentary on the recreation of Rudolf Laban's 1928 work *Die Grünen Clowns* at Trinity
Laban Conservatoire in London directed by Alison Curtis-Jones
in 2008.[37] Drawing on these experiences, I am currently involved
in researching the ballet *Ode*, originally performed by the Ballets Russes in 1928, for planned recreation in 2011, and developing a web-based resource on the work to act as an interface
for the spectator and a means of deepening access to the work
in its broadest sense and to its processes of recreation.[*] I come
at recreation from an unusual angle in that my major research
interest in dance has focused on scenography. I try to access a historical work through its set design and visual conception in order

---

[*]Following the passing of Lesley-Anne Sayers the project to recreate *Ode* has had to be
shelved, based as it was on her scenographic research—Anne Daye.

to understand the work's visual approach to and orchestration of space.

The challenge to researchers afforded by reconstruction of such works as *Le Pas d'Acier* is not just to interpret the surviving material through historiography, but also to produce an interpretation in practice that is valid in two respects: first, in terms of being true to the work as a whole as distinct from any one performance of it (like the premiere) and second, in terms of exploring and revealing the work's potential for future performance. If *reconstruction* is defined as seeking to repeat the parameters of an original performance, by *recreation* is meant practices that establish a freer relationship to an original work and an enhanced dialogue with the past. Such in-depth and analytical, but also highly creative, responses to earlier works have always enriched the arts: for example, in music Ludwig van Beethoven's *Diabelli Variations*; in visual arts Pablo Picasso's reworking and transformation of Édouard Manet's paintings or Diego Velasquez' *Las Meninas*, or David Hockney's version of Picasso's *Massacre in Korea* (2003); in dance Mats Ek's *Giselle* (1982) or Matthew Bourne's *Swan Lake* (1995). All of these are recreations of various kinds, and contribute to scholarly discourse and artistic innovation through exploration, transformation, and renewal. At issue here is not the simple case of one work being inspired by an earlier one, but the more complex one in which a new work emerges from a close analysis and creative dialogue with an earlier work and its contexts. Such works find a creative methodology, framework, and inspiration today through those processes of interaction. One of the fascinating things to come out of working closely with two such different works from the same period as *Le Pas d'Acier* and *Die Grünen Clowns* is that the legacy that comes to the fore is so much more than individual past works; it is the relationships between works and the artistic and sociocultural debates they address in vitally different ways.

In this paper I focus on these two very different approaches to recreation that I have been fortunate to witness or be closely involved with in recent years. My enthusiasm for re-creation and my belief in its value and vital importance to dance as an art form has come out of direct involvement with the processes of recreation and my experience as a spectator of the work of other practitioners. It has also been informed by the experience of working closely with Millicent Hodson and an ongoing dialogue with Valerie Preston-Dunlop.

Le Pas d'Acier 1927

Finding the Ballet

The possibility of recreating Sergei Prokofiev's *Le Pas d'Acier*, originally mounted on Serge Diaghilev's Ballets Russes in 1927, arose from my Ph.D. research into its scenography by Georgi Yakoulov.[*] Set in the chaos and famine of a postrevolutionary Russian railway station that transforms into a factory for the second act, *Le Pas d'Acier* was inspired by Russian constructivism, much in vogue in Paris during the early 1920s. While the ballet was based in the classical technique, it also drew movement inspiration from dramatic gesture and characterization, as well as Vsevolod Meyerhold's biomechanics and concepts of the machine. The ballet's construction was also influenced by cinema and montage. This was the era of Sergei Eisenstein's films, Alexander Rodchenko's photography, the machine dance, social and political revolution, utopian ideals, and geometric abstraction.[38]

A more personal context was the struggle of the individual creators—all of them Russian—to make a ballet about the ideals of the Russian Revolution. Prokofiev and Massine were both Russian exiles following the First World War and years of revolution. Yakoulov, Armenian by birth and residing in Moscow, was the only member of the team who was a Soviet citizen. The ballet was created just before Prokofiev made his first return visit to

---

[*]Anne Daye has edited the references for Sayers's portion of this article. Readers should see earlier publications by Sayers for full details of the sources used to recreate *Le Pas d'Acier*. Lesley-Anne Sayers, "*Le pas d'acier (1927): A study in the historiography and reconstruction of George Jakulov's set design for Diaghilev's 'Soviet Ballet,'*" doctoral dissertation, Bristol University, 1999; Lesley-Anne Sayers, "Re-Discovering Diaghilev's *Pas d'Acier*," *Dance Research*, vol. 18, no. 2 (Winter 2000), 163–185; Lesley-Anne Sayers, "Diaghilev's 'Soviet Ballet': Reconstructing Jakulov's Set Design for *Le Pas d'acier* (1927)," in Stephanie Jordan, ed., *Preservation Politics: Dance Revived, Reconstructed, Remade* (London: Dance Books, 2000), 30–40; model of the set of *Le Pas d'acier* constructed by Lesley-Anne Sayers, exhibited in *Diaghilev and the Golden Age of the Ballets Russes, 1909–1929*, at The Victoria and Albert Museum, September 25, 2010–January 9, 2011.

Soviet Russia in 1927, pending his permanent return in 1935. It is closely connected to the brief period of renewed contact between the Parisian and Russian avant-gardes during the Lenin years, and the liberalism of the New Economic Policy.

Le Pas d'Acier may be the closest ballet ever came to a constructivist work celebrating early Soviet and avant-garde ideals, and yet to this day it has never been staged in Russia. By the time the ballet was realized in 1927, it was already too late for such a work to meet with the approval of Stalinist artistic authorities. Too modernist for the Soviets, it was seen as Bolshevik propaganda in the West. Although it was one of the most performed works in Diaghilev's Ballets Russes repertory until the company's demise in 1929, the discomfort over its politics may at least partly explain its virtual absence from the canonical texts of dance history.* Accounts of the work suffered from a mixture of Cold War politics and artistic criteria stressing the values of neoclassicism and high modernism. With several utilitarian costumes and lack of "starring roles," the ballet was not popular with the dancers. In short, little trace of its colorful pyrotechnical and multimedia performance remained; Pas d'Acier was very much a "lost" work. However, archival research and practical, studio, and workshop exploration could be employed to access the interactive elements among the different media of the work and thus to uncover substantial aspects of the original. No known recordings in notation or film of the choreography exist, but even so, parts of this most ephemeral aspect of the work could, to some extent, be "found" through reconstructive methodologies. Examining the ballet's surviving source materials, engaging in historical-contextual analysis, making a working model of Yakoulov's set design, and exploring the possibilities of interaction among set, music, and dance yielded clues with regard to choreography.

---

*Audiences received *Le Pas d'Acier* with interest, particularly in London, and it remained in active repertory probably more because of Prokofiev's music than the choreography or the stage design. The following sources recount the reception of the work: Serge Grigoriev, *The Diaghilev Ballet, 1909–1929* (London: Constable & Co., 1953), 238–39; Nesta Macdonald, *Diaghilev Observed by Critics in England and the United States, 1911–1929* (New York: Dance Horizons, 1975), 348–51; Leslie Norton, *Léonide Massine and the 20th Century Ballet* (Jefferson, NC: McFarland & Co., 2004), 113–18.

Recreating Le Pas d'Acier *in 2005*

Prokofiev scholar Simon Morrison, professor of music at Princeton University, invited me from 2003 to 2004 to be artistic coordinator of the staged recreation of *Le Pas d'Acier* and to remake the original set design from the model I had built as part of my thesis on the scenography (Figure 5). There was no possibility of reconstructing the movement as Massine's choreography had been lost. Dame Alicia Markova, who had danced in the ballet at the age of sixteen, was still alive during the early stages of my initial research and recalled what she could; however, nearly seventy years had elapsed since the work's last performance. I was at the time very focused on questions about the set design, although Markova probably never saw the ballet from the front. What she remembered was her physical experience of how difficult it was to climb the rope ladders in bare feet and how distorted and angular Massine's choreography had felt; moreover, she volunteered how ugly and utilitarian the costumes for the factory scene had seemed to the dancers.

In recreating *Le Pas d'Acier* we found ourselves on a path that deviated from any established model of either reconstruction or recreation. Our ambition lay *toward* reconstruction: we wanted to explore the process undergone by those who created the original work. We had the music and we had the set design, which was essentially an apparatus for dancers to perform with and on, laying down strict pathways for the choreography. I had found a copy of the original scenario among uncatalogued papers at the Prokofiev Archive at Goldsmiths College in London. This scenario was profoundly revealing; it had been co-written in 1925 by Prokofiev and Yakoulov, in close collaboration, well before a choreographer entered the process. The music and a model set had been created for this scenario. It took some time to unravel the different source materials and to understand their place in the processes of creation.[*]

It was particularly fascinating to listen to the music with the original scenario and with the original set design before us, discovering and hearing how this work had originally been envisaged

---

[*]Lesley-Anne Sayers and Tim Rolt, dir., Le Pas d'Acier *1925: A Ballet by Serge Prokofiev* (London: IDM Ltd. in association with Rapid Eye Movies, 2006). The second DVD in the collection, *Rediscovering* Le Pas d'Acier *1925: A Documentary Film*, documents this stage of the recreation process particularly clearly.

Figure 5. Lesley-Anne Sayers's model of Georgi Yakoulov's 1925 design for *Le Pas d'Acier*. Photograph copyright © Peter Sayers.

in 1925. Prokofiev's music had probably never been heard as we were now hearing it: in interaction with Yakoulov's cinematic set design and the stage action. Sweet sellers, street vendors, sailors, and an orator with a book on an elastic band are among the vivid characters and stereotypes that people the first act of the original scenario and they can be readily identified in the music. The arrival of the train, so central to Yakoulov's design, and his cinematic use of theatrical gauze were also vividly present in Prokofiev's score.

My interest shifted away from the 1927 performance as such because the ballet had been radically altered when Massine took over the staging in 1927, and the train and gauze had been dropped. Ironically, more of the surviving source materials relate to the original unrealized collaboration than to the work as actually produced by the Ballets Russes. Records of the performance were enough to tell us about significant differences and adaptations, but while we could reconstruct the unrealized original set design, we had no records of the actual set used in performance and little information on Massine's adapted action. Surviving costumes came, obviously, from the performance.

All of these disparities serve to foreground how recreation involves interaction with a complex array of source materials. It was also necessary to experience artistic processes and to consider contextual materials in great detail in order to discover the complex identity of the work. While it would be a fallacy to believe that we could reproduce the 1925 work as originally projected or the 1927 adapted performance by Massine, what we could offer was a rich experience of the work, layered by multidimensional (and time-lapse) understandings of it.

For the Princeton production, Millicent Hodson created entirely new choreography, informed by the structure that the set design provided. She was aware of the original scenario, the music, and the research we had gathered on the work itself, the artists involved, and the work's artistic and sociocultural contexts. Hodson's in-depth knowledge of the period and of Diaghilev's Ballets Russes, as well as her reconstruction experience, greatly enriched our entry into the work. She began by introducing the student dancers from the advanced performance course at Princeton to scenes from Dziga Vertov's 1929 film *Man with a Movie Camera*, which facilitated their entry into the artistic terrain of the work.

The influence of film and its potential to inform the choreo-graphy was a serendipitous discovery stemming not from docu-mentary evidence but rather from practical exploration of the parameters set up by the set design.

My exploration of *Le Pas d'Acier* started life purely as research in scenography toward a doctorate. It was unusual to start an analysis of a ballet through a close study of the set design, but in this instance the set design turned out to be the key to open-ing the door on this lost work. As a complex piece of apparatus, intricately designed for action, it enabled key aspects of the per-formance to be discovered, as dancers interacted with its physical structures in conjunction with the music.

In keeping with the theory and aims of constructivism, the original set was intended to challenge the choreographer and dancers to use their bodies in athletic ways and to respond to the three-dimensionality of space. The choreographer should orches-trate space in a manner that draws on the principles of montage, as found, for example, in Sergei Eisenstein's films. In terms of de-vising the choreography for the recreation, Yakoulov's set design offered tremendous physical challenge and opportunity with its tracks for the dance: huge platforms to mount, ladders and stairs to be scaled, hammers to be wielded in the factory parts of the set, spaces within spaces to be inhabited, and powerful spinning wheels of enormous size.

Exploring the intended interaction between music and de-sign brought out the fascinating collaboration between designer and composer, and the music offered clues to cinematic visual effects. *Le Pas d'Acier* has much to tell about Prokofiev's devel-opment as a composer for ballet; his close work with Yakoulov on musical-scenographic interactions has rich implications for Prokofiev's later ballet and film scores.[39]

The recreation also affords insights into constructivists' utopian attitudes toward the machine—believed to offer mankind opportunities in a heroic rather than a dehumanized future. The Princeton performance and my documentary film add to our knowledge about the theatrical practices of Russian construc-tivism. While constructivist set design for plays in the dramatic theatre forms part of our understanding of this movement in art history, how the constructivist ethos played out in Soviet ballet is less well known.[40] Moreover, the research on and reenvisioning of

Le Pas d'Acier sheds further light on the depth of interest in constructivism in Paris and London in the 1920s. The constructivist mission was to impact on all aspects of life, but the movement is of necessity only partially understood when separated into media-specific histories. In recreating the work, the intersections among technology, design, music, dance, and theatre were brought into a single focus. One could see how Prokofiev and Yakoulov intended this convergence of media as a theatrical realization of constructivism. Not the least value inherent in the Princeton recreation of the work in 2005 arose from its multimedia relations and the fact that neither performers nor audiences in the 1920s were accustomed to experiencing works in which the scenography played so extensive and central a part (Figure 6).

If ever a ballet was primarily a set designer's ballet, *Le Pas d'Acier* is undoubtedly it. The work serves to remind us of the creative potential of the poetics of space,[*] and how developments in scenography and lighting have contributed to choreographic development. These lessons are easily lost or temporarily forgotten in any art form but particularly in one that is as ephemeral as dance performance.

Perhaps the most thrilling of our many discoveries in exploring this work was the extraordinary level of interactivity and multimedia theatre of the original. Today, of course, spectators would expect that, and it is no doubt why, at least in part, the work resonated with their experience in 2005. Whereas a reconstruction might be undertaken for purely historical interest, it is difficult to imagine why anyone would become involved in a recreation unless he or she felt that the work had a resonance in the present. For me, recreation is not primarily about preservation of a dance legacy or historical study; it is about transformation and renewal.

The Documentation and Dissemination of the Recreation

The recreation of *Le Pas d'Acier* was staged at the Berlind Theatre at Princeton in 2005. Quite separately from the production aspect

---

[*]Sayers clearly had specific insights into the phenomenological interpretation of the set in performance. Here, she makes an oblique reference to Gaston Bachelard, *The Poetics of Space: The Classic Look at How We Experience Intimate Spaces* (Boston: Beacon Press, 1994; orig. 1958)—A.D.

Figure 6. Factory scene from *Le Pas d'Acier* recreation (2005), performed by Princeton University dancers. Photograph copyright © Peter Sayers.

of the project, I had received an award from the Arts and Humanities Research Council in the U.K. to document the processes involved in the recreation, from which would emerge a DVD to be released in 2006.[41] I therefore embarked on a process of documentation, putting myself in the position of generating insights from the perspectives of both an insider and an outsider to the project. In 2008, after gaining the opportunity to document Valerie Preston-Dunlop's recreation of *Die Grünen Clowns,* I operated exclusively as an outside eye on the process. In making both documentaries, my interest has focused primarily on how best to create an interface for the spectator. I wished to address the kinds of questions many audience members may ask about this kind of historical work: What am I looking at and how close is this production to the original work? How have the directors of the project come up with this interpretation? What exactly is its relationship to the original work? All of these questions relate to a fundamental issue of concern to viewers both inside and outside the arts—the question of validity. To what extent does the recreated work bear a credible and cogent relationship to the work as intended by its original artists and as received by the audiences of the time?

In the documentary of *Le Pas d'Acier,* Morrison pairs the music with the scenario, bringing this relationship to light in a particularly compelling way. The curator of the Prokofiev Archive in London tells of my excitement in discovering the scenario among the quantity of papers in her care. Scenes of dance rehearsal show Hodson at work building the movement with the students, and these are interspersed with her talking directly to camera about the resources she used to reinvent the choreography.*

In embarking on the documentary of *Die Grünen Clowns,* my goal was at first to try to capture something of the creative process that is otherwise unseen by the work's audiences. I also wanted to glimpse the sources and strategies involved, having recognized that they were markedly different from my own in the

---

*Currently, as the only source available for understanding the process undertaken for the choreography, it is particularly valuable for students of the recreation.

Pas d'Acier project, as well as those I had observed in Millicent Hodson and Kenneth Archer's reconstructions of ballets from the 1920s. I was hungry to peruse photographs, descriptions of dances in critical reviews, and all the usual "outside-eye" materials that help reconstructors and recreators to establish validity in conventional terms. However, Preston-Dunlop often reminded me to avoid thinking like an "outside eye" and instead to engage with the creative procedures in the studio; only in this engagement, she insisted, lay the means to accessing the historical work.

I filmed classes of all kinds related to the project as well as studio rehearsals and the footage grew and grew. Preston-Dunlop and Curtis-Jones endured lengthy interviews in which the aim was to articulate exactly what was involved in all the processes taking place. We captured wonderful moments as the students creatively engaged with the project, transforming materials through their own individual qualities as performers and thoughtful artists. As I followed the recreation of *Die Grünen Clowns* during a few intense weeks in February 2008, a narrative emerged to reveal a reconstruction process, based on Laban's own methods, of making the work anew, especially with young performers of today. This part of the documentary records the dynamic processes of practical reconstruction in a manner that would not be possible in printed publication.

In the case of both documentaries, the filming of the performance offers a significant record to posterity, allowing dance historians and the general public greater access to two significant and altogether different works of modernist dance (albeit each performance of *Die Grünen Clowns*, being improvisational, is distinct). One should note that both projects were undertaken within educational institutions, specifically, programs for the study of the heritage of music and dance. Their primary function was to enrich the understandings and skills of undergraduate students. The documentaries serve as testimony to the engagement and transformation of the students involved in these projects. Such resources lend new insights into the embodied, experiential, and process-oriented nature of recreation, which can also inform the larger community of dance and music scholars, as well as a wider public.

Recreating *Ode*

Finding an Interface for the Spectator

My current interest in recreation focuses on the 1928 ballet *Ode*—composed by Nicolas Nabokov, choreographed by Massine, and designed by Pavel Tchelitchew—and encompasses the goal of making the processes of recreation transparent by placing them in the foreground from the outset.[*] Learning from past projects, I want to approach its documentation and dissemination in a different way. I want to ask to what extent does our *interaction* with source materials in varying formats impose structures that limit or stimulate frameworks that enhance the validity of the recreation and enrich the quality of the experience of the work? Related to this question are others about what it is we want to document about a dance work in general and a recreation in particular. Certainly, we can record the performance in a number of ways, but what about the creative processes and which aspects of them are important? When it comes to documentation, clearly, intention is very important, and questions such as who is the documentation for, for what purpose, and how should it be disseminated are key.

Ode may have been the first ballet to use film projections as part of its radical exploration of performance space. As such, it is an important precursor to the scenographic approaches very visible in dance today. *Ode* also provides an ideal focal point for tracing earlier interactions between dance and the visual arts. For example, via scenography *Ode*, like Renaissance dance, evokes ideas of Man's place within the cosmos. This ballet's audiovisual meditation on the nature of existence also echoed discourses that were coming to the fore as a result of evolving photographic techniques and technologies in scenography, which coincided with new conceptions of how the body resided in space. *Ode*'s geometric fascinations reflect the geometry of classical ballet, modernist abstraction, Bauhaus experimentation, and explorations of

---

[*]Although this project was not finished, the questions Sayers poses here are important for the direction of future studies in recreation and for the use of new media in the documentation of its processes and performances—A.D.

the body within spatial structures—known as choreutics in Laban studies.

As I develop a web resource on scenography for dance with *Ode* as its first case study, I am attempting to track the thinking that takes place as the researcher encounters the original source materials and contexts. As the recreation process proceeds, other artists and scholars involved in the project may contribute to the web resource, thus thickening the dialogue between practice and archive. One area of resonance for today's viewers of *Ode* might be its perspective on the body and sexuality; a powerful undercurrent in the ballet concerns the architecture of the male body, often veiled and abstracted. But this is only one of several ways in which contemporary discourse might vitally affect how we read a work. *Ode* also focuses on the majesty of nature, as revealed through photography and other media technologies—just as today we are astonished by images of the newly visible universe. *Ode* is preoccupied with man's relationship to nature and the environment, albeit in a very different way from how we are in our own time. Above all, *Ode* fastens on fundamental forms of all kinds—those found in Euclidean and sacred geometry, for example. In sum, the ballet is connected to discourses across the arts and sciences of its period that still have meaning for us today.

I do not believe that exploring related discourses in other disciplines threatens the validity of a recreation. Rather, I think it often yields ways of creating resonance for today's audiences. For me, validity can be present in a number of ways, but relates most closely to the quality of the dialogue that has taken place among recreators, performers, and spectators in a widening circle of knowledge.

At the end of the documentary on *Green Clowns*, the Trinity Laban students say that the experience of feeling connected to the original ideas, concerns, and issues surrounding the work made it come alive for them. Something Preston-Dunlop said has also stuck in my mind: the students "have to dare." With Laban's *Green Clowns* they certainly do have to dare, because for today's dancers it is challenging to explore the crude, the rude, and the grotesque; to scratch each other's bodies, spit, and make strange noises—all of which is demanded of this kind of avant-garde theatre connected to dadaism and expressionism. In a sense, though, in *any* recreation we have to dare—dare to get beneath the surface form of a work and really engage with its raison d'être, including its politics and sociocultural context. In other words, we must get at the life sources of its original innovations and its many possible versions. We have to dare to question, dare to take apart and explore the identity of the work, and dare to allow it to live through new interpretations and realizations. Hence, it seems vital to me that not merely the performance product be made visible, but also the pathways of interpretation—the archeochoreological journey.

We have moved beyond modernism's insistence that the spectator concentrate purely on contemplating compositional aspects of an artwork, and audiences grow increasingly aware of the complexities surrounding the issue of what constitutes the work of art. If art is more than a diversion, leisurely activity, or entertainment, then audiences need and want greater involvement in forging its meanings, as opposed to being its passive consumers. For the performers and (re)creators a work is always so much more than simply its performance, and yet often preservation and documentation efforts focus on the performance without giving sufficient attention to the creative processes underlying it. In recreation these creative processes, complex and multilayered, are restored to their place of central importance.

Notes

1. *The Fontana Dictionary of Modern Thought*, 2nd ed., ed. Alan Bullock, Oliver Stallybrass, and Stephen Tromley (London: Fontana Press, 1988).
2. Mike Pearson and Julian Thomas, "Theatre/Archaeology," *The Drama Review*, vol. 38, no. 4 (1994): 133–61.
3. Muriel Topaz, "Reconstruction: Living or Dead? Authentic or Phoney?" in *Preservation Politics*, ed. Stephanie Jordan (Alton, UK: Dance Books, 2000), 100.
4. Kenneth Archer and Millicent Hodson, "Confronting Oblivion," in *Preservation Politics*, 1.
5. Valerie Preston-Dunlop and Anna Sanchez Colberg, *Dance and the Performative* (London: Verve Publishing, 2002), 197–217.
6. Ibid., 202.
7. Norbert Servos and Gert Weigelt, *Pina Bausch Wuppertal Tanztheater or The Art of Training a Goldfish* (Cologne: Ballett-Bühnen-Verlag, 1984).
8. Rudolf Laban, *Modern Educational Dance* (London: Macdonald & Evans, 1948); Ministry of Education, *Moving and Growing* (London: Ministry of Education, 1952); Joan Russell, *Modern Dance in Education* (London: Macdonald

& Evans, 1958) and *Creative Dance in the Primary School* (London: Macdonald & Evans, 1965); Valerie Preston, *Handbook for Modern Educational Dance* (London: Macdonald & Evans, 1963).

9. *The American Invasion 1962–1972*, Luis Espana, prod., Valerie Preston-Dunlop, research dir., DVD (London: Verve Publishing, 2005).
10. Rudolf von Laban, *Ein Leben für den Tanz* (1935), trans. Lisa Ullmann, *A Life for Dance* (London: Macdonald & Evans, 1975), 105.
11. Valerie Preston-Dunlop, *In the Laban Tradition: Sylvia Bodmer*, videotape (1986), available in The Laban Collection.
12. Rudolf von Laban, letters to Susanne Perrottet, 1912–1913, The Laban Collection.
13. Detlev Peukert, *The Weimar Republic* (London: Penguin Books, 1993).
14. Laban, *A Life for Dance*, 48.
15. Valerie Preston-Dunlop, "The Seminal Years in Munich, 1910–1914," Part 1 and Part 2, *Dance Theatre Journal,* vol. 7, nos. 3 and 4 (1989): 1.
16. See Valerie Preston-Dunlop and Susanne Lahusen, *Schrifttanz: A View of Dance in the Weimar Republic* (London: Dance Books, 1990), which includes translations of the first academic journal on dance, *Schrifttanz*, published from 1928 to 1932 in Vienna by Universal Edition.
17. Laban, *A Life for Dance*, 99.
18. Evelyn Dörr, "Rudolf von Laban: Leben und Werk des Künsters (1879–1936)," unpublished Ph.D. dissertation, Berlin, Humboldt Universität, 273.
19. Laban, *A Life for Dance*, 108.
20. R. Hinton Thomas, *Nietzsche in German Politics and Society, 1890–1918* (Manchester, UK: Manchester University Press, 1983), 3.
21. *Tanzbühne Laban:* Kammertanz, program prospectus for 1924, The Laban Collection.
22. See *Recreating Rudolf Laban's* Die Grünen Clowns, *1928*, DVD, dir. and ed. Lesley-Anne Sayers, prod. IDM Ltd., 2008. Available from www.dancebooks.com.uk
23. Laban, *A Life for Dance*, 48.
24. Laban, *A Life for Dance*, 41, 42, 44–45.
25. *The Letters and Diaries of Oskar Schlemmer*, ed. Tut Schlemmer, trans. Krishna Winston (Evanston: Northwestern University Press, 1972), 156.
26. Laban, *A Life for Dance*, 34.
27. Laban, *A Life for Dance*, 41.
28. See the lyrics "It's All a Swindle," "Sex Appeal," and "The Smart Set" on *Entartete Musik: Berlin Cabaret Songs,* CD, Decca, 1997.
29. Laban, *A Life for Dance*, 41.
30. Bert States, *Great Reckonings in Little Rooms: On the Phenomenology of Theatre* (Berkeley: University of California Press, 1985).
31. A full discussion of the project appears in *The Dynamic Body in Space: Exploring and Developing Rudolf Laban's Ideas for the 21st Century*, ed. Valerie Preston-Dunlop and Lesley-Anne Sayers (London: Dance Books, 2010).
32. The *Loss of Small Detail* Project is available for study at the Laban Archive, Trinity Laban Conservatoire of Music and Dance, London.

33. See David J. Levin (dramaturge for *The Loss of Small Detail*), "Moving to Language: Ballet and/as Text in *The Loss of Small Detail*," in *Vom Wort zum Bild: Das neue Theater in Deutschland und der USA*, ed. Sigrid Bausinger and Susan L. Cocalis (Bern: Francke Verlag, 1992).

34. Sarah Rubidge, "Identity and the Open Work," in *Preservation Politics*, 212.

35. Anita Donaldson, "Thoughts from Hong Kong: Conference closing address," in *The Dynamic Body in Space*, 248.

36. Lesley-Anne Sayers and Tim Rolt, dir., Le Pas d'Acier *1925: A Ballet by Serge Prokofiev* (London: IDM Ltd. in association with Rapid Eye Movies, 2006). DVD 1 : *Le Pas d'Acier: Ballet*, DVD 2 : *Rediscovering* Le Pas d'Acier *1925: A Documentary Film*.

37. See Alison Curtis-Jones, "Historical Recreation and Current Practice: What Is the Relevance of Laban's Work for Today's Dance Artist?," *Movement and Dance: Magazine of the Laban Guild*, vol. 28, no. 1 (Spring 2009): 4–7; Lesley-Anne Sayers, dir., *Recreating Rudolf Laban's* Die Grünen Clowns *1928* (London: Barefoot-Dancer Productions in association with IDM Ltd., 2008).

38. See, for example, Camilla Gray, *The Russian Experiment in Art 1863–1922* (London: Thames & Hudson, 1962).

39. See also Leslie Norton, *Léonide Massine and the 20th Century Ballet* (Jefferson, NC: McFarland & Co., 2004), 116.

40. Elizabeth Souritz, *Soviet Choreographers in the 1920s* (Durham, NC: Duke University Press, 1990).

41. Sayers and Rolt, Le Pas d'Acier *1925*.

THE DANCING GAZE ACROSS CULTURES:
KAZUO OHNO'S *ADMIRING LA ARGENTINA*

MARK FRANKO

The eye comes always ancient to its work.
— Nelson Goodman, *Languages of Art*

Kazuo Ohno's 1977 butoh dance Admiring La Argentina *is studied as a Bergsonian reflection on "pastness" in performance. As the work questions the absolute quality of the present, it is initially compared with Paul Valéry's concept of La Argentina's dance as existing in the dimension of temporal immediacy. Ohno's relation to La Argentina is discussed as spirit possession, primal identification, cultural anthropophagy, productive consumption, and memorialization. Ultimately, the analysis leads to the premise of excorporation or heteropathic identification. The essay concludes with a 2007 meditation on Yoshito Ohno's homage to his father,* Emptiness (Kuu)*.*

It is often the case in modernist aesthetic theory that dancing qualifies as high art if and when movement appears to render the instant of its occurrence as pure and self-defining. In his tribute to the celebrated Spanish flamenco dancer Antonia Mercé (1890–1936), the poet Paul Valéry wrote, "[T]his person who is dancing encloses herself as it were in a time she engenders, a time consisting entirely of immediate energy, of nothing that can last."[1] For Valéry, La Argentina (Antonia Mercé's stage name) masters time, but also strangely obliterates it: her movements exude a present of their own making within which they disappear as into a void. Dance engenders an experience for which a gaze thrown back to the past has no place.

This essay is about a live performance constructed out of a gaze trained upon the past, and more specifically about dance as a means to memorialize. It moves between the self-contained present Valéry described in 1936—which was paradoxically the year of La Argentina's death, at the age of forty-eight, of rheumatic heart failure—and the past leaking into the present impressed upon the retina by visual memory that becomes, over time, a fragmented representation. What Japanese butoh dancer Kazuo Ohno did in his 1977 reenactment of Mercé—*Admiring La Argentina*—was to perform his memory image of her dancing in person in 1929. In so doing, he identified with a maternal principle that became an abiding theme of his work. Given the importance of the embodiment of women, and more particularly Ohno's incorporation of mothers, I shall draw on psychoanalytic theories of identification, including those of Jean Laplanche and J. B. Pontalis, Mikkel Borch-Jacobson, Max Scheler, and Kaja Silverman, later in this essay. While psychoanalytic theory, as developed by non-Japanese scholars, may at first glance appear out of place in a study on a Japanese artist, there are three compelling reasons for importing it into this narrative: Ohno was an international artist who performed extensively for Western audiences; this butoh artist ventured on cross-cultural excursions in his own work; psychoanalytic theory offers one form of explanation for the affective tie to the mother, a powerful motif in Ohno's work since he created *Admiring La Argentina*.

Moreover, the notion of devouring another also has a place within a postcolonial context that is pertinent here. The cultural divide that Ohno explores between Spain and Japan—flamenco and butoh—may also be conceived as a divide between the sexes and between mother and child. At the same time we are dealing with the question of ghosts, returning from the dead, and mourning. I hope to show in what follows that there is a place in these topics for psychoanalytic theory as well.[*] If one looks beyond a paradigm of cultural relativism alone, one sees that modernism (and hence questions of modernist temporality) has played a role in the assertion of national identity at local sites, and issues of appropriation through incorporation of others—in certain contexts cannibalism—has been a postcolonial strategy whose affect psychoanalysis recognizes and attempts to interpret.

---

[*]Although I have not seen *Admiring La Argentina* in live performance, I have viewed a film of this work and have seen live performances of other works by Kazuo Ohno. I am an American dance scholar, not a scholar of Japanese culture. I was captivated by Ohno's work when I first saw it in New York in the early 1990s, and I began to write about him. I have written about butoh from my perspective as a Western observer viewing his performances in the West. See Mark Franko, "Where He Danced," in *Dancing Modernism/Performing Politics* (Bloomington: Indiana University Press, 1995), 93–107.

"Pure" Perception and Delayed Mimesis

Argentina's dance was not only the subject of philosophical specu-lation for Valéry in 1936 but also an exemplar of metaphysical ac-tivity. His privileging of the exhaustive occupation of the present by the dancer's self-consuming immediacy banished all forms of physical instrumentality from dance modernism. It proposed the proper terms for the perception of dance as "pure"—understood as outside the everyday perception of movement and hence suffi-cient, in these terms, to his conception of dance as art.

Henri Bergson, on the other hand, critiqued the very possibil-ity of pure perception, which he claimed to exist "in theory rather than in fact," since it relied upon "*giving up every form of memory*, of obtaining a vision of matter both *immediate and instantaneous*" (my emphasis).[2] "Metaphysics," Bergson pointed out, was "mind striv-ing to transcend the conditions of useful action and to come back to itself as to a pure creative energy."[3] The name of this pure cre-ative energy was life (hence the enduring cliché, "dance is life"). "The dance is an art derived from life itself," stated Valéry, "since it is nothing more nor less than the action of the whole human body; but an action transposed into a world, into a kind of *space-time*, which is no longer quite the same as that of everyday life."[4] Bergson proposed an alternative *space-time* in which memory im-ages contribute to the construction of the phenomenal present, which is still and even more properly a present for this reason, albeit a present that cannot exist apart from images of the past.[5] Matter for Bergson was "an aggregate of images," and the act of perception in the present could not but activate the memory of earlier images.[*]

I shall argue that Ohno's evocation of Argentina stands in dialogue with Valéry's essay because Ohno's performance is Bergsonian in its conception. In *Admiring La Argentina* the then seventy-one-year-old dancer (born 1906) performed his memory of seeing the flamenco dancer at the Imperial Theater in Tokyo

---

[*]When it comes to discussing the relation of time to the image, Bergsonism, as Gilles Deleuze called it, is as important for Ohno's vision of La Argentina as it was for Deleuze's aesthetics of cinema. Deleuze calls Bergson's theory of memory "one of the most profound, but perhaps also one of the least understood, aspects of Bergsonism." Gilles Deleuze, *Bergsonism*, trans. Hugh Tomlinson and Barbara Habberjam (New York: Zone Books, 1991), 55.

in 1929.* *Admiring La Argentina* was in this sense autobiographical: it commemorated a personal perception that was also historical. Ohno's performance in the present held this image of La Argentina's performance up before our eyes: the immediate presence of his movements simultaneously recalled the past. Or we could say that the presentness of performance for Ohno was the "stage" upon which the memory image that had gestated within him over many years fitfully reappeared. Gilles Deleuze points out, "The recollection-image (*image-souvenir*) does not deliver the past to us, but only represents the former present that the past 'was.' "[6] And philosopher Suzanne Guerlac maintains that "the dancer figures the central notion of Bergson's thinking ... Real Duration."[†]

Ohno's cross-dressed performance—an elderly Japanese male dancer performing a forty-one-year-old Spanish female dancer—sets tensions into play. La Argentina was not young when Ohno saw her perform in Tokyo, and the ideal flamenco dancer is not a young woman.[7] In one segment of the dance as shown in the film *Kazuo Ohno*, made for Swiss television in 1982, Ohno moves to the sound of La Argentina's castanet playing.[8] That his embodiment of La Argentina is above all a recollection-image is underlined by her castanet playing on the 1935 sound track: La Argentina retains an indexical presence in the ambient sound. Ohno uses his hands to simulate castanet playing and evokes her *zapateado* (*zapatear* means to strike with a shoe) less frequently. He does not so much dance La Argentina as he dances his gaze upon her in the time of memory. This memory is necessarily selective: his movement is not a pristine representation but encompasses the dancing gaze of the remembering subject. Put

---

*La Argentina's appearance in Japan in 1929 was part of an extended international tour begun in 1928, one leg of which took her from San Francisco to Honolulu, Tokyo, Shanghai, Hong Kong, Saigon, Singapore, Manila, and Port Saïd. See "Chronology" in Ninotchka Devorah Bennahum, *Antonia Mercé, "La Argentina": Flamenco and the Spanish Avant-Garde* (Middletown, CT: Wesleyan University Press, 2000), 191. I am grateful to Bennahum for many aspects of her study of La Argentina.

†Suzanne Guerlac, *Thinking in Time: An Introduction to Henri Bergson* (Ithaca, NY: Cornell University Press, 2006), 50. "Paradoxcially," specifies Guerlac, "time becomes energy by passing, by losing itself in the very act of becoming, and by being stored through memory. There is a sense in which we are always already in the past" (p. 80). In her short discussion of the role of dance in Bergson's discourse, Guerlac invokes Valéry to support Bergson's views. In this essay, I see the two French writers as representing different positions on dance.

otherwise, *he sees in her a memory of himself seeing her or, better yet, an image of his perception of her as embodied in his actions in the present.* His action occurs, in other terms, through the memory of a perception imbued with affect and henceforth transformed into action. Although with Ohno we are in "a kind of *space-time,* which is no longer quite the same as that of everyday life," to use Valéry's words, the butoh dancer's is not so much a metaphysical as a nostalgic tracing. It inevitably evokes an absent presence. "At the very first sight of her," as Ohno recounted his spectatorship of 1929, "I was spellbound, as though totally bewitched by her charm."[9]

Extant film footage of two of La Argentina's dances, *Tango Tachito* and *La Corrida,* shows us something of her theatrical stage persona.[10] Ninotchka Bennahum analyzes the technique: "Both flamenco and Spanish classical technique require a controlled, vertical, yet elastic upper torso."[11] Unlike other flamenco dancers of the period (Carmen Amaya comes to mind), her gaze is not inwardly but outwardly focused (Figure 1). She was both extroverted and concentrated. Her extreme awareness of the audience she plays to is also typical of Ohno's brand of butoh, which in this sense is related to the popular elements of Kabuki.[*] The Spanish *zapateado* or stamping footwork might have reminded him of the stamping foot rhythms of *Ashibyoshi* in Noh, which can invoke the spirits of the ground.[12] Gunji Masakatsu has noted that *Ashibyoshi* "originated from a desire to pacify the spirits by stamping on a delimited symbolic space. In theater and dance, this symbolic space becomes the stage."[13] If La Argentina's *zapateado* reminded Ohno of *Ashibyoshi* in 1929, might he not also have immediately conceived of her relation to ghostliness?

One can note in the way Ohno works with and against the music a discontinuity, or what I should like to call *intermittent* or *delayed mimesis.* The film of La Argentina shows that she herself alternates *zapateado* with port de bras that extend from and

---

[*]"They [Tatsumi Hijikata and Ohno] also sought to incorporate Kabuki's intimate connections to the dark, taboo, repressed side of everyday life, and hoped that by taking on Kabuki's role of representing all that was seemingly unrepresentable in Japanese society, they might also appropriate Kabuki's 'particularly provocative technique of converting the socially negative into the aesthetically positive.'" Susan Blakeley Klein, *Ankoku Buto: The Premodern and Postmodern Influences on the Dance of Utter Darkness* (Ithaca, NY: East Asia Program, Cornell University, 1988), 37. With regard to the quotation above, Klein cites Masao Yamaguchi, "Theatrical Space in Japan, A Semiotic Approach" (unpublished manuscript).

Figure 1. La Argentina in a 1927 portrait (photographer unknown). Courtesy of Jerome Robbins Dance Division, The New York Public Library for the Performing Arts, Astor, Lenox and Tilden Foundations.

change the shape of her torso and back, describing arcs that revolve around her without propelling her through space. It is perhaps this use of the back, enhanced by the long waistline of her dress, which accentuates the torso by lengthening it, that is particularly modernist. *Zapateado*, as Bennahum describes it, typically works in counterpoint to the upper body: "The arms traced continuous circles, beginning at the shoulder joint, continuing to the elbow joint, and breaking at the wrist so as to leave the fingers free to form endless circles."[14]

Indeed, both actions tend to minimize the progression of the dance as locomotion in favor of movement held either below the body (in the feet) or above the body (in the arms over the head), and hence to diminish the sense of time passing. Ohno's mimetic delay seems to cite these qualities of La Argentina's dance, while blurring the difference between seeking her and actually finding her in these actions. That memory as image emerges in isolated flashes, so that La Argentina appears only momentarily through a kind of energetic fragmentation, works against the sensation that the present can be grasped in its purity through movement.* This dance does not enclose itself within a self-consuming present, but rather opens itself to a continued effort over an extended time. The movement is determined by a different attention—an attention to memory images—determined by the "rhythm" of memory itself as an irregular unfolding. The need to concentrate on channeling the memory image generates a delay factor in the performance. On stage, remembering itself takes time.

The Narrative of Origins

Ohno has discussed his evocation of La Argentina as part of a narrative of origins in several senses. Seeing her perform inspired him as a young man to become a dancer, and encountering her vanished image in the form of an abstract painting after his retirement from the stage inspired him to make his comeback in the 1970s.[†] But more radically, in his account the memory of La Argentina invited him to return to a prediscursive and

---

*This lack of purity is also noticeable in the danced genre itself, as noted by Klein: "[W]e might expect when Ohno comes on stage dressed in a flamenco costume and begins to dance to a tango, that we are going to see some kind of imitation 'Spanish' dancing. What we see instead are tattered bits and scraps of familiar yet strangely unfamiliar movement swirled together into a whole that paradoxically seems both seamless and discordant." *Ankoku Buto*, 43.

†Ohno began dance training at age thirty (Kazuo Ohno, "On the Origins of Ankoku Butoh: the dance of utter darkness," audiotape, Cornell University Library Media Center,

prehistorical body. "My intention in dressing as a woman onstage," he said, "has never been to become a female impersonator, or to transform myself into a woman. Rather, I want to trace my life back to its most distant origins. More so than anything else, I long to return to where I have come from."[15] In this statement, the origin of his dancing in the inspiration La Argentina gave him is confounded with the origin of life itself in the womb. The counterpart of Valéry's totalizing rhetoric in Ohno's discourse is the trope of the universe as a symbol of the womb. "I think frequently about the myth of the creation of the universe. I am obsessed with the universe as though I have to think of everything in terms of the universe: the colossal universe, and the opposite world: the uterus of my mother."[16] In the same talk, called the "Cornell Lecture," which took place during his season at the Joyce Theater when he first performed *Admiring La Argentina* in New York City in 1985, Ohno said, "Where is my arena of dancing? I resolved to dance in the womb of my mother." Katherine Mezur, a student of Ohno, has told me that Ohno started his workshops by asking his students to "eat your mother from the inside."[17] Ohno's identification with the historical figure of La Argentina was evidently an identification with the mother as a source of life. "I had always read about the creation of the world in the Bible. I had always accepted it as legend, but in Argentina's work I saw it realized in front of my eyes," he said in an interview with Jennifer Dunning.[18] In other terms, Argentina brought the universe and the womb together in one body. It is as if Ohno imagined the *zapateado* and the use of *castañuelas* (castanets) as the demiurge, a kind of making of the world from nothing—and here we could imagine that he shared a vision of the self-constituting presence of the dancer with Valéry.

This nostalgia of origins resonates with the historical character of butoh itself in postwar Japan as cultural nostalgia for a primordial state of Japanese identity that could reclaim (national) sovereignty, reject postwar modernization and consumerism, and

---

[CV2178]). His performing career began with a Tokyo recital in 1949 at the age of forty-three. After working with Tatsumi Hijikata in the late 1950s and 1960s on dance experiments that brought about the innovative style of *ankoku butoh*, Ohno first retired from the stage in 1967.

remain elemental in its plasticity.* In this sense, La Argentina became something of a fetish and functioned as a "vanishing auratic" or "modernist nostalgia," to use a construct for a phenomenon Marilyn Ivy has identified in Japanese society of the early 1970s.†
An interesting parallel may be drawn between the nostalgia for a primordial state of Japanese identity in Ohno's performance and La Argentina's dance as an expression of Spanish nationalism, especially at the time that Ohno saw her perform in the late 1920s. The way in which she melded Gypsy culture with modernist stylization (that is, folkloric with Spanish classical sources), as Bennahum is careful to show, was meant to epitomize the spirit of modern Spain for which La Argentina considered herself the ambassador both in her lecture-demonstrations and her performances. This concern for national identity resonates with an important aspect of postwar Japanese culture out of which butoh initially emerged, in which "the materiality of memory," in the words of anthropologist Yoshikuni Igarashi, became invested in discursive bodily tropes.[19] That is to say, memory relies on embodiment to represent its own content to itself. Yet, it is paradoxically a refusal to embody that both distances Ohno from impersonation and makes La Argentina appear in a vivid form through his gesture. As Ivy writes of butoh in general, "As a radically present or physically enacted nostalgia that nonetheless resists, precisely, being the representation *of* anything, it is dependent in part on this misreading, on the foreclosure of access, for its present, physical, imminent force."[20]

Before going any farther I wish to dispel the possible misconception that *Admiring La Argentina* is exclusively about the evocation of La Argentina. The piece starts with "Divine's Death," adapted from a scene in Jean Genet's novel *Our Lady of the Flowers* in which the character Divine, a male prostitute, dies of tuberculosis, choking on his own blood. This scene was restaged from

---

*I am grateful to Tom LaMarre for these formulations. "Plasticity" is a term used by Bennahum to characterize the modernist and metaphysical quality of La Argentina (*Antonia Mercé*, 67).

†"Thus the consuming and consumable pleasures of nostalgia as an ambivalent longing to erase the temporal differences between subject and object of desire, shot through with not only the impossibility but also the ultimate unwillingness to reinstate what was lost." Marilyn Ivy, *Discourses of the Vanishing: Modernity, Phantasm, Japan* (Chicago: University of Chicago Press, 1995), 10; "vanishing auratic," 12.

Tatsumi Hijikata's 1960 *Divinariane*, choreographed for Ohno.[*] Ohno became an avid reader at age sixty. Hijikata and he were heavily influenced by their readings in French literature, particularly the Marquis de Sade, Isidore Lucien Ducasse (Lautréamont), Arthur Rimbaud, Charles Baudelaire, Antonin Artaud, and Jean Genet as well as Georges Bataille and Henri Michaux. Moreover, Hijikata himself directed Ohno in *Admiring La Argentina*, giving this work a retrospective character in the annals of butoh. *Admiring la Argentina* was, therefore, not only a look backward to Ohno's activities with Hijikata in the early period of butoh in the late 1950s and early 1960s, but also, according to his son and collaborator, Yoshito Ohno, "the prototype of a butoh performance that could be staged over and over."[†] That is, it was something new: a self-consciously theatrical, and hence repeatable, butoh production. *Admiring La Argentina* was perhaps the work in which butoh dance assumed the capacity to remember itself and thus to repeat itself. Hence, its nostalgia has a self-reflective quality wherein the notion of the choreographic work both underlines the possibility of memory and embeds memory within itself as a choreographic trope.

The second section of *Admiring La Argentina* is "Rebirth as a Young Girl," which Yoshito Ohno describes as follows: "Kazuo, in the guise of a young girl, rises to his feet in precisely the same spot where the elderly prostitute died in the previous scene. The sequence comes to a close as this frail and childlike figure delicately vanishes into the upstage shadows."[21] Ohno's portrayal of the young girl is reminiscent of the paintings of Hans Bellmer. Several other sections follow, including "Daily Bread" and "The Marriage of Heaven and Earth," the first evoking the debts of butoh to German expressionist dance. Hence, although butoh has been associated with the return to a premodern Japan—and this is echoed in Hijikata's interest in the forgotten rural area of Tohoku in northwestern Japan where he was raised, and where

---

[*] See Stephen Barber, *Hijikata: Revolt of the Body* (n.p.: Creation Books, 2006). Barber writes, "[A]lmost the entirety of Tokyo's experimental art at the beginning of the 1960s was closely engaged with French culture" (p. 25).

[†] Kazuo Ohno and Yoshito Ohno, *Kazuo Ohno's World: From Without and Within*, trans. John Barrett (Middletown, CT: Wesleyan University Press, 2004), 166. The first butoh performance was reportedly Hijikata's *Forbidden Colors*, in 1959.

he and Kazuo Ohno danced in the film *Navel and A-Bomb*, directed by Eikoh Hosoe in 1960—European sources were of equal importance.[*]

The Painting

The memory of La Argentina's 1929 performance in Tokyo remained dormant, despite the powerful impression it had made on him, until Ohno imagined he saw the figure of La Argentina in an abstract painting by Natsuyuki Nakanishi at a Tokyo art gallery in 1976. "I was stopped dead in my tracks by an oil painting of geometrical curves painted on a zinc sheet ... I cried out to myself 'Ah Argentina ... it is you!' "[†] It was in this renewed act of envisioning—looking not at a live performance this time, but at a painting—that Ohno perceived La Argentina anew in a manner that mobilized him to action. "This unexpected encounter," Ohno summed up, was "what led me to resume dancing in public."

Perceiving the dancer within the abstract painting presented the possibility of moving from the abstract image ("the pure image" in Bergson's terms) to the memory image, and from there to action: the animation of the image on stage. For Ohno the image functioned as impetus (although the painting is anything but figurative), underlining Bergson's point that percepts are at least in part memory images and furnishing an example of what he calls the "sensori-motor power" of the image.[22] Affect that derives from memory invests perception with the possibility of action. Yet, it should be noted, the very abstraction of the image indicates a fading or disappearance of the memory itself. Most interestingly, Ohno perceived the past in the present experience of the painted image, not as a representation, but as a *present* ("Ah Argentina ... it is you!"): "*Practically*," writes Bergson, as if uncannily commenting on this state of affairs, "*we perceive only the past*, the pure present

---

[*]"Both Ohno and Hijikata were born and grew up in Northern Japan (Tohoku): Ohno was born in the fishing village of Hakodate in 1906; Hijikata was born Yoneyama Kunio in a farming village in Akita Perfecture in 1928." Klein, *Ankoku Buto*, 5.

[†]Ohno and Ohno, *Kazuo Ohno's World*, 184, note 4. The painter Nakanishi notes that he "had never met with La Argentina, and, besides, knew nothing about her."

being the invisible progress of the past gnawing into the future."[*]
Here, we are dealing with a present perception that contains the
recognition of the past within it.

The complex temporality of *Admiring La Argentina* that
emerges can be elucidated through what Deleuze, in his adaptation of Bergson, calls the crystal-image:

> [T]ime has to split itself in two at each moment as present and past, which
> differ from each other in nature, or what amounts to the same thing, it
> has to split the present in two heterogeneous directions, one of which
> is launched toward the future while the other falls into the past.... The
> crystal constantly exchanges the two distinct images which constitute it,
> the actual image of the present which passes and the virtual image of the
> past which is preserved.... We do not know which is one and which is the
> other.[23]

This double quality of perception informs *Admiring La Argentina*
because it is paradoxically a living, breathing performance proceeding in time ("launched toward the future") and a seeking or
replaying of images ("falls into the past") (Figure 2). The second
moment in the genesis of the work at the Tokyo art gallery introduced an intensification of affect that raises the stakes on the
conceit of memory itself. For, at this point, Ohno was no longer
admiring the dancer from a distance as when he was a spectator in 1929, but commencing an active quest to merge with her
through dance. Yet, the image was still present as a catalyst—if
not the memory image, then the painted image. Here it is worth
noting Ohno's affinity for photography in the context of his performance. As Toshio Mizohata writes, "Kazuo Ohno dances for
the photograph. ... The camera eye witnesses the coming to life
of *somebody else*."[24] For Ohno, posing for a photograph is a way
to inhabit a persona. Such a notion emphasizes the circular process between performance and image for him. What, after all, is a
photograph, if not a memory image in the making?

"Watching this piece," reports Yoshito Ohno, "I'm never quite
sure whether Kazuo is quietly possessing her spirit, or if Argentina herself has entered his body. ... As they begin to merge
and become as one, a metamorphosis takes place. Kazuo becomes

---

[*]Bergson, *Matter and Memory*, 150. "Toute perception est déjà mémoire. Nous ne percevons
pratiquement que le passé, le présent pur étant l'insaisissable progrès du passé rongeant
l'avenir." *Matière et Mémoire: Essais sur la relation du corps à l'esprit* (Paris: PUF, 2007), 167.

Figure 2. Photomontage of Kazuo Ohno and La Argentina by Eikoh Hosoe (1977). Reproduced with the permission of the photographer.

Argentina."[25] As a consequence of this metamorphosis the question arises: Who possesses whom?

The Agent of Possession

This question could be posed as a relationship between exotic beings, whose countries of origin, Argentina and Japan, form the background. Ohno's first dance teachers—Misako Miya and Takaya Eguchi—were instrumental in bringing tango to Japan in the 1920s; tango music is also present in *Admiring La Argentina*.[26] Marta Savigliano's discussion of how tango traveled from Argentina to Japan in the 1920s is predicated on the idea that both countries are mapped as equally exotic. "In dealing with each other," she writes, "those identified as exotics refer to the very categorizations that keep them bound and struggle to expand their identities through exotic re-appropriations."[27] The question of who possesses whom in *Admiring La Argentina* concerns such "exotic re-appropriations" or, at least, the witnessing of them. "Exotics," continues Savigliano, "negotiate their status as passionate objects so as to gain agency over their passionateness." What held the young Ohno spellbound may have been precisely the agon of possession of and by a passionate subject, exotic because her dance placed her in a self-conscious relation to her own passion. He imitates her passion in his dance in order to relive and understand himself.

In 1928 dance critic André Levinson said of La Argentina that she mastered her own exoticism: "Her intelligence has worked a subtle transformation of those curves, spirals, and ellipses, those interlaced ornaments and sinuous calligrams, which are the foundation of all Iberian *baile*. In her the spirit of the Occident triumphs over the lure of the Orient."[28] In Levinson's exoticizing gaze La Argentina is modernist because her passion, although potentially overwhelming to herself, is ultimately brought under control of and mastered by her Westernizing intelligence and her ability to stylize folkloric sources such as flamenco within the classical traditions of the eighteenth-century bolero school.[29] Most significantly, Levinson adds, "She bears in her the intoxicating poison, but also the antidote, rapture and poise."[30]

This agon of passion and self-possession is dramatically mirrored in Ohno's performance. If he *possesses* her, he becomes a subject whose performance is doubly reflected in her own: for Ohno bears within him both the sensorimotor experience of the visual image of La Argentina and the memory of its overwhelming effect upon him. "[The body] does not merely reflect action received from without," writes Bergson, "it struggles, and thus absorbs some part of this action. Here is the source of affection. We might therefore say, metaphorically, that while perception measures the reflecting power of the body, affection measures its power to absorb."[31] This, I would propose, is what we see in the moments of Ohno's dance that fail to keep La Argentina before our eyes. "Perception," argues Bergson, ". . . measures our possible action upon things, and thereby, inversely, the possible action of things upon us."[32] Ohno dances not only her, but also the impact she had upon him. Inasmuch as Ohno reproduces La Argentina's initial impression upon him, he could be said to master it; inasmuch as, in reproducing it, he relives his own subjugation to that reactivated memory image, he is mastered by it. The more that memory comes into play as a phenomenological given, the less discernible becomes the power relation.

Ohno's conceit of regression to an earlier, unindividuated state from which to embody La Argentina, or the feelings she inspired in him, indicates that his passion for her could not be controlled or tamed. According to Yoshito Ohno, "Kazuo considers La Argentina's dance an illustration of creation as described in the Old Testament's Book of Genesis."[33] The return to an unindividuated state of origin is, in psychoanalytic terms, primary identification. According to Laplanche and Pontalis, primary identification "does not wait upon an object-relationship proper—because it is the original form of emotional tie with the object." They elaborate, "This modality of the infant's tie to another person has been described in the main as the first relationship to the *mother*, before the differentiation of ego and *alter ego* has been firmly established. Such a relation would clearly bear the stamp of the process of incorporation."[34] Borch-Jacobsen treats primary identification as synonymous with primary incorporation:

> If I am the other, then *I no longer represent him to myself*, since the exteriority where he might have pro-posed himself to me, as model or object, as *Vorbild* or *Ob-jekt*, has vanished into thin air. And, at the same time, I have become unable to *represent myself*, to present myself to myself in front of

> myself: the other that I am no longer exists, has never been in front of
> me, since I identified myself with him from the start, since I assimilated,
> consumed, incorporated him from the very beginning.[35]

For Diana Fuss, this reveals the ambivalence in identification: "All active identifications, including positive ones, are monstrous assassinations: the Other is murdered and orally incorporated before being entombed inside the subject."[36] Her discussion of the body as crypt evokes another Freudian sense of incorporation—one associated with mourning and melancholy. Despite Ohno's discourse of a return to unindividuated origins, the theme of memory also gives credence to the idea that his relation to her is melancholic. "It came home to me," said Ohno, "that I will always seek after her, even after my ashes have been placed in an urn."[37]

The question of who possesses whom seems to confront us with two possibilities. If La Argentina "has entered his body" we should talk of spirit possession. This first scenario could be related to what Freud refers to in *Totem and Taboo* (1918) as animism.[*] La Argentina "returns," as it were, or becomes animate again, through Ohno. The implication is that she has entered his body to remain there: "Her memory has lived in the depths of my soul." She also becomes a memory that demands the work of mourning: "I longed so much to see her again."[38] There is an aspect of necrophilia in that he wishes to rejoin her in, as it were, a movement as death. "I want to enter into La Argentina's death," he said during an interview in *Kazuo Ohno*. On the other hand, if Ohno is "possessing her spirit," we are dealing instead with a form of cultural cannibalism, which, psychoanalytically speaking, is incorporation based on the oral model.

Placing butoh, on one hand, and Ohno's 1977 work, on the other, in the context of Japan in the wake of postwar American occupation inevitably leads the researcher to postcolonial politics. Savigliano describes the international travels of tango as a phenomenon of the appropriation of passion on a global

---

[*]Sigmund Freud, *Totem and Taboo: Resemblances Between the Psychic Lives of Savages and Neurotics*, trans. A. A. Brill (1918; reprint, New York: Vintage, 1960), 119. "Human beings have souls which can leave their habitation and enter into other beings; these souls are the bearers of spiritual activities and are, to a certain extent, independent of the 'bodies'" (p. 99).

scale, which is a way for the West (and even for Japan) to col-
onize movement resources with affective potential: we might
almost call it affective capital. Savigliano's phenomenon of "exotic re-appropriation" may be seen as a sort of cultural cannibalism that occurs as a result of this cultural appropriation.
Again, there is historically a connection to issues of incorporation
and melancholy. Concepts of cultural anthropophagism emerging
as early as Oswald de Andrade's *Cannibalist Manifesto* (*Manifesto
Antropófago*), which gained currency in the 1920s in the Brazilian avant-garde, are relevant here because *Cannibalist Manifesto*
is a text that "unites the search for national identity with the
modernist esthetic project."[39] The appropriation of modernism
to the ends of postcolonial self-definition points up the continuities already suggested in this essay between butoh, modernism,
and psychoanalytic theory. Literary critic and theorist Neil Larsen
calls the cultural cannibalism of the Brazilian avant-garde "consumptive production," a term he borrows from Karl Marx's *Grundrisse.** For Larsen the goal is actually not to reproduce exoticism
in a vicious circle of reappropriations, but to produce oneself
through the consumption of the other. Similarly, cultural critic
of cannibalism Eva Horn suggests that, when considered from the
psychoanalytic perspective, all love ineluctably suggests incorporation, and psychoanalysis consequently relies on a theory of
anthropophagism that it finds in anthropology.[40] In this way,
the postcolonial critical frameworks to which butoh inevitably
leads also places Ohno's ambivalent discourse in the domain of
cannibalistic incorporation. When love and hate become affects
difficult to distinguish from one another, psychoanalytic theory
recognizes the power motive within incorporation, as well as the
need to mourn.[41]

As with primary identification, cannibalism's mode of commingling is oral incorporation. Freud suggests that oral incorporation contains a power motive, since cannibalism works through
the idea of contiguity: "By absorbing parts of the body of a person
through the act of eating we also come to possess the properties

---

*Neil Larsen, "Modernism as *Cultural Brasileira*: Eating the Torn Halves," in *Modernism
and Hegemony: A Materialist Critique of Aesthetic Agencies* (Minneapolis: University of Minnesota Press, 1990), 81. As Larsen points out, once the "transcultural incorporation
has been achieved, then consumptive production can become productive consumption."
(pp. 81–82).

which belonged to that person."[*] Cultural anthropophagism, as film theorist Robert Stam notes, is "a devouring of all cultural stimuli in all their heterogeneity."[†] As Ohno reproduces La Argentina on stage he gains a part of her strength.[‡] It is worth noting that the international success of *Admiring La Argentina* not only put an end to Ohno's retirement from the stage, but also launched his second, by far more important, dance career at age seventy-one. Ohno's appearance at the avant-garde venues of the 1980 Nancy Dance Festival followed by the 1982 Avignon Festival, both in France, brought *Admiring La Argentina* to international attention.[42] One could say that his consumption of La Argentina made the Kazuo Ohno phenomenon possible, that he consumed her to produce himself. To "admire" Argentina is to do tribute to her, to eulogize her, to mourn her, to incorporate her as a melancholic, to reanimate her as a spirit, to devour her as a necrophiliac, yes, but also to ingest her as cannibal and appropriate her strength. Beyond Argentina or the (his) mother, Ohno's work confronts us with the cannibalization of Western culture as Other. In this way, it evokes butoh's original impetus to rediscover an indigenous, rurally based (hence folkloric) Japanese identity.

Heteropathic Identification

When one views the Ohno–La Argentina scene in the larger context of the work of which it is a part, one comes to realize, however, that the outcome of incorporation in this context cannot be exclusively power, for the roles of the male prostitute and the little

---

[*]Freud, *Totem and Taboo*, 107. The two ways that magic operates through animism, according to Freud, are similarity and contiguity. Similarity has to do with imitation, but contiguity replaces imitation with relationship. He wrote of the "devouring affection of cannibals as primary identification" in *Group Psychology* (see Mikkel Borch-Jacobsen, "The Primal Band," in *The Emotional Tie: Psychoanalysis, Mimesis, Affect*, trans. Douglas Brick et al. [Stanford, CA: Stanford University Press, 1992], 14).

[†]Robert Stam, "Of Cannibals and Carnivals," in *Subversive Pleasures: Bakhtin, Cultural Criticism, and Film* (Baltimore: The Johns Hopkins University Press, 1989), 145. Stam's account of cultural cannibalism relates it to Mikhail Bakhtin's carnival as it encompasses the blending of two identities: "The 'cannibalist' and 'carnivalist' metaphors have certain features in common.... Both evoke a kind of dissolving of the boundaries of self through the spiritual and physical commingling of self and other" (p. 126).

[‡]Freud noted of the primal horde devouring the father that "they accomplished their identification with him by devouring him and each acquired a part of his strength." *Totem and Taboo*, 183.

girl would work against such a conclusion. Psychoanalytic theorist Max Scheler likened the idea of incorporation on the oral model to what he calls *idiopathic identification*: "the total eclipse and absorption of another self by one's own, it being thus, as it were, completely dispossessed and deprived of all rights in its conscious existence and character."[43] As the antithesis of this, he proposed *heteropathic identification*, which is masochistic rather than sadistic. The latter achieves, in Kaja Silverman's terms, "the ultimate divestiture—the divestiture of self."[44] So, here is the possibility of a third interpretation of Ohno's appropriation of La Argentina, one that is neither animistic nor cannibalistic. As Silverman observes,

> Heteropathic identification is the obverse of idiopathic identification; whereas the latter conforms to an incorporative model, constituting the self at the expense of the other who is in effect "swallowed," the former subscribes to an exteriorizing logic, and locates the self at the site of the other. In heteropathic identification one lives, suffers, and experiences pleasure through the other.[45]

She likens heteropathic identification to masochistic ecstasy, in the etymological sense of being outside or beside oneself (*ekstasis*). In offering excorporation ("an exteriorizing logic") as an alternative to incorporation, Silverman provides a way of circumventing animism and cannibalism altogether. I would argue that what we are given to see is neither La Argentina impersonated nor Ohno appropriating her image, but rather his own identification with her as a process of self-dispossession. In his Cornell lecture, Ohno spoke of his relation to his mother as one of shame about his own willful behavior toward her as a young man. After her death, she reappeared to him in dreams as a caterpillar and a fish. He implies that she haunted him in this way. His ongoing relationship with her in her afterlife is an origin of his masochism, which might play out as his excorporation of himself.

Perhaps here, in the guise of conclusion, I should return to Valéry to ask whether Ohno's dancing gaze itself does not comprise a certain metaphysical activity, which, rather than existing in the purity of a fully invested present, occupies instead a continuous space of exile. Ohno's vision of Argentina shows not "life itself" in its "immediate energy," but rather a space to which the subject has willfully exiled himself, a space in which affect trumps the regression to origins with the will to self-estrangement. Appropriating another culture is then to recognize oneself, both psychoanalytically and culturally, as occupying an exteriorized site of identification. The pure and self-defining instant is, under these circumstances, impossible. Yet, it does constitute an experiential present.

Epilogue

Kazuo Ohno died on June 1, 2010, at the age of 103. From the beginning of his work in butoh, death-in-life and acts of memorialization were a key motif of his work, and as he grew older and more infirm, he began to memorialize himself. His aging body increasingly became the subject and the theatrical wager upon which his work was based.

By the time he was 101 years old and stricken by Alzheimer's disease, he had retreated from the stage he had inhabited since the late 1940s. Yoshito Ohno performed an homage to his father and longtime performance partner as part of the "Kazuo Ohno 101" festival that took place at the Japan Society (in conjunction with CAVE's Third Biennial New York Butoh Festival, October 21–November 21, 2007). The work is called *Emptiness* (*Kuu*) and is, at first, a solo in which Yoshito, himself a youthful sixty-nine years old, appears motionless, and practically stricken one could say, on a bare, brightly lit stage, entirely decked in white curtains with a white floor. Standing with his back toward us, hunched over from the neck so that his shaven head appears like a truncated piece of anatomy, he wears an off-white shirt and pants. It becomes clear that this off-white fabric is a kind of flesh, as the silk shirt catches the tension of his arms and the sinews of his back. The tips of his ears are bright red. Deafening chords of the organ ring out, making me think of the program note: "*Kuu* is the body itself." The organ seems to resonate with the internal space of the body before us, passing through it and suggesting that breath is a pulling in and exhaling of volume that already exists around us. The program notes explain: "I AM ONLY OTHERS." Clearly, the emptiness is within Yoshito as well as on the stage: the effect of the absence of others, notably of his father. As the organ piece modulates into a nimble arpeggio, and its volume diminishes, I have the thought of circulation—movement within the body projected aurally onto the stage. If choreography is movement, it is here displaced onto sound, which itself suggests internal bodily motion. The stage is in a sense empty despite the figure that occupies it: the choreography being that of sound apprehended as the body's drama with its own interiority, understood as spatial materiality. Another stage exists within this immobile body: one that could be host to the invisible and the absent. This is a clever and effective construct for homage.

Next comes a series of scenes not unlike those of many Ohno (father and son) productions: each section is marked by distinctive costume and music. The vocabulary is limited: walking, running, hopping. Yoshito wears no makeup, and he exhibits none of the complex facial play of expression typical of Kazuo. In fact, Yoshito is a stockier figure than his father and, seen from straight on in this piece, he resembles Jean Genet. This is, perhaps, not fortuitous, since the work of Hijikata was influenced by Genet's writing.

In one section Yoshito appears bare-chested, gently gyrating his torso. Elsewhere his body appears clenched like a fist. His fingers and wrists are not fluid; he uses them to great effect when holding a paper tissue and manipulating it so that it appears to become a flower, a bird, or a hat. That is, the movement of his hands is complex, but always instrumental, just as his presence on stage is always highly skilled, yet styled to "partner" the presence of Kazuo rather than to make a statement on his own. As he has written, "[Kazuo's] performances generate the feeling of being drawn from a great depth in himself. By comparison, when most dancers—and I count myself among them—perform any given movement, it tends to stop dead at a certain point. This explains why my expression often comes across as lacking in something."[46] That being said, the opening scene with his back to the public must be recognized as a tour de force. Yoshito has written of the performer's use of the back in Ohno's work: "The back ... can be as nuanced as the face in the way it indicates emotion."[47] He adds that the back should have eyes, and this is clearly the case at the beginning of *Emptiness*, in which Yoshito performs motionless with his back facing us for at least twenty minutes.

The final part of the program is ushered in by a slide show containing images of Kazuo in the present time, very old and weak. Although one knew Ohno was not to be present on stage, these images come as something of a shock. This artist who had so audaciously used his aging body to amazing effect in a complex denial of and subjection to time is now shown as beyond such explorations. The photographic images show him mostly with his eyes closed, resting, and occasionally with Yoshito at his side. Kazuo is a remarkable subject in that he, too, is motionless, not simply by virtue of his appearance in the still image, but because he is slowly fading away. The sense of emptiness emerges—the absence of Ohno on stage rendered more poignant—as the *beginning* of the absence of life. Some of the projected images show a tiny hand puppet resembling Kazuo placed next to his face.

The puppet image is picked up in the final scene of *Emptiness* where Yoshito works the hand puppet on stage, while his image is captured on live feed and projected from an angle onto the back wall. Thus, we have two images again on stage, a magnified image of the puppet that mimics the remarkable complexity of Kazuo's hands, and a live image, somewhat to the side of the stage, in which we perceive Yoshito's gift of partnering. In this section, unlike in any other, his whole facial expression comes alive with concentration, an expression less severe than that of his dancing. He says, "Thank you" to the public and, suddenly, it is over. The evocation of absence is, itself, gone.

The Kazuo puppet in the hands of his son is at first an unlikely if ultimately moving image that allows Yoshito to evoke his absent father affectionately and refocus the center of attention on the elder Ohno as a figure whose embodiments had always been mysterious. It also recalls, in the uneven moments of his evocation of La Argentina, a subtle puppetlike jerkiness in his movement, which is even perceptible, if one looks closely, in the movement of La Argentina as seen on the extant film as well as in Kazuo's evocation of her. The puppet also serves to point out that Yoshito had been more than a partner. As we can learn from *Kazuo Ohno's World*, the son was in fact the director of the father's performances as well as his performative partner. "Any attempt to predict how Kazuo will move, or what he will do onstage," he wrote, "is fruitless. . . . This come-what-may attitude, even in public performance, enables him to thrust deeper into himself."[48] Yoshito was able to organize the overall effect of Kazuo's improvisatory methodology, to divide it into scenes that structured its suggestive poetry. He clearly complemented the work of his father in more ways than one. "Given that a dance," he also wrote, "for him at any rate, has no need of predetermined sequences or movements, his modus operandi doesn't require him to establish a choreographic structure or vocabulary."[49] As the "stage manager" exemplified in the puppeteer figure, Yoshito exposes, as part of the tribute, this role that contributed immeasurably to Kazuo's success.

Yoshito's own performance of *Emptiness* benefited from such structuring, from the clarity of scenic variation. *Emptiness* refers to stagecraft, to the stage itself as a craftily organized space that still lacks a raison d'être, which is, in turn, the antipathy of such craft: the ability to *embody*. Emptiness is not just a feeling of loss, it is the condition of the stage itself in Kazuo's absence: a stage that awaits fullness. As such, the stage is crafted as a frame, just as the tiny Kazuo puppet articulates its gestures against the foil of Yoshito as puppeteer and projected shadow. One begins to understand the motif of whiteness and off-whiteness: all in Kazuo's absence is screen, stage, place prepared for his appearance, counterpart carefully set up for his powerful improvisations.

After seeing *Emptiness*, I wrote these words:

> Kazuo Ohno, whose dance career began in earnest by reanimating or incarnating, in a heteropathic mode, others long absent—notably La Argentina—exists now in a paradoxical fold. Although still alive, he is no longer performing, and so how he is still "with us" or continues to share our reality needs reexamination. Who will do for him what he did for La Argentina? In awaiting an answer to that question, Yoshito Ohno shows us that all performance is essentially built on absence and emptiness. This is the mysterious formula for Kazuo Ohno's afterlife—as it was always already the premise of La Argentina's legendary performances to suggest that another Spanish culture could be visible in her dance through an unusual amalgamation of folk elements and classical stylization. Together (at last?) Kazuo Ohno and La Argentina seem to suggest that dance itself in its personal and cultural project is heteropathic identification.

Acknowledgments

Earlier versions of this paper have been read at the Getty Center for Research in Arts and the Humanities, the Society of Dance History Scholars (San Francisco), the Dance Studies Working Group at the University of California at Berkeley, The Centre for Interdisciplinary Research in the Arts at Manchester University, the Dance

Department of Roehampton University, and the Society for the Humanities, Cornell University, in the context of the workshop "Critical Mobilities." I wish to thank John Solt, Toshio Mizohata, Eikoh Hosoe, Katherine Mezur, Nanako Nakajma, Timothy Murray, Dee Reynolds, Janet Wolff, Seeta Chaganti, Catherine Soussloff, Alexandra Kolb, Joellen Meglin, and the anonymous readers of *Dance Chronicle* for their critiques and responses, which helped to bring this essay toward its current form. Any errors, however, are exclusively my own.

Notes

1. Paul Valéry, "Philosophy of the Dance," in *Aesthetics*, trans. Ralph Manheim (New York: Pantheon Books, 1964), 203. Valéry's engagements with dance have recently received critical attention from Véronique Fabbri in her *Danse et philosophie: Une pensée en construction* (Paris: L'Harmattan, 2007).

2. Henri Bergson, *Matter and Memory*, trans. N. M. Paul and W. S. Palmer (New York: Zone Books, 1991), 34. *Matière et mémoire* was originally published in French in 1939.

3. Ibid., 15.

4. Valéry, "Philosophy of the Dance," 210, 198.

5. "Matter, in our view, is an aggregate of 'images.'" Ibid., 9.

6. Gilles Deleuze, *Cinema 2: The Time-Image*, trans. Hugh Tomlinson and Robert Galeta (Minneapolis: University of Minnesota Press, 1989), 54.

7. I am grateful to one of the anonymous readers for this point.

8. *Kazuo Ohno* was shown at the New York Butoh Festival, Martin E. Segal Theatre, The Graduate Center, City University of New York, New York, in October 2005. See also Ninotchka Devorah Bennahum, *Antonia Mercé, "La Argentina": Flamenco and the Spanish Avant-Garde* (Middletown, CT: Wesleyan University Press, 2000), 170.

9. Kazuo Ohno and Yoshito Ohno, *Kazuo Ohno's World: From Without and Within*, trans. John Barrett (Middletown, CT: Wesleyan University Press, 2004), 150. One could say this dance takes place between her charm and his bewitchment.

10. A film of these dances is held at the Cinémathèque de la danse, Paris.

11. Bennahum, *Antonia Mercé*, 37.

12. See Carl Wolz, "The Spirit of Zen in Noh Dance," in *Dance Research Annual VIII: Asian and Pacific Dance: Selected Papers from the 1974 CORD-SEM Conference* (New York: CORD, 1977), 57.

13. Gunji Masakatsu and Selma Jeanne Cohen, "Virtuosity and the Aesthetic Ideals of Japanese Dance and Virtuosity and the Aesthetic Ideals of Western Classical Dance," *Dance as Cultural Heritage, Dance Research Annual XIV* (1983), 89. I thank Joellen Meglin for referring me to the articles of Wolz and Masakatsu.

14. Bennahum, *Antonia Mercé*, 41.

15. Kazuo Ohno, quoted in Yoshito Ohno, "Food for the Soul," in *Kazuo Ohno's World*, 76

16. Kazuo Ohno, "On the Origins of Ankoku Butoh," Cornell Lecture, Cornell University, Ithaca, New York, 1985.

17. Katherine Mezur, conversation, San Francisco, July 2009.

18. Jennifer Dunning, "Birth of Butoh Recalled by Founder," *New York Times*, November 20, 1985, C27.

19. Yoshikuni Igarashi, *Bodies of Memory: Narratives of War in Postwar Japanese Culture, 1945–1970* (Princeton, NJ: Princeton University Press, 2000), 5. I am grateful to Katherine Mezur for suggesting this book to me.

20. Marilyn Ivy, *Discourses of the Vanishing: Modernity, Phantasm, Japan* (Chicago: University of Chicago Press, 1995), 168.

21. Ohno and Ohno, *Kazuo Ohno's World*, 155.

22. Bergson, *Matter and Memory*, 63.

23. Deleuze, *Cinema 2: The Time-Image*, 81.

24. Toshio Mizohata, "Introduction," in *Kazuo Ohno's World*, 4.

25. Yoshito Ohno, *Kazuo Ohno's World*, 166.

26. See Ohno and Ohno, *Kazuo Ohno's World*, 147.

27. Marta Savigliano, *Tango and the Political Economy of Passion* (Boulder, CO: Westview Press, 1995), 169.

28. André Levinson, "Argentina," in *Dance Writings from Paris in the Twenties*, ed. Joan Acocella and Lynn Garafola (Middletown, CT: Wesleyan University Press, 1991), 96.

29. See Javier Suárez-Pajares and Xoán M. Carreira, eds., *The Origins of the Bolero School, Studies in Dance History*, published by the Society of Dance History Scholars, vol. 4, no. 1 (Spring 1993).

30. Levinson, "Argentina," 99.

31. Bergson, *Matter and Memory*, 56.

32. Ibid.

33. Yoshito Ohno, quoted in *Kazuo Ohno's World*, 167.

34. J. Laplanche and J.-B. Pontalis, *The Language of Psychoanalysis*, trans. Donald Nicholson-Smith (New York: W. W. Norton & Co., 1973), 336.

35. Mikkel Borch-Jacobsen, "The Primal Band," in *The Emotional Tie: Psychoanalysis, Mimesis, Affect*, trans. Douglas Brick et al. (Stanford, CA: Stanford University Press, 1992), 23.

36. Diana Fuss, *Identification Papers* (London: Routledge, 1995), 34.

37. Kazuo Ohno, *Kazuo Ohno's World*, 185.

38. Ohno and Ohno, *Kazuo Ohno's World*, 185.

39. Leslie Bary, "Oswald Andrade's 'Cannibalist Manifesto,'" in *Latin American Literary Review* 19/38 (July–December 1991), 35.

40. Eva Horn, "Leichenschmaus: Eine Skizze zum Kannibalismus in der Psychoanalyse," in *Verschlungene Grenzen: Anthropophagie in Literatur und Kulturwissenschaften*, ed. Annette Keck, Inka Kording, and Anja Prochaska (Tübingen: Gunter Narr Verlag, 1999), 297–308. I thank Alexandra Kolb for referring me to this essay.

41. See the Brazilian film directed by Nelson Pereira dos Santos, *How Tasty Was My Little Frenchman* (1971). I thank Catherine Soussloff for calling this film

to my attention. On the consubstantiality of hate and love in oral incorporation, see Borch-Jacobsen, "The Primal Band," 12.

42. See Ichikawa Miyabi, "A Preface to Buto" (1983) in *Ankoku Buto: The Premodern and Postmodern Influences on the Dance of Utter Darkness*, by Susan Blakeley Klein (Ithaca, NY: East Asia Program, Cornell University, 1988), 69.

43. Max Scheler, quoted in Kaja Silverman, *Male Subjectivity at the Margins* (London: Routledge, 1992), 264.

44. Silverman, *Male Subjectivity*, 265.

45. Ibid., 205.

46. Yoshito Ohno, "Food for the Soul," in *Kazuo Ohno's World*, 11.

47. Ibid., 40.

48. Ibid., 62.

49. Ibid., 167.

CELEBRATIONS DURING A TRADITIONAL WEDDING ON THE ISLAND OF RHODES

PATRICIA RIAK

This article ethnographically reconstructs the sousta *as danced during a traditional wedding celebration on the island of Rhodes during the interwar period (1925–1940). I describe how courtship occurring when youth danced was imbued with meaning by the traditional celebration. The wedding ritual and related dance performances reveal the social dynamics connected to courtship and how the* sousta *played the primary role as signifier of the socially and religiously mediated experience of romantic union.*

This paper uses a processual approach to the study of dance ritual in order to understand the meaning of a dance—the *sousta* of Rhodes—as embedded in a wider ritual complex for life-cycle transformation. In his seminal 1969 book, *The Ritual Process: Structure and Antistructure,* Victor Turner defines society as an entity, flowing and changing, that creates transformational social tasks for the individual.[1] Of particular importance is the change of social status brought about through "life-crisis" rites that involve the experience of liminality and *communitas.* A "betwixt and between state" for the individual, liminality functions as the antithesis of status in the structural domain.

Figure 1 diagrams Victor Turner's theory of ritual structure, illustrating the collapse of structure in the liminal phase, which stands between separation and re-aggregation as an unstructured, undefined, in-between state. Whereas the phases on either side of liminality are apparently stable, whole states, the liminal period is essentially one of "statelessness"—hence Turner's term "anti-structure." Liminality reshapes ritual personae to create new social configurations, transferring power to people who take on new positions in society. Turner considers *rites de passage* to be a dialectical process rather than a logical sequence. *Communitas* serves to reinstate societal values dialectically through the experiences of structure and anti-structure. As Turner proposed, *communitas* can

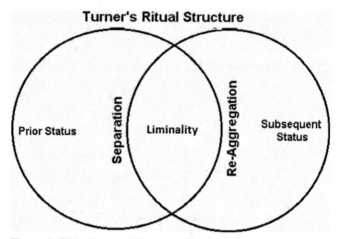

Figure 1. This diagram illustrates Victor Turner's theory of ritual structure.

often dramatize difference. Initiates "work" on emotions associated with sexuality and gender in relation to marriage and fertility. This splits the experience of *communitas* with regard to what men and women feel, so that *communitas* becomes sexually schismatic. In the *sousta* this split occurs with poignancy when men sing and women do not. It is the intention of this article to place more emphasis on the notion of gender difference in the liminal state, as well as the heightened intensity of emotion in *communitas*, which implicitly make the state of liminality more diverse than Turner implied.

Methodology

The French structural linguist Ferdinand de Saussure developed a theoretical approach that posited the presence of the binary system in cultural life. However, the problem with such an approach is that it suppresses the ambiguous spaces and overlaps between the proposed binaries. Poststructural approaches have argued that such dichotomies create hierarchies, especially when one side of the binary is understood as dominant. In ethnographic inquiry, paradigms that present the ethnographer as working in a culture deemed "exotic" in relation to his or her own culture represent the binary logic of Self/Other. However, some ethnographers work from a "nostalgic" position in which field research is associated with personal history to represent a more integrated logic of Self/Self. Such work may be classified as "native," "indigenous," or "auto-ethnographic" in genre. However, it could be argued that this model merely erects a new dichotomy between the "traditional" or "old style" (etic) and the "contemporary" or "new style" (emic) ethnographer.

Nevertheless, an in-between space may be found in the situation of the bicultural ethnographer, who works within the frameworks of both the country of ethnic origin and the diasporic country where he or she was born and brought up. The bicultural ethnographer, driven by nostalgia, participates in interpretive ethnographic inquiry in the country of ethnic origin and the diasporic country; however, the nostalgic self-interpretations may not be the same in the two field sites. Migration from a "home country" results in a sense of selfhood as Self/Other-Self. Life experience has fragmented the sense of family. For the first-generation children of the immigrants, in the culture of origin, the conception of "home" seems reversed in time because of traveling back to grandparents (Other-Self).[*] Language barriers are typically difficult. What is experienced in the daily life in the non-native society supercedes the sense of family history in the native country, and the first language is typically that of the former. Personal yearnings for the nostalgic as a result of the lack of everyday ties to the native country of heritage create sensitive personal environments for those who find themselves at the crossroads of cultures as a hyphenated self (Greek-Australian), especially if they are able to travel to meet family in the native country of heritage as many cross-cultural children do. Nostalgic ethnographic inquiry results if a cross-cultural child becomes an ethnographer and engages with some work related to the Self and the Other-Self, bridging the sense of divide.

In this research study, I engage with family members and villagers from the region of my personal/cultural heritage. My aim is to understand Greek wedding rituals and the dance performances contained within them on the island of Rhodes. In my family,

---

[*]My own initial ethnographic fieldwork in Greece, for example, reconstructs the time period when my grandparents and their young family were not yet fragmented as a result of emigration.

I heard a story about my paternal grandfather being awarded a prize for best dancer of the *sousta* when he was a young man. It was awarded to him in 1947 when the island region was given its independence from Italy. Stories became a way of getting to know him, as he died when I was young. My father (his son) was a professional ballet dancer of the Russian school who choreographed Zorba performances for television and theater in Australia. My personal connection to these members of my family enhances my nostalgic position in relation to Greek culture, and this connection is deepened through my studies of Greek dance (Figure 2).

In 1997 I stayed in the vacated home of my paternal grandparents, without expecting to rely on more formal introductions. Although most relatives of my father's generation have left, old networks provide informants. Initially I rely on Olympia, age fifty-six, a neighbor married to my father's closest childhood friend in the village.* Through her I initiate contact with the village social circle. She tells me to go to see her aunt Anastasia (eighty-three), who, I discover, was my grandmother's neighbor during World War II. Anastasia refers me to her sister-in-law Stamatia (also eighty-three), whose husband was the village mayor during the late 1940s. Olympia also refers me to her uncle Stellios (eighty-five), a veteran dancer and godparent of my grandmother's younger daughter. Stellios in turn refers me to Mihalis (eighty-three), whose father's family was involved in caretaking a local Kattavian monastery, and also to Dimitris (seventy-nine) and Kyriakos (ninety-one), both traditional folk musicians before 1950. Dimitris's eldest daughter is my grandmother's godchild. Of my own accord I go to see Elisaveth (seventy-four), who was my grandmother's other neighbor until her mother died in 1985 and her sister's younger son inherited the house. Elisaveth refers me to Flora (seventy-five), an active member in the local church, and Maria (seventy-three), the oldest coffee-shop owner in the village square, who, I remember, used to give me soft drinks when I was a child playing there. Maria refers me to her aunt Anastasia (eighty-seven) who, I discover, was also my grandmother's first cousin. On my own I go to see Hetopoula (sixty-five), who is still one of my grandmother's neighbors; I remember playing

---

*The actual names of the informants are used for this article as all the informants were willing to have their true identities revealed.

Figure 2. This photograph shows the dance troupe from the village of Kattavia during independence celebrations at the Diagoras Stadium in Rhodes in 1947. The performance of the *sousta* was won by my grandfather, who is located third from the left. A copy of the photograph was kindly given to me by the sister of my godfather, located fifth from the left in the photograph.

with her sons as a child at the local Greek school. (My grand-mother's youngest daughter christened her eldest son.) I also go to see Manolis (eighty-two), who, now living in the United States, is holidaying in the village. I later find out that he is married to my godfather's sister. He in turn refers me to Stamos (seventy-three), who is also vacationing. He had been the village's mandolin player before migrating to Australia in the 1950s.

Some informants are not reached through family networks. Miltiadis (eighty-three and a widower) often comes to visit me at the house and stays for coffee. He is from the village of Sianna but, after marrying a Kattavian woman, he remained in Kattavia. Fotini (seventy-two) is the only Kattavian above the age of seventy I know who lives in Rhodes City. She lives next to the apartment I am renting in the capital. She spends all her weekends in the village, so I am able to visit her in the capital as well as in the village. She is my grandmother's younger cousin, orphaned during the war and placed in my grandmother's care in the postwar period.

In the oldest age group (seventy plus) the sense of national identity was formed before large-scale tourism took hold of the island.* Because tourism has been decisive in the development of the local and national economy, the two younger groups have ex-perienced an emphasis on national as opposed to regional dances. Members of the oldest age group have established their families and their work in the village. Many of these people still live in their marital homes and have an excellent recollection of what hap-pened during the interwar period. Villagers older than seventy were close to twenty at the time of island independence (1947), and so about ten years old in 1937. They are able to recall lived experiences of the weddings and dances from that time, as many learned to dance between the ages of ten and fourteen. Some have primary knowledge from even earlier. As my sample age was on av-erage above seventy-five, the experiences documented come from

---

*The onset of Greek international tourism offers the two younger age groups opportuni-ties to make money, so they migrate to the city. Subsequently, they often have no direct knowledge of the *sousta* and its place in village celebrations during the interwar period. People between the ages of twenty and forty-nine live in the capital and only return to the village for ritual celebrations. The *sousta* danced during the interwar period is no longer performed. Women of the youngest age group dance a variation of *sousta* from the capi-tal, but no males dance the *sousta* at all. When village members resettle in the capital city, cultural practices are often reconstituted there.

the years 1925 through 1940, a time when the northern region of the island was beginning to be developed for the purpose of Italian tourism (beginning in 1926). During the interwar period, the royalist governor of the island, Governor Lago, wanted to maintain local Greek culture by organizing, for example, the Kremasti Dance Competition (1923–1935 or 1936). However, during World War II the fascist Governor Devecci felt that it was necessary to eradicate Greek culture. Most of the interviewees married members of their own village during the period of this war and did so according to established village traditions.

Sousta in the Village: Historical Background and Current Demise

Bonding within the community occurs when children engage in the process of watching and learning how to dance the *sousta*. Stellios remembers that this process functioned as a form of play. Before public entry into the community as ritual dancers, young children spent years practicing the dance with each other. They were invited to learn the dance by older children who had begun to dance at ritual celebrations. Dimitris, Kyriakos, and Stellios agree that the young male dancers (*kavalieri*) first entered the ritual celebration at the age of fourteen and young female dancers (*koustieres*) at the age of sixteen. The three steps of the *sousta* consisted of two jump steps going forward and one jump step going back. A *kavalieros* prepared to dance for longer periods of time because he had to learn to design (*skedhiasei*) his own steps (*tsalimia*) for the lead dancer position (*embros*) in the dance circle (*kiklos*). Stellios remembers that in 1928 he was ten when his older brother, who had been taught by two older girls, taught him the *sousta*. He remembers that young people prepared to dance the *sousta* during the summer, when they would gather in small groups at the threshing floors (*alonia*) situated between the patron church, the Old School, and the smaller neighborhood squares around the village. Learning the dance either after or during school holidays created platonic friendships. When at puberty, however, youth entered into ritual celebrations as dancers, platonic relationships changed into romantic ones. They felt that their social worlds were changing as they entered into the role of young adults, and the community recognized the young dancers as eligible marriage partners. Moral codes now had to be adhered to and the dance became an expression of this adherence even as it legitimized courtship. The *sousta* played an integral role in this socialization process.

The *syrto* dance has since become representative of Dodecanesian identity, but before Independence the *sousta* claimed this position. When I dance with the youth of the village during ritual celebrations, we dance the *syrto*. When I ask the young people why they do not dance the *Kattaveni sousta* anymore, they reply that they feel that the *syrto* represents what it means to feel young and Dodecanesian. This response gives precedence to regional identity over more local village identity. I join the Kattaveni youth at their favorite saint's-day festival—for Saint John—in the village of Profilia with Panayis, a Kattavian man and his family. I watch the Kattaveni youth at Profilia get up to perform the Cretan *pentozali* and the *kotsari* (dances they also performed at the festival of St. Paraskevi in our village). Panayis tells me of his dance education in the village in the late 1970s and early 1980s. He remembers he was taught these two dances along with the *kalamatiano* [the Panhellenic dance] and the *syrto* at primary school in order to perform them during National Day celebrations. My elder informant Stellios recalls that in 1935 students in the village learned *kalamatiano* and *vlaha* at school. The *sousta* was not taught as a national dance in the school curriculum either before or after Independence. Stellios remembers that, although the *kalamatiano* was taught as part of the village school curriculum, it was not danced nearly as much as *sousta* by the youth. This was because the Dodecanese island region was not yet independent.

At the Old School on Easter Sunday in 1997, I observe that older women perform the *sousta* during the celebration. No one gets up to dance when the musicians first play the *sousta* music. A group of women gets up to dance *Rodhitiki sousta* when the musicians play the *sousta* music a second and final time, and I also join in. Coming back to the table after the dancing, Olympia tells me that all the women are members of the Kattaveni Women's Cultural Organization. The lead dancer is the president of the organization. Olympia also mentions that nine of the twelve dancers who got up to dance live in the capital of Rhodes and come back to the village to organize the village celebrations for Easter. The Kattaveni Women's Cultural Organization organized the celebration dance the *Rodhitiki sousta* of the capital for the Easter Sunday celebration in the Old School. Before Independence, males performed to honor females in the dance. When I ask these women why they choose to dance the *Rodhitiki sousta* and not the *Kattaveni sousta*, they explain that it represents the locality of their residence in the capital. They identify with a newfound regionalism among the Dodecanesians after Independence; for them it is important to perform a dance representing the entire island, rather than the village, because of the island's annexation to Greece after 1947. Prior to Independence, they considered local dances specific to villages on the island of Rhodes important in defining, in a sort of regional mosaic, a Dodecanesian identity under foreign occupation.

After Easter, when our village celebrates the saint's-day festival of Saint George, again I observe that the *sousta* is performed only once. It is no longer performed at the beginning and the end of the festival as it was prior to Independence. The *kalamatiano* and the *syrto* are now the most popular circle dances, followed by the *kritiko*.

Reconstructing the Wedding Ritual of the Interwar Period

The importance of community in the traditional wedding is evident. The wedding began with rites involving the whole village and ended with more socially restricted family-related rites, marking a transition from widespread social recognition to private consummation of the marriage. The wedding rites were performed for seven days in a particular sequence: (1) display of a dowry, (2) making of wedding bread, (3) adornment of the bridal bed, (4) shaving of the groom, (5) bathing of the bride, (6) dressing of the bridal couple, (7) procession to the church with song and dance, and (8) the wedding feast (Figure 3).

The *Kamara*

The *kamara* is a Rhodian house with a particular architectural design, named after the dividing wall running through the center of the house in the form of a large archway. The *kamara* was built in the villages of Lindos and Damatria until about two hundred years ago, when it spread to other villages.[2] The front and back areas of the home are divided into two discrete parts, which the archway

Day 1 Wednesday	Day 2 Thursday	Day 3 Friday	Day 4 Saturday	Day 5 Sunday	Day 6 Monday	Day 7 Tuesday
Village		Family	Village			Family
Koskinisma	*Prozimia*	*Pasmata*	*Kalesma*	*Stolisma*	*Koumbaricia*	*Feast of Parthenia*
		Welcoming	*Bathing of Bride*	*Wedding Celebration at the Kamara*		
		Krevatia				
		Mbatichia				
RITUAL STAGE 1		RITUAL STAGE 2	RITUAL STAGE 3			RITUAL STAGE 4

Figure 3. This chart illustrates the days of the wedding celebration (ritual) in the village.

connects even while separating one side of the house from the other; the result is four rooms. The father gifted the *kamara* to the bride as part of her dowry (*prika*).

Figure 4 illustrates how the dancing took place in the center of the *kamara* with women aggregated in the back half and men in the front half. Young women sat on the benches (*pangi*) and along the front of the storeroom for wheat (*arekla*) and the bedroom (*krevati*), closest to the dance space. Young men stood around the dance space. Older men gathered in the kitchen area (*soufa*) and older women (with young children) in the *arekla* and *krevati*. In short, young men and women positioned themselves close to the central dance space, with older men and women placed peripherally. This arrangement emphasized that the dance space was for young people and the role of the dance was to facilitate courtship.

The Ritual Sequence

The first stage of the wedding occurred on Wednesday and Thursday and involved the preparation of food by the village. The *koskinisma* and *prozimia* rites prepared the wedding loaves for baking. On Wednesday wheat was ground and sifted and firewood was collected for the oven. Anastasia, Stamatia, Flora, and Fotini recall that married women transported the wheat to the flourmill, grinding the flour three times. Closely related married male relatives would travel to the mountains to collect wood for the oven and this continued into Thursday. On Thursday night, young, single women sifted and kneaded the dough around a rectangular wooden box (*skafi*) and the village came to watch. Kyriakos recalls that it was customary for observers to throw candy and walnuts into the *skafi* for the young women to eat while they were kneading the dough. Coins were also thrown into the dough and as the young women bent over to pick out the coins their faces were dunked into the dough. Flora recalls that a handkerchief was brought by the young women and, although the money was a gift to them, it was collected in the handkerchief and given to the bride. Dimitris remembers that portions of dough were reserved for the married men who collected the wood, and the married women would fry the dough to make flat dough cakes (*tighanites*). The loaves were left to rise overnight and on Friday they were baked in the outdoor oven. The traditional wedding dish of

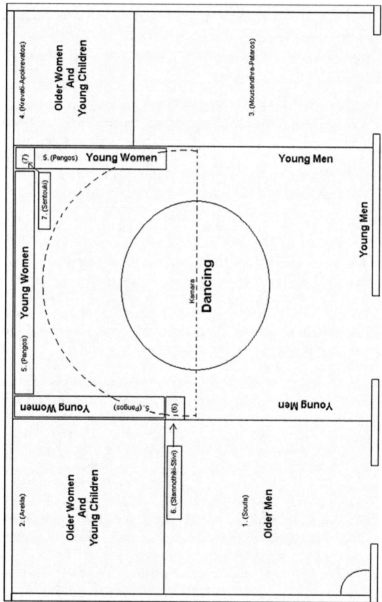

Figure 4. This diagram illustrates the placement of dancers in the *kamara* during the wedding celebration.

meat and potatoes (*stifadho me patates*) was cooked in two barrels (*tenzera*) in the courtyard of the bridal home and left to simmer until Saturday. Fotini recounts that the first ritual stage prepared the future unions of other young couples through the display of young single women kneading the dough. It drew public attention to young women as potential marriage partners for village men.

The second stage of the ritual built toward the coming ceremonial and celebratory components of the wedding that involved family members. This stage included rites for the formal coming together of the families before the wedding ceremony that represented and enacted the binding of the families. Dimitris, Kyriakos, and Stellios recall that during the shaving of the groom (*pasmata*), relatives watched while he, his best man, and the brothers of the bride and groom were shaved in preparation for the formal welcoming. A musician was also present and the family sang songs to the groom.[3] Once the wedding dish was prepared and simmering and the wedding loaves baked, it was time for the family of the bride to welcome the groom and his family. In the early evening a parade commenced from the home of the groom; he set off on a donkey with his family following and carrying his trousseau (*prikia*). Dimitris recalls that, with village musicians accompanying them, the parade passed through the village square so that the trousseau was displayed to the village. The mother of the groom gave her son a gift to give to the bride when he arrived. Anastasia remembers that the gift was usually an aluminum pot or frying pan. Once the parade approached the new bridal home, both families began to sing to one another. Flora recalls that the family of the bride held large church candles (*lambadhes*), and the mother of the bride held a bottle of holy water (*kani*), which she sprayed on the groom and his family when they entered the home. The bride and her mother served beverages in the courtyard before they entered the bridal home. Anastasia recalls that the mother of the bride pinned a handkerchief on the left shoulder of each musician as they also prepared to enter.

The dressing of the bridal bed (*krevatia*) with the trousseau of the bride symbolized the prosperity of the bridal couple. Young women and female relatives of the bride and groom dressed the marital bed as family members watched and older women sang songs of farewell to the bride. Money was thrown on the bed as a sign of good fortune, sugar almonds (*koufeta*) to symbolize a sweet life, and grains of rice to symbolize "good seed." A young boy thrown onto the bed conveyed the wish that the first-born be a son to carry on the family name of the groom. Flora recalls that before the *krevatia*, the mother of the bride displayed the *prikia* on the benches (*pangi*) in the bedroom (*soufa*) before the families. The *batichia*, an agreement between the father of the bride and the father of the groom concerning the dowry, was negotiated during the *krevatia*. The negotiation concerned a plot of land to be farmed by the groom, that he might provide for his new family; it was to be a gift from the parents of the bride in addition to what had already been requested by the parents of the groom. It was customary for the parents to honor the new couple with a pair (*zevghari*) of horses. The parents of the groom gave a stallion and the parents of the bride gave a mare.

The bride and groom were separated during the rites of the first two ritual stages. The bride stood in the corner of the room and was not allowed to participate in the dressing of her bridal bed. Although the groom was present during the *batichia*, he could not speak during the negotiations. During the procession of the groom and his family to the bridal home, the groom had to ride a donkey a distance away from his family. Both the bride and groom stood passively apart from these events, indicative of ritual separation before the wedding ceremony.

The third stage of the ritual brought together the entire village for the wedding ceremony and celebration. A time of maximum communal involvement and celebratory dancing, it was an intense and ecstatic stage in which the spirit of communal fusion heightened. The Saturday before the wedding was known as the day of inviting (*kalesma*). As Kyriakos recalls, that morning saw the adding of the *prikia* of the groom to the display in the marital home and the slaughtering of twenty lambs. Dimitris and Stellios recall that the intestines (*patsadhes*) were washed and cleaned to make a soup served after the dancing on Sunday night. Elisaveth and Maria recall that the *kalesma* commenced in the afternoon when two groups of women—the bride and the young women, and a group of older women—carried a basket (*panieri*) of sugar almonds. They gave almonds to every village home as an invitation to the wedding. Accompanied by a violin player, each group invited people from opposite ends of the village. Young women were on display in a ritual debut.

The bathing of the bride occurred in the evening. Fotini recalls that it was customary for three young women to "pass through" the water once the bride finished bathing. The young women had to be single and healthy with both parents living. They acted as a prophylaxis, warding off bad luck. As a purification rite, the bathing cleansed and separated the bride from her old world and prepared her for her journey into marriage. The day of the wedding began with the dressing and adornment of the bride and groom (*stolisma*) at opposite ends of the marital home. The mothers of the bride and groom offered an appetizer made of chicken kidneys cooked in tomato sauce (*sikotakia kokinista*) to the guests. Then the matron of honor (*koumbara*) and the bride's friends dressed her, singing as they did so.[4] Again, the friends who dressed her had to be single and healthy with both parents alive, to avoid bad luck. All informants mentioned that it was customary for the father of the bride to help her into the wedding dress.[5]

After the *stolisma,* the procession of bride and groom and their families began at the bridal home and ended at the church. The groom[6] and his family first proceeded to the church with the bride and her family following suit, all the while accompanied by song and music.[7] The nuclear families of the bride and groom created lines with relatives following them, singing songs to the bride and groom before they reached the church.[8] Each individual procession stopped at the village square, where they met to unite as one procession before going on to the church.

Before the holy dance of matrimony took place, it was customary for the best man (*koumbaros*) to place a piece of material, which had been brought to the church by the family of the bride, over the bride and groom. This acted to bind the couple spiritually. It was a gift to the bride from the *koumbaros*, and she would make a dress from this piece of material to wear eight days after the wedding. The cloth was left on the bridegroom for the Dance of Isaiah (Holy Dance of Matrimony) and the *koumbaros* guided the bride and groom around the Royal Table. The congregation threw *koufeta* over the couple symbolizing a sweet union. This, the most significant rite of the wedding ceremony, demonstrated the elevation of status. The bride and groom became queen and king symbolized by the wedding crowns they wore during the marriage crowning service.

Flora and Stellios mention that after the wedding ceremony, the entire village went to the marital home to kiss the wedding crowns (*stefania*). The priest returned to the home, chanting all the way with the church choir, as the bride and groom and *koumbaros* led the village procession.[9] Just before the procession left the church, the bride would drop a handkerchief behind her. It was believed that the unmarried young woman who picked it up would become the next bride. Fotini recalls that upon returning to the bridal home, the priest stood in front of the main entrance to bless the couple before they entered. The groom had to break a pomegranate with his foot at the threshold of the door, placed there by the mother of the bride. The fruit was a symbol of fertility and by breaking it the couple would "multiply to the number of the seeds in a pomegranate" (*na plithoun osi ine i karpi tou Rodhiou*).[10] Beforehand, when entering the front gate, the priest presented the married couple with a walnut dipped in honey to eat. Anastasios Vrontis states that the groom must first dunk a finger into a cup of honey and smear the form of the cross on the door of the house with the bride following suit. He adds that eating the walnut dipped in honey symbolized a "sweet and wholesome life."[11]

The village was then invited into the marital home to pay their respects to the couple. When expressing their best wishes, guests placed money onto a tray that held the wedding crowns. If they were not closely related to the couple, they kissed the wedding crowns. If guests were close relatives, they kissed the couple. There was also an icon in the tray that had been given to the bride by her mother as an heirloom; it was also the first item listed in the dowry agreement (*anglavi*). Stellios recalls that in the evening guests were served the wedding dish of *stifadho me patates*. The soup made of *patsadhakia* was served for supper to guests remaining after the dancing.

The following day was the rite of the *koumbarichia*, in which the bride, the groom, *koumbaros*, and young men, accompanied by musicians, collected chickens from the village houses; these were given as a gift for the family feast on Tuesday. Stellios remembers that the chickens were tied to a wooden pole (*kontari*) carried by two young men. The chickens were placed in the courtyard of the marital home and later slaughtered by the young men for the feast. (A pair was spared and given as a gift to the married couple.) A few of the chickens were roasted on Monday afternoon in the coffee house (*kafenio*), where the best man and the young men ate. Drinks were served and the expense was paid by the *koumbaros*, giving the occasion the name *koumbarichia*. This event bestowed public recognition on a new spiritual relationship—a kinship between the groom and his *koumbaros*. Elisaveth remembers a gift of food consisting of beans, chickpeas, rice, macaroni, and sweet sesame seed toffee (*melekouni*) being given by the bride to the *koumbaros* after the *koumbarichia*.

During the celebrations in the *kamara* on Monday evening, guests would bring a plate of rice and *melekouni* to the couple, which was then redistributed to the guests in the *kamara*. Kyriakos remembers that at the end of the celebration a meal of rice and meat (*pilafi*) was served to the guests, then the bridal couple was "put to bed" by the *koumbaros*, who "locked" them into their new home. Dimitris and Stellios remember that sometimes the bedroom door was taken off its hinges by friends of the groom and turned into a table, where they would sit waiting for the groom to retrieve it. The groom would promise his friends plenty of meat and wine so that the door would be put back on its hinges.[12] In the evening young guests were invited to the best man's house before locking the couple up into their marital home, and there they built a little boat (*karavaki*). The young guests were expected to bring decorations for the *karavaki*. The small boat was made of wood and was decorated with flowers, lit candles, sugar almonds, and apples. It was decorated by the bride, placed on a tray, and displayed by two singers to everyone. The guests took something from the boat to eat while singing.[13]

The final stage of the wedding ritual had to do with female honor (*timi*). Female *timi* took a dramatic form on Tuesday, the day celebrating the rite of the Feast of Virginity (*parthenia*). Anastasia remembers that early Tuesday morning the *koumbaros* returned to the bridal home with the mothers of the bride and groom and a violinist. When the mothers showed the bloodstained sheets to the fathers, the Feast of Virginity commenced with music and song, together with a meal of chicken and rice.[14] Close family members of the bride and groom shared the meal to honor the virginity of the bride; it marked their first meal

Day/Dance	Pair	Group	Group	Group	Group	Group	Group
Day 5 Sunday	*Monakhiki Sousta*	*Sousta*	*Sousta*	*Sousta*	*Sousta*	*Sousta*	*Sousta*
Day 6 Monday	*Monakhiki Sousta*	*Sousta*	*Sousta*	*Sousta*	*Piperi*	*Vlakha*	*Vatani*
Process	*Beginning*		*Middle*			*End*	

Figure 5. This chart illustrates the sequence of dances during the wedding ritual, showing that on Sunday only the *sousta* was performed, representing courtship negotiations among the youth. On Monday three other folk dances culminated the ritual. Performed by older, married men and women, these dances suggested that the transition to the married status—a change of social status—occurred at the beginning of a new week.

together as a couple in the marital home with their immediate families. The display of the bloodstained sheets during the *parthenia* honored the bride for being a virgin and the occasion united the families for the final time during the wedding ritual. This final meal solidified an honorable bond; it conveyed the idea that the marital bond had begun as an honorable one.

The Sequence of the Dances

During the wedding ritual, dancing took place on Sunday and Monday evenings (Figure 5). The *sousta* was the main dance of the wedding. Performed at the beginning of the dance sequence on both Sunday and Monday, it drew attention to the coupling of young people during the celebration. Dancing represented a climax during the wedding, marking a transition from honoring single people on Sunday to honoring married people on Monday. Young men and women performed the *sousta* with the bride and groom on Sunday. The dancing on Sunday had an exclusively courting character for youth, but on Monday night the youth and married couple danced with older married women and men. All informants describe the *sousta* as an honorable dance (*timitikos horos*) precisely because of the role it played during the *ghamos*. Stellios mentions that during the saint's-day festival they would perform mainly *kalamatiano* and *syrto*, while during the wedding they would perform mainly *sousta*, *vlaha*, and *vatani*. The dance allowed them to bond and communicate, and the village was able to observe this romantic love played out during the performance of the dance. As well as unifying the community and consolidating religious faith, it acted to unify man and woman socially, giving definition to both honor (*timi*) and love (*aghapi*) in the community.

Courtship and Dance

The *ballo* is a couple dance of the Greek islands whose function is to facilitate courtship; it is made up of traditional elements of courtship, such as attraction, flirtation, display of masculine prowess and feminine virtue, pursuit, rejection, and eventual capture or surrender. One characteristic that links both Cretan *sousta* and *ballo* is that dancers break from the dance line to form couples, who then dance together in a number of dance forms. In the simplest form of *ballo*, one couple at a time dances through a series of spontaneous movements. In a more complicated repertory, many couples dance but each as if they were alone. The *ballo* can be introduced by another island dance called the *syrto*, in which three or five people dancing the *syrto* go into the *ballo*, leaving "the odd man out." In the most complicated form of the *ballo*, a number of couples, roughly spaced in two circles facing each other or in promenade position, go through various movements, the women moving with footwork opposite to the men.[15] More specifically, Theodore Petrides argues that the Cretan *sousta* is the Cretan form of *ballo*, in which a circle or a contradance formation is introduced. Dancers split up into couples but maintain their original formation and at the end of the dance link up.[16]

There are three forms of the *ballo*. In the first form, men are located in the inner circle and women in the outer circle, and as couples they face the line of direction. They hold opposite hands (in a regular handhold) or left hands with right hands resting on their hips. In promenade position they dance with opposite footwork (the man starting on left, the woman on the right). In the second form, couples stand in an open circle chain with regular handhold and dance a *syrto* before breaking up into separate couples. The footwork of the men and women is identical. In the third form, also in an open circle chain formation, one couple at a time

breaks from the circle to dance in the center while the other couples continue to do the *syrto* around them.[17] The reconstruction
of the *sousta* from the island of Rhodes indicates that, although it
is a courtship dance, it is unlike the Cretan *ballo*. For one thing, its
pairs are formed at the end, not the beginning, of the dance and,
for another, the couples do not break from the circle formation
to dance the *sousta*.

Performing Courtship: Concealing and Revealing Identity in the Sousta

For the dance to be socially binding, courtship was mediated
through the principal values of female honor (*timi*) and male
grace (*hari*), which entailed four means of concealing identity.
First, a young man indirectly invited a young woman to dance so
that her identity would not be explicitly revealed. Second, after
the invitation, the two did not dance directly beside one another.
Third, the male tail position (*oura*) acted to conceal the final
female in the dance circle (*kiklos*) so that a female was not the last
dancer. The final and most significant expression of concealment
occurred when the young man concealed the identity of the
young woman he loved by singing songs that did not reveal her
identity. Revealing the identity of the young woman meant that
a courtship couple was acknowledged and another wedding
would take place in the village. *Timi* was always adhered to during
the dance so that revelation was a cumulative process normally
culminating in the singing of love songs (*kantadhes*). Revelation
could also occur with the invitation being directly given to a
young woman whom a man loved, but all informants mentioned
that this rarely occurred.

The Sousta and Concealing

The formation of the dance unit (*omadha*) was an exciting time
for all who were going to enter the dance. Courtship was felt
strongly among all dancers, but it was an especially confusing time
for young women, as they would be made to feel uncertain of
whether courtship intentions were going to be directed toward
them or not. Young men concealed their intentions as best they
could. The young man introduced an element of tension when he

offered his handkerchief (*mantilaki*) to a young lady. To play down any possibility of an advance the young lady invited her friends to dance alongside her. All got up to dance and formed an *omadha*. As a result of feminine caution, a female never accepted the invitation of a male by herself. The *omadha* acted to camouflage any possible affection and this is why the male instigated its formation and the female completed it (Figure 6).

When a young man invited a young woman to dance, he invited her directly. However, this did not necessarily mean that he was attracted to her. Direct invitation functioned to conceal rather than reveal courtship interests. Stellios explains that a young man did not always end up positioned in the same *omadha* as the young woman to whom he was attracted. A young man would often invite a young woman to dance in the hope that the woman he was actually attracted to might trail as part of the *omadha* he was forming. For example, a young man might decide to invite his sister to dance, knowing that she would choose the friend he was interested in to accompany her in the *omadha*. His sister and the young woman to whom he was attracted might or might not have known of his intentions. The same situation applied to a young man inviting a female cousin or a god-sister or the sister of a good friend. However, the young man might also have asked a good friend of his to invite the young woman he was attracted to. This young woman may have thought that the young man inviting her was attracted to her when this was not the case. The young man who invited this young woman may have been attracted to her

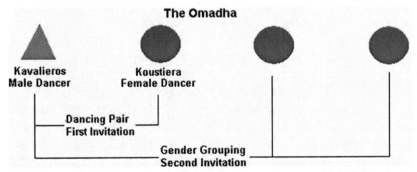

Figure 6. This diagram illustrates the structure and arrangement of dancers in the *omadha* (color figure available online).

friend who accompanied her as part of the *omadha*, so that both young men's affections remained concealed. Anastasia remarks that young women entered the dance not knowing *how* an invitation arose or *whether* an invitation was really meant for them or not. Because courtship was concealed it became a very strong undercurrent in the dance. At the outset, the male was an instigator of courtship proceedings and all young women who entered the dance were aware of the possibility of courtship intentions in every male dancer. Anastasia concludes that the dance led young women into an ambience of courtship activity. They were honored by the *timi* expressed to them through the white handkerchief and this was the only direct invitation to courtship. The *mantilaki* shrouded the rest of courtship activity in mischief.

During the *sousta*, the male assumed highly active and less active roles. The role of lead dancer (*embros*) was primarily one of revealing, and that of the tail dancer (*oura*) primarily one of concealing. The position of *embros* expressed virility, revealing to everyone how well the leader could dance. The position of *oura* protected the honor of the *koustiera*, first, by dancing behind her and, second, by *anonymously* singing songs to her (Figure 7).

There existed a polarity between the roles of the *embros* and the *oura* in the *kiklos*. The *oura* embodied the notion of *timi*, in contrast to the virility expressed by the *embros*. The role of the *oura* was that of chaperone to the last *koustiera* in the line; he protected her *timi* because he "sealed" the *kiklos* in the honorable sense. Displaying self-control and civility, he symbolized "the gentleman," whereas the *embros* symbolized "the man" (Figure 8).

Kyriakos explains that when male dancers performed in the *kiklos*, they sang to the young women but hid the object of their affections, sustaining the secret. They produced lyrics that would not give away the identity of the young woman they loved. This kept young women alert and listening to the lyrics to sift through and sort any meaning that might be directed their way. Often lyrics were so general that they might appear to be aimed at anyone in a group of women. Singing in such a way functioned as a game of hide-and-seek. Behind their lyrics the men hid the object of their affections, which the women sought to find out during the dance. Examples of the hidden meaning of a love song (*kantadha*), expressed here as a four-line poetic verse, are reflected in a love song designed and sung by Stellios. He sang the two

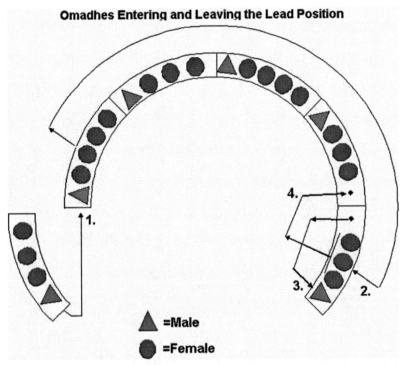

Figure 7. This diagram shows how a new *omadha* enters to assume the lead position in the *kiklos* (1); the former lead *omadha* disengages and relocates to the end of the *kiklos* (2); the male dancer of this *omadha* now assumes the tail position (3); and the female dancers attach themselves to the *omadha* in front of them (4) (color figure available online).

following songs for the young women he loved in the years 1938 through 1939.

sto diplomerakliki sou	in your happiness doubled
marenome ke liono	I wilt and I melt
ego gapo se kardhiaka	I love you with my heart
ma dhen to fanerono	but I dare not make it appear

While the *kantadha* reflected the happiness he felt when thinking about a particular young woman, there was no indication as to the identity of the young woman, which he dared not reveal. Some

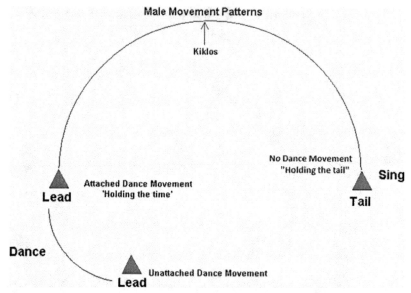

Figure 8. This diagram shows the relations among male role, movement pattern, and position in the *kiklos* (color figure available online).

time later while dancing, he made it known through another *kantadha* that the young woman he loved was positioned somewhere to the left of him in the *kiklos*. This could point to a female dancer (*koustiera*) in his *omadha* or another *omadha* in the *kiklos*.

stin zarmi mou tin plefra	on my left side (in the dance)
ke akomi para pera	and a little further along
vasta to astro tis afgis	holds the star of the earth
ke o ilios tis imeras	and the sun of the day

The Sousta *and Revealing*

Like the indirect invitation to dance, *kantadhes* could also hide the identity of the young woman. Thus, the *kantadha* revealing the identity of the young woman, like the rare direct invitation, became a public demonstration of courtship between couples during the dancing. Once the *kantadha* revealed the identity of the young woman, it was then appropriate for the young man to ask for her hand in marriage. When a particular young man and woman felt mutual love, dance events were the only occasions where they could declare their love for each other, secretly. Even for young people in love, the public expression of this love did not give a clear indication to others, especially if one of their parents would not approve of the potential match. Fotini's father was a teacher and he did not want her to marry a farmer. The farmer Fotini loved would communicate with her about their love in his *kantadhes* at the dances. Their love was unrelenting and he continued to sing to her until he married her. Fotini recalls one of these songs sung for her:

ama aghapas likrina	if you really love me
dhixe mou simadhi	show me a sign
otan kratoume sto horo	when we hold hands in the dance
sfixe mou to kheraki	squeeze my hand

When they danced together Fotini often secretly squeezed the hand of the young man she loved, behind the *mantilaki*. She recalls that squeezing hands was a sign reaffirming their love.

Miltiadis sang songs to the young woman he loved. However, he designed a *kantadha* that pinpointed her identity publicly because he wanted to propose to her. Soon after singing this *kantadha* he married her:

kokkino foremeni mou	my red dressed one
kafe to karsomeni	brown are your stockings
ap olles tis Kattavenes	of all the Kattavian women
esi ise i penemeni	you are the praised one

This *kantadha* pointed to the clothing she wore. Miltiadis warns that such *kantadhes* could be used only to express the intention of marrying. The *kantadha* acted as a form of public promise. Such songs indicate that after the dance was complete, the couple (*zevghari*) had formed. Dance with song heightened solidarity and further climaxed when the identities of young women were revealed. Song-dance vehicles encouraged a social bonding that broke the code of concealment. There was a strong sense of liminality felt in the social states of both young men and young women, as the song shared among them acted as a catalyst, changing their social status from single to married. The changed social status of the dancer was recognized once the dancing was finished.

The dancing assisted in creating a new social identity, while song expressed the state of liminality and resulted in transformation.

The informants Dimitris, Kyriakos, Stellios, Anastasia, and Fotini affirm that *kantadhes* sung in the *kamara* were also sung to young women outside their windows late at night after a saint's-day festival (*paniyiri*). A young man, more often than not intoxicated, would throw a stone at the bedroom window of the young woman he loved and then hide and wait for her to open her window, whereupon he sang a *kantadha* to her. Often young men would do this in groups to give each other confidence. Stellios remembers that one of the young men knew how to play the mandolin, and he would accompany another singing a *kantadha*. It was these private *kantadhes*, sung after the *paniyiri*, that often gave away the identity of the young men, as all informants remember that sometimes young men hid their feelings and sometimes they did not, depending upon whether they wanted to reveal their identity or not. All male informants note that when their love for a particular young woman grew, they would eventually reveal themselves, and private conversations would develop after a *kantadha* had been sung to the young woman under her bedroom window. Depending upon what the young man told the young woman outside her window, and what she told him, he would continue at the next opportunity to sing to her, either after another *paniyiri* or during the dancing in the *kamara* during a wedding. If a young woman reciprocated his love, he did not need to hide his identity, unless the woman wanted him to or he felt it was the right thing to do. Expressions of love, then, depended very much on the intentions and actions of the young man. Revealing the identity of the young woman he loved during a *kantadha* at the wedding may have been the result of intimate conversations under the young woman's window, or it may have emerged from a series of *kantadhes* or a combination of both. The *kantadha* at the wedding would reveal a young woman and was a prelude to a young man asking for her hand in marriage. The *kantadha* was an important form of courtship play alongside the dance and outside of it. However, singing a *kantadha* under the bedroom of a young woman was generally not allowed, and often mothers aware of the event would wait until a *paniyiri* and take this opportunity to rather sternly tell the young man to go home. Stellios and Dimitris recall that often mothers would throw cold water from a bucket out of a window of the house as a way of telling the young men to go away.

Stellios and Dimitris recall that the *sousta* played a critical role in the public affairs of the village and not just for the private affairs between two young people. In folk tradition a bowl called a *koupa* was used in conjunction with the dancing to collect money for the civic affairs of the village. In the course of the dancing, when a spectator praised a lead dancer (*embros*) by shouting "*koupa* for the lead," the church council members would move toward the shouting observer, who would then place money into the *koupa*. The church council member holding the *ouzo* (Greek aniseed liqueur) would then head toward the lead dancer, offering him a drink with the spectator's compliments. Accepting the drink, the dancer toasted the spectator's health and resumed dancing. The collection of the money assisted with the maintenance of the patron church of the village and neighboring monasteries belonging to the jurisdiction of the village.* Mihalis, Dimitris, Kyriakos, and Flora remember that the small monastery of Saint George of the Bride always had the *koupa* at its *paniyiri* because it was a poor village monastery and had often been damaged by Turkish occupiers and, later, Italian occupiers. The contributions were also important because they helped to pay the wages of local priests and teachers whose wages were not paid by the Turkish or the Italian state before independence. These contributions unified the village in praise of local *sousta* dancers, whose performances helped to maintain civic life.

The first dance performed before the wedding ceremony was a version of the *sousta* called the *monahiki sousta*. It was performed publicly in the village square by older female relatives of both bride and groom. It lasted a few minutes, serving to bind the families of the bride and groom as one procession. Before meeting in the village square, the families left the bridal home in separate processions. A circle formed around the dancers that reflected the unifying of the families. The notion of binding and linking was a consistent theme in the performance of the *sousta* during the wedding. The fact that married female relatives danced the *monahiki sousta* was significant. The dance was referred to as a

---

*For example, Stamatia and Stellios recall that in 1926 there was an earthquake and the bell tower of St. Paraskevi fell. At the *paniyiri* the following year, the *koupa* collected the money required to build a new bell tower for the church.

couple (*zevgharoti*) dance because two females danced facing one another, holding their right arms up, and sharing a *mantilaki*. Married female—not male—relatives represented married status and the binding of two families in the community.[18] Fotini explains that women performed this dance because they were associated with the idea of *timi*. The fact that women danced this version of the *sousta*, even incorporating the *mantilaki*, supports the idea that honor was linked with women during the wedding ritual.

The bride and groom did not dance together at the village square because they were still in a state of "separation." When approaching the church, the bride's *sousta* took the form of a circle dance performed in the church courtyard by the entire village in one large *kiklos* with the bride as the lead dancer.[19] It was called "the bride's *sousta*" because she was placed in the leading position and relatives, who had initially followed her in the line, came to the lead to "dance the bride" (Figure 9). There was an order of lead dancers for the performance, at least initially: first the bride's father, mother, and siblings, and, after the immediate family, in random order a number of "lead dancers" who were usually her extended family. The groom then followed suit with his family in the same initial order. Hence, while the groom and his family headed the processions when leaving the home, the bride and her family headed the dances at the church.

The *piperi* or "pepper dance" was a male dance performed during the latter part of Monday evening. Young and old men would perform it by rubbing parts of their bodies on the floor as if pepper were irritating their skin. The dance leader sang a question: "How do the devil's monks rub the pepper?" (*Pos to trivoun to piperi tou dhiavolou i kaloyeri?*).[20] The lead dancer would give the answer by shouting out a particular part of the body, whereupon the other dancers would dive to the ground and rub that particular body part on the ground. This sequence would continue as the lead dancer called out another part of the body and so on. He held a large kerchief (*mantilla*) knotted at one end, and if a dancer did not do as he was told, the lead dancer would playfully hit him with the *mantilla*. The *piperi* was a comical dance, the hitting of dancers with the *mantilla* being done in jest, making dancers and spectators laugh. Moreover, the lead dancer often referred to private parts of the male. Alluding to the profane nature

Figure 9. The bride's *sousta* as performed in the church courtyard of Ayia Paraskevi in the village of Kattavia, 1952. Personal collection of the author (color figure available online).

of male desire, the dance had decidedly sexual overtones—hence the reference to the devil.

Young and older women performed the second dance done on the latter part of Monday evening, the *vlaha*. Hands were linked as in the *sousta*, and, although the dance steps were those of the slower *syrto* dance, they still consisted of two steps forward and one step backward, as in the *sousta*. The men sang while the women danced: "On the sand and at a Turkish spot, Turkish spot, I find married and single women. Peasant girl, oh peasant girl, your hair I wish I could have" (*Ton amon amon ke ton tere tere, vrisko ke pantremenes ke lefteres. Vlaha mori blachan ta mallia sou na kha*). The words allude to female beauty as a counterpoint to male desire.

The final dance of Monday evening was the *vatani*—performed *only* during the *ghamos*, as noted by all the informants—traditionally the last dance before the bridal couple went off to consummate their union in their marriage bed.[21] The bridal couple led the dance, followed by the *koumbaros*, their parents, and other older relatives. Young men and women were not allowed to dance the *vatani*. It was in a song-dance format with the older men and women singing of good wishes and praising the new couple.[22] The *vatani* was linked to the *sousta* by a series of direct contrasts, inversions, and oppositions. Hands were linked as in the *sousta*, but the steps were exactly the opposite of those of the *sousta*, with one step forward and two steps backward. Interestingly, the *vatani* was also known as the "down dance" (*kato horos*),[23] and the *sousta* was known as the "up dance" (*pano horos*). Moreover, the *vatani* was slow, while the *sousta* was fast. Whereas older dancers performed the *vatani* with the newly married couple, younger dancers performed the *sousta* with the bride and groom. Hence, the *kato horos* clearly represented the bride and groom's change of status from single to married; it functioned as a rite incorporating the newly married couple into the married community before they entered the marital bed. The dancing in the *kamara* publicly acknowledged the bride and groom as man and wife.

There was a definite structure to the sequence of dances performed on Monday evening. Older men danced the *piperi* with single young men, and older women danced the *vlaha* with single young women, which served to mark these young people as potential spouses. In other words, young people were incorporated into the community of older, married village members in these dances to steer youth in the direction of marriage. However, the final dance—the *vatani*—was reserved exclusively for older people and the bridal couple. Hence, the dance that completed the entire sequence of dances during the wedding ritual or *ghamos* was one in which a recently married couple danced with older married dancers. The dance sequence clearly marks the shift from courtship to marriage and shows the couple and the young people being reintegrated into society with their status transformed and their gender roles affirmed.

This paper has demonstrated how a particular Greek dance, the *sousta* of Rhodes, expressed the values of honor (*timi*) and grace (*hari*) during the wedding ritual (*ghamos*) in the interwar period. What informants remembered was how the process bound performers in distinctive ways to socially legitimate gender relations. During the dance, a man revealed himself as graceful and concealed the woman to protect her honor. The *sousta* ultimately revealed the courting couple, resolving the tensions that had built up in the social drama played out in the *kamara*. This revelation was expressed in dance and song as the active work of men. The cultural values of *timi* and *hari* were given form through the dance in a number of distinct and progressive social stages of separating, connecting, associating, and isolating. The dance moved from a static period, in which the dancers were separated by gender in opposite sections of the *kamara*, until the dance teams began to form. Here, the individual man displayed his *hari* to the women through the designs of his dancing and singing. Yet, the focus of the dance was to conceal his desire for a particular female dancer. Only at the very end of the performance was the couple isolated and seen as a romantic pair, although the formation of the couple was the goal of the courtship process. Performing the *sousta*, the couple concealed, revealed, negotiated, and finalized the social outcome of becoming a romantic pair.

Employing Victor Turner's theory of social process, in which negotiation brings about a social outcome in ritual, the processual approach taken in this paper shows how dance may contribute to social development. The fact that the *sousta* included singing, with inherent commitments and bonds in the power of words, and that it was performed at the most elaborate Greek ritual—a wedding—validates the idea that social processes do occur *through* dance performances, not just *around* them. The singing also represented an expression of male identity and the role of *hari* in romance. Dance embodied central cultural values in Greece, such as *hari* and *timi*, which amalgamated and harmonized in the revitalization of a Greek village community.

This article is dedicated to my husband, Efstratios Hadjikonstantinou.

A Note on the Transliteration

The system used for the paper is outlined below.

Alphabet

Aα = a	Nν = n
Bβ = v	Ξξ = ks
Γγ = gh or y (followed by short e or i)	Oo = o
Δδ = dh or d	Ππ = p
Eε = e	Pρ = r
Zζ = z	Σσ = s
Hη = i	Tτ = t
Θ θ = th	Yμ = u
Iι = i	Φφ = f
Iκ = k	Xχ = h or kh
Λλ = l	Ψψ = ps
Mμ = m	Ωω = o

Digraphs

αι = e
ει = i
ου = ou
οι = i
ωι = oi
αυ = af
ευ = ef

Consonant clusters

μπ = b, mb, or mp
ντ = d or nt
γκ, γγ = g or ng

Notes

1. Victor Turner, *The Ritual Process: Structure and Antistructure* (London: Routledge, 1969).
2. See Anastasios Vrontis, *Rodhitikos Ghamos* (Rhodian Wedding) (Athina: Notaras, 1932), 10–15.
3. For a Kattavian song sung during this occasion, see Vrontis, *Rhodhitikos Ghamos*, 36.
4. For an account of a song, see Athina Tarsouli, *Dhodhekanisos* (Dodecanese) (Athina: Alfa, 1947), 120–21.
5. "To Htenaki" was a Rhodian song sung for the bride during the *stolisma*. See Yerasimou Dhrakidhou, *Rodhiaka* (Rhodian) (Athina: Ksatsikounaki, 1937), 66–68. See also Pavlou Ghneftou, *Dimotika Traghoudhia tis Rodhou* (Demotic Songs of Rhodes) (Rhodos: Prisma, 1980), 80–81; and Theodhoros Papandhreou, *I Malona tis Rodhou* (Malona of Rhodes) (Rodhos: Papandhreou, 1986), 163–64. See Vrontis for a Kattavian song sung during this rite (*Rodhitikos Ghamos*, 42–48 and 48–52). For Rhodian songs sung after the dressing, see a later account of the *stolisma* in Papandhreou, *I Malona tis Rodhou*, 164–65.
6. For an account of singing to the groom during this occasion, see Dhrakidhou, *Rodhiaka*, 65–66. See also Tarsouli, *Dhodhekanisos*, 120–22.
7. For songs sung for the occasion of taking the bride to the church, see Dhrakidhou, *Rodhiaka*, 69–70.
8. For songs sung during this procession, see Vrontis, *Rodhitikos Ghamos*, 52–55.
9. For songs sung to the bridegroom from the church to the bridal home, see Dhrakidhou, *Rodhiaka*, 72. For later accounts of singing, see Papandhreou, *I Malona tis Rodhou*, 167.
10. Vrontis notes that this is a remnant of an ancient ritual because the pomegranate was symbolic of the wedding of the Goddess Hera. See Vrontis, *Rodhitikos Ghamos*, 57.
11. Ibid, 57.
12. Ibid., 69.
13. For songs sung during this rite, see Vrontis, *Rodhitikos Ghamos*, 65–68.
14. For an account of Rhodian songs sung during this ritual event, see Vrontis, *Rodhitikos Ghamos*, 85.
15. See Theodore Petrides, *Greek Dances* (Athens: Lycabettus Press, 1975), 121.
16. See Petrides, *Greek Dances*, 122.
17. See Theodore Petrides and Elfleida Petrides, *Folk Dances of the Greeks* (Bailey: Folkstone, 1974), 13.
18. Vrontis states that the *monahiko* was danced by young people in the village square, followed by the *sousta* (*Rodhitikos Ghamos*, 47 and 55). For a later account of the *monahiko* danced in the village square see Papandhreou, *I Malona tis Rodhou*, 167–68.
19. For a later account of the *sousta* danced in the church courtyard, see Papandhreou, *I Malona tis Rodhou*, 168.

20. For an account of the *piperi* song and dance see Vrontis, *Rodhitikos Ghamos*, 60–70; see also Papandhreou, *I Malona tis Rodhou*, 175, and Tarsouli, *Dhodhekanisos*, 116. Papandhreou also gives a very interesting account of a dance called the *skoupa* performed by youth on Monday night in the village of Malona (*I Malona tis Rodhou*, 177).

21. Vrontis indicates that the *vatani* dance was performed after eating (*Rodhitikos Ghamos*, 59).

22. For an account of *vatani* songs, see Vrontis, *Rodhitikos Ghamos*, 59–61. For an account of songs sung to the bride and groom see Tarsouli, *Dhodhekanisos*, 120–21.

23. For an account of the *kato* at a Rhodian wedding dance, see Papandhreou, *I Malona tis Rodhou*, 173–74.

A CREATIVE PROCESS IN ETHIOPIAN-ISRAELI DANCE: ESKESTA DANCE THEATER AND BETA DANCE TROUPE

RUTH ESHEL

Dancer, teacher, and choreographer Ruth Eshel has worked extensively with the Ethiopian Jewish community in Israel (known as Falashas or Beta Israel), developing a creative process and contemporary choreographic approach to the traditional Ethiopian eskesta (shoulder dancing). Discussion of selected dances and different choreographic methods reveals a number of issues and responses arising in the course of this fifteen-year artistic journey. Questions and experiences uncovered through this exploration offer perspectives on cultural formation and preservation specific to the Beta Israel but also more broadly applicable to other immigrant groups, beyond the population and work discussed here.

Ethiopia. University of Addis Ababa Theater (December 10, 2011). Eight of the Beta Dance Troupe dancers are standing in a line, facing the audience. The dance *Opus for Shoulders* commences with a motif of shoulder dancing (*eskesta*) in unison so that the audience's attention can be drawn to the changes that this movement phrase undergoes in direction, length, and pauses that freeze the movement. At one point the dancers stand in a tight circle descending into a deep plié as they perform *eskesta*, the movement becoming soft and melting. While bouncing in deep plié they encourage one another, shouting vowels in their native tongue, Amharic,* while one or another dancer jumps and "melts" again. As they gather energy the dancers spread in space like fireworks competing with one another in the energy of their jumps and vibratory shoulders. The dance ends with the formality of a canon in which half the dancers advance in a low walk adorned with *eskesta*, crossing the stage from right to left, while the other group, after eight counts, repeats variations of the same phrase, advancing in a quadrangle that crosses the

---

*Amharic is the official working language of Ethiopia.

approaching dancers on the same side-to-side axis.[1] The dance is accompanied by the dancers' recorded voices, speaking Amharic syllables. Henok Yared reviewed Beta's program of contemporary *eskesta* dance as a "Dance Performance that Opens a New Era of *Eskesta*," while another headline noted that "Israel's Beta Dance Troupe Brings Unique *Falasha* Insight."[2] *Falasha* is Amharic for "stranger"—the name given by Ethiopians to their Jewish population—yet Beta Dance Troupe is composed of Israelis of Ethiopian descent who immigrated to Israel as children. They returned to Addis Ababa to dance their version of *eskesta*, incorporating the changes they had experienced.

This article reflects on my dance work with the Ethiopian community in Israel beginning in 1991 and continuing to the present. Prior to this work, I was known as a dancer and choreographer in what were considered avant-garde recitals at the end of the 1970s, and later as a dance researcher focusing on the history of dance in Israel. My work with the Ethiopian-Israeli community, the subject of this essay, has occupied my focus from 1991 to the present. This work, shared with dozens of dancers of the Ethiopian community, has explored the establishment of a contemporary choreographic approach to the traditional *eskesta*. In the course of this creative process many questions have arisen, some familiar to other choreographic processes, some unique to this one: How can we discover and stimulate the creative powers, within both the dancers and me, of which we are often unaware? Can the dancers express themselves in their new society, yet keep connected to their roots? How far may one dare take creative freedoms in service of artistic expression and still maintain what I think of as the "DNA" of the culture from which this movement material emerges? What are the best ways to work with dancers who have no previous formal dance training to create contemporary material from this traditional dance form? What differences are reflected in the group's creative processes and repertory between work with dancers who joined the group as adults, only a few years after immigrating to Israel, and those who grew up in this country? Can dance create a bridge between people from different cultures? These questions, and the experiences their exploration yielded, may apply to cultural formation and preservation among immigrant groups in other locations.

The Ethiopian Jews

The Ethiopian community in Israel is an ethnic group of Jews whose existence was little known outside their native land until the beginning of the nineteenth century. They lived in north and northeastern Ethiopia in small villages spread over a wide territory among a Muslim and predominantly Christian ruling population.[3] Between the thirteenth and sixteenth centuries they fought and resisted several attempts by Christian Ethiopian emperors to subjugate them and impose Christianity. The last independent Falasha stronghold, in the Semien Mountains, was finally defeated in the seventeenth century, followed by mass suicides to avoid forced religious conversion. Of those who remained, most converted to Christianity (this converted group was later known as Falashmura or Beit [house of] Avraham), but a handful maintained their religion and called themselves Beta [house of] Israel. These Falashas did not mingle with the Christian Ethiopians and suffered low social status, anti-Semitism, and blood libels. Yet they were devout in their Judaism, as they knew it from the First-Temple period.[*]

After establishment of the state of Israel in 1948 this population's determination to immigrate to Israel increased and was regarded as the realization of the dream of generations. However, immigration was suspended owing to the debate in Israel about whether the Beta Israel were actually Jews, since their practices diverged widely from those of modern Judaism. Only in 1973 were they recognized as Jews by Israel's rabbinical authorities, but by that time Ethiopia had become a Communist country and the population was denied the right to leave. As the condition of Beta Israel worsened, the Israeli government decided to wait no longer but rather to smuggle the population out of Ethiopia. Under Operation Moses, conducted during the first half of the 1980s, large numbers of the community crossed the border on foot and under cover from Ethiopia to the Sudanese desert, walking hundreds of miles north to reach an improvised refugee camp and wait for aircraft to arrive, also under cover, to fly them to Israel.[4]

---

[*]Although dating is not entirely clear, the First Temple was built by King Solomon, perhaps in the tenth century BCE, and destroyed in the sixth century BCE, at which time the Jews were exiled from their land and several tribes of Israel were lost from historical record.

During the harsh and dangerous trek through the desert, some 5,000 members of the community died from hardship, robbers, rape, and imprisonment. When, at the peak of its effectiveness, the secret airlift was leaked to the media, the operation was discontinued. Those left behind moved to Addis Ababa, waiting hopefully for the Ethiopian government to allow them to leave. Only in 1991, on the eve of a revolution and perceptible danger to the Ethiopian Jews' well-being, the regime, on the verge of toppling, allowed Israeli aircraft to use the Addis Ababa airport for thirty-six hours. Beginning on May 24, Israeli planes transported more than 14,000 Ethiopian Jews to Israel in what was known as Operation Solomon. Currently, there are approximately 150,000 Israeli members of the Ethiopian community living throughout the country.

Dawn Horwitz points out that "the music and dance these Ethiopian Jews have brought with them have played a role in their lives, sometimes as a unifying force, sometimes a comforting one, sometimes a defiant one and sometimes an embarrassing one."[5] Several dance groups established by the Ethiopian community in Israel have claimed to be "keepers of tradition," modeling their dancing on video disks of Ethiopian folk dances performed in Addis Ababa to entertain tourists. How "authentic" is the dancing from these sources? Robert Nicholls has remarked on the tourist's "voyeur stance," a "search for local color" that often leads to a "decline in cultural and artistic standards" as performers strut for "the benefit of goggling strangers."[6] Traditional dances are not static but are always evolving, so that whatever is regarded as "authentic" and "traditional" will reflect culture in a certain period and is subject to change.[7] Folklorist Felix Hoerburger has used the term "folk dance in its first existence" to describe the "original tradition" that functions chiefly as an integral part of community life where dances are learned in a natural way as part of everyday living, whereas "folk dance in its second existence" is a "conscious revival or cultivation of folk dance" with fixed figures and movements, taught by professional teachers.[8] Similarly, Anthony Shay identifies the "parallel traditions" of folk dance "in the field" and in theatricalized forms.[9] Lois Ellfeldt distinguishes another category, that of "contemporary creative dance," in which "significant movement sequences are drawn out of human experience and the very act of moving. Form develops from the manipulations of these movements according to the dictates of the choreographer."[10] In the early years, some of my works created with Eskesta could be described as "folk dance in its second existence." Yet, as I felt more confident, my work became increasingly embedded in the last category. This shift also reflects a change in Ethiopian community dance in Israel that connects to a comment by the African philosopher Paulin Hountondji; he notes that Africa's developing relationship with the cultural traditions of other continents need not be "a process of Westernization or of acculturation," but rather can be understood as an opportunity for "creative freedom, enriching the African tradition itself as an open system of options."[11]

Community Dance and Stage Dance in Israel

My work with the dance groups Eskesta and Beta is one of the meeting points in the convoluted relationship between ethnic dance and stage dance in Israel, a relationship always reflecting ideologies and political changes.[*] In 1882, at the beginning of the Jewish settlement in Palestine or Eretz Israel (the biblical "Land of Israel"), there was an aspiration in the Yishuv (the Jewish communities existing between 1882 and 1948) to create a Hebrew culture that would be different from Jewish culture identified with the Diaspora and that would create a bridge between contemporary Israel and ancient Israel.[12] Upon their immigration to Eretz Israel, Jewish dance artists from Russia and Central Europe, connected with both Ausdruckstanz (expressive dance) and classical ballet, tried to create a Hebrew dance for the stage while seeking inspiration from the small Yemenite community that had been trickling into the land since 1905. These artists regarded the Yemenite Jews, who had lived in isolation and were little exposed to foreign influences, as continuing the Jewish history that had been discontinued by exile 2,000 years earlier. Similarly, the artists' imaginations were fired by the local Arabs and Bedouins, whose ways of life had

---

[*]This essay does not address the relationship between folk and stage dance in Israel. Today, for reasons beyond the scope of this article, the term "folk dance" is generally used for choreographed Israeli folk dances created in that land in the 1940s and thereafter, while "ethnic dance" generally refers to the community dances that immigrant Jews from the Middle East, Asia, and Africa have brought with them, as well as the dance of ethnic minorities in Israel (e.g., Arab or Druze).

seemingly remained unchanged, and were considered as possible representations of life in biblical Israel.[13]

When World War II broke out, cultural ties with Europe were severed and Eretz-Israeli dance artists became isolated for more than ten years. This separation from Europe increased reliance upon local talent and creativity, and there were many dance performances in the styles of Ausdruckstanz and "Hebrew dance" given by teachers and their students. Artists were driven to create, and there was public demand for their works.[14] Upon establishment of the state of Israel in 1948 an estrangement between ethnic dance and stage dance occurred. The country was flooded by waves of Jewish refugees from Arab countries, Holocaust survivors from Europe, and Jews from elsewhere throughout the world. The country became a Tower of Babel culturally and linguistically. This situation led to a "melting pot" policy: rather than fostering the heritage of each distinct community, the goal would be creation of a common core for all communities out of which, it was hoped, an Israeli culture would be generated.

It was not until the first half of the 1950s that dance companies from abroad began to appear in Israel, including the Martha Graham Dance Company in 1956. That tour evoked an intense response; Israeli modern dancers adopted Graham's style and Ausdruckstanz was rejected as old-fashioned. Connections to "the ethnic" were further perceived as a drawback that might color the dance work with locality and provinciality, while dance artists were looking to ascend the peak of international art. Interest in creating a Hebrew or Israeli dance also waned as a result of the belief that one cannot force such a development and this dance would be naturally created with time. A notable exception was the Inbal Dance Theater that Sara Levi-Tanai founded in 1949 with members of the Yemenite community, creating contemporary dance for the stage inspired by Yemenite culture. Dance critic Giora Manor remarked, "Great folk dance choreographers such as Igor Moiseyev or Amalia Hernandez 'domesticated' folk dance to fit the modern stage. Mainly, they solved the spatial problems of many folk dances performed in a circle, thus excluding spectators from the central arena. Unlike them, Sara Levi-Tanai has 'dissolved' ancient folk dance traditions and built her own original choreographic structures from the basic folkloric components."[15] From its start, Inbal's artistic goals inspired debate. The Ministry of Education expected Inbal to preserve the traditional Yemenite folklore and were disappointed to see that Levi-Tanai was creating "nonauthentic" dances. The dance community regarded Inbal as a purely ethnic troupe. Yet abroad, Inbal Dance Theater was accepted enthusiastically as a representative of Israeli artistic dance during the 1960s.[16]

In the 1970s the "melting pot" policy in Israel collapsed and was replaced by "Social Pluralism." According to Dina Roginsky, "Contrary to the former absorption model, which attempted to annul the ethnic-cultural difference of oriental Jews so they might 'assimilate' into the Israeli society and culture, the new absorption model desired to do just the opposite—to actively 'foster' this culture."[17] In response, the enterprise of fostering the dance of communities and minorities began in 1971. The document "Culture Certificate—Vision 2000" articulates this change in Israel's cultural policy. As Dan Ronen states, "The principle of heterogeneity was accepted as a value, based on equality of cultural opportunities, and equal opportunity for all existing cultures in society to develop and maintain their existence."[18]

While the relationship between folk dances and dances of various communities underwent change and experienced reciprocal fertilization, stage dance continued developing on an independent course without any connection to ethnic or Israeli folk dance. In the course of the 1990s, a few Israeli choreographers, identified with modern dance and working with professional dancers trained in Western techniques, employed motifs connected to ethnic culture: Moshe Efrati adopted movement elements from Sephardic* Jewish culture, Liat Dror and Nir Ben Gal integrated components of belly dance into their work, and Renana Raz was inspired by the Druze debka. Barak Marshal is notable in that he regularly combines motifs of Hassidic, Yemenite, and pop-culture dance.[19]

Considering this background, the creative work done in Eskesta Dance Theater and Beta Dance Troupe for fifteen years is unusual. This has been a creative process performed with the community members, none of whom were then profes-

---

*The term "Sephardim" refers to Jews who fled or were expelled from Spain in or around 1492, many of whom settled in Middle Eastern countries as well as North Africa, the Levant, Brazil, and various European centers.

sional dancers, at a time when historic memory still exists in the dancers' bodies. That memory is growing weaker and is about to vanish.

Documenting Ethiopian-Israeli Dance

My contact with members of the Ethiopian-Israeli community began in 1991, initiated by Gila Toledano, then the director of the Dance Library of Israel at Beit Ariela in Tel Aviv and, for twenty-six years prior to that, the close assistant of Sara Levi-Tanai. At the time Toledano approached me, the media were filled with documentaries about Operation Solomon. That same year a large influx of immigrants from the former Soviet Union brought many Russian folk dances to Israel, but that dance was familiar, while the dance of the Ethiopian community was, for me, a virgin field.

Between 1991 and 1993, armed with a Super 8 video camera, I visited caravan sites that were set up throughout the country in order to temporarily house the influx of immigrants from Ethiopia and the former Soviet Union.[20] I conducted interviews, recorded musicians, and observed and taped a range of movement activities. These included the *eskesta* dances in festivities (weddings and bar-mitzvah celebrations), the movement accompanying prayers of Yom Kippur (Day of Atonement) and funeral ceremonies, everyday activities such as hair-braiding, tying the baby to the mother's back, and baking the Ethiopian *injera* bread, and the curiosity of the community members gazing with amazement at visiting Israeli dance ensembles featuring girls in tight jeans wriggling through jazz dances.

Prior to the documentation period, I had done some reading about African dance[21] and had investigated literature on identity construction, representation, and embodiment through dance.[22] Particularly influential in my research has been Theresa Buckland's statement, "Dance is a culturally constructed mode of human action,"[23] and the comment by Glendola Yhema Mills, assistant artistic director of Kariamu & Company, "Historically, dance descriptions by anthropologists, historians, and dance critics are replete with references to the power, focus, and energy that is present in African dance as a social form, but lack the same attention to technical skills and the discipline required of high-level performers."[24] I read a sizable body of literature written on the Ethiopian Jews in the last decades,[25] but none has included dance.* Some research on Ethiopian dance has been done by Hungarian ethnomusicologists who worked for a time at the National School of Music in Addis Ababa.[26]

After three years of documentation and research I transferred the dozens of hours I had filmed to the Dance Library of Israel with notes, descriptions, and analyses of events. At this point, I began to dream of establishing an Ethiopian dance troupe, modeled on the work of Sara Levi-Tanai. This dream materialized two years later, a subject to which I shall return shortly.

Analyzing the *Eskesta*

The *eskesta* appears in folk dances of several Ethiopian areas with differences in motifs and in its place in the dance. The Amharic *eskesta* danced by the Ethiopian Jews is usually performed in a circle with participants moving their shoulders, rebounding in knee bends, clapping, and making hissing sounds.[27] The excitement increases when two soloists compete with one another in an improvised virtuoso *eskesta* for a few seconds, soon replaced by others. Sometimes, at the climax of excitement, the whole group jumps up and down, clapping hands, their shoulders dancing *eskesta*, and everyone moving in a circle en masse, engulfing the soloists as if swallowing them. There is no specific time or cue for the dance to start or end. The dancing is accompanied by melodic vocalization, clapping, drumming, and other traditional instruments. This dance serves for many festivities, although the words of the dance-song change. Kariamu Welsh Asante has noted, "Many of the dances in Africa are what I call 'multipurpose' dances. These dances change their context according to the event and therefore the responses also change."[28]

In my work I focused on the movement of the *eskesta* itself, and not on a specific folk dance of a particular area. The *eskesta* involves various upper-body parts—the top of the shoulders, the neck, the scapulae, and head. The movement of the shoulders is usually initiated in the shoulder blades. In improvisation, the

---

*Since that time, I published the article "Dance," in *Ethiopia*, ed. Hagar Salamon (Jerusalem: Ben-Zvi Institute, 2007), 111–18.

eskesta reveal rich motifs distinct from one another in rhythm, direction, and qualities. The shoulders move vertically (upward and downward), sagittally (backward and forward), and diagonally (twisting, with one forward and the other backward). The shoulder movement can be symmetrical or asymmetrical. The neck and head can move with the shoulders or in opposite directions.

Musicologist Tibor Vadasy suggests three vertical "stations" (spatial points) for the *eskesta*: one between the shoulder's natural position to its highest possible point and two leading from the natural position to the lowest point; furthermore, there are three horizontal stations on the way forward and two for movement to the back.[29] I have observed that movement between the stations can travel in a straight line or in a partial or full circle toward the next station or skipping over stations. The circular movement enables connections between the vertical and sagittal dimensions. According to Vadasy, the dancers alternately integrate two variations on the *eskesta* into the same dance. One consists of improvisations on shoulder motifs passing between two or even three stations; these movements are fragmentary, quick, and concluded with a sharp halt. The second type of *eskesta* variation is a continuous shoulder-blade movement, generally horizontal, between two proximate stations, creating a trembling or vibrating effect that can be performed by both shoulders together or one alone. Various rhythmic motifs give vitality and force to the *eskesta*. These are typically short, rich rhythmical units in a 2/4 meter, in some cases repetitive and in others changing constantly as the soloists demonstrate their virtuosity, unifying rhythm and movement to create the dance.

Establishing Eskesta and Beta Dance Troupes

In 1991 I was invited to give dance courses at the University of Haifa as part of the faculty of humanities, although the university has no dance department. The courses included dance in Israel, twentieth-century dance, and an introductory movement composition class. Several female students of Ethiopian descent enrolled in the composition course but their shyness inhibited their creative expression. With establishment in 1995 of the Theater Study Circle at the university, my courses were integrated into that program, in which four male students of Ethiopian origin appeared. While they paid little attention to my instructions in the course, rather doing whatever they pleased, what they did was wonderful. I suggested establishing a dance group. They did, and brought their friends, male and female, from the university. Thus, in December of 1995, Eskesta Dance Theater was born. After a decade, in 2005, internal changes at the faculty brought about the end of the company within the framework of the university. A group of the dancers and I then established Beta Dance Troupe at Neve Yoseph community center in Haifa, at the heart of a heavily Ethiopian-Israeli neighborhood. The community center regarded the adoption of the troupe as both a contribution to society and a way to strengthen its own standing. Peggy Phelan has written, "Certainly under-represented communities can be empowered by an enhanced visibility" in the cultural field.[30] During the troupe's rehearsals the studio doors are left open in order to enable community children to see the dancers, and those who appear are invited to enter and watch the rehearsals. Since many of the youngsters want to disown traditional dance and music, preferring to dance hip-hop, our intention is to instill in them interest and pride in their culture as they watch our work.

The size of the group ranges from six to eight dancers who rehearse twice a week, three hours each time. In the early days of Eskesta Dance Theater, most of the participating dancers had come to Israel through the Sudan desert in Operation Moses. A small number arrived as youngsters with Operation Solomon and had been in Israel only three or four years prior to joining the dance group. They spoke Hebrew with a heavy Amharic accent. At that time, Ethiopian cultural expression differed markedly between men and women, the latter being shy and restrained while the former were full of confidence and creativity. Among the recent members of Beta Dance Troupe, some dancers arrived as young children in Operation Solomon, while others were born in Israel. The women are as strong as the men and all speak Hebrew as their native tongue. Some do not even know Amharic drumming or language but the *eskesta* that they dance in festivities continues to be part of their bodily learning and memory. Some have become reacquainted with their culture through their connection to the dance troupe.

I told the first cast of Eskesta's dancers that my goal was to form a different dance group from those they watched on

Ethiopian videocassettes. It would not be a folk dance troupe and we would make no claims of "authenticity" or "representation." Since I was a lecturer at the university and an authority in their eyes, they trusted me and I hoped that, through the creative processes, they would understand that we were talking about a kind of work in which there was much room for their personal expression. Their friends often came to rehearsals, and the enthusiasts among them asked to join the group, while others complained that we were not performing "authentic" Ethiopian dance. It is interesting to note that this first group of dancers in Eskesta Dance Theater, when interviewed by the media, always emphasized that they represented Ethiopian culture, as if such a response were expected of them, although they knew that we were proceeding on a different artistic path. When asked in the course of media interviews whether they would prefer to dance the traditional dances, they responded that, although they loved those dances, in Eskesta they had the opportunity to be part of the creative process. Dancer Zena Adhenen was a member of the first troupe and reflected on his transition during that period: "Before, I only danced and moved 'mechanically' at weddings and clubs. In the group I realized for the first time that dance had more power of expression than what I had known in the past. I wanted to combine what I knew and what I did not know. The group gave me another dimension to discover in myself and the strength to engage in art in the coming years."[31] Minalu Degai, who had performed with folk dance troupes in Ethiopia and in the Ethiopian-Israeli Bahalachin Dance Troupe (a traditional ensemble), has remarked that in those companies she danced "traditional dances with which I grew up and I was told how to dance them. Here [with Eskesta], I can create, and it is such a wonderful gift."[32] The dancers are, thus, articulate in their recognition of Eskesta's different objectives from those that a folkloric company would typically embrace.

While the troupe was received enthusiastically by native Israelis, the reactions of some of the Ethiopian community varied from astonishment to annoyance. The responses to this work by the community members resurrected the tension between authentic and nonauthentic expression that arose in the work of Inbal Dance Theater. Dancer Revital Fekadu remarked, "At the beginning, it was not so clear what we were doing because it was not the dance we used to dance in Ethiopia where there is only folk dance. Yet I felt very good about what we were doing. I understood that dance is not only folk dance, but we were afraid of what the Ethiopian community would say. With time, as we performed and received good feedback, it encouraged us. Also, the community has gone through changes and started to understand that dance can also be art."[33] Similarly, Zehava Baruch recalls, "We were connected to what we were doing because we danced from within, but we did not know how the Ethiopian community would accept it. My brother called me and said, 'What is this? Are you crazy?' In Ethiopia there is no creative contemporary dance. When I met with my parents I told them that what we were doing was like theater, because they saw a play in Ethiopia on the stage, and then they understood what we were doing."[34]

Choreographic Processes

Upon commencement of rehearsals with Eskesta Dance Troupe, I made several fundamental decisions to which I have adhered through the years: the dancers and I would work as a collaborative team, experimenting with *eskesta*, new subject matter, and new imagery; we would also collaborate with professional musicians and costume and lighting designers; we would not borrow movement material identified with the lexicons of ballet, modern dance, jazz, hip-hop, and other such recognizable forms; the choreography's technical demands would be based on the dancers' natural movement abilities. Thus, the lexicon of movement material would be drawn from two parallel sources: the dancers' natural, free, expressive movements and the expansion of *eskesta* from within its own vocabulary by exploiting contemporary compositional devices. The former is more intuitive and emotional and the latter more objective and analytical. These two sources—polar opposites on the same creative continuum—support and enrich each other during the creative process.

In the first months I suggested *eskesta*-related subject matter familiar to the dancers, such as festivities, prayers, and mourning, all tied to life-cycle events and each offering a different lexicon of movement. I told them that through improvisations we would explore expressive areas of which the dancers might be unaware, drawing from their somatic memories to reveal what might be hidden or not articulated verbally. Some improvisations were intended to uncover the rich reservoir of possibilities in the *esk-esta* and to expand the lexicon of movement from within its current form. I see these explorations as related: the more one reveals what is hidden within, the more one needs a broad choice of movements, and at the same time, the broader movement lexicon encourages exploration of new subject matter. In a similar way, Sarah Rubidge, working with a Ugandan dance troupe, remarked about her experience, "It was like being a guide in a terrain that neither the dancers nor I knew, a terrain we were creating together as we developed our ideas."[35]

I rejected musical accompaniment of pop songs by well-known Ethiopian singers, asking instead that the dancers drum traditional rhythms. I wanted to avoid the influence of the powerful and currently familiar songs on the dancers, which called forth partylike social dancing. I encouraged them to listen to themselves and find out what the pure rhythms evoked. From the very beginning I emphasized that, rather than trying to impress me, the dancers' movements should emerge from the body's "hunger" to move expressively, and not out of a rational decision. Dancer Yoseph Tagenia recalls, "We learned how to listen to the 'silence' within us and from there to burst out."[36] When a dancer concentrated on his or her own inner experience, a free dialogue between the dancer and the drummer developed and it was possible even to stop the drumming so that the dancer could continue plunging quietly into him or herself and explore what was deeply concealed.

Already in the documentation period, as well as in the composition course, I realized that abstract instructions related to space might paralyze the dancers' creativity. Similarly, Danielle Bélec recalls that if Robert Dunn asked his students to work with an effort quality during an improvisation, "he often found himself shifting away from the terminology of the LMA [Laban Movement Analysis] system to an image or personal association."[37] As substitute for abstract instructions, I told stories and used images taken from Ethiopian culture. For example, instead of asking the dancers to dance while changing level, I asked them to imagine that they were entering a river in order to purify themselves before Sabbath, and that they were diving to the bottom and rising up from the water to look at the sky. This kind of work brings to mind the claim of philosopher Mark Johnson that imagination is prior to reason as the basic meaning-making operation and, further, that metaphors and our understanding of them are grounded in bodily experience.[38] Dunn, on the other hand, encouraged students to start with the bodily experience and allow the image to emerge and become sharper.[39] With Eskesta, we worked in both ways: sometimes, based on choreographic guidelines, I appealed to the dancers' imaginations with culturally inspired images, while later in the creative process, after discovering the movement material, I might return to abstraction in the choreographic staging.

We gave substantial focus to work with objects familiar to the dancers from the Ethiopian culture, such as sticks used for walking or carrying merchandise, plaited baskets, or the *chera*, short sticks with horsehair attached at the ends, held by respected elders as a status symbol. During the prop work, the dancers showed me how these items were used in the Ethiopian villages and then I asked them to set off on a creative voyage using the objects according to their imaginations—to dissociate and return freely to the familiar context—while I offered suggestions. I discovered that through work with these kinds of props it was possible to gradually impart abstract compositional values. The very act of taking a familiar object and transforming it, using it in another context, demanded considerable reflection on the nature of props in traditional dance. Tagenia remarked, "Working with the props was interesting. We did not have any problem using them differently than their original function."[40]

From the *eskesta* combinations generated in the improvisations some phrases appeared that stood out in their originality or virtuosity. I wanted to catch those phrases, analyze and engrave them, so they might serve as "bricks" for constructing the movement lexicon or new dances, as Sara Levi-Tanai had done in her work with Inbal. As with Inbal in its early stages, the Ethiopian dancers found it hard to repeat the movements they had performed a few seconds earlier. The special movement burst out unselfconsciously, shone, and immediately faded away—vanished. Therefore, we attempted to videotape rehearsals in order to give the dancers an opportunity to observe the movements they had performed and try to repeat them. However, the dance phrases that had erupted spontaneously turned into foreign material when the dancers watched the video and tried to imitate them or

Figure 1. Johnny Brahanu and Shmuel Bero compete, dancing *eskesta* (1996). Photograph by Arik Baltinester. Courtesy of Arik Baltinester (color figure available online).

learn all over again how to perform them. I found, too, that after I had analyzed those movement phrases and then taught them to the dancers, they appeared forced. I realized that the assignment of "fishing the *eskesta*," as I called it, and expanding the vocabulary was more complicated than I had anticipated (see Figure 1).

Works

After four months of exploratory rehearsals the dancers became impatient and demanded that I dictate to them what to dance "as in the Ethiopian videocassettes," so that we could begin performing. I realized that I was beginning to lose their trust and patience and that an immediate change of direction was essential before they all left and the project dissolved. I decided to abandon, temporarily, attempts to expand the vocabulary and, rather, to engage in the general framework of new choreography within the context of events familiar to them.

To meet the dancers' needs, I created "guideline maps" for the general structure of dances that recalled the composition methods of John Cage, who gave scripts with general assignments to his collaborators, leaving space for the musicians' decisions and for chance encounters.[41] My "guideline maps" created a general structure that determined which dancers entered; from where; when they advanced, in which direction in space; and whom they encountered. Within this general set of guidelines, I developed smaller units of instruction for each dancer. For example, in the dance *Courting*, in which the dancers show off to one another, talk, and quarrel using *eskesta*, the instructions were based on transitions that connected couples with contrasting qualities. For example, "When you encounter dancer A, you surround him and have a certain image, and when you encounter dancer B, you dance back to back and have a different image. Then you both approach dancer C, form a circle, and perform jumps in a clockwise direction." I told them not to see just the movements of the dance but to regard these instructions as a means to express themselves. This creative form released the dancers from the pressure of needing to repeat the *eskesta* sentences accurately. The imagery functioned as Dunn stated: "[When] you change an image or cue, you are changing the whole quality of the movement."[42] These instructions led to a structured dance with a through line performed according to the instructions, but the choreography left much room for the dancers' creativity. The instructions had to be clear and simple and I had to guard against the dancers' tendency to break the frameworks and do whatever they desired, thus dissolving the structure of the choreography.

This structure of guidelines for staging the macro-form, while the dancers provided the micro-elements, had the benefit of both "participatory dance" and "presentational dance."[43] According to Elsie Ivanovich Dunin, the former applies to dances performed by those who participate spontaneously; these dances tend to focus on the experience of the dancers themselves. On the other hand, presentational dance encompasses planned performance on the stage.[44] Andriy Nahachewsky points out that when the same dance is notated in Labanotation there is significant difference between the "participatory" and "presentational" form: the

Figure 2. Johnny Brahanu, Zena Adhenen, Shmuel Bero, Geto Tesfay in *Prayer Dance* (1996), choreographed by Ruth Eshel. Photograph by Arik baltinester. Courtesy of Arik Baltinester (color figure available online).

"participatory is complex and rich with communicative material in its 'microscopic' movement elements (eye contact, variations in touch, etc.), while the presentational is quite standardized and regular at this level. This is often desirable in presentational dance as the focus there lies in its 'macroscopic' structure (phrases, formations, etc.)."[45] I found that the structure offered by the guidelines I had provided combined benefits of both the micro/participatory form and the macro/presentational form. I continued to use this model between the years 1995 and 1998. The dances of this period appear connected to the "authentic village" repertory of the group, with traditional costumes and live drumming (see Figure 2).

Maharo *(1998)*

In conversations with the dancers the subject of the harsh voyage in the desert during Operation Moses, in which some of them had participated, often arose. Thus emerged the idea for *Maharo* [Amharic for "In Their Memory"], a dance formed as a sequence of theatrical scenes about that journey. At the beginning of the creative process I invited Ilana Ben Tov-Israeli, a creative writing instructor, to meet with the dancers.[46] Under her guidance they told and wrote their personal memories and stories they had heard from their parents. For example, all of them recalled their parents telling them that in order to reach Jerusalem they would have to cross a big, dangerous river and many people would die on the way. The river symbolized the difficulties that had to be endured; for the dancers the Sudan desert and its dangers became that river. We improvised on overcoming physical and imaginary obstacles. Zehava Baruch, five years old when she walked the Sudan desert, remembered how the group hid during the day, afraid of soldiers, robbers, and rapists, and walked quietly through the nights. She wrote a song describing her experience, each verse ending with the line, "That they will not know, that they will not see that we are Jews." There happened to be mats in the studio for use by the physical education students. We took the mats and began improvising with them, creating imaginary walls to hide behind (see Figure 3).

Others wrote about the fear of snakes and lions during the journey, and how helpless they had felt. Instead of improvising

Figure 3. *Maharo.* (1998), choreographed by Ruth Eshel. Yeshalem Fekadu, Orna Yihias, Zehava Baruch, and Revital Fekadu as women in the desert, wrapped in big shawls, covering their babies; an exhausted man, danced by Tesfahon Alamo, crawling with a stick. Photograph by Dina Guna. Courtesy of Dina Guna (color figure available online).

on the theme of "fear," I suggested that the dancers improvise on the quality of strength—the strength of those feared animals and the sensation of being strong. Tagenia recalled, "You told us to be lions, to project strength and roar loudly. Not to be ashamed. To dare. We are a very introverted community and suddenly I could be a lion, so powerful, both physically and mentally. We took this feeling we had experienced in the improvisations to our daily life."[47] In the course of the following years, the use of metaphor became integrated into the choreographic process. Later, I found confirmation for this process in George Lakoff and Mark Johnson's theory: "Since much of our social reality is understood in metaphoric terms, and since our conception of the physical world is partly metaphorical, metaphor plays a very significant role in determining what is real for us . . . . A given metaphor may be the only way to highlight and coherently organize exactly those aspects of our experience."[48]

The dance begins with the travel prayer *Samaeni*, a request that God hear one's prayer. The dancers sing in Geez, the holy

Figure 4. *Maharo.* Yossi Tagenia, Johnny Brahanu, and group, dancing with mats. Photograph by Dina Guna. Courtesy of Dina Guna (color figure available online).

language of Beta Israel, while walking in a convoy after the *Kes*, who is the Ethiopian rabbi.* This prayer is among those taught us by *Kes* Yirmiyahu Pikado as part of the community prayers preservation project carried out by the dance troupe. The work includes a dance of women in the desert wrapped in large shawls, as if covering their small children on their backs (see Figure 4). Their steps have a feeling of heaviness as they advance with shawls fluttering like birds in a panic. Scenes include hiding from robbers while manipulating the bundles on their backs; a duet of men in which one carries his friend across an imagery obstacle (the "river"); a love duet of caresses from afar without any physical contact between the man and the woman, performed to live singing by one of our dancers; and a group performing the "authentic" *eskesta* in moments of joy. The work ends with the burial service, *Maharo*, which asks God to accept the souls of the dead who passed away on the journey, as the dancers hold green branches, customary at the death of children[49] (see Figure 5).

For *Maharo*, most of the dancers chose expressive natural movement to tell their stories, except for the joyous *eskesta* dance where traditional movement was used. While Sarah Rubidge employed a similar strategy in using autobiographical material as the basis of her work with the Ugandan dance community, she had a different experience: "Most of the dancers chose to use traditional dance movements, carefully selected from the range available to them, interpolated with original movement images."[50] Maybe the reason for the difference was Rubidge's selection of a range of traditional movements for her dancers, while we were still investigating the evasive *eskesta*. In retrospect, I find that the images were sometimes too literal, but the movement was honest and the dancers were telling their story. Dancer Ester Maharat commented, "In the group I revealed myself. Sometimes it had a therapeutic effect."[51]

In that same year, the dance group was invited to Ethiopia on the occasion of Israel's fiftieth anniversary. The troupe performed the repertory of folk-derived dances created in our first years, as well as *Maharo*, before the cultural elite of the country. In

---

*Many words in the prayers are similar to Hebrew. For example, *samaeni* in Geez and *shma'eni* in Hebrew both mean "hear me."

Figure 5. *Maharo* ends with a burial service, the dancers holding green branches, customary at the death of children. First row: Yossi Tagenia, Telahon Malako and Asubalu Alamo. Second row: Johnny Brahanu as a *Kes*, holding a *chera*. Third row: Revital Fekadu, Yshalem Fekadu, Zehava Baruch and Orna Yihias. Fourth row: Alamo Tesfahon and Trudel Kidna. Photograph by Dina Guna. Courtesy of Dina Guna (color figure available online).

the course of conversations, we learned that there was a struggle in Ethiopia between those seeking to preserve traditional dance and those who wished to take new paths. We brought our humble example of searching in new directions. The positive reactions to the dances we presented strengthened us, but I did not know how to continue from there. I was familiar with this feeling—not knowing how to move forward—from the years I had performed as a dancer/creator of my solo programs. From that experience, I knew that we had to go on working, to open the internal attention channels and not push anything toward definition in order to avoid diverting by rationalism what might emerge spontaneously and unexpectedly.

The difficulty of investigating—or, as I thought of it, "fishing"—the evasive *eskesta* remained, and I felt that I had to put aside this endeavor and enrich the movement lexicon with additional Ethiopian materials. In 2002 I invited Abdu Negash, resident choreographer of the Ethiopian National Theater, to work with the group for a month and a half. I had visited Ethiopia the previous year and Negash had given me a cassette documenting dances of Ethiopian tribes. From this, we selected the dances he would teach. Working with Eskesta in Israel, Negash abandoned the traditional structure in some cases in favor of unison. Anthropologist Michael Herzfeld has argued that "nationalism is directly predicated on resemblance, whether biogenetic or cultural. The pivotal idea is that all citizens are, in some unarguable sense, all alike."[52] With Negash's approval, we created polyphonic compositions on these materials but we retained the element of repetition as one of the characteristics of much African dance.

Among the dances that were created during Negash's residency was one deriving from the Ethiopian Guragé tribe, a dance very popular in the Ethiopian-Israeli community. Characteristic of this dance is its quick kicking movement forward, accompanying a fast repetitive movement of the shoulder blades and the elbows, creating the sensation of flight.[53] Negash also taught us a dance of the Benishangal Ethiopian tribe in which a kind of cloth tail is tied to the female dancers' swaying hips, and a dance of the Ethiopian Sidama tribe, with head movement such as turns and tilting back and forth. The work with a senior Ethiopian teacher and choreographer thus enriched our knowledge of diverse Ethiopian dance styles. Negash also reinforced the *eskesta* technique of our dancers who had left Ethiopia as children and felt they needed to refresh what the body had started to forget.

The encounter with these new movement materials evoked a number of insights: first, the more the movement lexicon was analyzed and defined, despite its technical difficulty, the less significant was the difference between its performance by a dancer who was a member of the community and one who was not. It also became clear that the more defined the movement was, the more the variations we created on it led us toward dance solutions that recalled the familiar lexicon of jazz movement. Thus the group lost its movement uniqueness and the dancers were revealed as lacking currently expected levels of technique. On the other hand, with a complex and evasive fabric of movement and rhythm, circumscribed in a limited area of the body, as in *eskesta*, it is possible to travel long distances from the source and still remain within the framework of what I think of as the movement DNA.

Opus for Shoulders *(2001)*

While free, expressive movement became part of our regular rehearsals, expanding the elusive *eskesta* vocabulary continued to be difficult, as noted above. Yet the *eskesta* symbolized for the dancers their roots and distinguished them from other ethnic communities. I realized that a productive direction might be to choose a basic and simple phrase as the raw material to be developed. For the greatest creative freedom in the variations, I chose to develop the composition in silence. There were sections where the *eskesta* was performed in unison, contrasted with sections of solo *eskesta* virtuosity (see Figure 6). Having constructed the dance, I looked for music. At first, I thought the dancers could drum the Ethiopian rhythms and the composition would be danced accordingly, but the drumming of the group's dancers was basic and repetitive and, with time, this made the movement heavy. On the recommendation of composer Oded Zehavi, head of the music department at the University of Haifa, I invited Dganit Elyakim, a composition student, to compose music for the dance. Her first inclination was to create contemporary music for traditional Ethiopian instruments but the idea was rejected for practical reasons: there were no musicians in the group and I could not finance players for only one dance, not to mention the organizational difficulties of bringing them along to performances.

Thus, the idea occurred to me to use the dancers' voices; I had recently returned from a trip to Indonesia where, on the island of West Papua, I encountered a tribe whose entire dance was performed by the group sitting in a circle and moving their shoulders, accompanied by singing of what sounded to me like repetitive syllables. Inspired by my report of this encounter, Elyakim chose interesting-sounding Amharic syllables that are related to the images we used in the dance, thus coloring the movement with certain qualities. For the dance's title, I borrowed a term from the music world, *Opus,* in order to indicate that this was an abstract piece. The dancers found different ways of interpreting this abstraction and giving it meaning. Dancer Mazal Demoza

Figure 6. *Opus for Shoulders* (2001), choreographed by Ruth Eshel. Ma'ayan Raskay, Wagau Geteneh and Nir Elazar. Photograph by Ofer Zvulun. Courtesy of Ofer Zvulun (color figure available online).

commented, "I like this dance because it does not look like a traditional Ethiopian folk dance. It is an abstract dance that is based on my Ethiopian roots, and that is important to me. I was born in Israel and grew up in a modern life style. I also like dancing it because it is a challenge, since it requires precision."[54] Degai stated, "For me the sections we dance together remind me of Ethiopia where you are educated to obey—to obey your parents, to obey the choreographer, to obey the leader, while the individual parts in the dance connect me to my life today where I have the possibility to say 'No, I want to do something else.' "[55] Thus, the interpretive "logic" upon which "meaning is constructed" for each dancer varied according to their experience and stance.[56]

Opus for Heads *(2002)*

In the course of our work, the dancers continued to bring in songs by Ethiopian pop singers, and after having refused for years to create dances to them, I finally felt there was sufficient movement lexicon and rich experience to create a dance whose point of departure was music. That is, the choreography could stand equally with the music. I selected a song by Aster Aweke, analyzed the music, including its varying phrase lengths, and decided that I could work with it choreographically, in a reverse creative process from the one we had experienced so far. In order to discover new options of head and neck work I had the female dancers seated on chairs, so that the richness of the work would focus on the head and not on locomotion through space (see Figure 7).

The dance opens with four women "dancing" with the head precisely and in unison, matching the music as the phrase lengths shift between eight and twelve beats. Within the strict framework of uniformity there are windows in which the dancers "talk" among themselves freely by means of the *eskesta*. This creates a colorful dance of girls who might be sitting at a party, holding a movement conversation among themselves, flirting with the guests from afar. For the dancers, however, it was much more than

Figure 7. *Opus for Heads* (2002), choreographed by Ruth Eshel, danced by Ester Maharat, Minalu Degai, Aviva Nagosa and Ma'ayan Raskay. Photograph by Ofer Zvulun. Courtesy of Ofer Zvulun (color figure available online).

a light, colorful dance, as Chen Reta remarked: "I entered the stage and sat on the chair looking beautiful, showing my pretty shoulders, my femininity, as if I was saying 'I am a woman,' no more shy or afraid."[57] For Mazal Demoza, this dance meant something different: "Each time I enter the stage to dance *Opus for Heads* I know I need to impress the audience more than do the two other dancers. That means to be stronger and to project more. I know I can impress those who watch me by dancing and I do not need words."[58]

Nefas *(2003)*

In 2003 my experiences with meditation led me to a new work, *Nefas*, which means "wind" in Amharic or *ru'ach* (soul) in Hebrew. The dance consisted of eight solos, matching the number of dancers in the group. Meditation inspired me with serenity and encouraged me to let chance take its course. I worked with each dancer separately, which reduced the pressure that a group presence creates. Themes were generated during rehearsals out of images that could emerge from the dancer's character, life experience, or particular technical preferences or strengths. Imagery played an important role, as it did for Anna Halprin, who has reflected that "the process of connecting with our internal imagery involved 'dancing' the images that welled up from the unconscious as another way of connecting the mind and the body."[59] When I suggested an image as a starting point for a dance or in order to color a movement, I encouraged the dancers to find their own images or to "translate" my imagery in a way that made it theirs, thus building a bridge between myself, born and raised in Israel and imbued with Western culture, and the dancers, who came from another country and culture. Dancer Dege Hanoch-Levi told me, "When I understood deeply your image, I could change it and take it to a place that suited me. This way it wasn't just a movement, but rather it projected inner truth."[60] A casual item of clothing lying on the floor or a piece of music, belonging to the previous teacher, that I happened to find in the studio could be the starting point. I believe that any point of departure is but the ignition of an engine and if I do not interfere, it will bring to the surface authentic solutions reflecting the dancer and myself at that moment.

Each dance was generated from a different point of departure, matching the qualities and personality of that dancer, created with its own particular imagery and movement vocabulary. There was a constant cycling back and forth between the movement and the image. For example, the point of departure for the solo by Amen Chole was his ability to perform movement from the Guragé national dance with impressive virtuosity: the movements of his shoulder blades backward and forward created the image of an eagle in flight.[61] I gave Hanoch-Levi a *chera*, which always appeared to me a remarkable object, combining the toughness and inflexibility of the stick and the flow of the horsehair "tail" attached to it.[62] The image underlying this solo was of the *chera* as a magical paintbrush with which the dancer colored the world. Hanoch-Levi recalls, "The image of being a goddess painting the world with the *chera* meant, to me, responsibility. I have a job to do, something beyond everyday life, and it puts me in a higher spiritual place."[63] For Chen Mamo I created the solo, "I am Mamo." I knew about her dream of becoming a medical doctor and her long struggle to achieve that goal. For her I wanted to create a piece projecting determination, which I believe was accomplished in her dancing. I teased her, insisting that her name was not Mamo, refusing the name given to her upon immigrating to Israel.[*] In the dance she moves her head from side to side persistently, over and over again, as if saying with the movement accompanying the sound of her name that this, and only this, is her name. Mamo has commented to me, "At the beginning I did not understand why you repeated that my name was not Mamo. Personally, I had no problem with my name, but gradually I started to understand and I took it to my personal life experience, asking myself if I knew strongly enough to insist on doing things my way."[64] Perhaps, for some, the imagery could be a guide to future action.

With the short and very delicate Gila Bitualin I created a dance that has the movement quality of a butterfly or a fresh infatuation, whereas Gilat Bayenne, a tall female dancer well aware of her beauty, danced as if she were the Queen of Sheba, advancing while moving her shoulders and head, projecting confidence in

---

[*]Upon reaching Israel, many Ethiopian immigrants adopted Israeli names, wishing to become Israelis. Later, some regretted doing so and returned to their birth names.

her power. With Reta, I worked with the image of respect, as I was interested in gestures showing respect in the Ethiopian community. Reta noted that, "while dancing it, I thought about the virtue of respect in our community—respect for parents and for old people. Especially, I was thinking about grandmother who raised my small brother and me after my mother died and my father left."[65]

The solo dances were created without music or rhythmic accompaniment, so that the dancers would be attentive to themselves and the images that nourished the improvisation. This time, as in the past, the method involved processing, selecting, developing, and carving each movement, all shaped by a particular, evocative image. The music used in performance was composed by Oded Zehavi, based on drumming (performed by Keren Zehavi) and on the vocal improvisations of Chole and Hanoch, dancer-singers, inspired by the images and metaphoric words shaping each solo. For the costumes, Noga Weise selected a natural-white Chinese silk material that flutters during movement, creating a sense of spiritual flow (see Figures 8 and 9).

Beta Today

At this time, the dancers participating in Beta either were born in Israel or immigrated here as very young children. In the Ethiopian community today the troupe is respected and well received. Adhenen has remarked, "What we did in the troupe reflects the change the Ethiopian community underwent while building a bridge between the two cultures. I am different today. When I immigrated to Israel, Western music sounded false to me. When I saw a Western dance on television I thought 'What is this?' I am different today. Now, I like it and I'm moved by it. The expectations today are different than in the past."[66]

Recently, Tzvika Hskias, the first professional dancer who has emerged from the Ethiopian community in Israel, has joined the group. He danced with Ensemble Batsheva (the junior company of Batsheva Dance Company) and performed works by Ohad Naharin and others. Yet for him, being a member of Beta Dance Troupe means returning home. As a professional dancer who is exposed to a variety of movement styles, he came to appreciate the originality of the shoulder dancing for its creative potential:

Figure 8. *Nefas* (2003), choreographed by Ruth Eshel, with Minalu Degai dancing "Sheba." Photograph by Ofer Zvulun. Courtesy of Ofer Zvulun (color figure available online).

Figure 9. *Nefas*, with Hanni David dancing with a *chera*. Photograph by Ofer Zvulun. Courtesy of Ofer Zvulun (color figure available online).

"*Eskesta* is so different from other folk dances. I wanted to expand the vocabulary without 'spoiling' it with foreign movements but rather to strengthen, support, and refine it with my Western technique and professional education. When I dance *eskesta* and transfer its rhythm to other parts of my body I feel connected to the authentic part of me."[67] Working with Hskias, obstacles to creative solutions dissolve, something that was not possible earlier, yet we must guard against the technical virtuosity of contemporary dance overwhelming the intention of expanding the movement from within the form and ethnic movement becoming mere ornament.

I am working with Tirza Sapir, formerly head of the Dance and Art School at the Kibbutzim College and an expert in Eshkol-Wachman Movement Notation, to analyze and notate the *eskesta* components and some of the variations created in the course of my work with the dance troupes. I anticipate that the notation and analysis will reveal new directions for creative work, including maximized use of shoulder possibilities, discovering unpredicted variations, and achieving greater levels of precision.

In reflecting on my work with the Ethiopian-Israeli community, I can identify two courses of research in our efforts to create contemporary traditional dance that reflects both the dancers' new lives and their roots. The first emerged from looking inward toward the intuitive, natural, and expressive movement of the dancers, and the second has been expansion of the *eskesta* movement lexicon based on its form and structure. During the creative process the two courses flow freely, nourishing one another and, eventually, blending. The research continues.

Notes

1. See Beta Dance Troupe—*Shoulders*, http://www.youtube.com/watch?v=J6_QUQU2KBg (accessed June 13, 2011). Video by Kibbutz Ramat-Yohanan studios, 2009.
2. Henok Yared, "Dance Performance that Opens a New Era of *Eskesta*," *The Ethiopian Reporter* (December 14, 2008), and Tagu Zergaw, "Israel's Beta Dance Troupe Brings Unique *Falasha* Insight," *The Capital* (December 14, 2008).
3. See Hagar Salamon, ed., *Oriental Jewish Communities in the 19th and 20th Centuries: Ethiopia* (Jerusalem: Ben-Zvi Institiute for the Study of Jewish Communities in the East, 2008)

4. See "Operation Moses, Part 1," Anti-Defamation League of B'nai B'rith, Kastel Films, 1987, http://www.youtube.com/watch?v=TOGxF_CsnG4 (accessed June 13, 2011).

5. Dawn Lille Horwitz, "Ethiopian Dance in Israel," in *Jewish Folklore and Ethnology Review,* ed. Judith Brin Ingber, The Jewish Folklore Section of the American Folklore Society, vol. 20, nos. 1–2 (2000): 98. See also the *eskesta* exposed to other cultural influences in Ruth Eshel's Documentary Project, 1992, http://www.youtube.com/watch?v=BIfJDZV5hnY (accessed June 14, 2011).

6. Robert Nicholls, "African Dance: Transition and Continuity," in *African Dance,* ed. Kariamu Welsh Asante (Eritrea: Africa World Press, 1996), 52.

7. See, for example, Adrienne Kaeppler, "Recycling Tradition: Hawaiian Case Study," *Dance Chronicle,* vol. 27, no. 3 (2004): 293–311; Andriy Nahachewsky, "Once Again: On the Concept of 'Second' Existence Folk Dance," *Yearbook for Traditional Music,* vol. 33 (2001): 17–28; Jill Crosby, "A Felt Authentic Grounding: Intersecting Theories of Authenticity and Tradition," in *Choreographies of Migration, Patterns of Global Mobility,* Proceedings of the Congress on Research in Dance, 40th Annual Conference, New York, 2007, 24–28.

8. Felix Hoerburger, "Once Again: On the Concept of 'Folk Dance,'" *Journal of the International Folk Music Council,* vol. 20 (1968): 30–31, and "Folk Dance Survey," *Journal of the International Folk Music Council,* vol. 17, pt. 1 (1965): 7–8.

9. Anthony Shay, *Choreographic Politics: State Folk Dance Companies, Representation and Power* (Middletown, Conn.: Wesleyan University Press, 2002).

10. Lois Ellfeldt, *A Primer for Choreographers* (Los Angeles: National Press Books, 1967), 4.

11. Paulin Houtondji, *African Philosophy: Myth and Reality* (Bloomington: Indiana University Press, 1983), 166.

12. See Zohar Shavit, *The Construction of Hebrew Culture in Eretz Israel* [Hebrew] (Jerusalem: The Israel Academy for Science and Humanities and The Bialik Institute, 1998).

13. See Ayala Goren-Kadman, "Debka and Its Metamorphoses: Affinities between Arab Debka Dancing and Jewish Debka Dancing in Israel," *Dance Today* [in Hebrew: *Mahol Ahshav*], no. 3 (November 2000): 10–15; Ayala Goren-Kadman, "Is There a Future for Ethnic Dance in Israel?" *Dance Today,* no. 15 (October 2008): 15–17.

14. See Ruth Eshel, *Dancing with the Dream: The Development of Artistic Dance in Israel 1920–1964* [Hebrew, with an abstract in English] (Tel Aviv: Sifriat Hapoalim Press, 1991), 28–37; Giora Manor, *The Life and Dance of Gertrud Kraus* [Hebrew and English] (Tel Aviv: Hakibutz Hameuhad, 1978); Nina Spiegel, "Cultural Formation in Eretz Israel: The National Dance Competition of 1937," *Jewish Folklore and Ethnology Review,* vol. 20, nos. 1–2 (2000): 24–38.

15. Giora Manor, "The Yemenite Dance Materials of Sara Levi-Tanai," *Jewish Folklore and Ethnology Review,* vol. 20, nos. 1–2 (2000): 88. In the same volume, see also Sara Levi-Tanai, "A Private Testimony," 93–98.

16. Gila Toledano, *A Story of a Company: Sara Levi-Tanai and Inbal Dance-Theater* (Tel Aviv: Resling, 2005), 126–29; Giora Manor, *Sara's Ways: Sara Levi-Tanai and Her Choreography* (Tel Aviv: The Multicultural Ethnic Center Inbal and the Dance Library of Israel, 2004).

17. Dina Roginsky, "Double Dance: Folk and Ethnic Dance in Israel" [Hebrew], *Dance Today*, no. 4 (November 2000): 18; Dina Roginsky, "The National, the Ethnic and In-Between: Sociological Analysis of the Interrelations between Folk, Ethnic, and Minority Dances in Israel," in *Dance Discourse in Israel* [Hebrew], ed. Dina Roginsky and Henia Rottenberg (Tel Aviv: Resling, 2009), 95–125. All quotations in English from Hebrew sources are my translations.

18. Dan Ronen, "Dance for Everyone: On Multi-Culture in Israel and Its Influence on the Development of Dance," *Dance Today*, no. 3 (November 2000): 4–10 [English translation, 84–89]. See also Dan Ronen, "Folk Dances as an Inspiration to Artistic Dance," *Dance Today*, no. 11 (December 2004): 75–81.

19. See Yonat Rotman, "In between East and West: Oriental Landscapes in the Dances of Moshe Efrati and Barak Marshall," in *Dance Discourse in Israel*, 127–55.

20. See Eshel's Documentary Project, YouTube.

21. For example, Kariamu Welsh Asante, ed. *African Dance—An Artistic, Historical and Philosophical Inquiry* (Trenton, N.J.: African World Press, Inc., 1994), and Robert Nicholls, "African Dance in Transition," *The World & I*, vol. 10 (1988): 459–62.

22. See, for example, Theresa Buckland, "Dance, Authenticity and Cultural Memory: The Politics of Embodiment," *Yearbook for Traditional Music*, vol. 33 (2001): 1–16; Theresa Buckland, "All Dances Are Ethnic, but Some Are More Ethnic Than Others: Some Observations on Dance Studies and Anthropology," *Dance Research: The Journal of the Society for Dance Research*, vol. 17, no. 1 (Summer 1999): 3–21; Jane Desmond, ed., *Meaning in Motion: New Cultural Studies of Dance* (Durham, N.C.: Duke University Press, 1997); Jane Desmond, "Terra Incognita: Mapping New Territory in Dance and 'Cultural Studies,'" *Dance Research Journal*, vol. 32, no. 1 (Summer 2000): 43–53; Susan Leigh Foster, ed., *Corporealities: Dancing Knowledge, Culture and Power* (London: Routledge, 1996).

23. Buckland, "All Dances Are Ethnic," 4.

24. Glendola Yhema Mills, "Is It Is or Is It Ain't: The Impact of Selective Perception on the Image Making of Traditional African Dance," *Journal of Black Studies*, vol. 28, no. 2 (November 1997): 145.

25. For example, Steven Kaplan, *The Beta Israel: Falasha in Ethiopia—From Earliest Times to the Twentieth Century* (New York: New York University Press, 1992); Kay Kaufman Shelemay, *Music, Ritual and Falasha History* (East Lansing: Michigan State University Press, 1986); Stephen Spector, *Operation Solomon: The Daring Rescue of the Ethiopian Jews* (New York: Oxford University Press, 2005).

26. Martin György, "Dance Types in Ethiopia," *Journal of the International Folk Music Council*, vol. 19 (1967): 23–27; Tibor Vadasy, "Ethiopian Folk-Dance I," *Journal of Ethiopian Studies*, no. 8 (July 1970): 119–46, "Ethiopian Folk-Dance II: Tegré and Guragé," *Journal of Ethiopian Studies*, no. 9 (June

1971): 191–217, and "Ethiopian Folk-Dance III: Wällo and Galla," *Journal of Ethiopian Studies*, no. 11 (1973): 213–31.

27. See Eshel's Documentary Project, YouTube, particularly the sections where children dance *eskesta* at Kibbutz Bet-Oren (0:54–2:00) and where two soloists compete in *eskesta* dancing at a bar mitzvah (4:48–6:00).

28. Kariamu Welsh Asante, *Zimbabwe Dance* (Trenton, N.J.: African World Press, 2000), 115.

29. Vadasy, "Ethiopian Folk Dance I," 123.

30. Peggy Phelan, "Broken Symmetries: Memory, Sight, Love," in *The Feminism and Visual Culture Reader*, ed. Amelia Jones (London: Routledge, 2003), 110.

31. Zena Adhenen, interview by the author, March 1, 2011.

32. Minalu Degai, interview by the author, May 1, 2011.

33. Revital Fekadu, interview by the author, May 4, 2011.

34. Zehava Baruch, interview by author, February 1, 2011.

35. Sarah Rubidge, "Re-addressing Traditional Dance in Contemporary Uganda," in *Proceedings*, Society of Dance History Scholars Conference, University of Oregon, June 18–21, 1998, 155.

36. Yoseph Tagenia, interview by the author, February 10, 2011.

37. Danielle Bélec, "Robert Ellis Dunn: Personal Stories in Motion," *Dance Research Journal*, vol. 30, no. 2 (Autumn 1998): 26.

38. Mark Johnson, *The Body in the Mind: The Bodily Basis of Meaning, Imagination, and Reason* (Chicago: University of Chicago Press, 1987).

39. Bélec, "Robert Ellis Dunn," 28.

40. Tagenia, interview.

41. James Pritchett, *The Music of John Cage* (Cambridge: Cambridge University Press, 1993), 197–200.

42. Quoted in Bélec, "Robert Ellis Dunn," 27.

43. Adrienne Kaeppler, "Dance and the Interpretation of Pacific Traditional Literature," in *Directions in Pacific Literature: Essays in Honor of Katherine Loumala*, ed. Adrienne L. Kaeppler and H. Arlo Nimmo (Honolulu: Bishop Museum Press, 1976), 199–200.

44. Elsie Ivanovich Dunin, quoted in Andriy Nahachewsky, "Participatory and Presentational Dances as Ethnochoreological Categories," *Dance Research Journal*, vol. 27, no. 1 (Spring 1995): 1.

45. Ibid.

46. See Ilana Ben Tov-Israeli, *Let Me Talk: Creative Writing with Ethiopian Youth* (Tel Aviv: Tag Press, 1997).

47. Tagenia, interview.

48. George Lakoff and Mark Johnson, "Metaphors We Live By," in *The Production of Reality: Essays and Readings on Social Interaction*, ed. Jodi O'Brien (Newbury Park, Cal.: Pine Forge Press, 2011), 112.

49. Beta-Eskesta Selected Repertoire, http://www.youtube.com/watch?v=-W49Wd1dMBQ&feature=related, *Hallelujah* (0:18–0:38), the song *How Much Pain*, and the prayer *Maharo* (0:39–1:42) (accessed June 16, 2011).

50. Rubidge, "Re-addressing Traditional Dance in Contemporary Uganda," 157.

51. Ester Maharat, interview by the author, March 20, 2011.

52. Michael Herzfeld, *Cultural Intimacy: Social Poetics in the Nation State* (London: Routledge, 1996), 27.

53. Beta-Eskesta Selected Repertoire, http://www.youtube.com/watch?v=-W49Wd1dMBQ&feature=related, *Gurage* (2:08–2:33), *Sidama* (3:00–3:12).

54. Mazal Demoza, interview by the author, February 20, 2011.

55. Degai, interview.

56. Janet Adshead-Lansdale, "Dance Analysis in Performance," *Dance Research: The Journal of the Society for Dance Research*, vol. 12, no. 2 (Autumn 1994): 16.

57. Chen Reta, interview by the author, February 28, 2011.

58. Demoza, interview.

59. Anna Halprin, *Moving toward Life* (Hanover, N.H.: Wesleyan University Press, 1995), 65.

60. Dege Hanoch-Levi, interview by the author, March 3, 2011.

61. Beta Eskesta—*Nefas* (part one), Amen Chole dancing "The Eagle," http://www.youtube.com/watch?v=4EZiclxOKW0&feature=related (accessed June 16, 2011).

62. Beta Eskesta—*Nefas* (part two), Dege Hanoch-Levi dancing "Chera" (1:43–2:01), http://www.youtube.com/user/16166746?feature=mhee#p/u (accessed June 16, 2011).

63. Hanoch-Levi, interview.

64. Chen Mamo, interview by the author, February 28, 2011.

65. Reta, interview.

66. Adhenen, interview.

67. Tzvika Heskias, interview by the author, April 1, 2011.

DANCE AND DIFFERENCE: TOWARD AN
INDIVIDUALIZATION OF THE PONTIAN SELF

MAGDA ZOGRAFOU and STAVROULA PIPYROU

This article is concerned with Pontic dance, particularly as part of the celebrations of Panayía Soumelá, as a marker of identity for the Pontians in Greece. Adopting a historical perspective, we explore how markers of identity are intimately related to the systemic overvaluation of the Pontian Self. We argue that a strong Pontian referential system is based on the cultivation of clear markers of identity. Drawing on the concept of "the narcissism of minor differences," we conclude that it is major differences that may promote individualization and cultural tolerance, enabling the Pontian Self to reflexively engage with the difference of the Other.

Discussions about sameness and difference are at the core of social studies, especially in light of ethnic and nationalistic developments, in Europe and all over the world, which bring to the fore issues of difference and sameness not only between, but also within groups. Of special interest from an anthropological point of view are the ways people theorize, politicize, and eventually materialize their difference, which, in the unfolding of nationalism, may take different forms and follow different paths. Markers that were once emblematic for particular collectivities may no longer hold. Here we explore the contextual nature of difference within the Greek state with reference to Pontian collectivities, and examine its materialization vis-à-vis the developments of Greek nationalism. More specifically, we focus on Pontic[*] dance as a system of constructing and materializing difference for the Pontians who live within the Greek state.

---

[*]The Pontians are a population that originate from the historical area of Pontus in Anatolia, originally located around the southern and eastern coasts of the Black Sea. Along with other Orthodox Christian populations, Pontians were exchanged between Turkey and Greece as a result of the Lausanne treaty in 1923. In this essay, we refer to Turkish- and Greek-speaking Pontians and not to the Pontian subjects of the former U.S.S.R. In employing the terms Pontic/Pontian in this article, we follow the practices of David Bruce Kilpatrick in "Function and Style in Pontic Dance Music" (Ph.D. dissertation, University of California, Los Angeles, 1975).

Our theoretical endeavor in this article is to examine dance as a system of differentiation. From a historical perspective the way that Pontians construct and materialize their difference within Greek society has not been monolithic and has followed different paths according to national and international developments. Thus, we are concerned with critical questions about processes of maintenance and reconstruction of Pontian identity over the period of relocation to Greece. Our research reveals the development of Pontic dance as a strong self-referential system of Pontian identity around which revolve and evolve identity markers such as ethnicity. Further, through a deep examination of the meanings in Pontic dance, which hold and inform different political perspectives in different contexts, the notion of difference itself is made problematic. Precisely because we do not adopt the notion of difference unproblematically we deal with degrees of difference and, more specifically, with minor and major differences.

How may minor differences be transformed into major differences and vice-versa? Some researchers have suggested that minor differences between collectivities may channel aggression and lead to bitter conflicts.[1] While the notion of minor differences has been associated with ethnic and national conflicts, here we claim that major differences may boost individualization and promote cultural tolerance. By individualization we mean a strong self-referential system that enables the actors to reflexively engage with the difference of the Other.

By combining a historical perspective with ethnographic material collected during long-term fieldwork,[*] we examine Pontic dance with special emphasis on performances that take place in the context of celebrations of the Madonna of Soumelá, or Panayía (All Holy One) Soumelá, as she is called in Greek. We show that the materialization of difference within Pontian collectivities takes various forms at different historical stages. Additionally, the ways Pontian collectivities cast and recast their identity markers is directly related to wider national and international political phenomena.

---

[*]Magda Zografou has been conducting fieldwork on Greek Pontian communities since the mid-1980s, Stavroula Pipyrou since 2004.

Dance in Greece has often been theorized in relation to the construction of identity.[2] As a means toward articulating social, hegemonic, and structural relationships and the construction of difference—national, ethnic, gender, or genealogical—dance provides scope for human agency in choreographing transgressions of symbolic borders and thus securing personal and collective interests. In dance studies, the production of difference has usually been studied through contexts of conflict and particularly of ethnic and nationalistic disputes. These studies have emanated from the explicit politicization and ethnicization of identities in the Greek state as an epiphenomenon of the turmoil of ethnic identities in the Balkans and Europe. At present, both Pontic dance and Panayía Soumelá herself constitute major and clear-cut systems of individualization of the Pontian Self. While Panayía Soumelá is undoubtedly a symbol of "Pontianness," it is equally employed as a political means by which Pontians trace common cultural ground between themselves and other Greek populations. It has been suggested that religious sites are loci of emotional attachment and are also imbued with political meanings that "reflect and assert an intimate relationship between the material and the divine worlds."[3] Nevertheless, neither Pontic dance nor Panayía Soumelá have always constituted major differences in the sense that we explore here. By tracing their "genealogies"* we hope to show how difference is materialized and contextually evaluated.

Exploring Differences

As discussed above, it is minor differences that, in contexts of conflict, may be highlighted as means of differentiation and, ultimately, of aggression. These differences, precisely because they are minor, may provoke confusion instead of clarifying the reasons why conflicts between collectivities develop. Here, we interrogate the opposite side of the argument and ask whether major differences can eventually boost individualization and promote cultural tolerance. While the present study is contextualized

---

*Here we refer to "genealogy" in the Foucauldian sense. Thus, we do not seek to uncover linear developments in the history of the Pontian communities; rather, we are interested in contradictory developments that uncover the workings of power in shaping Pontian identities.

within the formulation of identities in the Greek state, we draw inspiration from the work of Sigmund Freud, among others, concerning understandings of how difference is socially constructed and expressed.

Similar to other refugees from the Black Sea and Asia Minor, the Pontians were relocated to Greece from Anatolia following the forcible exchange of Christian and Muslim populations between Greece and Turkey as dictated by the Lausanne Treaty (1923). These displaced populations, by no means homogenous either in language or culture, were resettled around Greece, especially in depopulated areas, in order to provide a "Greek" presence to nationally contested areas such as Macedonia.[4] Local populations, hostile to these refugees, tended to dismiss them based on ethnic and ideological criteria, labeling them as "Turks" or "Turk-seeds"[5] or "leftists," as in the case of the Pontians who, during the Russian-Turkish wars of the nineteenth and twentieth centuries, had moved farther into the region of Caucasus.[*] At the same time, the refugees themselves often promoted a discourse of superiority in relation to mainland Greeks while sustaining a rhetoric of "paradise lost" in respect to their places of origin, lost properties, and constructed concepts of homeland for decades after their relocation.[6]

Subjected to the nationalistic process of the newly consolidated Greek nation-state, the Pontians, like other refugees, engaged in selective remembrance and forgetting in shaping their identities as simultaneously privileged and disadvantaged members of Greek society.[7] Equally crucial to this process was the often idealized memory of *patridha* (fatherland) as a symbolic context for identity-making.[8] To their new environment Pontians brought their histories, personal accounts, documents, images, and "precious symbols," all of which would work as "places of memory."[9] The displaced Pontians reconstructed their collective system of

---

[*]The majority of Pontians were fervent supporters of Eleftherios Venizelos, a prominent Greek politician who served multiple terms as Prime Minister. Nevertheless, among the leaders of the newly founded (1918) Communist Party of Greece (KKE) were many of Anatolian origin. Inevitably, those among the refugees who had any background connected to Communism, such as the Pontians who had moved into the region of the Caucasus, were stigmatized as leftists. See Richard Clogg, *A Concise History of Greece* (Cambridge: Cambridge University Press, 1992), 106.

representation by shaping categories of identity relating to collective history, language, religion, and dance.

As we have argued elsewhere, wider as well as smaller collectivities may engage in historical constructivism, thus appropriating history and "histories" in order to address questions that relate to their dancing identity.[10] By adopting a comparative stance between Pontians and Cretans, we argued that collectivities may construct their signs of difference by privileging or devaluing aspects of their "cultural stuff" in direct relation to national politics.[11] For example, it is interesting to note that while both Pontians and Cretans materialized their difference as the sine qua non of Greekness, they each successfully cultivated a rhetoric of uniqueness-cum-difference regarding their dancing performances. Despite the fact that they drew inspiration from different categories, each population was quick to create a "product" branded as having ancient Greek origins and yet too culturally specific to be mistaken for something other than Pontian or Cretan.[12] The manner in which Pontic dances developed in modern Greek society is parallel to the way Pontian identity itself came to be constructed and expressed in various stages of modern Greek history; both were caught in an ideological matrix that sought simultaneously to display and conceal, balance and regulate sameness and difference.

The "Narcissism of Minor Differences"

Before answering the question of how Pontians successfully cultivated individualization within the Greek nation, an interrogation of the role of degrees of differentiation (that is, minor or major differences) between collectivities is appropriate. Keeping in mind the relative nature of difference, we explore the contexts where minor differences are transformed into major differences and vice versa. Finally, we ask if it is difference or sameness that draws people together or pulls them apart. While this question is by no means easy or one-dimensional to answer and touches upon the ontological status of the production of difference, we would like to explore its heuristic value.

Freud developed the concept of the "narcissism of minor differences" gradually over his three studies, *The Taboo of Virginity*

(1917), *Group Psychology and the Analysis of the Ego* (1921), and *Civilization and Its Discontents* (1930), coloring it every time with different attributes. Initially intended to explain psychoanalytically the production of difference on the individual level, the idea of a morbid self-love[13] would justify individual aggression as a means of prevailing over establishing fellowship and would challenge the idea of a love that people are supposed to feel toward one another. In *Group Psychology and the Analysis of the Ego*, Freud departed from the individual level and discussed the narcissism of minor differences in relation to groups residing in close proximity. "Closely related races keep one another at arm's length; the South German cannot endure the North German, the Englishman casts every kind of aspersion on the Scot, the Spaniard despises the Portuguese."[14]

The final time that Freud deals with the concept is in *Civilization and Its Discontents*, where he argues that minor differences between individuals and groups lend themselves particularly to the context of bitter disputes. Externalized aggression, in his analysis, refers to particular contexts where a considerable number of people are bound in love so long as there are other people outside that group to receive the manifestation of their aggression. The narcissism of minor differences was the effect of a process of magnifying once-small differences that now come to operate as reminders of why people are apart. Despite the fact that aggression can be a factor in group cohesion, Freud does not clarify exactly what can be classed as minor or major difference. He states, however, that "We are no longer astonished that greater differences should lead to almost insuperable repugnance, such as the Gallic people feel for the German, the Aryan for the Semite, and the white races for the colored."[15] This final comment suggests that all difference is problematic and thus context-dependent.

In the social sciences the concept of the narcissism of minor differences has lent itself to the development of a theory of conflict. More particularly, the works of Anton Blok and Michael Ignatieff explore the construction of difference in contexts of ethnic conflict and particularistic nationalism. Ignatieff, referring to the conflicts and nationalist revivals in Serbia and Croatia, notes that "there is nothing in our natures that makes ethnic or racial conflict unavoidable. The idea that different races and ethnic groups can coexist in peace and even goodwill is not a hopeless illusion. Even long-standing, apparently adamantine antipathies of the ethnic war zones turn out, on closer examination, to be expressions of fear created by the collapse or absence of institutions that enable individuals to form civic identities strong enough to counteract their ethnic allegiances."[16] Ignatieff attributes the revival of conflict to the loss of differences and the resulting need to create "inauthentic" ones. It is precisely the inauthentic and fantastic quality of ethnic identities that triggers violent reactions of defense. The narcissism of minor difference is thus a leap into collective fantasy that enables threatened or anxious individuals to avoid the burden of thinking for themselves or even thinking of themselves as individuals. Tolerance depends, critically, on being able to individualize oneself and others, to be able to "see" oneself and others—or to put it another way, to be able to focus on major difference, which is individual, and to relativize minor difference, which is collective.

Being able to see oneself and others this way relies heavily on the workings of self-consciousness and on making difference visible to others. Such seeing is not a mere reflection of difference, not just looking back at yourself and celebrating your uniqueness, but rather engaging with the Other and accepting the difference. The weaker the self-referential system the more important is the need to reinvent collective identities. Having a strongly cultivated self-referential system relies heavily on the capacity to develop noncontradictory and clear systems of signs. In his influential essay on the materialization of difference, Paul Sant Cassia has further argued that the medium for communicating difference, and the system of signs employed, "may itself precipitate certain areas of distinction that may not be evident through another system of signs, much like writing can display distinctions that may not appear in speech. Individuals may thus themselves be confused about the nature of their difference from, and similarity with, others. Such slippages can occur particularly when people may be using one register to talk about difference only to be contradicted, or subverted, by another register."[17]

In light of these insights it is interesting to consider the ethnographic accounts from an area of Greek Macedonia provided by Ioannis Manos[18] in order to examine the relationship

between minor differences, individualization, and cultural tolerance. He refers to the highly politicized district of Florina, where
modern subjects are caught between Greek nationalistic and local ethnic claims and ascriptions. While Manos discusses the pivotal role of individual agency through dance as a subversive force
against rigid state structures, other interesting insights can be
extracted. The proliferation of the politics of difference in the
area, especially after the Balkan wars, is explained by the workings of very similar but opposing nationalistic processes between
the neighboring nations of Greece, Bulgaria, and the Former Yugoslav Republic of Macedonia (FYROM). Recently, the formation
of the political movement MAKIBE[*] and the subsequent Rainbow
party played a pivotal role in the claims of a Macedonian national
minority in the area. Tensions on the local level were exacerbated
by the dispute between Greece and FYROM concerning the naming of the latter.

Much like the Croats and Serbs studied by Ignatieff, Manos's
actors focus on giving shape to categories pulled out of the cultural stuff that characterizes the area in an introverted and "narcissistic" manner, as described by Freud. Among other systems of
signs, they choose dance in order to articulate their conformation
with or opposition to nationalistic discourses raised by the Greek
state on the one hand and ethnic Macedonian claims on the other.
Yet, a contradiction soon becomes apparent. Despite the fact that
people of Florina recognize the Greek and Macedonian dancing
repertories as "referring to the same step patterns danced with
different songs and melodies," performing the one or the other
dance becomes a strict boundary marker between the collectivities.[19] In that sense, difference is structured upon minor rather
than major differences. Local culture is forced into a politicization
that demands that any shade of difference be highlighted, exacerbated, magnified. As a result of the fact that the dancing stock
entails an ambivalence in itself (is it Greek or is it Macedonian?),
dance performances do not provide a one-dimensional, exclusive,
and, for that matter, clear identity message. In this case language

---

[*]The Macedonian Movement for Balkan Prosperity (MAKIBE) was founded in 1991. The
political party Rainbow, which succeeded MAKIBE, was founded in 1994. See Ioannis
Manos, "To Dance or Not to Dance: Dancing Dilemmas in a Border Region in Northern
Greece," *Focaal: European Journal of Anthropology*, no. 41 (2003): 21–32.

is employed as the semantic catalyst that distinguishes between those dances perceived as national Greek and those considered as national Macedonian. Thus, the same dance acquires different connotations when it is assigned a Greek or a Macedonian name. Manos sensitively describes the case of an elderly woman who as a girl performed a dance then attributed to the Macedonian repertory but now attributed to the Greek. Caught between ambivalent systems of signs, this woman is herself the embodiment of aporia provoked by the evaluation of differences and similarities in the same dance, performed at different stages of her life.

This last observation is important in evaluating the predicament of the local dancing repertory, which becomes a hazy marker of boundaries among the local populations. Thus, the subjects' aporia is reflected in the title of Manos's paper, "To Dance or Not to Dance." The degree that the dancing stock—despite the effort at both Greek and Macedonian ends—is able to create narcissistic markers within the populations is reflected in the subjects' choice to join or abstain from the highly politicized local festivities. Manos is explicit: "The only striking difference between the two feasts was that the local dances, mentioned above, were announced in Greek at the 'Greek' feast and in Dopia at the 'Macedonian' feast. Similarly, many of the songs, some of which were identical, were sung in Greek at the 'Greek' feast and in Slavic at the 'Macedonian' feast. At both feasts, adult participants conversed with each other in both Greek and Dopia. In fact, members of the same family participated in both feasts."[20]

If we return to Ignatieff's observations regarding the dynamics of minor differences, we can argue that, had the local groups established between themselves major differences so that the dancing product or other cultural stuff was clearly distinguished, then tolerance rather than conflict might be at work. While this is by no means a certain result, the antithesis could also be argued that it is then the loss, rather than the cultivated national categorization of difference, that leads to dilemmas and, in the end, local conflicts. In that case, "it is not difference that needs to be nationalized, but rather nationalism that needs difference."[21]

How, then, do groups materialize and communicate their differences? What mediums of distinction are employed and are these clear enough to create individualization? Furthermore, what is the predicament of difference within nation-states? Do mediums of distinction hold the same degree of significance over the course of time or is their impact influenced by other historical and political factors? We address these questions in light of Panayía Soumelá and the Pontic dance as markers of difference exclusively attributed to the Pontians.

The Pontian Panayía

On August 15 the Greek Orthodox Church celebrates the Feast of the Dormition.[*] On the same day the Pontians celebrate Panayía Soumelá, a hallmark of cultural identity for Pontians from all over the world. Despite the fact that the icon of Panayía has been brought from its original religious site in Trabzon, Turkey,[†] to Vermio in the province of Veria in northern Greece, the actual name of Panayía Soumelá is lent to a variety of religious locations and civic associations worldwide, thus allowing for the creation of imagined kinship links to Pontian communities otherwise unconnected geographically and politically.

While the Church holds a formal position concerning the interchangeability of all representations of the Panayía, ethnographic accounts show that an excessive localism has led to different and idiosyncratic representations of the Mother of God.[22] In that sense, images of the Panayía and other religious figures such as saints may become the pivot, the hub, of the emotional and cultural relations of diverse collectivities. As argued emphatically by a sixty-four-year-old Pontian, "Panayía Soumelá is the Panayía of the Pontians. We think that she is special. ... Other Panayies are good too, but our own Panayía is above all (*t'emeteron ē Panayía en apan ap' ola*). ... Panayía Soumelá is the protector of the Pontians only. We have our Panayía in Vermio, who must understand that we—with a lot of love—brought her from Pontus. In the same manner that she used to protect us in Pontus she

---

[*]This feast commemorates the death of the Virgin Mary and her assumption into heaven.

[†]According to the Turkish newspaper *Hürriyet* (March 17, 2010), the Turkish authorities granted that the Orthodox Patriarch in Istanbul could perform the religious celebration of the Dormition in the historic monastery of Panayía Soumelá in Trabzon in 2010. The celebration, on August 15, 2010, was a glorious event broadcast live in both Greece and Russia. The monastery reopened after eighty-eight years, having been closed since the exchange of Christian and Muslim populations between Greece and Turkey. This may have been a strategic move by the Turkish government to conform to human rights demands in order to accelerate accession to the European Union.

protects us now in Greece."[23] While religious sites in the collective imagery may be loci of sentiment, one must be careful not to overlook the intimate relationship between the local refractions of divine grace and the political status of the communities concerned.[24] In that sense, a contextual evaluation of the history of Panayía Soumelá is essential, its ruptures as well as its continuities, in order to understand the gradual transformation of the Pontian Panayía from a minor to a major difference. The history of the Pontian Panayía starts in the fourth century when the monks Varnavas and Sofronios brought the icon of the Panayía from Athens to Melá Mountain in the province of Trabzon, Pontus. On this site the monks built a monastery that soon became an important religious and intellectual center that flourished predominantly in the era of the Empire of Trepizond, from the thirteenth to the fifteenth centuries.[25] Panayía Soumelá herself was a highly celebrated figure and locus of devotion and love. Lyric narratives color the festivities in this beloved figure's name, and all adjacent populations—Christian and Muslim alike—visited the church in her honor. Equally interesting are stories relating to the Panayía's journey from Pontus back to Athens, which clearly highlight the strong attachment between her and the Pontian people. In the Pontian imagery, Panayía Soumelá is kin, "one of them." As such, Soumelá is directly related to issues of the Pontian political identity as well as to international claims concerning the recognition of the Pontian genocide by the Turks between 1914 and 1923. After the exchange of populations between Greece and Turkey, Panayía Soumelá, too, became a refugee among those who came to Greece. As a "refugee Panayía"—a term first employed by Filon Ktenidis (1950) and elaborated on by Giorgos Vozikas (2008)[26]—Soumelá closely relates to the history of the Pontians before and after their relocation to Greece.

More than a religious persona, Panayía Soumelá came to be regarded as kin, an ancestor, thus creating an ancestral link between past and present Pontian generations.[27] As was the case with other religious figures whose relics were brought by the refugees of Anatolia, Panayía Soumelá is seen as a victimized refugee. As a victim, forced out of her ancestral lands, she demands compensation and the appropriate recognition by the Greek state. The "politics of victimization" extends to any Pontian kin, human or divine.[28] Panayía Soumelá thus embodies two conflicting attributes, protector and victim, but definitely a Pontian kin. These semantic elaborations color Pontian culture allochronically, for they allow the Pontian imagination to reconfigure difference both spatially and temporally. This is important if we are interested in exploring the construction of Pontian identity vis-à-vis religious symbols, especially in the course of the nationalistic processes in Greece.

The icon of Panayía Soumelá was transferred to Greece in 1931 and kept in the Byzantine museum of Athens until 1951. Under pressure from the civic association "Panayía Soumelá," founded in Thessaloniki in 1951, the idea emerged of recreating a religious site in Greece that would resemble the original monastery in Trabzon. Through the association's journal, *Pontiaki Estia* (Pontic Hearth), prominent Pontians including intellectuals addressed crucial questions related to their history, economy, and politics after their relocation to Greece. Under the influence of the late Filon Ktenidis, editor of the journal, Panayía Soumelá was brought to the center of political developments regarding Pontian ethnoreligious identity in Greece. Furthermore, the association insisted that the new monastery of Panayía Soumelá in Veria[*] (Figure 1) should maintain an independent administrative status in order to regain its historical, ethnic, and religious dimension, so crucial to Pontians around the world.

The current legal status of the monastery is one of the most contested and controversial issues for Pontians today. Since the Royal Decree 924/1966 in 1966, the Holy Monastery of Panayía Soumelá is recognized as a public body of religious and beneficiary character under the supervision and control of the Ministry of Education. Members of the association "Panayía Soumelá" usually constitute the administrative body of the monastery, a fact that provokes much discontent among Pontian federations. In 1977

---

[*]The location in Veria was carefully chosen to recreate the ambience of the church's initial site on the mountain of Melá in Trabzon. The procession that followed the transfer of the icon to the newly constructed monastery in Veria was elaborate, with the inclusion of the Greek national army highlighting the political significance of the event. The Panayía was given back her agency in an apotheosis of religious, political, and popular fervor. On the concept of agency and political ritual as used here, see Marc Abélès, "Modern Political Ritual: Ethnography of an Inauguration and a Pilgrimage by President Mitterrand," *Current Anthropology*, vol. 29, no. 3 (1988): 391–404.

Figure 1. The monastery of Panayía Soumelá in Vermio, Veria, Greece (1985). Courtesy of Magda Zografou (color figure available online).

the charter of the Church of Greece was passed and the royal decree was abolished. Institutions like Panayía Soumelá were designated as sanctuaries under supervision of the Church of Greece. Yet administrative control of the monastery has not changed.

For Pontian participants, the celebration of Panayía Soumelá provokes the "effervescence" so eloquently described by Émile Durkheim.[29] It is a succession of liturgy, speech, and dance, clearly incorporating many of the "*distinguishing* marks of ritual."[30] The festivities of Panayía Soumelá start well before the celebration day. Each year, up to fifty thousand pilgrims of all ages, irrespective of social and economic status, gather in the designated space around the monastery under the trees. Some are regular pilgrims; others are visiting the monastery for the first time. Most come to fulfill a personal vow to the Panayía. Many bring their traditional musical instruments and gather in small groups to play music and dance. These unofficial events give the celebrants the opportunity to see each other while dancing. We conceptualize "to see while dancing" as a dialogical discourse where the dancers evaluate, constitute, and reconstitute their difference, sameness, and individualization in an intersubjective manner. Furthermore, this sharing of time between the celebrants, as well as between the celebrants and the Panayía, accords with an ethos that characterizes the relationship between religious figures and people in Greece: on the eve of the festivity of Panayía Soumelá the priest, after completing mass, inaugurates the civic celebrations with a *tik* dance, thus blurring the boundaries between human and divine intent, sacred and profane discourses.

On the premise that modern rituals can never escape political mediation,[31] we consider the festivity of Panayía Soumelá a contemporary act through which the politics of difference are played out. As Jill Dubisch notes in relation to the Panayía of Tinos, another famous Panayía of Greece, specific shrines are imbued with nationalist dimensions. This closely relates to the issue of Greekness, which "was by no means resolved with the establishment of the first Greek state, for there remained many who were defined, and who defined themselves, as Greeks but lived outside that first state's boundaries, a situation that determined much of Greece's destiny for the hundred years following the Greek War of Independence."[32] According to Nikos Marantzidis, "the myth of the dilemma 'language or religion' successfully accommodated identity issues during the Ottoman Empire especially when national identities were under construction. It further contributed critically to the incorporation of the refugee populations into the Greek national state, thus operating as a tool towards the transformation of their identity."[33] This observation is important to our understanding of the creation of Greek national consciousness through common religious figures such as Panayía; it applies to the Turkish-speaking Pontians of Western Pontus as well as to other Orthodox Turkish-speaking populations.

The simultaneous celebration of the day of Annunciation (March 25) with the day of Greek independence from the Ottoman Empire (achieved in 1821) demonstrates the inseparable relationship between nationalism and religion in Greece.[34] The persona of Panayía is thus directly implicated in the dynamics of Greek nationalism, making it a national symbol. This explains the prominence of the military presence at religious celebrations. It can be argued, then, that Panayía Soumelá was important for the

Pontian collectivities not only as a "Pontian persona," but also as a needed mediator who could negotiate the relationships between Pontians and other Greek populations equally devoted to various representations of the Panayía. At the macro level the celebration of Panayía Soumelá is a "public space"[35] where Pontians from Greece and around the world, subjected to different and conflicting state policies, gather on common ground to "see each other" through dancing. As such, ambivalent local perceptions (such as the managing of economic and political aspects of Pontian identity in Greece) as well as ideological positions related to wider contexts (for example, the contestation of Turkey's entrance into the European Union and Turkey's recognition of the Pontian genocide) can be successfully accommodated. In this case, accommodation is not the same as homogenization, owing to the fact that the festivity allows hegemonic as well as discontented or marginal voices to be heard equally.[36] An example of this occurred during the celebration in 2009, when prominent political figures, government officials, members of the opposition party, and local authorities all asserted the importance of Panayía Soumelá for the Greek nation. Declarations, like "Panayía Soumelá, the Mother of All Greeks," were coupled with political messages that directly related Panayía with the present economic and political crisis in Greece. Speakers pleaded to Panayía to "enlighten" both the government and the opposition so that they might rule wisely, and her intervention was petitioned for Greece's swift recovery from economic turmoil. This rhetorical capitalization of the festivity by participating politicians gave a national flavor to the Pontian Panayía.

Dance and Individualization

The festivities of Panayía Soumelá incorporate religious and civic performances. The civic celebrations begin following an elaborate procession of the icon of Panayía Soumelá around the church, accompanied by a military group, a band, and political figures representing the government as well as the opposition parties. Civic elements involve staged artistic performances of Pontian singers and dance troupes who have come from all over Greece and abroad in order to present their work to such a diverse audience. The dance troupes are allowed two to three minutes to perform and are selected the day prior to the celebration. According to a member of the Panayía Soumelá board, this procedure is needed for a variety of reasons, foremost, because it is not possible for all the invited troupes to perform since they are so numerous: "During the first years of the celebrations after 1974, the troupes that were invited were around ten and now they are more than fifty." Selection is also dictated by aesthetics. A committee of experts in Pontian arts and history is charged with the task of selecting troupes according to criteria of style, vivacity, authenticity in movement, and performance.

The rejection of some troupes unavoidably provokes conflict and discontent. The committee in such cases is proactive. They have established a rotational scheme on the grounds that troupes that have performed previous years must give way to new ones, while groups that have been rejected are promised a spot for a coming year. The dances are usually chosen primarily for their vivacity. This has resulted in a preference for specific dances such as Serra and Kotsari, which are dynamic, while other, subtler dances are overlooked. According to some older teachers who used to participate in the festivities, the performances are now more or less homogenous in terms of style owing to the pressure that the troupes feel to produce performances that will rouse the audience. Especially since the 1990s, more dance variations have been added, largely because of the pressure to come up with new, vivacious variations. In the political context this change occurred simultaneously with the explicit politicization of identities in Europe and the long-term presence of the Greek socialist party in government, which soothed wounds between collectivities that had played a leading role in the Greek civil war following the Axis occupation.[37]

If Panayía Soumelá, interwoven with the ruptures and continuities of Pontian history, is a powerful medium of distinction and individualization of the Pontian Self, so is Pontic dance. During the period of the relocation to Greece, dance performances became discourses where collective meaning was produced and affirmed. The management of dance identity in various stages paralleled the development of Pontian identity within the Greek state and the workings of Greek nationalism. The decades of the 1920s and 1930s were characterized by tensions between the local and refugee populations, the significant developments resulting from the agrarian reforms during the interwar period, and the worldwide economic crisis of 1929.[38] In the crucial period of the Axis occupation (1941 to 1944), the civil war that followed (1945 to 1949), and the Cold War, Pontian identity was structured mainly according to ideological dispositions crafted during this time[*] as well as by economic and social mobility,[†] and it gradually shifted away from issues of refugee identity as its core. During the 1950s and 1960s the political situation was more favorable toward elements of folk culture and Pontians eventually established their first civic associations with the aim of promoting a common identity and advancing political and economic claims. These positive developments were interrupted during the dictatorship in Greece (1967 to 1974), when many Pontian associations were closed down. When the dictatorship ended, Pontians commenced with fervor where they had left off but it was during the 1980s that major developments took place.

In this light, Magda Zografou identifies two main periods of managing Pontian dancing identity: before and after the 1980s.[39] The first period is characterized by tendencies toward incorporation within Greek public institutions, mainly reflected in music and dance. In this period, the creation of a common Pontic repertory and its subsequent homogenous interpretation, which undermined local stylistic variations, were conscious efforts by the Pontians to regulate sameness and difference within the host nation and to reinforce a common Pontian sense of belonging.

---

[*]Prevalent ideologies in this context were structured around alterities. The political right wing contrasted the national-minded (Ethnikofrones) with "traitors" to the nation, while the left wing projected concepts of patriots versus collaborators-reactionaries. See Nikos Marantzidis and Giorgos Antoniou, "The Axis Occupation and Civil War Bibliography: Changing Trends in Greek Historiography: 1941–2002," *Journal of Peace Research*, vol. 41, no. 2 (2004): 224.

[†]During the 1950s and 1960s a massive rural-urban migration swept through Greece and other European countries. Pontians who relocated to nearby cities and to Athens were considered "second-class" citizens, a trend echoed in other parts of Europe regarding rural populations that migrated to cities. See Kalliopi Panopoulou, "The Dance Identity of the Vlachs of Lailias Village and Its Transformations over Three Generations," *Yearbook for Traditional Music*, vol. 41 (2009): 166–86, especially p. 170; Keith Brown, "Anamesa sto kratos kai tin ypaithro," in *Taftotites sti Makedonia*, ed. Basil K. Gounaris, Iakovos D. Michailidis, and Giorgos V. Agelopoulos (Athens: Papazizi Publications, 1997), 171–95; and Stavroula Pipyrou, "Urbanities: Grecanici Migration to the City of Reggio Calabria, South Italy," in *History and Anthropology*, vol. 21, no. 1 (2010): 19–36.

Conforming to the nation's instrumental role in rhetorically disseminating "the need to preserve tradition ... Dance troupes were transformed into guardian angels of the national dance tradition and a means of preserving the Greek national identity."[40] As a result, Pontic dances with "Ottoman" connotations such as *male-male* (*horos me ta mantilia*, scarf dance), performed by the Metetzidiotes living at the frontier of Cappadocia, and dances shared with Armenians were excluded from the official Pontic dance repertory. The management of Pontian dancing identity was as much a top-down as a bottom-up process. In that sense, "official" dance discourses, represented mainly by the Pontian civic associations, and "unofficial" ones, represented by the everyday people, were constantly intermingling. These discourses created a self-referential dancing system at once narcissistic and ambivalent. As noted above, the creation of a common Pontic dancing repertory had a threefold effect. First, it promoted a common Pontian sense of belonging that was reflected in the homogenous interpretation of the dances; second, it projected outward an ideology of cultural specificity; and third, it cultivated deterministic assumptions about who is capable of performing a Pontic dance. Yet discrepancies created paradoxes, such as the obscuring of the origins of specific dances and the fact that non-Pontians are capable of performing Pontic dances.

The desire for incorporation into the Greek state on the one hand and preservation of what was considered authentically Pontian on the other structured Pontian identity around idealized categories such as Pontian history and moral virtues that exalted the Greekness of the Pontians.[41] Ioannis Kaskamanidis argues that before the 1980s Pontian identity was narcissistic in the sense of introversion and overvaluation[*] of the Pontian Self. Despite the fact that we maintain that, at least through dance, Pontians exhibited their intention to incorporate into the state, Kaskamanidis's argument has value for our discussion here. The idea of "symbolic capital"[42] in the form of staged dance performances, discussed above, accords with Freud's notion of the "narcissism of minor differences" in the sense that Pontians looked to their dance performances to evaluate themselves as different.

---

[*]This term relates to identity formation as a fluid and open-ended process.

In a somewhat similar manner, everyday actors reflexively played out the game of differentiation and sameness. In their attempt to regulate sameness while also carefully cultivating their difference, Pontians adopted local dances that accorded with their aspiration to be classed as meaningful members of Greek society. The elements that were introduced, including certain customs and musical instruments, were perceived as belonging to a pan-Hellenic repertory, thus bringing Pontians under the same nationalistic umbrella as other Greek populations. Similarly, in their attempt to connect themselves with ancient Greek ideals, the cornerstone of Greek nationalism, Pontians readily recognized a number of their dances as "pure" and "authentic" remnants of a Hellenic past when all Greeks shared a common dance repertory. Such decontextualized dance in Greece was a result of the workings of Greek nationalism, which stressed a uniform and linear spatiotemporal continuity between ancient Greeks and present subjects, with ancient Greek mythologizing at the center of its conceptualization. Thus, dances such as Syrtos Kalamatianos were comfortably incorporated into Pontian dance celebrations not only as a result of the Greek educational curriculum, which Pontians and non-Pontians shared, but also because it is perceived as a pan-Hellenic dance with ancient Greek origins.

In the 1980s, Greece came face to face with European modernization. Having survived World War II, a civil war, the resonance of the Cold War on Greek politics, and a military junta, the nation entered a period of political and cultural extroversion. The advent of a socialist government in 1981 initiated an era of political and cultural awareness as well as identity-making in relation to Greece's European counterparts. In this context local communities engaged in an even more dynamic manner with cultural and political activity, employing their historical resources to meet "sophisticated" European standards.[43] Under socialist leadership, "the ideology of returning to [its] roots," as the safest stance from which Greece could face Europe, became ever stronger.[44] The new socialist government was supported by the majority of Pontians.* As Richard Clogg noted regarding the success of the newly founded socialist party, it was the social rhetoric combined with

---

*Despite the fact that a considerable number of Pontian collectivities voted against the socialist party, the new government, especially under the leadership of the late Andreas Papandreou, was indeed favored by the majority of Pontians. See Nikos Marantzidis, *Yiasasin*

an uncompromising policy toward Turkey that "struck a responsive chord with a significant segment of the electorate."[45] More than that, the socialist prime minister himself, the late Andreas Papandreou, visited the monastery of Panayía Soumelá as an act of publicly acknowledging the support that his party received from the Pontians in the general elections of 1981. This visit successfully promoted the importance of the Panayía Soumelá monastery in the Greek national conscience. We believe that this decisive move transformed it from a "minor" to a "major" difference in the sense that the Pontian Panayía was nationally acknowledged and its particularistic connotations were slightly loosened.

This positive climate boosted Pontian cultural matters at the national level. Next to the already existing and institutionalized national dancing associations, new ones were created with the aim of displaying and promoting local dance identities through a reenactment of "traditional" culture.* In this sociohistoric framework, Pontian dance identity started materializing on the national level as a celebration of difference. The incorporation of Pontic dance into the school curriculum was a major advance of the era with enormous political connotations. Additionally, after great pressure from the Pontian associations, Pontic dance was included in the closing ceremony of the 2004 Olympic Games, officially displaying to the world that Pontian culture was considered Greek.

Finally, Pontians were able to reevaluate their systems of reference from within. Dances with Turkish names, initially approached with scepticism, are no longer taboo. Gradually, empirical research by both professional and amateur dance scholars introduced new dances to the associations from areas such as Bafra, Turkey. Contact with dance troupes from the historic area of Pontus in Turkey further enriched the existing dance repertory. Thus, dances such as Tsourtougoulou, from the mining area of Kiumous Maten, Giouvarlandoum, performed in Ak Dag Maten, Tamsara,

---

Millet/Zito to Ethnos: Prosfigia, Katoxi kai Emfilios, ethnotiki tautotita kai politici simperifora stous Tourkofonous ellinorthodoxous tou Ditikou Pontou (Irakleio: Panepistimiakes Ekdoseis Krētis, 2001).

*The Panpontian Federation of Greece, founded in 2004, is the official representative body of 340 Pontian associations. The other central representative body, with 170 member associations, is the Panhellenic Federation of Pontic Associations, founded in 1972. There are also the Federation of Pontian Associations of Southern Greece and the Federation of Pontian Associations of Northern Greece.

Ters, and variations on existing dances or dances invented according to known motifs have raised the number of current Pontic dances to over ninety. The introduction of dance seminars all over Greece, with the aim of educating new dance teachers, rapidly disseminated more "localized" dances that had often been completely unknown to dance professionals and researchers. This development was welcomed despite the unavoidable discontent expressed by older Pontian dance teachers who complained about "all these dances that we have not even heard of."[46]

Panayía Soumelá and Pontic dance did not always constitute major differentiations for the Pontian collectivities. At the time of the Pontians' relocation to Greece, the Pontian Panayía and Pontic dance both reflected back on the Pontian Self only to confirm its difference vis-à-vis the rest of the Greek collectivities. Eager to be part of a modern Greek society, Pontians gradually embraced Greek nationalism as they managed to cast themselves as worthy Greeks. In so doing they loosened particular connotations of their identity markers and gradually established their individualization based on a more reflexive (and not reflective) referential system.

Concurrent with political developments at the European level regarding the plurality of identities, new generations of Pontians have successfully politicized Pontian identity and transformed their self-referential systems and the signs that comprised them. In that sense both Panayía Soumelá and Pontic dance were transformed into major differences as an epiphenomenon of developments in Pontian identity. While difference may be manipulable and flexible it cannot be completely plastic;[47] minor differences may be structured around categorical and, for that matter, dichotomous ascriptions but major differences allow for a considerable mixing of identity markers that simultaneously conserve the seeds of their initial difference. Through systems of signs such as Panayía Soumelá and Pontic dance, the Pontian Self strives for individualization. By constituting major differential systems the Pontian Self looks at the Self only to be able to look at, recognize, and engage with the difference of the Other.

We would like to thank David Henig of Durham University for his valuable comments on this work and Lynn Matluck Brooks for her meticulous editing of the article.

Notes

All translations in this article are by Magda Zografou and Stavroula Pipyrou.

1. See Anton Blok, "The Narcissism of Minor Differences," *European Journal of Social Theory*, vol. 1, no. 1 (1998): 33–56; Sigmund Freud, *Group Psychology and the Analysis of the Ego* (London: Hogarth Press, 1921); Sigmund Freud, *Civilization and Its Discontents* (London: Hogarth Press, 1930); Michael Ignatieff, *The Warrior's Honor: Ethnic War and the Modern Conscience* (New York: Owl Books, 1997); Pål Kolstø, "The Narcissism of Minor Differences-Theory: Can It Explain Ethnic Conflict?," *Filosofija i Drustvo*, vol. 33, no. 2 (2007): 153–172; Paul Sant Cassia, "Guarding Each Other's Dead, Mourning One's Own: The Problem of Missing Persons and Missing Parts in Cyprus," in *When Greeks Think about Turks: The View from Anthropology*, ed. Dimitrios Theodossopoulos (London: Routledge, 2007).

2. Jane Cowan, *Dance and the Body Politic in Northern Greece* (Princeton, N.J.: Princeton University Press, 1990); Elisabeth Kirtsoglou, *For the Love of Women: Gender, Identity and Same-Sex Relationships in a Greek Provincial Town* (London: Routledge, 2004); Ioannis Manos, "To Dance or Not to Dance: Dancing Dilemmas in a Border Region in Northern Greece," *Focaal: European Journal of Anthropology*, no. 41 (2003): 21–32; Kalliopi Panopoulou, "The Dance Identity of the Vlachs of Lailias Village and Its Transformations over Three Generations," *Yearbook for Traditional Music*, vol. 41 (2009): 166–86; Stavroula Pipyrou, "To lipothimise to tsamiko: H diapragmateusi tis emfilis tautotitas, tis somatopiimenis mnimis kai tis istorias mesa apo khoreutikes epitelesis stin Kalloni Grevenon," *Proceedings* of the Third International Conference of Culture and Civilisation, University of Serres, Greece (Serres: Afoi Charalambidi 2006); Magda Zografou, "The Politics of Dance: The Incorporation of the Pontic Refugees in Modern Greek Culture through the Manipulation of Dancing Practices in a Northern Greek Village," *The Journal of Mediterranean Studies*, vol. 17, no. 1 (2007): 1–22; Magda Zografou and Stavroula Pipyrou, "Dancing in History: Socio-Political Aspects of Dance Identity of Two Distinctive Groups in Greece," *Studia Choreologica*, vol. 10 (2008): 25–41.

3. Jill Dubisch, *In a Different Place: Pilgrimage, Gender and Politics at a Greek Island Shrine* (Princeton, N.J.: Princeton University Press, 1995), 65.

4. See Michalis Meraklis, *O sigxronos Ellinikos laikos politismos* (Athens: Kallitehniko kai Pneumatiko kentro "Ora," 1983), 51; Dimitrios Pentzopoulos, *The Balkan Exchange of Minorities and Its Impact upon Greece* (Paris: Mouton & Co., 1962); Eleutheria Voutira, "Population Transfers and Resettlement Policies in Inter-war Europe: The Case of Asia Minor Refugees in Macedonia from an International and National Perspective," in *Ourselves and Others: The Development of a Greek Macedonian Cultural Identity since 1912*, ed. Peter Mackridge and Eleni Yannakakis (Oxford, U.K.: Berg, 1997).

5. Renee Hirschon, *Heirs of the Greek Catastrophe: The Social Life of Asia Minor Refugees in Piraeus* (Oxford, UK: Clarendon Press, 1989), 30–31; Anastasia Karakasidou, *Fields of Wheat, Hills of Blood: Passages to Nationhood in Greek Macedonia, 1870–1990* (Chicago: University of Chicago Press, 1997), 157, 159, 160–61; Elisabeth Kirtsoglou and Lina Sistani, "The Other Then, the Other

Now, and the Other Within: Stereotypical Images and Narrative Captions of the Turk in Northern and Central Greece," *The Journal of Mediterranean Studies*, vol. 13, no. 2 (2003): 189–213, especially 203–4; Stephen D. Salamone, *In the Shadow of the Holy Mountain: The Genesis of a Rural Greek Community and Its Refugee Heritage* (New York: Columbia University Press, 1987), 101; Voutira, "Population Transfers," 120.

6. Hirschon, *Heirs of the Greek Catastrophe*, 15–17, 30–33; Renee Hirschon, "Mnimi kai taftotita: Oi Mikrasiates prosfyges tis Kokkinias," in *Anthropologia kai parelthon: symvoles stin koinoniki istoria tis neoteris Elladas*, ed. Euthimios Papataxiarchis and Theodoros Paradellis (Athens: Ekdoseis Alexandria, 1993), 327–30; Elisabeth Kirtsoglou and Dimitrios Theodossopoulos, "Fading Memories, Flexible Identities: The Rhetoric about the Self and the Other in a Community of 'Christian' Refugees from Anatolia," *The Journal of Mediterranean Studies*, vol. 11, no. 2 (2001): 406–8; Dimitrios Pentzopoulos, *The Balkan Exchange of Minorities and Its Impact Upon Greece* (Paris: Mouton & Co., 1962), 205; Stephen D. Salamone, and Jill B. Stanton, "Introducing the Nikokyra: Identity and Reality in Social Process," in *Gender and Power in Rural Greece*, ed. Jill Dubisch (Princeton, N.J.; Princeton University Press, 1986), 101; Voutira, "Population Transfers," 120; Zografou, "The Politics of Dance;" and Zografou and Pipyrou "Dancing in History."

7. Zografou, "The Politics of Dance;" Theodoros Paradellis, "Anthropologia tis mnimis," in *Diadromes kai topoi tis mnimis: Istorikes kai anthropologikes prosegiseis*, ed. Rika Benveniste, and Theodoros Paradellis (Athens: Ekdoseis Alexandria, 1999); Kirtsoglou and Theodossopoulos, "Fading Memories, Flexible Identities."

8. Patricia Fann, "The Pontic Myth of Homeland: Cultural Expressions of Nationalism and Ethnicism in Pontos and Greece, 1870–1990," *Journal of Refugee Studies*, vol. 4, no. 4, Special Issue: The Odyssey of the Pontic Greeks (1991): 340–56; Hirschon, *Heirs of the Greek Catastrophe*; Hirschon, "Mnimi kai taftotita"; Karakasidou, *Fields of Wheat, Hills of Blood*, 150–51; Peter Loizos, *The Heart Grown Bitter: A Chronicle of Cypriot War Refugees* (Cambridge: Cambridge University Press, 1981).

9. Marc Augé, *Non-places: Introduction to an Anthropology of Supermodernity* (London: Verso, 1995), 25.

10. Zografou and Pipyrou, "Dancing in History." On historical constructivism, see James Faubion, *Modern Greek Lessons: A Primer in Historical Constructivism* (Princeton, N.J.: Princeton University Press, 1993).

11. Fredrik Barth, ed., *Ethnic Groups and Boundaries: The Social Organization of Culture Difference* (London: Allen and Unwin, 1969), 13.

12. Zografou and Pipyrou, "Dancing in History."

13. Kolstø, "The Narcissism of Minor Differences-Theory."

14. Freud, *Group Psychology*, 101.

15. Ibid.

16. Ignatieff, *The Warrior's Honor*, 7.

17. Sant Cassia, "Guarding Each Other's Dead," 114.

18. Manos, "To Dance or Not to Dance."

19. Ibid., 30, n. 2.

20. Ibid., 21.

21. Sant Cassia, "Guarding Each Other's Dead," 114.

22. William Christian, *Person and God in a Spanish Village* (Princeton, N.J.: Princeton University Press, 1972); Dubisch, *In a Different Place*; Carmelo Lisón-Tolosana, *Belmonte de los Caballeros: A Sociological Study of a Spanish Town* (Oxford, U.K.: Clarendon Press, 1966); Stavroula Pipyrou, *Power, Governance and Representation: An Anthropological Analysis of Kinship, the 'Ndrangheta and Dance within the Greek Linguistic Minority of Reggio Calabria, South Italy* (doctoral dissertation, Durham University, UK, 2010); Eric Wolf, ed. *Religion, Power and Protest in Local Communities: The Northern Shore of the Mediterranean* (Berlin: Mouton, 1984).

23. In accordance with the "Ethical Guidelines for Good Research Practice" of the Association of Social Anthropologists of the United Kingdom and Commonwealth, the authors have chosen to protect the identity of informants quoted in this article. See http://www.nomadit.net/asatest/ethics/guidelines.htm (accessed March 15, 2011).

24. Michael Herzfeld, "Icons and Identity: Religious Orthodoxy and Social Practice in Rural Crete," *Anthropology Quarterly*, vol. 63 (1990): 109–21.

25. For a detailed historical account of Pontic Greeks before the exchange of populations between Turkey and Greece, see Anthony Bryer, "The Pontic Greeks before the Diaspora," *Journal of Refugee Studies*, vol. 4, no. 4, (1991): 315–34.

26. Filon Ktenidis, "H prosfix Panayía," *Pontiaki Estia,* vol. 7–8 (1950); Giorgos Vozikas, "'Prosfix Panayía': Sinifanseis stin Anasistasi tou Proskinimatos tis Panayía Soumelá sto Vermio," in Manolis Sergis, ed., *Pontos: Themata Laografias tou Pontiakou Ellinismou* (Athens: Alitheia, 2008), 115–32.

27. For comparative accounts see also Jon Mitchell, *Ambivalent Europeans: Ritual, Memory and the Public Sphere in Malta* (London: Routledge, 2002); and Pipyrou, *Power, Governance and Representation*.

28. Pamela Ballinger, *History in Exile: Memory and Identity at the Borders of the Balkans* (Princeton, N.J.: Princeton University Press, 2003).

29. Émile Durkheim, *The Elementary Forms of the Religious Life*, trans. Joseph Swain, 1915 (London: George Allen and Unwin, 1915), 206–14.

30. Maurice Bloch, *Ritual, History and Power: Selected Papers in Anthropology* (London: Athlone Press, 1989), 21. Italics in the original.

31. Marc Abélès, "Modern Political Ritual: Ethnography of an Inauguration and a Pilgrimage by President Mitterrand," *Current Anthropology*, vol. 29, no. 3 (1988): 391–404.

32. Dubisch, *In a Different Place*, 166.

33. Nikos Marantzidis, *Yiasasin Millet/Zito to Ethnos: Prosfigia, Katoxi kai Emfilios, ethnotiki tautotita kai politici simperifora stous Tourkofonous ellinorthodoxous tou Ditikou Pontou* (Irakleio: Panepistimiakais Ekdoseis Kritis, 2001), 49.

34. Dubisch, *In a Different Place*, 172; Paul Sant Cassia and Constantina Bada, *The Making of the Modern Greek Family: Marriage and Exchange in Nineteenth-Century Athens* (Cambridge: Cambridge University Press, 1992), 4.

35. Magda Zografou, "Anamesa stin ensomatosi kai ti diaforopoiisi: Diadikasies sigrotisis kai diapragmateusis tis pontiakis tautotitas kai i dynami tou xorou," in Sergis, *Pontos: Themata Laografias tou Pontiakou Ellinismou*, 170.

36. David Kertzer, *Ritual, Politics and Power* (London: Yale University Press, 1988).

37. Nikos Marantzidis and Giorgos Antoniou, "The Axis Occupation and Civil War Bibliography: Changing Trends in Greek Historiography: 1941–2002," *Journal of Peace Research*, vol. 41, no. 2 (2004): 223–31.

38. Richard Clogg, *A Concise History of Greece* (Cambridge: Cambridge University Press, 1992); Voutira, "Population Transfers and Resettlement Policies."

39. Zografou, "The Politics of Dance."

40. Ioannis Manos, "The Past as a Symbolic Capital in the Present: Practicing Politics of Dance Tradition in the Florina Region, Northwest Greek Macedonia," in *New Approaches to Balkan Studies*, The IFPA–Kokkalis Series on Southeast European Policy, vol. 2, eds. Dimitris Keridis, Ellen Elias-Bursac, and Nicholas Yatromanolakis (Dulles, Va.: Brassey's Publishers, 2003), 35.

41. Ioannis Kaskamanidis, "Diapragmateusi me to parelthon gia ton kathorismo tou parondos kai to skhediasmo tou mellondos: H tautotita ton elladiton Pontion kata ton 20o aiona," in Sergis, *Pontos: Themata Laografias tou Pontiakou Ellinismou*, 193.

42. Pierre Bourdieu, "The Forms of Capital," in *Handbook of Theory and Research for the Sociology of Education*, ed. John G. Richardson (New York: Greenwood, 1985), 248.

43. Cowan, *Dance and the Body Politic in Northern Greece*, 63, 74.

44. Jane Cowan, "Idioms of Belonging: Polyglot Articulations of Local Identity in a Greek Macedonian Town," in *Ourselves and Others*, ed. Peter Mackridge and Eleni Yannakakis, 164.

45. Clogg, *A Concise History of Greece*, 179.

46. Interview, Pontian dance teacher from Kars, Turkey.

47. Sant Cassia, "Guarding Each Other's Dead."

Index

Page numbers in **bold** represent figures

abstract expressionism 135
Adam, M. 42
Adams, L. 7, 28
Adams, M. 7, 27–9
Adhenen, Z. 242
Admiring La Argentina (Ohno) 3–4, 171–96
Ailey, A. 70–1
Algo, J. 134
Alltag und Fest (Laban) 137
Alton, K. 43, 49
American Ballet Theatre 93, 114
American Dance Guild 98
American Dance Legacy Institute 51
American Institute of Indian Studies 83
American-Scandinavian Foundation 77
Anderson, J. 45
Andrade, O. de 187
Andrew W Mellon Foundation 69, 75
Angiolini, G. 99
anthropophagism 188
Antony Tudor Ballet Trust 37
ARCHEION (database) 31
archeochoreology 130–41, 168; in action
    133–41; body as living archive 137–8;
    definition 130–1; locating/study of
    archival materials 133–4; product/
    process 138–41
Archer, K.: and Hodson, M. 131–2, 165
Archive Fever (Derrida) 58
archives: Canada 8–34; choreographers 2;
    Clara Thomas (York) 31; Hamburg
    Communist Collection 135; Interpreters
    116; Jerome Robbins Dance Division
    Film 82, 86, 87; Lost Choreography
    116; Manitoba 8, 18, 23, 26; Prokofiev,
    S. 158, 164
archivists 27–31; grassroots 28–9;
    perspectives 27–31; and source diversity
    50–4

Aroldingen, K. von 115
Art of Movement Studio 137
ashibyoshi (stamping foot rhythms) 175
Ashley, M. 116
Ashton, F. 3, 76, 104–5, 120–3, 131;
    Trust 37, 120–3; upkeep problems 121;
    work revivals 122
Asian dance 79–86; Archive 80
Astor, J.J. 92
Astruc, G. 73
Ausdruckstanz tradition (Laban) 132–3,
    138, 148–50, 235
Avant-Garde Dance exhibition 92
Aweke, A. 256

Baker, P. 2, 35–63; approach to dance
    preservation 46, 54–6; biography 38–
    45; Creator authority 56–60, *see also*
    Choreographer's Trust
Balanchine Catalogue 116
Balanchine, G. 3, 78, 83, 92, 99, 104–9,
    120, 125; Foundation 105; Trust 37,
    105, 114–17, 123
Ballard, S. 2, 12, 19, 22–7, 31–2; *homeagain*
    17; *Landscape Dances* 26; Legacy Project
    and works 22–7; *Prairie Song* 22–4
ballet 64–103
Ballets Russes 150, 154–7, 160; de Monte
    Carlo 74
Ballett Frankfurt 5
Barthès, R. 53
Baruch, Z. 243, 249
Baryshnikov, M. 38–40, 79
Basil, Col W. de 74
Bass, A. 92
Batsheva Dance Company 259
Bausch, P. 132; Tanztheatre 147
Bay Area Lawyers for the Arts (California)
    111

Bayenne, G. 258
Beatty, P. 21
Beethoven, L. van 155
Bélec, D. 244
Bellmer, H. 180
belly dancing 237
Benesh system 121, 131
Benishangal tribe (Ethiopia) 253
Bennahum, N. 175–9
Berber, A. 150
Bereska, D. 134, 138
Bergson, H. 173–4, 181–2
Berlin Akademie der Künste 150
Berlin Choreographisches Institut (Laban) 133, 140
Berlind Theatre (Princeton) 162
Beta Dance Troupe 4–5, 231, 240–3, 259–62, *see also Eskesta* Dance Theatre
Bharata Natyam 49
Bhattacharya, N. 42, 49, 58–9
Bibliothèque et Archives Nationales du Québec (BAnQ) 8
Bibliothèque Nationale 75
Billion Dollar Baby 106
Bird, B. 133
Bitualin, G. 258
Bizarrer (Laban) 138
Blok, A. 272
Bode, R. 136
Bodmer, S. 134, 137
Bolshoi Ballet 114
Borch-Jacobson, M. 172, 185
Bourne, M. 148, 155
Bournonville 100
Bourscheidt, R. 92
Bowring, A.: and Lindgren, A. 2, 35–63
Brahms Waltzes (Baker) 41–2, 46–7, 52, 55
Branitzka, N. 74
Braveman, A. 124
British Ballet 76; romantic 95
Brochu, S. 42, 48, 56
Brooks, L. 3, 64–103; and Meglin, J. 1–5
Browne, R. 2, 11, 16–22, 25–32; *A Living Legacy* 25; *Ceremonies* 21–2; *Edgelit* 18; *Mouvement* 19–20; *Sunstorm* 19; and WCD 16–22
Brownley, J. 65
Bruhn, E. 76
Brute (Baker) 43–51, 55
Buckland, T. 238
Building your Legacy: Archiving Handbook for Dance (Adams) 28
Bulletin (NYPL) 68
Burashko, A. 41–5

butoh dance (Japan) 172–5, *see also* Ohno, K.

Cage, B. 87
Cage, J. 41, 56, 119, 247
Canada 6–34; Council for the Arts, Dance section 9, 18–19, 22; Dance Festival (Ottawa) 15; and Dance Heritage 6–34, 29; Heritage Department 9; Integrated Dance Database (CIDD) 28; Modern Dance Festivals 25; National Ballet 39, 42–4, 48–9; National Library 9; public archives 8–34; Social Sciences and Humanities Research Council 21, *see also* choreographers
Cannibalist Manifesto (de Andrade) 187
Capezio Award 65
Carlson, T. 119
Carr, R. 96
Castelli, V. 118
Chaffee, G. 72–3
Chai Folk ensemble 26
Chaos, Fight and Liberation (Laban) 144
Charleston Ballet, The (Guest) 106
Chole, A. 258–9
choreographers 2; archives 2; legacy plans overview 113–25; legacy preservation case studies 6–34; perspectives 11–27; trusts 104–29
Choreographer's Trust 2–3, 35–63, 104–29; letter of agreement 54–5; and Peggy Baker 38–45; performances 41–5
choreutics (space studies) 137
Civilization and its Discontents (Freud) 272
Clara Thomas Archives (York) 31
Clogg, R. 285
Cohen, S.J. 46
Cold War 157, 285
Cole, J. 70
Columbia University 69, 74; Oral History Research Office 69
Concert, The 118
Congress Library 91
Connerton, P. 51, 58
constitutive elements concept 45
constructivism 161
Cook, R. 106
Cooney, S. 43, 48–9, 55–7
Copeland, R. 45
copyright 87, 110–13; and rights of ownership 110–13
courtship: Greek celebratory dance 215–28; *sousta* performance 216–28, **217–20**
Creative Post, Inc. 13

culture: Pontic dance 271–6
Cunningham, M. 3, 56, 71, 93, 104, 133;
Dance Foundation 119; Living Legacy
Plan 105–8, 119–20; Studio/Repertory
Group 119; Trust 113, 119–20, 123
Curtis-Jones, A. 145–51, 154, 165

Dalcroze, E.-J. 136
Dalinsky, M. 106
*Dance Chronicle: Studies in Dance and the
Related Arts* 1, 98
Dance Committee 92–3
Dance Heritage Coalition (DHC) 1, 8
Dance Index (Kirstein) 88, 95
Dance Library of Israel (Beit Ariela) 96,
238
Dance Masters of America 98
Dance Notation Bureau (DNB) 51, 71,
119
Dance NYC 112
Dance Resources in Canadian Libraries
(National Library) 9
*Dance, a Short History of Classic Theatrical
Dancing* (Kirstein) 88
dance writing: forms 91
Dancer's Congress (1928) 136
Dancing Balanchine/Watching Balanchine
lecture series 116
Danny Grossman Dance Company 2, 10
Danse Collection Danse (DCD) 2, 7–8,
12, 18, 36; role 27–9; workshops 14–15
Dante Sonata (Ashton) 122
Day on Earth (Humphrey) 131
Decade of Acquisitions, A (Kirstein) 86
Degai, M. 242, 255
Deleuze, G. 174, 182
Demoza, M. 254–7
Denham, S. 74
Denishawn Collection 70
Der Blaue Reiter 135
Der Schwingende Tempel (Laban) 137
Der Spielmann (Laban) 137
Derrida, J. 58
Devi, R. 82
Diabelli Variations (Beethoven) 155
Diablo Ballet (California) 115
Diaghilev, S. 73–6, 150, 156–60
Dictionary Catalog of the Dance Collection
(Kirstein/Oswald) 89–91
Die Grünen Clowns (Green Clowns) (Laban)
3, 135, 138–48, 153–5; *Klub der
Sonderlinge* 146; *Krieg* 143–4, **143**;
Maschine 141–3; re-creation (Preston-

Dunlop) 3, **139**, 141–6, **142–5**, 164–7;
Romanz 144–6, **145**; sections 141–6
Diversion of Angels (Graham) 147
Divinariane (Hijikata) 180
Dodge, R.P. 66
Don Juan 140
Don Quijote 78
Doobs, R. 72
D'Orleans Juste, R. 41
Dowell, A. 120–1
Dowler, G. 121–2
Dror, L. 237
Dubisch, J. 280
Duncan, I. 40–1, 67–8; collection 93;
studio 80
Dunham, K. 71
Dunin, E.I. 247
Dunleavy, R. 115
Dunn, R. 244–7
Dunning, J. 178
Duport, L. 94
Dyson, A. 120–1

Eames, M. 95
Earle, D. 21
Efrati, M. 237
Eguchi, T. 184
Ein Leben für den Tanz (Ullman) 136
Eisenstein, S. 156, 161
Ek, M. 148, 155
Ekstatischer Zweimännertanz (Laban) 138, 141
Ellfeldt, L. 234
Ellis, W. 121
Elssler 78, 92
Elyakim, D. 254
Emptiness (Ohno) 190–3
Endangered Dance: A National Dance
Heritage Forum (Toronto) 2, 10–11,
14, 17, 22–7; performance themes 24–5
Enigma (Ashton) 122
Erdman, D. 68
Eretz Israel 235–6
Eshel, R. 4–5, 231–66
Eshkol-Wachman Movement Notation
262
Eskesta Dance Theatre (Ethiopian-Israeli)
4–5, 231–62; analysis 239–40; and Beta
Dance Troupe 231, 240–3, 259–62;
choreographic process 243–6;
establishment 240–3; guideline maps
247; *Maharo* 248–54, **249–52**; *Nefas*
257–9, **260–1**; *Opus for Heads* 255–7,
256; *Opus for Shoulders* 231, 254–5, **255**;
Prayer Dance 248; variations 240

Ethiopian National Theatre 253
Ethiopian-Israeli dance 4–5, 231–66;
  Bahalachin Troupe 242; and *Eskesta* 4–
  5, 231–62; and *Falasha* 232; history 5;
  Jewish community 233–5
eukinetics 137
eurhythmy (Steiner) 136
excorporation 189
expressionism: abstract 135

family heritage: Rhodes 4, 216–28
Feist, H. 134
Fekadu, R. 242
Feld, E. 113
Fenley, M. 38
Fiddler on the Roof 87
Filene's Department Store 88
Final Report: Legacy Project (Ballard) 22
Five Brahms Waltzes (Ashton) 122
flamenco dance 171–2; ideal 174; and
  zapateado (foot stamping) 174–8, *see also*
  Ohno, K.
Flatow, S. 115
Fokine, M. 73
folk dancing 4–5, 26; *eskesta* 4–5, 231–62;
  Folklorama ethnic celebrations
  (Winnipeg) 26; *sousta* 4, 197, 203–5,
  216–28
folklore: Yemenite 236–7
Fonteyn, F. 121
Fonteyn, M. 75, 93–4, 120
Fonteyn, P. 121
Ford Foundation 89, 92
Former Yugoslav Republic of Macedonia
  (FYROM) 274
Fornaroli, C. 72
Forsythe, W. 5, 132, 147, 152–3;
  Foundation 152
Fortier, P-A. 38–40
Foucault, M. 35
Four Seasons, The 49
Frank, E. 134
Franko, M. 3–4, 171–96
Freedgood, A. 68
French Court and Opera Ballet exhibition 91
Freud, S. 186–7, 270–2, 284
Frid, N. 42, 45
Frohlich, J-P. 118
Fundação Calouste Gulbenkian 99
Fuss, D. 186

Gal, N. 237
Gamson, A. 41
Garden, The (Stroud) 25

Gates, L. 39–40
Gaukelei (Laban) 137, 140
Genet, J. 179, 191
Gert, V. 150
Giselle (Ek) 74, 148, 155
Goldschmidt, H. 74–5
Goodman, N. 45
Gordon, B. 83
Gould Foundation 92
Graff, M. 92
Graham, M. 3, 42, 58, 69, 92, 119, 133,
  147; Center 112, 123–5; Dance
  Company 84; living legacy 125; School
  of Contemporary Dance 123; tax/salary
  problems 124; trademark 112–13, 124;
  Trust 123–5
Graham, W.B. 66
Grant, A. 120–1
Greece, celebratory dance 197–230; *ballo*
  215–16; and courtship 215–28; dance
  sequence 214–15; family networks and
  identity 202–3; historical background
  203–5; *Kamara* 205–7, **208**;
  PanHellenic/Cretan 204; ritual
  sequence 205–14, **206**; *sousta* (Rhodes)
  197–223; *syrto* and *vlaha* 204, 215, 226;
  wedding ritual reconstruction 205–15
Greek War of Independence (1821–32)
  280
Green Table, The (Jooss) 131
Grider, C. 41, 46–9
Grossman, D. 21; Danny Grossman
  Dance Company 2, 10
Group Psychology and the Analysis of the Ego
  (Freud) 272
Grundrisse (Marx) 187
Guerlac, S. 174
Guernica (Picasso) 43
Guest, I. 95
Guragé tribe (Ethiopia) 253; national
  dance 258

Haifa University: Theatre Study Circle
  240–1
Haight, K. 19–20
Hall, F. 1
Halprin, A. 257
Hamburg Communist Archive Collection
  135
Hamburger Nachrichtung 135
Hanley, E. 42
Hanoch-Levi, D. 257–89
Harrington, R. 43, 48–50
Harvard Theatre Collection 73

Hassan, A. 42
Hawaii University: Dance Research Congress 98
Hawkins, E. 93
Hendl, S. 118
Herd, J. 26
Hernandez, A. 236
Herzfeld, M. 253
Hijikata, T. 180, 191
Hockney, D. 155
Hodson, M. 154–6, 160, 164; and Archer, K. 131–2, 165
Hoerburger, F. 234
Holden, K. 41, 47–9
Holm, H. 68
Hookham, L. 121
Horgan, B. 106, 114–17
Horn, E. 187
Horst, L. 68, 92
Horwitz, D. 234
Hosoe, E. 181–3
Houghton, E. 92
Hountondji, P. 235
Howard, J. 26
Howard, T. 41, 46–9
Hskias, T. 259
Hughes, R.M. (La Meri) 80
Humphrey, D. 68–9, 131–3
Hutchinson Guest, A. 106, 116, 148

idealism 45
identity: Pontic dance 268–9, 282–5
idiopathic identification 189
Igarashi, Y. 179
Ignatieff, M. 272–5
In a Landscape (Baker) 41, 45, 48, 52–5
In the Night (Robbins) 118
Inbal Dance Theatre 236–7, 242, 245
Individuality in the Dancer (Baker) 52
individualization: and Pontic dance 281–7
Internal Revenue Code (section 509) 107
International Council of Kinetography Laban (ICKL) 131
International Dance Day 26
International Festival of Dance Academies 99
International Theatre Institute (ITI) 99
Interpreters Archive 116
Irma Duncan Collection 68
Israeli community dance 235–8; belly dancing 237; Sephardic culture 237; Yemenite folklore 236–7, see also Ethiopian-Israeli dance
Ivanochko, S. 43–4, 47–9

Jacob's Pillow 76–7
Jacobson, D. 122
Japan: butoh dance 172–5
Jerome Robbins Dance Division: Film Archive 82, 86; Foundation 105; Recorded Moving Image Archive 87; Trust 105–9, 117–18, see also New York Public Library
Jewels (Balanchine) 114–16
The Jewish Dancing Master and Theatrical Society exhibition 92
Joffrey Ballet 87
John D. Rockefeller III Fund 80
Johns, J. 120
Johnson, D. 76
Johnson, H. 69
Johnson, M. 245; and Lakoff, G. 250
Jones, H. 42, 53
Jooss, K. 131, 134, 147
Jordan, S. 131
Julliard School 39, 65

Kabuki 175
Kaeja, A.: and Kaeja, K. 2, 11–16, 27, 30–2
Kaeja d'Dance (Toronto) 11–16; Asylum of Spoons 14; Making Dance philosophy 16; Resistance 13
Kalamatianos, S. 285
Kammertanzbühne (Chamber Dance Group) 130–44, see also Laban
Kandinsky, W. 135
Kariamu & Company 238
Kaskamanidis, I. 284
Kattaveni Women's Cultural Organization 204
Kaye, N. 76, 79
Kazuo Ohno 174, 186
Kazuo Ohno's World 192
Keith, J. 134
Khmer dance 83
Khomeni, Ayatollah R: M. 84
Kibbe, B. 111
Kibbutzim College: Dance and Art School 262
Kim, N.S. 113, 123–4
King, B. 71
King, E. 41
Kirkland, G. 93
Kirov Ballet (Maryinsky) 114
Kirstein, L. 70, 78, 86–9, 92, 95
Klee, P. 135
Klingenbeck, F. 133
Knust, A. 134

Kochno, B. 91
Kokoshka, O. 135
Koperkultur groups 136
Kremasti Dance Competition 203
Kreutzberg, H. 132
Krystall (Laban) 138
Ktenidis, F. 277–8
Kudelka, J. 38
Kuhn, L. 119

La Bibliothèque de la danse de Vincent Warren 8
La Corrida 175
La Sonnambula (Balanchine) 114
La Valse (Ashton) 121
Laban, R. 3, 130–51, 154, 165;
    Ausdruckstanz 132–3, 138, 148–50,
    235; Center (London) 132–3, 137; and
    Kammertanz Works re-creation 130–
    51; lost heritage 146–7; Movement
    Analysis (LMA) 244; sources and
    context 135–7
Labanotation 91, 106, 116, 131
LaFrance, C. 2, 6–34
Lajarte, de T. 75
Lakoff, G.: and Johnson, M. 250
Lambert, C. 75
Laplanche, J. 172, 185
L'Après-midi d'un Faune (Nijinsky) 148
Larsen, L.B. 77
Larsen, N. 187
Las Meninas (Velasquez) 155
Lasky, G. 95
Lausanne Treaty (1923) 4, 270
Le Clercq, T. 115; Trust 115
Le Pas d'Acier (Prokofiev) 3, 154–5; design
    159; documentation and dissemination
    162–5; finding the ballet 156–7; re-
    creation (Princeton) 3, 156–65, **163**
Le Sacre du Printemps (Nijinsky) 131
Leatherman, L. 69
Legacy, Transition and Succession report (Arts
    Council) 9–10
Lenox, J. 92
Lent, P. 119
Les Noces 148
Levi-Tanai, S. 236–9, 245
Levinson, A. 184
Lewis, A. 26
Library-Museum of the Performing Arts
    (NYPL) 65
Lieberman, W.S. 92
liminality 197–8, 221–2
Limón, J. 65
Lindgren, A.: and Bowring, A. 2, 35–63

Listening to the Worlds Inside and Out (Baker)
    52
Loesch, I. 134
Loeser, G. 134
London Contemporary Dance Theatre
    133
Loss of Small Detail, The (Forsythe) 152;
    maps 152–3
Lost Action (Pite) 5
Lost Choreography Archives 116
Lowry, W.M. 89
Lubovitch, L. 38–9
Lubow, A. 120

Macaulay, A. 125
McBride, P. 115
McCray, P. 80–2, 92
McNeil, W.H. 1
Macpherson, S. 40
Madden, D. 141
Maharaj, B. 82
Maharat, E. 251
Makarova, N. 79
Mamo, C. 258
Man with a Movie Camera (Vertov) 160
Manet, E. 155
Manitoba: Archives 8, 18, 23, 26; Arts
    Council 22
Manor, G. 236
Manos, I. 273–5
Marantzidis, N. 280
Markard, A. 131–2
Markova, Dame A. 158
Marotte (Laban) 138–41
Marsch (Laban) 138, 141
Marshal, B. 237
Martha Graham Dance Company 84,
    236; Trust 110, 123–5
Marx, K. 187
Masakatsu, G. 175
Mason, F. 112
Massacre in Korea (Picasso/Hockney) 155
Massine, L. 154, 158–60, 166
Medau, H. 136
Meglin, J.: and Brooks, L. 1–5
Mellon Foundation 92
Menaka Thakkar & Co 49
Mensendieck, B. 136
Mercé, A. 171–2
Merce Cunningham Trust 37, 107–9,
    119–20
Metcalf Foundation 35, 58
Meuller, H.L. 80
Meyerhold, V. 156

Mezur, K. 178
Mille, A. de 78, 113
Miller, E. 81
Milloss, A. 134, 140
Mills, G.Y. 238
Mirzoeff, N. 49
Miya, M. 184
Mizohata, T. 182
modernist nostalgia 178–9
Moir, M. 30–1
Moiseyev, I. 236
Möndane (Laban) 138
Monte Veritá 134–5
Moore, L. 72, 76–8, 94
Morris, M. 38–40
Morrison, S. 158, 164
Movement for Canadian Dance Heritage 29
Mozart 106
muscular bonding 1
Museum of Modern Art (MoMA) 70, 88
Music for Piano and Solo Dance (Baker) 43

Nabokov, N. 166
Nacht (Laban) 137, 148–51; re-creation issues 148–51; scenes 150–1; theme 148–9
Nahachewsky, A. 247
Naharin, O. 259
Nakanishi, N. 181; and *La Argentina* painting 181–4
Nancy Dance Festival (1980) 188
Nann, A. 43, 49
narcissism: and Pontic dance 271–6, 284
National Endowment for the Arts 87, 92
National Resource Centre for Dance (Guildford) 149
National School of Music (Addis Ababa) 239
nationalism and culture: Pontic dance 271–6
Navel and A-bomb (Hosoe) 181
Negash, A. 253
Nesmith, T. 57
Neue Sachlichkeit (New Objectivity) 136
Nevins, A. 69
New York Asia Society 83
New York City Ballet (NYCB) 68, 80, 86–8, 93, 114, 118, 125; exhibition 92; Robbins works 118
New York Herald Tribune 67
New York Public Library Dance Collection (NYPL) 3, 117–18; American Modern Dance 67–71; background 65–

6; ballet records 71–9; exhibitions and Committee 91–4; founding 64–103; Friends category 93; Jerome Robbins Dance Division 64–103; Lenox/Astor Collections 66; Oswald as teacher and mentor 94–6; preservation and cataloging 88–91; research libraries 92; Schomburg Center for Research in Black Culture 71; Spencer Collection 82; visual documentation 86–8; World Dance 79–86
New York State Council on the Arts 87, 92
New York Times 65, 70
New York University 66
Newton, C. 122
Nicholls, R. 234
Nichols, M. 97
Nietzsche, F. 140
Night Shadow (Balanchine) 114
nihilism/anarchy 135–6
Nijinsky, B. 148
Nijinsky, V. 66, 73, 131, 148
Noguchi, I. 69
Non Coupable (Fortier) 40
North, M. 133
North Star (Lubovitch) 39
nostalgia: modernist 178–9
Nureyev, R. 78
Nutcracker 116

Oben und Unten (Laban) 138
Obrist, H. 135
O'Connor, T. 38
Ode (Laban) 150, 154; re-creation 166–8; themes and undercurrents 167
Ohno, K. 3–4; and *Admiring La Argentina* 171–96; French literature influences 180; heteropathetic identification 188–90; legacy and *Emptiness* 190–3; and modernist nostalgia 178–9, 184; and Nakanishi's painting 181–4; narrative of origins 177–81; passion and possession 184–8; pure perception/delayed nemesis 173–7, 185
Ohno, Y. 171, 180, 190–3; and *Emptiness* 190–3
Olympic Games (2004) 286
Operation Moses 233, 241, 248
Operation Solomon 238
Orchidée (Laban) 138
Oswald, G. 3; after retirement 97–101; and Asian dance 79–86, **84–5**; biography 65–6; New York Public

Library Dance Collection founding 64–103; as teacher and mentor 94–6
Other Dances (Robbins) 118
otherness 140
Ottman, P. 42–3, 58
Our Lady of the Flowers (Genet) 179
ownership rights 110–13

Pabst, I. 74, 92
Page, R. 77
Palucca, G. 132
Panayía Soumelá celebrations 4, 267–91; history and ritual 276–81; Holy Monastery 278; and victimization 277–8, *see also* Pontic dance
Papandreou, A. 286
Parent, M. 42, 45
Paris Opéra Ballet 118
Parkes, R. 84–6
participatory dance 247–8
Pavlova, A. 73, 92
Pearson, M. 130
Peggy Baker Dance Projects 43
Pennington, C. 107, 117–18
Pennsylvania University: Rare Book and Manuscript Library 96
Perreault, J-P. 8
Peters, K.: and Peters, G. 133–4
Peterson, Judge J. 111
Petipa, M. 90–2
Petrides, T. 215
Pew Foundation 92
Phelan, P. 241
Piasecki, M. 25
Picasso, P. 43, 155
Pikado, Y. 251
Pilkington's Tile Factory workshops 142–3
Pipyrou, S.: and Zografou, M. 4, 267–91
Pite, C. 5
PJS Richardson Collection 75
plagiarism 87
plurality 37
Plymouth University 152; Institute of Digital Art and Technology 152
Pontalis, J.B. 172, 185
Pontic dance 267–91; conflict and troupe rejection 282–5; differences 269–76; identity 268–9, 282–5; and individualization 281–7; and narcissism 271–6, 284; nationalism and culture 271–6; the Panayía 268–9, 276–81; Serra/Kotsari 282; Turkish origins 280–1, 286–7
poverty of access 1

presentational dance 247–8
Preservation Politics 131
Preston-Dunlop, V. 130–56, 164–7; and Laban's Kammertanz Works 130–54; and Sayers, L-A. 3, 130–70
private foundations 92
Prokofiev, S. 3, 45, 154–6; Archive 158, 164
Protas, R. 123

Quigley, C. 29

Rachel Browne Theatre 25
Rainer, Y. 147
Rambert, M. 76
Rauschenberg, R. 120
Raz, R. 237
RCA Victor studios 73
re-creation 3, 130–70; archeochoreology 130–41; ballets (from 1920s) 154–65; digital age documentation 151–4; and Laban's Kammertanz Works 130–3
recollection-image (*image-souvenir*) 174
Reese, G. 65
Regeny music 150
Rencher, D. 121
Research in the Humanities (NYPL) 94
Reta, C. 257
Reynolds, N. 106, 116
Rhodes: family heritage 4, 216–28
Riak, P. 4
rights: ownership 110–13
Ritual Process, The (Turner) 197
Robbins, J. 3, 79, 86–7, 104; Trust 37, 105–9, 113, 117–18, 123
Robinson, E. 26
Robinson, T. 25
Rockefeller Foundation 89, 92
Rodchenko, A. 156
Rogge, L. 133
Roginsky, D. 237
Ronen, D. 237
Rosicrucianism 141
Rowat, T. 9–11, 29–31
Royal Academy of Dance (London) 75
Royal Ballet 75, 91, 94, 104–5, 121–2; Birmingham 105, 122, 131
Royal Danish Ballet 76–7
Royal Winnipeg Ballet (RWB) 25–6
Rubidge, S. 132, 153, 244, 251
Runge, J. 41, 47–9
Russell-Roberts, A. 120–1
Russian Revolution (1917) 156

Sachs, C. 66
Saddler, D. 93
St Denis, R. 67, 84, 90
Sanctum (Baker) 42, 49, 53, 58–9
Sangeet Natak Academy (Kerala) 82
Sant Cassia, P. 273
Sapir, T. 262
Saussure, F. de 198
Savigliano, M. 184–7
Sayers, L-A. 150, 154–65; *Le Pas d'Acier* re-creation 154–65; and Preston-Dunlop, V. 3, 130–70
Scheler, M. 172, 189
Schlemmer, O. 136, 150
School of American Ballet 88
Schulman, A. 66
Schuman, W. 65
Scriabin 45
Self/Other, logic 199
Sephardic culture 237
Servos, N. 132
Shaw, B. 120–1
Shawcross, N. 96
Shawn, T. 67, 70, 77, 84, 92
Shearer, M. 75
Shewchuk, A. 19–20
Siegel, M. 1, 106, 125
Silverberg, J. 42, 45
Silverman, K. 172, 189
Sinha, D. 42
The Sleeping Beauty 76
Smith, C.S. 64–6, 79, 92
Snell, G. 133
Society for Canadian Dance Studies 9
Society of Dance History Scholars 99
Somes, M. 120–1
Sorrin, E. 114–17
sousta 4, 197, 203–5, **225**; concealing 216–20; courtship performance 216–28; **217–20**; and family heritage on Rhodes 4, 216–28; nostalgic ethnography 4; revealing 220–8, *see also* Greece, celebratory dance
Sparshott, F. 111
Special Libraries Association 90
Spencer Collection 82; Asian Dance Images 82
Sperling, A. 119
Spohr, A. 26
Stage Directors and Choreographers Society (SDC) 124
stagers 118
Stamm, R. 188

States, B. 151
Steegmuller, F. 68
Steinberg, R. 41
Steiner, R. 136
Stravinsky and the Dance exhibition (1966) 91
Stravinsky, I. 148
Stroud, T. 25
Study of Dance Collections in Canada (Rowat) 9, 29–30
Sulzberger, J. 92–3
surface forms 3
Swan Lake (Bourne) 74, 90, 148, 155
Swinston, R. 119
Sylvia (Ashton) 122
Symphonic Variations (Ashton) 131

Taboo of Virginity, The (Freud) 271–2
Tagenia, Y. 244–5, 250
Taglioni, M. 90, 99
Tangente Centre de documentation (Montreal) 8
Tango Tachito 175
Tanzschrift (Laban) 136
Taylor, P. 71
Tchelitchew, P. 166
Ten Suggestions (Morris) 40
Terry, W. 67, 70, 92–3
Thomas, H. 46
Thomas, J.M. 131–2
Tilden, S.J. 92
Tinos Panayía 280
Titan (Laban) 137
To Dance or Not to Dance (Manos) 275
Toledano, G. 238
Topaz, M. 131–2
Toronto: Dance Theatre 38, 43; Performing Arts centre 12; Reference Library 8, 12–13
Toscanini, A. 72
Toscanini, W. 72–3, 93
Totem and Taboo (Freud) 186
Tov-Israel, I. 248–9
Triadic Ballet (Schlemmer) 150
Trinity Laban 3, 147, 152–4, 167
Trio 147
trusts 104–29; Antony Tudor Ballet 37; Ashton 37, 120–3; Balanchine 105, 114–17, 123; charitable 109–10; choreographers 104–29; Cunningham 113, 119–20, 123; Graham 123–5; Jerome Robbins Dance Division 105–9, 117–18; living 107; Martha Graham Dance Company 110, 123–5; Merce Cunningham 37, 107–9, 119–20; private 108–9; Robbins 37, 105–9, 113,

117–18, 123; and trustee role 107, *see also* Choreographer's Trust
Tudor, A. 79
Turkey: Pontic dance origins 280–1, 286–7
Turner, V. 197; ritual structure theory 197–8, **198**, 227
Two Pigeons, The (Ashton) 122

Ulanova, G. 92
Ullman, L. 136–7
Unfold (Baker) 43–5, 51
United Nations (UN) 98
University of London Press Ltd 111; and University Tutorial Press Ltd case 111

Vadasy, T. 240
Vaill, A. 117–18
Valéry, P. 171–5, 178, 189
Valois, N. de 75, 121
Van Camp, J. 123–4
Varone, D. 38
Vaughan, D. 71, 104
Velasquez, D. 155
Vertov, D. 160
victimization: and Panayía Soumelá celebrations 277–8
Video Archives Project 116
Video vs Imagination (Baker) 52
Viganò, S. 92
Vozikas, G. 277

Walter Reade Theatre 98
Wangh, A.W. 96
Warner, M.J. 21, 29
Warsitz, E. 149–50
Watt, N. 41
Weber, L. 106, 119

wedding ritual reconstruction: Greek 205–15
Weidman, C. 68–70, 133
Weise, N. 259
Welsh Asante, K. 239
White Oak Dance Project (Morris) 38–40
White Studio 70
Wiener Neustadt Military Academy 135
Wigman, M. 41, 92, 132
Willems, T. 152
Winnipeg Contemporary Dancers (WCD) 8, 12, 16–27; and School (SCD) 16–27
Winnipeg Dance Preservation Initiative (WDPI) 25–6
Winter, M.H. 95
Wolz, C. 98
World Dance Alliance (WDA) 97; Americas Center 98; Global Assemblies 98
World Wars: I (1914–180 134, 144, 156; II (1939–45) 132, 137, 203, 236, 285
Wright, H. 93

Yakoulov, G. 3, 154–6, 158–62; set design 161–2
Yang (Baker) 42, 48, 52, 55–7
Yared, H. 232
Yemenite folklore 236–7
Yeoh, F. 2–3
Yom Kippur 238
Your Isadora (Steegmuller) 68

Zehavi, O. 254, 259
Zografou, M. 283; and Pipyrou, S. 4, 267–91
Zorba dance 200